Ballymurphy and the Irish War

Ciarán de Baróid

PLUTO PRESS • London

IRISH BOOKS AND MEDIA INC • Minneapolis

This edition first published 1990 by Pluto Press
345 Archway Road, London N6 5AA
and in the USA by Irish Books
and Media, Inc.
1433 Franklin Avenue East
Minneapolis, Minnesota 55404-2135
Tel. (612) 871-3505

First published in 1989

British Library Cataloguing in Publication Data
De Baroid, Ciaran
    Ballymurphy and the Irish War.
    1. Belfast, history
    I. Title
    941.67

    ISBN 0-7453-0445-1 (UK)

Library of Congress Card Catalog number
90-80322
Data applied for
    ISBN 0-937702-12-9 (USA)

Typeset by Stanford Desktop Publishing
Printed in Great Britain by
Billing and Sons Ltd, Worcester

Contents

To the people of Greater Ballymurphy
and the oppressed everywhere

Acknowledgements

We are grateful to Pacemaker Press for permission to reproduce the following photographs: Confrontation in Ballymurphy in June 1970; Paratroopers moving into the Ballymurphy Estate on May 14th after the weekend bombing of Kelly's Bar; IRA guard of honour at funeral of Kevin Delaney January 1980; to the *Belfast Telegraph* for British Troops invading Ballymurphy, Easter 1970.

Every effort has been made to obtain permission for the use of photographs. Where this has not been possible, grateful acknowledgement will be made in subsequent editions.

Foreword

In my childhood, self-praise was viewed as one of the deadly sins, and we were often quietly cautioned with the saying, 'If your work speaks for itself, let it!' The combination of talent, personality and objectivity needed to make that saying work is very rare, and very wonderful.

Ballymurphy and the Irish War speaks for itself, with all the eloquence and intensity of human beings telling the truth of their existence and the reality of their world; and it speaks without being moulded to fit any preconceived ideas, political theories or social attitudes.

This book is history as history should be documented in all our communities. The apparent ease and confidence with which reality confronts even a disbelieving reader is a testament to the skill of the author, Ciarán De Baróid.

Ciarán has worked on the ground, in the background, and has, in my recollection, never said a great deal. Now he has set down this work – the story of the Upper Springfield community – and in speaking, he leaves us silent with respect.

Without *Ballymurphy and the Irish War* people might never know or believe these things happened. As a record of fact, it will be remembered, and referred to, when we are long forgotten.

Bernadette McAliskey

Glossary

Active Service Unit (ASU): IRA cell on active service.

Alliance Party: Centrist, middle-class, liberal unionist party, founded in 1970.

'B' Specials: Part-time branch of the Ulster Special Constabulary, founded in the North of Ireland after partition. Disbanded in 1970 and replaced by the Ulster Defence Regiment.

Ballymurphy Tenants' Association (BTA): Working-class tenants' body, founded in 1963 to agitate for improved living conditions in Ballymurphy.

Belfast Areas of Need (BAN): Study group established by British government in 1978 to look at social and economic deprivation in Belfast.

Belfast Urban Study Group (BUS): Campaign group attempting to prevent the construction of urban motorways that would destroy traditional communities.

Catholic Ex-Servicemen's Association (CESA): Vigilante group established in 1971 to protect nationalist areas of Belfast.

Central Citizens' Defence Committee (CCDC): Vigilante group established in nationalist areas in 1969, following August pogroms.

Child Poverty Action Group (CPAG): British voluntary body monitoring levels of poverty.

Citizens Advice Bureau (CAB): Voluntary advice-giving body.

Citizens' Defence Committees (CDCs): Constituent parts of CCDC.

Communist Party of Ireland (CPI): Moscow-oriented party, influential in development of 'stages theory' by Sinn Fein during 1960s.

Concerned Community Organisations (CCO): Belfast-based umbrella group of community organisations, established in 1983 to fight the 'supergrass' system.

Cumann na gCailini: Girls' branch of Republican Movement. Similar to Guides.

Cumann na mBan: Women's branch of the IRA.

Dail Eireann: Originally established as republican parliament after the Westminster elections of 1918. Second Dail elected during the War of Independence in 1921. The Free State Dail, founded after the Treaty of 1921, is the forebear of today's Dail Eireann.

Democratic Unionist Party (DUP): Far-right unionist party formed by Ian Paisley in 1971 as a successor to his Protestant Unionists.

Divisional Mobile Support Unit (DMSU): Quick-reaction unit of Royal Ulster Constabulary.

Emergency Provisions Act (EPA): Repressive legislation that replaced the Special Powers Act.

Fianna Eireann: Boys' branch of Republican Movement. Similar to Scouts.

Fianna Fail (Soldiers of Destiny): Party established by Eamon de Valera after split with Sinn Fein in 1926.

Fine Gael (Tribe of the Gael): Descendants of pro-Treaty party Cumann na nGaedhal. Had links with the fascist Blueshirts during the 1930s.

Gaelic Athletic Association (GAA): Body founded in late nineteenth century to promote Gaelic sport.

Gardai/Garda Siochana: The 26-County police force, established after creation of Irish Free State.

General Officer Commanding (GOC): Commander of British forces in Six Counties.

Irish National Liberation Army (INLA): Founded in 1976. Amalgamation of 'People's Liberation Army' and former Official IRA members.

Irish People's Liberation Organisation (IPLO): Breakaway group from INLA, founded in 1986.

Irish Republican Army (IRA): (Oglaigh na h-Eireann). Underground army that has fought for an independent Ireland since 1919. Split in 1969/70 into Official IRA (OIRA) and Provisional IRA (PIRA). Official IRA declared truce in 1972 but still maintains a profile in nationalist areas of the North and in the 26 Counties. Provisional IRA launched war against the British in 1970 and maintains it to the present day.

Irish Republican Socialist Party (IRSP): Formed after 1974 split in Official Sinn Fein. Closely allied to INLA.

Local Enterprise Development Unit (LEDU): Government body designed to stimulate the growth of small industries through the provision of grants.

Loyalist Association of Workers (LAW): Political umbrella of loyalist workers.

Military Reconnaissance Force (MRF): Undercover units of British army, probably SAS.

National H-Block/Armagh Committee: Founded in 1979 to campaign for political status for republican prisoners in the H-Blocks of Long Kesh and Armagh women's prison.

Noraid: US fund-raising group supporting Republican Movement.

Northern Ireland Civil Rights Association (NICRA): Anti-discrimination body established in 1967. Involved in early civil rights agitation. Eventually dominated by the (Officials') Republican Clubs and CPI.

Northern Ireland Office (NIO): British administration centre in the Six Counties. Based at Stormont Castle outside Belfast.

Northern Resistance Movement (NRM): Established by People's Democracy and the Provisionals in 1971 to oppose internment and demand abolition of Stormont.

Officer Commanding (O/C): Leadership term used by IRA.

Official Unionist Party (OUP): Descendants of Unionist Party formed in the late nineteenth century to oppose Home Rule in Ireland.

'Official' used to distinguish it from the DUP and from Faulkner's
short-lived party of 1973–4.

Orange Order: Exclusively Protestant and loyalist organisation, formed
in 1795 to oppose the alliance of Presbyterian and Catholic peasants.
Closely linked to the Unionist Party.

Peace People: Peace campaign launched in 1976 to end the war in Six
Counties. Its one-sided condemnation of violence rapidly lost its
support in nationalist areas.

People's Democracy (PD): Civil Rights group established in Queen's
University, Belfast, in 1968. Became non-doctrinaire New Left Party.
Still active but small.

People's Liberation Army (PLA): Early armed supporters of Irish
Republican Socialist Party.

Relatives' Action Committee (RAC): Local committees, mostly
women, established in 1976 to fight for political status for republican
prisoners.

Relatives for Justice: Anti-'supergrass' group established in 1983.

Republican Clubs: Initially set up to circumvent ban on Sinn Fein.
After 1970 split, became the Northern branch of Official Sinn Fein and
then the Workers' Party. Favours indefinite union with Britain and the
restoration of Stormont.

Royal Ulster Constabulary (RUC): Overwhelmingly loyalist Six-
County police force, established after partition.

Secret Intelligence Service: Exterior arm of British intelligence (MI6).

Sinn Fein: Republican party founded in 1905 by Arthur Griffith.
Politically identified with IRA since 1919. Split in 1970 into Official
Sinn Fein and Provisional Sinn Fein. Official Sinn Fein later became
the Workers' Party. Provisional Sinn Fein is the present day Sinn Fein.

Social Democratic and Labour Party (SDLP): Founded in 1970
and immediately replaced old Nationalist Party. Opposes republicanism, favours eventual unity of Ireland but simultaneously upholds
the loyalist 'veto'.

Special Air Service (SAS): Secret 'dirty tricks' unit of British army.
Active in Six Counties since beginning of Troubles.

Special Support Unit (SSU): SAS-trained units of RUC, involved in
the Armagh death squad killings of 1982, and in other RUC undercover operations.

Stormont: Seat of government in the North of Ireland.

Troops Out Movement (TOM): Small but active British coalition of
left, campaigning for British withdrawal from Ireland.

Ulster Defence Association (UDA): Largest loyalist guerrilla organisation; claimed 50,000 members in early 1970s. Never banned despite
much involvement in sectarian killings, many carried out under cover
name of 'Ulster Freedom Fighters'.

Ulster Defence Regiment (UDR): Loyalist militia that replaced 'B'
Specials in 1970, under control of British army. Many members have
links with loyalist guerrilla groups.

Ulster Freedom Fighters (UFF): Name often used by UDA killer squads when claiming operations.

Ulster Security Liaison Committee (USLC): Intelligence co-ordinating body established by Maurice Oldfield.

United Ulster Unionist Council (UUUC): Unionist co-ordinating body opposing power-sharing.

Ulster Volunteer Force (UVF): Name of loyalist army organised by Edward Carson to oppose Home Rule and support partition. Re-emerged in mid 1960s as loyalist death squad, carrying out random attacks against nationalists. Became fully active from 1972. Often uses cover name 'Protestant Action Force (PAF)'.

Ulster Workers' Council (UWC): ad hoc amalgamation of loyalist workers established in 1974 to oppose power-sharing. Organised general strike that brought down the power-sharing executive in May 1974.

Vanguard: Right-wing loyalist group set up by William Craig to oppose reforms and the imposition of direct rule by Britain.

Westminster: Seat of British parliament in London.

Whitehall: Seat of British government in London.

Workers' Party: Descendant of Official Sinn Fein and the Republican Clubs. Condemns IRA as 'terrorists' despite its own links with Official IRA. Had seven members elected to Dail in 1989. Very little electoral success in North.

Introduction

> Were history what it ought to be, an accurate literary reflex of the times with which it professes to deal, the pages of history would be almost entirely engrossed with a recital of the wrongs and struggles of the labouring people.
>
> James Connolly

To describe the Irish war as a conflict between Catholics and Protestants is about as honest as portraying the Vietnam war as a conflict between Christians and Buddhists. This narrative therefore steers clear of such misleading, British-inspired terminology. Instead, the broad terms of 'nationalist' and 'loyalist' are used to describe those sections of the Northern population who oppose or support British imperialism in Ireland.

In using the word 'nationalist' I am aware of its many unsavoury connotations, but none the less find it the most suitable term of convenience to cover the anti-imperialist population, within which are to be found nationalists, republicans, socialist-republicans, socialists, communists and anarchists. As a result of an accident of history most happen to be of Catholic origin, but they also include Protestants, agnostics and atheists. None of them are fighting for or about religion.

The focus of this story is a small tightly-knit community of some 12,000 people spread over eight housing estates in one square mile of West Belfast. The whole area is collectively known as Ballymurphy, Greater Ballymurphy or the Upper Springfield. Its epicentre is Ballymurphy estate. For the purpose of this book, Ballymurphy estate will at all times describe the smaller entity. The following pages attempt to record the life of that community through a 40-year period, 20 of which have been years of war.

In Ireland Ballymurphy is a name guaranteed to evoke strong reactions directly betraying the listener's politics. On my own arrival in Belfast in early 1972 I made the mistake of innocently asking a Citybus inspector where I could get a bus to Ballymurphy. 'They don't run any buses to Ballymurphy', he snarled, 'they burn all the buses in Ballymurphy!' I never again asked such an unguarded question. For the next 13 years I watched the Ballymurphy story unfold with an ever-increasing conviction that someone should write it all down. In the autumn of 1985, I set myself the task, feeling that any attempt was better than none. At last, three and a half years later, the story has at least been written down in some form before the participants and victims become too scattered or go to their graves. That is the main concern. Otherwise, a generation hence, nobody would believe any more that it actually happened.

Much of the material is based on the recollections of those who experienced the events described. However, nothing has been included without having first been checked for accuracy against existing documentation. Where no such documentation can be found, exhaustive research has been carried out locally to ensure that the account given is based on a general consensus. All interviews have been cross-checked over and over again to eliminate error and provide the truest possible picture of what happened over the 40-year period described.

The nature of the Irish conflict means that many of those who provided invaluable insights and information cannot be named. Nevertheless they will know that I am grateful for their trust and their time. Others who can be mentioned include Frank, Marie, Malcolm, Leslie, Melanie, Anita and Cora who provided helpful comments and criticisms; Gerry, who cleared the way for much of the research; the staff at the Central and Linenhall libraries; Ann, Maureen, Eugene, Frankie and Jim for their endless rounds of inquiry on my behalf; and all who agreed to be interviewed. In many cases families were reliving heartbreaking experiences, often involving the loss of a loved one. To them I am especially indebted. And especially to Cora, who suffered the perennial clatter of the typewriter in stoic silence.

Ciarán de Baróid
Belfast
1 March 1989

Prologue

Vincie Clarke was unusual as far as Ballymurphy went. Not many people in the area could boast a family business: in fact only half the 'working population' could boast a job. Vincie Clarke therefore considered himself a lucky man as he turned his coal lorry into Ballymurphy Road on the afternoon of November 16th 1970.

His delivery run stretched from the red-brick houses of Whiterock where he lived, up through the cluster of aluminium huts that made up Westrock to the box houses of Springhill, the rows of garden-houses packed into Ballymurphy Estate and New Barnsley, and the ugly grey flats of Moyard right on the slope of Black Mountain. A little sprinkling of his business also took him into the fancier owner-occupied houses of Dermott Hill and Springfield Park. Littered with the rubble of the recent riots, the place looked even greyer than usual as the chilly evenings stretched towards winter. On Ballymurphy Road, at the junction with Westrock Drive, Vincie Clarke's truck broke down. He cursed and got out to apply his mechanical skills to the problem.

As he worked on the engine, a car drove up Westrock Drive and stopped at the Ballymurphy Road junction, its occupants having spotted the immobilised coal lorry.

Vincie Clarke recognised the two men, Arthur McKenna and Alexander McVicker: in the Upper Falls and Ballymurphy areas of Belfast everyone knew McKenna and McVicker. For many years both men had led a circle of heavies who ran the pitch-and-toss in Beechmount Brickyard and a card school over Watson's shop on the Falls Road. There was a constant battle of wits between themselves and 'Pig Mineely' of the Royal Ulster Constabulary who had set himself a life crusade against pitch-and-toss and card schools. When the lookouts shouted: 'Here comes the Pig!' scores of feet could be heard clattering through Beechmount before the motorbike-mounted enemy could scoop the pot. So unpopular were the exploits of Pig Mineely that his house resembled Fort Knox in days when such fortifications were rare in the city of Belfast. And the fortifications remained long after the notorious spoilsport had left the RUC.

The McKenna and McVicker outfit was also involved in minor racketeering. They fenced stolen goods, lent money at exorbitant rates of interest, ran small protection rackets, and when the opportunity arose, invested their talents in burglaries and robberies. Generally acknowledged as rough diamonds, not to be crossed if you valued limb and property, they maintained a stranglehold over Greater Ballymurphy. A former fellow-traveller would later comment:

Very few people would take them on, because if you did it never ended. If one of them got in a fight they weren't happy until the other bloke ended up a hospital job. Then they'd wreck your house as well. That's how they controlled this whole area; they just terrorised the whole place.

By late 1970 the two Ballymurphy men had also begun to cross swords with a new organisation – the Provisional Irish Republican Army – in the course of their extortionist activities. It was a fatal error.

Shortly after Vincie Clarke had broken down across the street from her home, 51-year-old Kate Hall set off for St Peter's School in Whiterock where she worked as a cleaner. She waved to Vincie Clarke, then continued on down Westrock Drive.

I never seen McKenna and McVicker coming in the car, but I heard later that they'd stopped to talk to the wee fella Clarke. They knew one another well, you see. Then another car came alongside them and it was the Boys. I was away past it by that time but I heard the shots. Next thing was the whole place was in uproar with everyone out on the street saying McKenna and McVicker were shot. Vincie Clarke had dived in under the truck to get away from the bullets.

Arthur McKenna and Alexander McVicker had been shot dead by the Provisional IRA. The local population was stunned. Bad and all as things were, nothing like this had ever happened before.

Some people went home to be physically sick.

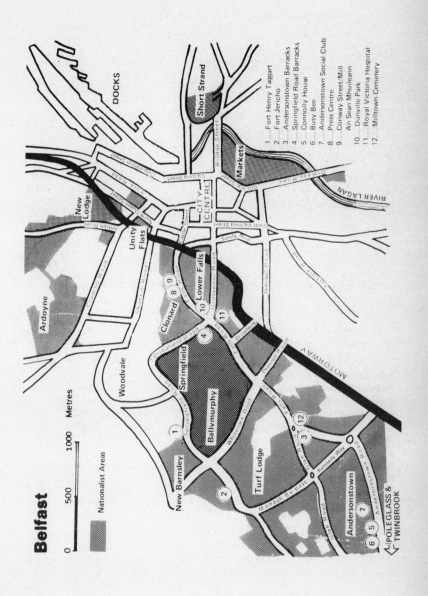

Belfast

0 500 1000 Metres

Nationalist Areas

DOCKS

Short Strand

1....Fort Henry Taggart
2....Fort Jericho
3....Andersonstown Barracks
4....Springfield Road Barracks
5....Connolly House
6....Busy Bee
7....Andersonstown Social Club
8....Press Centre
9....Conway Street/Mill
10...An Sean Mhuileann
11...Royal Victoria Hospital
12...Milltown Cemetery

Markets

RIVER LAGAN

New Lodge

Unity Flats

CITY CENTRE

Ardoyne

Woodvale

Clonard

Lower Falls

Springfield

Ballymurphy

New Barnsley

Turf Lodge

Andersonstown

MOTORWAY

POLEGLASS &
TWINBROOK

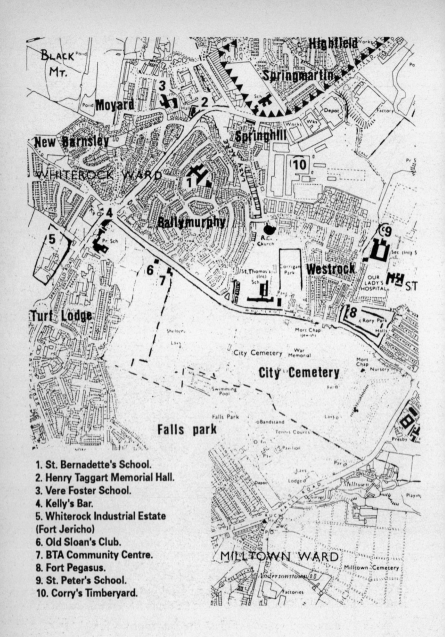

1. St. Bernadette's School.
2. Henry Taggart Memorial Hall.
3. Vere Foster School.
4. Kelly's Bar.
5. Whiterock Industrial Estate
(Fort Jericho)
6. Old Sloan's Club.
7. BTA Community Centre.
8. Fort Pegasus.
9. St. Peter's School.
10. Corry's Timberyard.

An IRA Volunteer on sentry duty in the Ballymurphy Estate, 1971

British troops invading Ballymurphy, Easter 1970

Confrontation in Ballymurphy in June 1970

Paddy McCarthy, the BTA's first youth worker, who died during internment week 1971

Ten-year-old Carmel Fegan and Frank Cahill, secretary of Ballymurphy Tenants' Association, presenting cheques to Belfast Corporation's loan bond scheme in 1967

An IRA guard of honour at the funeral of IRA Volunteer Kevin 'Dee' Delaney, on Ballymurphy Road in January 1980

Paratroopers moving into the Ballymurphy Estate on May 14th after the weekend bombing of Kelly's Bar

Part I
Under Siege

1

The Easter Riots

We don't want to be defended by an army who surrendered
When the kids of Ballymurphy came to play
                                        Belfast street song, 1970's

The 'Troubles' came to Ballymurphy in Easter 1970. Previously, since the pogroms of August 1969, the area had maintained a fragile peace with neighbouring loyalist New Barnsley through the medium of the Springfield Joint Committee. Relationships between the people and the British army had also been relatively relaxed. Shortly after the first barricades had gone up back in August, the 1st Light Infantry Battalion had moved into the Henry Taggart Memorial Hall on the New Barnsley side of the Springfield Road. Its commanding officer, Major James Hancock, was a man versed in tact.

On the morning of his arrival he had come up to one of the barricades at the upper end of Ballymurphy and asked permission to enter. He was refused and he and his men left. He returned the next day and was again refused. On the third day he was allowed through. He met with a number of people operating a relief centre for incoming refugees at St Bernadette's School in the centre of the estate. From then on Hancock liaised with the Ballymurphy community through its leadership and managed to sustain a cordial relationship with the estate's residents.

However, things were beginning to change in the weeks leading up to Easter. The bad news was first brought to St Bernadette's by the local commander of the Royal Scots, the regiment then based at the Henry Taggart Hall. Frank Cahill, a slightly built, 45-year-old, bespectacled man who had for many years been secretary of Ballymurphy Tenants' Association, was co-ordinating the relief centre. He listened in disbelief. The Junior Orangemen were planning a rally in Bangor for Easter Tuesday – and as part of the day's activities one of the lodges was going to come marching out of New Barnsley on to the Springfield Road. As the Grand Master of the lodge lived in New Barnsley, the Orangemen were insisting that the parade set off from his home in keeping with tradition.

Frank Cahill, his neighbour Johnny McCullough, and a number of others who had been keeping the lid on Ballymurphy for the past seven-and-a-half months, asked the officer if the people in New Barnsley had gone crazy. There had never been a parade out of that estate. To hold one now, after 18 months of inter-communal violence in which thousands of people had been burned out of their homes in other parts of Belfast, would be the height of madness. The Ballymurphy people would

3

accept no responsibility for the outcome. The Royal Scots officer said he would go back and talk to the loyalists.

Over the next three weeks negotiations continued between the military and the two communities, but by Easter Monday the issue was still unresolved. The Ballymurphy leaders were insisting that the parade be prevented from coming out on to the dividing line. They would have enough on their hands trying to prevent a reaction to the party tunes without having Orangemen in full regalia staging a provocative display along the length of the Springfield Road. The New Barnsley people were adamant that the parade was going ahead, but gave an assurance that no tunes would be played until they were well out of earshot of Ballymurphy.

On his final visit before the parade took place, the Royal Scots officer told the Ballymurphy leaders: 'You have my word, there will be no party tunes.' The Ballymurphy people shrugged their shoulders and tried one last time to persuade the officer to prevent the parade, but to no avail.

Next morning, Tuesday, March 31st, with Ballymurphy tense and apprehensive, the Orange bands assembled in New Barnsley – and struck up loud and clear. Within minutes the music had attracted large numbers of young people from Ballymurphy up to the Springfield Road. By the time the Orangemen came marching out of New Barnsley – as the Royal Scots commander, standing in the middle of the road, threw his hands in the air and shouted about his word being made worthless – there was nothing anyone could do to avoid confrontation. A young Ballymurphy man threw half a brick and struck one of the Orange drummers, setting off a shower of missiles in both directions. Although the RUC and military rushed in to usher the Orangemen down the Springfield Road in no slow order, the damage was done.

Skirmishes broke out between the locals and troops, and the fragile peace of the previous months was shattered beyond retrieval. The events that would lead to an all-out offensive by Irish nationalists against British occupation forces in Ireland had been sparked off by a single reckless act that had just taken place on the perimeters of Ballymurphy.

That evening, as the Junior Orangemen returned from Bangor, the scattered fighting of the day erupted into serious rioting. Crowds had gathered on the Springfield Road; and when the Orange bands appeared they were attacked. The Royal Scots, backed by jeering flag-waving loyalists, immediately turned on Ballymurphy, and the first major engagement between the British army and Irish nationalists for two generations was under way. The British would later claim that only 70 soldiers and a small force of RUC were on the Springfield Road during the early part of the night's rioting. The people of Ballymurphy remember a much larger force. Either way, the troops took a severe hammering. Then, some time after 10pm the fighting was interrupted by the whine of columns of Saracen armoured cars coming up the Springfield Road. A large contingent of the 1st Light Infantry, with Hancock in charge, had been sent to reinforce the Royal Scots.

'What happened here?' Hancock wanted to know as his troops spread out. 'Ask him', Geordie Shannon from Turf Lodge replied, pointing to the officer who had sanctioned the morning's parade.

By then the nationalist crowd stretched the entire length of Ballymurphy, facing Hancock's troops, and missiles were still flying. Within minutes the second stage of the night's rioting had taken off. Army 'snatch squads', armed with clubs and shields and backed up by troops with automatic rifles, charged the crowd. The Ballymurphy people fought back with broken paving stones, bottles, hurleys and catapults, drawing the troops into the dark streets and alleys of the estate where they could mount ambushes in their own familiar territory.

An Irish Tricolour was fixed to a pole, and as the night wore on and the battles moved from street to street, the whole Ballymurphy community, though confused and frightened by the military invasion, threw its full resources behind those who were engaging the troops. At one point Jim Sullivan, the custodian of Official IRA interests within Belfast's Central Citizens' Defence Committee, and Paddy Devlin, MP for the area, arrived to appeal for restraint, but the rioting went on until the early hours of the morning.

. On Wednesday, April 1st, Ballymurphy, neighbouring Springhill, and loyalist New Barnsley were tense amid the debris of the night before. By evening large crowds had again gathered in Ballymurphy, this time prepared for a fight with the military. At 8pm a group of youths stoned an army vehicle at the top of the Whiterock Road. Soldiers immediately descended on Ballymurphy in unprecedented force, a thousand troops being deployed in an area of one square mile around the estate. The crowd, again armed with stones, bottles and sticks, broke in the face of the huge troop reinforcements and retreated into the estate. From then on the battle raged in every entry and on every corner of the semi blacked-out streets.

Troops of the 1st Light Infantry Battalion and the 2nd Battalion of the Queen's Regiment, wearing gas-masks and carrying clubs and shields, and supported by Saracen armoured cars and more troops carrying rifles, launched another invasion into the estate. The young people defending the area retreated before the assault, then regrouped in small bands spread out over a wide area, thus stretching the troops and denying them the opportunity of concentrating their massive strength into one drive.

Again, the successful attack-and-retreat tactic of the previous night was used against the army. This time, however, the military, who had taken a nasty pasting on the Tuesday night, were determined to give Ballymurphy a bloody nose. They opened up with salvos of CS gas – cartridges and grenades launched by soldiers and armoured cars – and as the push into the estate intensified, the salvos became an incessant barrage, swamping the area in a choking acrid cloud so dense that the people of the Falls Road, a mile away, suffered its effects.

In the homes of Ballymurphy it caused havoc and terror as people fainted and retched and tried to protect their children. The young people in the streets replied with stones and petrol bombs, and an even fiercer determination than the night before. As the British army snatch-squads broke from the lines of troops, now also hurling stones and bottles, their opponents countered with their own snatch-squads. Groups of young men, armed with hurleys, waited in the dark entries between the houses until the army squads had rushed past. They then cut off their line of retreat, and pitched hand-to-hand battles ensued. Some shots of unconfirmed origins were also fired, but there were no casualties.

As the riot progressed nationalist reinforcements came in from the Falls, Turf Lodge, Andersonstown and Ardoyne. Medical assistance also arrived and a casualty centre was set up in St Thomas' secondary school to treat injured civilians, while military casualties were treated at the Henry Taggart base. Many of those treated that night at St Thomas' were victims of the gas. Being the indiscriminate weapon that it is, its use by the British was designed to dole out collective punishment to the entire rebellious community.

The gas seeped into every house in Ballymurphy, causing more casualties among innocent non-combatants than among combatants, who were parrying its effects with home-made remedies originally developed in the Bogside. The end result was to open a chasm, that would never again be bridged, between all the people of Ballymurphy and the British army. As cannisters of gas exploded in people's bedrooms and living-rooms, often causing impact-injury to occupants, an indelible message was left behind: the British troops, who had taken on the role of the RUC, had also taken on their methods.

In Ballymurphy's 'Bullring' Seamus and Minnie McGuigan, who had lived in the estate since 1967, watched the street-fighting from inside through their landing window. Their four children lay huddled in nearby bedrooms. A cannister of gas came through one of the bedroom windows and filled the room with smoke. Their youngest child, Francis, who was almost two years old, was in the room and suffered severe effects from the saturation of gas. He became violently ill with vomiting and diarrhoea – the well-known effects of CS gas – and never recovered. On April 6th, he was rushed to hospital and died the following day. The clinical cause of death was put down as 'pneumonia'. The 'Troubles' had claimed their first Ballymurphy victim. Minnie McGuigan remembers how:

> The gas was everywhere. We were all choking. It was early in the morning, and the fighting had come right through the estate, and as always happened, it ended up in the Bullring. Since there was so much gas we didn't realise at first that a cannister had actually come into the house ... Afterwards they told us that the gas had nothing to do with our Francis' death. But we know that, until the CS gas came through our window, our Francis was a healthy child. We know what caused his death.[1]

Meanwhile, the Reverend Ian Paisley had arrived in New Barnsley earlier in the night with some followers to evacuate children from the estate. Paisley's actions, which precipitated the full evacuation of New Barnsley by the loyalist community, would have been difficult to explain in the light of what had occurred so far. There had been no intimidation of the New Barnsley community, other than the accidental breaking of windows in two houses when stones aimed at the military had overshot their targets. The Ballymurphy leaders, with the support of the Republican Movement, had given assurances through the Springfield Joint Committee that there would be no incursions by nationalists provided there were no attacks on Ballymurphy; and this had held for the past two nights. However, Paisley was standing for election in the Bannside by-election in a fortnight for the Stormont seat formerly held by ex-Prime Minister, Terence O'Neill, and being a man never to miss the opportunity of a good political gimmick, he no doubt would have seen beneficial publicity coming from the New Barnsley intervention.

On Thursday, April 2nd, the Royal Scots, decimated and demoralised, were withdrawn from the area and replaced by the Gloucester Regiment, brought in from Derry. As truckloads of youths and young men converged on Ballymurphy to take on the British army for the third night running, the IRA sent in units from all over the city – to try to stop the rioting. At this stage, the Provisional IRA in Belfast, who were still reorganising, feared that they would be drawn, unprepared, into direct confrontation with the British army, and wanted to avoid such a development.

At the same time, the local Ballymurphy unit was content to let events find their own pace, recognising that the riots, and the British army's overkill response, were uniting the people as never before, and demoralising the British military whose mammoth resources could not subdue the army of young people who faced them. The division between the two could be seen as the outsiders threw a line of IRA vigilantes along the Springfield Road to prevent any fresh outbreaks of rioting, while young republicans on the inside plotted as to how they could thwart the vigilantes' plans. What the Ballymurphy enthusiasts did was quite simple: they went back through the estate and reassembled at Springhill Avenue, facing the loyalist estate of Springmartin. When news of this reached the vigilantes, they left a skeleton force positioned on the Springfield Road, and sent the bulk of their number to the top of Springhill Avenue. There, they found opposing crowds of loyalists and nationalists waving flags and jeering at one another across the Springfield Road, and a large force of soldiers with armoured support ready to move on the nationalists. The republican vigilantes stepped in between the troops and the nationalist crowd and began to advance down Springhill Avenue. As they did, the soldiers and the nationalists began to stone one another and the rioting erupted, catching the vigilantes – many of whom were injured – in the middle. As the gas poured into Springhill, fleets of Knights of Malta ambulances moved children and pensioners from Springhill and Ballymurphy to St Thomas' and St Kevin's schools. As the trouble worsened, 13 nationalist families, intimidated out of Moyard by loyalists, arrived in Ballymurphy where they were rehoused in the Whiterock Road chalets, erected as emergency accommodation during the pogroms of the previous August; and two hundred loyalist families followed Paisley out of New Barnsley. From then on New Barnsley was a nationalist estate and Moyard soon followed, so that the nationalist stronghold of Greater Ballymurphy began at the perimeters of Springmartin, which remained the frontline loyalist estate in the fierce inter-communal conflict of the coming years.

The Easter riots at Ballymurphy ended in the early hours of Friday, April 3rd, when the IRA finally managed to persuade the rioters to call off their actions. Immediately afterwards, the British army General Officer Commanding (GOC), Sir Ian Freeland, announced that, in future, petrol-bombers could expect to be shot dead. In response, the Provisional IRA warned Freeland and the British government that such action would draw republican fire. In a statement, they declared that:

> The trouble in Belfast last week arose solely because of the coat-trailing of Orange bands who were allowed to march and play in areas where the local people objected, and the subsequent clashes with British troops occurred when the residents of Ballymurphy defended their homes... The full resources of the Provisional Army Council will be used to protect our people against attacks from both crown forces and sectarian bigots.[2]

The worm was beginning to turn.

References
1.   Minnie McGuigan of Ballymurphy (1985 Interview).
2.   *Freedom Struggle – the Provisional IRA* (1973), p. 24.

2

Early Days

The Ballymurphy story began in May 1947, when the Estates Committee of Belfast Corporation acquired some 59 acres for house-building at the foot of Black Mountain which, along with Divis and Cavehill, forms the 1,200 ft escarpment that curtails the city's westward expansion. By the time building began the Corporation was under intense pressure to step up its housing programme. The city's housing shortage had been greatly exacerbated during the Second World War when all development was suspended and many houses were destroyed by bombing. When the war ended the huge homeless population, further swollen by large numbers of returning servicemen, was spread out over several hastily erected pre-fabricated bungalow-estates and huts which had been occupied by troops during the war.

In the post-war spirit of renewal, large subsidies were made available to help local authorities provide houses quickly and in large supply. However, materials were scarce and strictly controlled. To solve the problem, the Ministry of Health and Local Government and the Belfast Corporation Housing Committee decided to experiment with non-traditional designs and materials so that available skills and supplies could be stretched to their absolute limit. In this atmosphere of frugality and adventure, Ballymurphy estate was planned and built.

By May 1948 the first plans for the new estate had been submitted by the architect. It was envisaged that 436 houses would make up the lower end; but in a revision ordered by the Ministry of Health and Local Government this was increased to 493, despite part of the site having been given over to the Water Commissioners for a reservoir and pumping station. In the end 501 houses were built in this part of the estate, using the 'no-fines' concrete method instead of the traditional red brick that had characterised Belfast housing since the establishment of the city.

'No-fines' dwellings were constructed by pouring a honeycombed mixture of cement and aggregate into shutters and skimming the finished result with grout. The lack of a cavity in the quickly-constructed shells would later result in acute problems of cold, dampness and ill-health in Ballymurphy. Another innovation, brought about by a dearth of skilled plasterers, was the introduction of a new type of internal partition that was easy, cheap and quick to erect but did little for the solidity of the houses. The Bullring shops, and the flats that rose above them, in the centre of the estate were an afterthought that came about in 1952. The remainder of the estate – 159 houses in 'Orlit' blocks – was completed in the 1950s. In this latter type of housing a quick-drying concrete

9

was used. But it was discovered less than 30 years later that the chemicals in the mix caused the steel reinforcements of house beams to rot, reducing the lifespan of the Orlit houses to 45 years – they will have to be demolished before 1997.

The overall result of using shoddy and often untested materials, unskilled labour, short-cut methods and the cramming of dwellings was to sow the seeds of problems that would one day catapult Ballymurphy on to the world stage in a way that could hardly have been imagined by those who planned the initial adventure.

Lack of foresight, however, was not to be a monopoly of those who planned and built Ballymurphy. The management of the estate also reflected an appalling incompetence and lack of understanding of how human beings and the environment in which they live interact with one another. In the first place, most of the residents allocated to Ballymurphy in its infant days were young married couples, many of them ex-soldiers and their wives who either had, or were soon to have, large numbers of children, creating a population bulge that was to last a quarter of a century. This, coupled with a complete lack of recreational and play facilities, was to give rise to serious problems of vandalism. Further, to add to the difficulties of coping with streets full of bored youngsters, there were no shopping facilities, nor was there a church or primary school. The early education of the estate's children was restricted to a daily half-day sponged from other schools in West Belfast, linked to Ballymurphy by a bus service that was nearly a mile away on the Falls Road.

Poverty too was endemic. With almost half the families subsisting on state benefits, many had acquired massive debts, and money-lending was rampant at strangling rates of interest. The money-lenders often took possession of a family's Children's Allowance books on a permanent basis, delivering them to the post office each week so the money could be drawn and handed over, thus forcing the family into a living standard well below the accepted poverty line. Even those in Ballymurphy who were working often had to rely on state benefits to shore up inadequate incomes. At that time such benefits were discretionary, so there was the added humiliation of having to argue the case at the local office, and the attendant stigmatisation.

As a result of the discriminatory nature of the Six-County state, poor housing invariably became the living quarters of nationalists. This was quickly to come about in Ballymurphy. In a system of patronage dominated by the loyalist population, those with 'pull' tended to be of that tradition; and those with pull wanted out of Ballymurphy. The fact that a sizeable lump of what was originally planned as Ballymurphy had already been sold to the Catholic Church no doubt accelerated the process, and by 1955 the two acres of land reserved for a Protestant primary school had also been sold to the Catholic Church. All educational facilities were now in their hands, so that henceforth Protestants would feel they didn't belong in Ballymurphy.

Another development that would have a profound effect on the future of the estate was also taking place. The Ministry of Health and Local Government had ordered the closure of the city's remaining wartime huts to coincide with the completion of Ballymurphy. Forced speedily to accommodate their occupants, the Estates Committee rehoused a number of them in the new estate. Many of those families are now widely acknowledged to have had problems of their own that were intensified by the living conditions in which they now found themselves.

Problem pursued problem and the area quickly acquired a bad reputation. The media were quick to take note; and a pattern of attributing to Ballymurphy the behaviour of others from neighbouring estates soon emerged. Images of a violent lawless community were taking shape. As the attitudes of outsiders and statutory bodies became increasingly hostile and alienating, the people of the area became increasingly aware of that alienation and what it meant to have a Ballymurphy address. Traders, the RUC, publicans and employers treated the estate as the consummate social pariah. It was not a place in which to settle down. In his exhaustive study of Ballymurphy, completed in 1973, Tony Spencer points out that:

> In time, despite the high rents, this bad reputation undermined the attempts of the more responsible tenants to bring about improvements. Whether they wanted jobs, public services or credit, they found it was a heavy liability to have a Ballymurphy address. So, many of those who could have contributed to its improvement moved elsewhere, while others avoided it altogether and sought homes on estates that had a better reputation. Whether by accident or by design, the estate had by the late 1950s become a sort of clearing house for Catholic Belfast. The 'best' potential tenants were creamed off by the Northern Ireland Housing Trust, the 'worst' were offered houses in Ballymurphy, and those in between went to other Corporation estates.[1]

Therefore, by the late 1950s, Ballymurphy had become a transit location, from which the more ambitious families speedily extricated themselves. As a result, the entire community was permanently unstable and unable to establish any form of community network that could begin to tackle the area's mounting problems. The continuous drain of the 'better' families took with it the most likely source of local leadership and left behind despair and apathy, and bewilderment at the rapid turnover of neighbours. Twelve thousand families are reported to have passed through Ballymurphy's 660 houses in 14 years! It was impossible to guarantee any continuity of programme or membership in any initiative under such circumstances.

Meanwhile, a constant barrage of vindictive propaganda had become the acceptable response of a society intent on considering the people of Ballymurphy as rightly occupying the bottom rungs of the social ladder. The problems of isolation, poverty, money-lending, unemployment and poor housing that now bedevilled the place were re-created so that guilt was shifted from those who caused the problems to those who were their victims. Popular myths were developed: that the people in Ballymurphy kept their coal in the bath; used their doors and window-frames as firewood; never washed from one end of the year to the next; engaged in epidemic partner-swapping; and as a result were too lazy to work. Ballymurphy had become the classic scapegoat.

A further factor maintaining poor conditions in Ballymurphy was that its predicament had long suited politicians of all hues. The unionists could use it to rationalise their abuse of power; after all, nationalists did not deserve equal status. The nationalists could hold it up as an example of how unfairly the artificial Northern minority were treated under British/unionist rule. Ballymurphy, meanwhile, continued to decay.

The final factor was that unionist control of Belfast's administration was guaranteed. There was therefore no motivation for ensuring the well-being of the opponents' constituents, or investigating the underlying causes of their problems. Spencer was to discover that: 'The permanent officials most concerned were apparently unaware of the factors that caused the Ballymurphy problem. They simply lacked the necessary professional knowledge.'

The voice of protest, when it was finally raised, was a forlorn one that seemed hopeless in the extreme.

The Ballymurphy Tenants' Association (BTA) was formed in 1963, at a meeting held in St Bernadette's School. By now there were two primary schools, a church, a doctor's surgery and shops in the area, but as yet no recreational or community facilities, and no organisation around the issues confronting the people. The few previous attempts at a tenants' association had all failed, quite often at about the same time as their limited funds disappeared. Nevertheless the 1963 meeting attracted a 70 per cent turn-out of households, illustrating the pent-up frustrations of the community, and a body of 25 was elected to the new BTA. 'At that time this place was like a leper colony', Hugh McCormick, the founding secretary, later explained; 'We just had to get up and fight back.' There were many issues to be tackled, but the BTA concentrated on the immediate priorities: repairs to houses, the organisation of social functions that would hopefully engender some community cohesion, fund-raising towards a building that would belong to the people, and an educational programme aimed at politicising local people.

Soon the new BTA proved itself an organisation to be reckoned with. Members met with the superintendent of Belfast Corporation's Estates Department, and it was agreed that their Repairs Sub-committee should channel all repairs directly to the Corporation's repairs manager. As a result the Repairs Section of the Corporation was flooded with housing complaints from the BTA. The Corporation's staff were unable to deal with the avalanche, so the BTA campaigned for a local yard and a housing manager based in the area.

Social functions also began to materialise on a regular basis with the double purpose of providing facilities for the community and funds towards the desired community centre, a hut somewhere in the area, envisaged as 'a centre of communication for the area, and a place where the needs of the community, particularly the young, could be accommodated'.[2] At the end of the first year the BTA's account showed the healthy balance of £437. With each subsequent boost to the account the BTA became more ambitious as to the type of centre it would provide for the area.

In 1967 the BTA's architect, Sean Mackle, had told them that with £6,000 (£1,000 more than they already had in their account) they would have enough capital to embark on a reasonable building, for which Mackle had already donated a design. The total cost would be £15,000, leaving £10,000 still to be found. (From then until the building was completed, Mackle was to play a tantalising game of carrot and donkey with the BTA. Every time they got near the goal, he donated a new design for a bigger, more elaborate and more expensive centre, until they finished off with plans for a two-storey building costing £100,000.)

The Education Sub-committee chose to tackle another immediate problem: although there were now two primary schools in the area (St Bernadette's built by the Catholic Church in 1960; and St Aiden's opened by the Christian Brothers in 1961), they were not large enough to take all the children of the estate, which meant children attending schools in other parts of the city. School transport for those children did not exist, so attempts were made to remedy this. But, as the children were spread about so much, this proved an impossible task. The sub-committee then began to look at the more complex politics of who controlled the schools attended by the children of the estate, and why local people – the parents – were denied opportunities to influence the education of their children. The debate that thus began has been a recurring, unresolved theme ever since.

The Youth Sub-committee of the BTA began to mount pressure for outdoor facilities for the young; they pressed for play space in the district and organised night-time social activities for teenagers. A disco, however, had to be abandoned after a gang of outsiders arrived in a van one Sunday night and jumped out brandishing guns. As time went on the Association began to notch up an impressive catalogue of victories, forcing the Corporation to carry out maintenance and improvements to the estate. In the mid-1960s, the BTA took on the role of tenants' advocate. It became a way of life for some members of the Association's executive to spend every Friday at the rent office representing tenants who were in arrears. Their intervention was largely successful in preventing evictions and making sure that essential services were not cut off on families.

For the first time, those who had stepped forward into positions of leadership were staying put, demonstrating an act of faith on their part and representing a symbol of hope for the community. The Association was growing in awareness and political astuteness as issues were taken on and analysed. The increased politicisation in turn added new issues and the development of greater efficiency, new tactics of protest and more streamlined methods.

In 1967, after four years of struggle, the BTA decided to tackle the problem of Ballymurphy's image. They realised that this was necessary if they were ever to succeed in holding on to any kind of stability within the community, and they were all in agreement that progress within the estate was dependent on doing just that. For several months beforehand, Ballymurphy had been at the butt-end of a barrage of unfavourable publicity, much of it in line with the scapegoating and stereotyping that had gone before.

So in order to counter the rash of bad publicity and simultaneously lay the foundations for an all-out fund-raising drive, a public relations consultant was employed. At first, when the firm was approached with details of the BTA assignment, they were somewhat taken aback. They had never before heard of a tenants' association's employing a public relations consultant; and they had heard and read plenty about Ballymurphy to know the extent of the PR job they would be undertaking. None the less, they agreed to have a go, and suggested a three-month full-blooded drive – they were eventually to stay for two years.

From then on, the sophistication of the BTA operation was stepped up considerably. An Appeals Committee was established and headed by Sir Graham Larmor, one of Belfast's leading linen merchants, who was already associated with youth work in Sandy Row. The Northern Ireland Association of Youth Clubs encouraged the work and lent the committee a more expansive front than its Ballymurphy base would have allowed. At the launching of the appeal in October 1967 the press release prepared by the PR firm set the tone:

> The estate had been an example of early post-war planning and suffered a reputation for hooliganism and rowdy behaviour. Considering that it had more than 3,000 children and yet absolutely no recreational facility of any kind, this was not surprising.[3]

Sir Graham Larmor added 'We have now, I hope, learned our lesson that planning must not just put up boxes for people, but must also give space in which to grow and develop as citizens.' But, regardless of Sir Graham's hopes, the nationalist community was still to face the agonies of Divis, Moyard, Unity and Derry's Rossville Flats, all designed and built by people who would never have to live in them.

At the same time, the publicity counter-offensive began to make itself felt. A new type of article relating to Ballymurphy crept into the newspapers on an apparently inexplicably regular basis, taking over from the 'hooliganism', 'wanton destruction' and 'coal-in-the-bath' image fostered over the previous decade and a half. Now, the newspapers finally began shifting the blame back, after their 15-year onslaught, from the victims of the Ballymurphy syndrome to its perpetrators. In October 1967 the *Belfast Telegraph* wrote:

> The Ballymurphy story is a familiar one – houses rushed up by the Corporation in 1950 to accommodate families from all over Belfast, who had been bombed out in the war ... and nowhere for the young people to amuse themselves or for the older ones to meet socially.

The result at one end of the age scale today is frustration and loneliness, at the other, boredom and vandalism ... But Ballymurphy is taking itself in hand ...[4]

In the months ahead Ballymurphy's image improved daily, its 'civic spirit' further embossed by the BTA's investment of £5,000 in the Corporation's loan bond scheme and the image of ten-year-old Carmel Fagan, in her Irish dancing costume, presenting the cheque to the Lord Mayor. As early as 1964 the tenants' association had participated on the Lord Mayor's Committee on Vandalism, and was now seen as a body that understood that problem and the others they were trying to tackle. By 1967 Ballymurphy was etching its way into the social history of Belfast, emerging as an authority on its own problems and an inspiration in the field of radical community politics. Twenty years on, it still holds that position.

The BTA was also in a healthy financial position. With Mackle's plans having gone through umpteen convolutions, it had its sights on a two-storey building with two halls, offices, a coffee-bar, showers and a workshop. The members also felt that they had done their share and were entitled to some form of government aid, particularly as it was proposed to allocate five nights a week to youth activities that qualified for Ministry of Education grants. A meeting was arranged with the permanent secretary to the minister, but there were obstacles. Grants for youth activities were subject to two conditions – no drink and no gambling on the premises – which the BTA considered ridiculous. Alcohol was a normal part of most adult functions, and bingo, which was classed under gambling, was much in demand on the estate. It was decided not to avail of the grant.

In time, following pressure from the BTA, the Ministry relented. They reinterpreted the deeds of convenant so that the question of gambling and alcohol became a matter between the owners of buildings and those who granted the licences, and the BTA got its grant. A total of £15,000 came from the Ministry of Community Relations, established as the North went over the brink, and over £56,000 from the Ministry of Education. Substantial sums in those days.

In the meantime the struggle to improve the estate's conditions and image continued. In 1968 a credit union opened in the area. This curbed the activities of the money-lenders, but it could only cope with a limited membership and many people were still forced into the clutches of the profiteers. (In 1985 the Upper Springfield Resource Centre exposed and smashed an illegal money-lending racket in Whiterock, where people were being charged annual interest rates of up to 200 per cent. The money-lenders fled, leaving behind uncollected capital of some £15,000.) At about the same time, a local Corporation yard was opened at the top of the Whiterock Road (to be destroyed, unfortunately, during the riots of 1970); and following BTA suggestions, a block of senior citizens' bungalows was built. The Association also mobilised substantial pressure – including local GP Dr McSorley who rated driving through

Ballymurphy a health hazard – and demanded of the Corporation that the roads and pavements, neglected for 18 years, be repaired. The Corporation conducted a survey and found that nothing short of complete resurfacing was needed. The BTA threatened action if this wasn't done immediately; and within a week heavy machinery had moved in.

The same lack of maintenance applied to street lighting. Only four lights worked in the whole area, although in many cases all that was required was a bulb. The BTA threatened legal action. As Corporation tenants they were entitled to proper lighting. Again the threat worked. Another complaint to the BTA from the more horticultural Ballymurphy residents was that all the fertile topsoil had, during the building of the estate, been removed to the grounds of Stormont Castle and the Ormeau Embankment! Not until 1983, however, would the gardeners of Ballymurphy have this soil replaced as part of an eventual refurbishing scheme.

As a result of all the publicity and the excellent public image of the then BTA chairperson, Frances McMullan – one of the few Protestants left in the estate by the late 1960s – many outsiders were attracted to Ballymurphy. Some were philanthropists who quickly became disillusioned and fled. Others such as the Child Poverty Action Group (CPAG) were more resilient. The CPAG was based in Queen's University, and it, like everybody else, was becoming aware that something was very much amiss in the cluster of houses at the base of Black Mountain. It approached the BTA, in the person of Nicholas Ragg, offering to set up an advice centre. Before doing so, however, it decided to discuss its proposal with the Citizens Advice Bureau (CAB), based in the city centre at Bryson House. The CAB stated that there appeared to be no great need in Ballymurphy. It had only dealt with three cases from the area in the past year.

Nick Ragg and his colleagues were, on the strength of that one assertion, absolutely convinced of the need. The CAB, they reasoned, was incorporated into a bureaucratic structure in a large city office block, and was therefore intimidating to most working-class parents. As a result the vast majority of people in Ballymurphy had nowhere to turn when confronted with a problem.

CPAG set up its advice centre in St Aiden's School. In its first year it dealt with over 500 cases involving a vast range of problems. The centre was to operate for the next seven years, until in 1974, the CAB opened a branch in the Bullring which was staffed by Anna Andrews, a local woman of infinite compassion, who made the CAB work in Ballymurphy.

The year 1969, a bombshell in the political life of the Six Counties, saw the realisation of the BTA's dream. Work on the community centre commenced. After six years, the efforts of the tenants' association were bearing fruit. Since Graham Larmor's untimely death, Dr H.S. Corscadden had taken over as patron of the appeal. As President of the Ulster Merchant Bank, the new patron was able to facilitate the BTA with a bridging loan at 9.5 per cent interest and guarantee an equivalent interest on their deposit of £10,000. This was a major factor in deciding the starting date of the building.

Day by day the people of Ballymurphy were now seeing their own community centre rising steadily from the waste ground above the City Cemetery. The BTA had shown that, with motivation and determination, great things were possible. The principles of 'discussion, resolution, decision and action' had triumphed over seemingly insurmountable odds. The first stage of the building was completed in 1970; and its first activity was a summer playscheme run by the Belfast Quakers – the BTA's first involvement with young people since the disastrous end of its youth section in 1965. Soon the community centre had become a focal point of Ballymurphy. Social functions were well supported and the BTA was always on hand to attend to any problems that might crop up.

In November 1970 the association employed Paddy McCarthy as its first full-time youth worker. But, by then, the 'Troubles' had come to Ballymurphy.

References

1. Spencer, AECW, *A Tale of Two Surveys* (Queen's University of Belfast, 1973), p. 2.
2. Frank Cahill, former BTA secretary (1976 Interview).
3. Press release by Irish Public Relations Consultants, October 11th 1967.
4. *Belfast Telegraph*, October 11th 1967.

3

Belfast in Flames

On the eve of August 13th 1969, the picture in Derry looked grim to nationalists in Belfast. The city was burning. The RUC and loyalist mobs had the Bogside under siege. CS gas was being poured into Free Derry. 'B' Specials, armed with rifles, were poised for what looked like a pending massacre of the people behind the barricades. Something would have to be done before it was too late.

Large crowds began to muster on the Falls Road. To show solidarity with the Bogsiders, and as a protest against the RUC onslaught in Derry, they decided to band together and march on Springfield Road Barracks to hand in a hastily prepared petition. The RUC at Springfield Road told them to go to Hastings Street, as RUC headquarters for the area had been temporarily transferred. The crowd, still expanding and growing increasingly angry, marched back down the Falls.

At Hastings Street a group of teenagers began to stone the barracks. In response, District Inspector Cushley ordered the RUC's Commer armoured cars on to the street. The crowd scattered, to reform again at midnight at Springfield Road Barracks. Convinced that they had earlier been duped into an ambush, they attacked the building with stones and petrol bombs. The RUC inside opened up with guns and wounded two men. As the crowd fled, fire was returned by two armed IRA men. In nearby Leeson Street, shots were also fired at the RUC, and a hand grenade was thrown.

In an alarmingly short time, protest against the events in Derry had given way to gunfights between the RUC and people from Belfast's main nationalist stronghold. Although the disturbances petered out shortly afterwards, the fact remained that guns had been used by nationalists against the RUC – a major escalation in the ten-month old conflict.

The next day was Thursday, August 14th, the day 8,500 'B' Specials were mobilised across the North, the day British troops trundled into Derry to lift the siege of the Bogside, the day the 'B' men shot dead John Gallagher and wounded two other nationalists during a riot in Armagh. West Belfast, and the more isolated nationalist pockets were on tenterhooks with rumours of invasion. The mobilisation of the 'B' Specials had confirmed that the loyalist state was gathering its forces, regular and irregular, for a full offensive against the risen nationalists. Barricades were thrown up across the small streets off the Falls. An RUC patrol moving up Percy Street was showered with petrol bombs from Divis Flats.

Then, towards nightfall, a loyalist mob that had been gathering for some hours on the Shankill Road swept down the 'mixed' Percy and Dover streets towards the Falls.

The invasion had begun.

Nationalist homes in the mixed streets were petrol-bombed, their occupants beaten up, while many of the fleeing residents were wounded by loyalist gunmen. As the mob reached the Falls, attacking St Comgall's School, a loyalist was hit by IRA automatic fire, one of the few defensive actions taken by the IRA that night. The RUC immediately opened up on the nationalist area, spraying the narrow streets and the blocks of Divis Flats with heavy calibre Browning machine-gun fire from Shorland armoured cars. Two people were killed in Divis Flats.

Simultaneously, the small nationalist enclave of Ardoyne in North Belfast came under arson and gun attack by the same combined forces of loyalists and RUC. The RUC killed three nationalists, while the mobs, including many 'B' Specials, burned down three whole streets.[1] The following morning, August 15th, 150 nationalist homes lay gutted; six people were dead, including a nine-year-old boy in Divis; and 150 others were wounded by gunfire. Ireland was shocked and horrified. After 10 months of intercommunal rioting and RUC attacks on civil rights marchers, war had come to the Six Counties.

In Belfast, nationalists were frightened and angry. They also felt badly let down by their last line of defence, the Irish Republican Army. 'I Ran Away' was scrawled on walls across Ardoyne. Many republicans shared the nationalist contempt.

As far back as 1967, when the Northern Ireland Civil Rights Association (NICRA) was founded, sections of the organisation had foreseen such a response from the RUC and 'B' Specials. Realising that any bid for civil rights would inevitably become linked to the question of national rights, they had sent a delegation to Dublin to ask the IRA if it could provide protection in the event of an armed knee-jerk by the state. The IRA had said yes.

During July and early August of 1969, as the rioting gradually increased in Belfast, and nationalist areas came under sporadic loyalist fire, community leaders had again approached the Belfast IRA, most of them old veterans of earlier days, for protection. They in turn sent word to Dublin, asking for an immediate transfer of guns and ammunition from the 26 Counties; but the guns and ammunition were not there. Most had been sold to the Free Wales Army.

The sale of the IRA arsenal was a reflection of what had been happening within the republican leadership since the collapse of the Border Campaign in 1962. Cathal Goulding, who had been imprisoned in England from 1953 to 1961 for his part in an arms raid, was the new Chief of Staff. In 1963 Goulding met with Roy Johnston, a computer scientist and socialist with strong links with the Communist Party of Great Britain and the much smaller Communist Party of Ireland (CPI).

Johnston had been involved with the Connolly Association in London. When he returned to Dublin in 1963, he brought with him a new vision of republicanism, one that Goulding was willing to adopt as the way forward for the IRA. Johnston argued that Sinn Fein would have to forgo its romantic past and recognise the Dail, Stormont and Westminster. As the ensuing controversy raged, he and Goulding were busily encouraging republicans to become involved in trade unions, co-operatives, housing groups and the general social movement with a view to demonstrating the correctness of the socialist/republican approach to issues.

Meanwhile, Johnston and his CP allies were perfecting the 'stages theory', still being pursued today by the Workers' Party, descendants of Official Sinn Fein, one of the two parties to emerge from the political fracturing of republicanism in 1970. The stages theory goes something like this. First, a capitalist democracy would be established in the Six Counties by working through the loyalist and nationalist working class on civil liberties and civil rights issues, resulting in intercommunal working-class solidarity. Next, the radicalised fused working class of the North would be married to its Southern counterpart, now also radicalised by Sinn Fein's political programme; with capitalism working well, and the border and national question removed from Irish politics, Ireland would have a strong indigenous bourgeoisie and a united, politicised industrialised labour force. At this third stage, the Irish working class would overthrow capitalism throughout the island.

Somewhere along the line, it was either decided that this would be done without the use of force, or that the guns would all be rusty before it came about. Either way, the weapons were sold; and in August 1969, as the Falls Road and Ardoyne burned, the naivete of the Dublin leadership was coming to roost on the heads of Northern nationalists. Goulding and Johnston's CP-inspired stages theory may have had no room for the loyalist working class engaging in all-out pogroms against the nationalist working class; but nobody had bothered to fill the loyalists in on the idea.

With the whole of the Lower Falls resembling a blitz zone, and palls of smoke still hanging over the gutted nationalist streets, British troops came marching up the main road on the afternoon of August 15th 1969, pointing their rifles up and down the narrow streets with no idea of why they were there, or who they were supposed to be sorting out. But more was to come. Bombay Street, completely nationalist, was razed to the ground that night in full view of British troops, as were more homes in Ardoyne. In all, six people were killed and 200 homes burned out during the two-day RUC/loyalist invasion of the nationalist enclaves of Belfast. Hundreds more were wounded.

One of the people on the Falls Road during the night of August 14th was Frank Cahill, secretary of the BTA, and a prominent member since its foundation, who, like many in Ballymurphy, had come originally from the Falls and still had relatives living there. Sixteen years after that violent night, he recalled the events that were to suck Ballymurphy onto centre stage in the war that had come to the North:

That night (August 14th) I was away with a group from here, helping a Protestant community over in Greenisland to run a bingo function; and Jimmy Burns and I, we were talking about the tension. There was so much about that we were thinking we might come back over the mountain rather than in through the city. Jimmy, he said: 'Well, that car of mine will do it but your van would never get there.' So he came over the mountain and I came in through the city; and there wasn't a sinner about. The centre of the city was absolutely deserted; and as we came up through the Grosvenor, right to the Springfield, there wasn't a person on the road.

Then, about half twelve, we were having a cup of tea when I went out to the gate. There were some people out there and they were saying that rumours were rampant about the place – of areas being attacked and so on. And people were congregating in Springhill. There were attacks coming from Corry's timberyard, the occasional shot being fired. It was felt it was the 'B' Specials and people were in an awful state, looking for protection – there was no protection here – and the decision was made that it would be very wise to advise the people that the safest place would be their homes, to stay indoors. If there was going to be an attack at all, there was no equipment here, and there was no military movement to protect the area.

Things were happening on the Falls at that time, the burning and that, and we weren't aware of that at all. It was happening further down, and that was why we hadn't seen anything at the Springfield Road. So, later on then, I went down to my brother, Tom, and he and I went down to see my mother and father, to see if they were all right. Then it was decided that Tom and I would go in towards town. At that stage we learned what was happening.

The thing had fairly well calmed down, but people were in a state of shock, and in a situation where they were desperately trying to set up a defence. They feared there were going to be more attacks. The mills were burning at the time. The loyalist snipers had taken positions on the roofs and they were firing into the nationalist areas. They were so high that there was no defence against that at all, so the people had set fire to the mills. [2]

On the morning of August 15th, with the shock waves still coming in from the Lower Falls and Ardoyne, Frank Cahill went to work amidst the stunned uncertainty of nationalist Belfast. He came home at lunchtime to an estate that was in consternation.

I was having a cup of tea here and I was approached by three or four women who came in and said, 'For Christ's sake come out of your work, things are happening in Ardoyne and they're happening all over the place'.

Later that evening, we had the first influx of people, we had the refugees arriving in here some time about 3 o'clock in the afternoon. Luckily, we had taken some precautions the night before – we had taken a decision to have the schools opened – in the event that we might have to cope with the problem. (At the time the people in authority in the schools, they were treating our demand as some kind of panic, that there was no need for it, and they wouldn't open the schools. However, we, the local people, opened the schools and had them prepared.)

So I got in the van and went back down to where I was working – I had to go through the shipyard – and whenever I got down to Queen's End and into the shipyard, all the workers from the shipyard were out on the road. It was the trade union movement that had called for that particular action to try and stop any intimidation. However, it frightened me enough to leave the van and get the hell out of it. I was expecting that everyone (the Catholics) would be put out – I wasn't aware of the purpose of the action. Then, whenever I got home, the place was in turmoil with families arriving in from all over the place. So, at that stage an organisation had to be set up.[3]

That evening, nine people met at St Bernadette's School, a meeting initiated by three local women, Nora McCafferty, Ethel McAllister and Nelly Clarke. The purpose: to organise relief for the families flooding into Ballymurphy, and to organise basic defence.

The first concern of the group was that there were a number of loyalist families in the area, and they would have to be approached individually and given reassurance that they would get the protection of the local people.

The next step was the formation of a women's corps to organise food and clothing for the incoming refugees, many of whom had nothing but the clothes on their backs. After that, there was the question of bedding, medicines, communications and transport. Ballymurphy was rounding the most crucial bend in its history.

The relief operation now springing into action was centred around St Thomas', St Aidan's and St Bernadette's schools, the first two fully under the control of the Ballymurphy people. Offices, assembly halls and kitchens were opened up as the women went from door to door for a cup of sugar here, a quarter of tea there, until enough food had been collected to provide an evening meal for the area's sudden population increase. People began to drift into the schools to offer assistance. And, more significantly, barricades went up around the estates.

Everybody came out into the streets and they built barricades at every corner – the whole thing was crazy. But people said, 'Let them do it; at least people feel that they have something to do and that they are providing some protection.' They'd build a barricade here, and another one at the bottom of the street; and every corner was the same, with the result that the emergency services couldn't get into the place, you couldn't get transport in. So, that had to be taken on board the next day. People went out and looked around and decided, We'll remove all the barricades inside the estate, and we'll leave one entrance and one exit. And we'll strengthen the barricades on the outside of the estate.[4]

At the same time, three shotguns were acquired for defence. For maximum preventive effect, these were brought up to the top end of Ballymurphy, facing predominantly loyalist New Barnsley, and poked out through the barricades.

That evening, as Bombay Street was reduced to ashes, Ballymurphy and every resource it could muster was being taxed to its limits.

References
1. *Sunday Times* Insight Team, *Ulster* (Penguin, 1972), p. 136.
2. Frank Cahill of Ballymurphy (1985 Interview).
3. Ibid.
4. Ibid.

4

Emergency

By nightfall on August 15th, Ballymurphy was in a state of flux. The trickle of families that had begun to arrive in the afternoon had grown to a deluge as Bombay Street burned and nationalist homes across the city came under attack. Although a certain amount of work had been done in anticipation of a possible problem, nothing of the scale of what was happening had been expected.

Vehicles were pouring in from every direction, bringing shocked and hysterical families who had just been burned out of their homes, or had managed to flee with a few possessions before loyalist arsonists had reached them. Some had friends or relatives in the area, but many had headed for Ballymurphy simply because it had as yet been untouched and was considered a safe haven. Nothing could have been further from the truth, as those furiously organising in the estate understood only too well.

Across the Springfield Road lay loyalist New Barnsley, now also barricaded off; behind that were the mixed flats of Moyard; and beyond Moyard were Springmartin and Highfield, the most western outposts of the Shankill bastion of loyalism. Springmartin sat on a hill, overlooking Ballymurphy and Springhill, its blocks of flats commanding an excellent view and affording an ideal vantage point to snipers. It would be easy for the loyalists to launch an attack, sweeping into Springhill from Springmartin, and Ballymurphy from New Barnsley. Without guns the area would be impossible to defend, and Goulding in Dublin was still showing no signs of sending the guns.

Meanwhile, the glint of gunmetal could be seen at barricades and windows on the far side of the Springfield Road. In a desperate bid to bluff their neighbours into believing Ballymurphy to be an armed fortress, the unfortunate carriers of the estate's three shotguns were sent running from barricade to barricade to make much display of their weapons. Large numbers of young men and women were also dispatched to the barricades as Ballymurphy's community leaders concentrated on sorting out the turmoil within the rather shaky ring of defence. It is claimed by many an older Ballymurphy resident that their first grey hairs appeared in the week that came in the wash of August 15th 1969.

Right through that Friday night, and on through Saturday, August 16th, the flood of refugees continued to pour into Ballymurphy. Two hundred families were billeted with friends and relatives by Saturday night, as St Bernadette's, St Thomas' and St Aiden's schools coped with the overflow. St Bernadette's and St Thomas' were both staffed by the growing relief organisation, St Aidan's by the Christian Brothers who

24

owned the school. The respect earned by the Brothers over the next ten days was to last to the present, as was the case with the nuns of St Louise's and St Rose's schools on the Falls Road.

At first there had been a confused response to the emergency. Forty-eight-year-old Jimmy Burns, who became relief co-ordinator at St Thomas', found himself caught up in the gut reaction to the burning and shooting in the Falls and Ardoyne.

> People had come up from Clonard looking for men to go down and help with the fighting. A group of us were about to go when Paddy McGuinness stopped us in the street and says, 'That's the worst thing you could do. We're going to need mature, experienced people here to organise relief'. St Thomas' was then opened and things started to happen spontaneously – people going out on to the road and stopping bread vans and food lorries and bringing them to the school.[1]

At the same time the people of Ballymurphy had taken it upon themselves to provide food and bedding for the incoming families; but by Saturday they were bled dry and the relief committee, now including most members of the militant BTA, had taken over. The spontaneous hijacking of food vehicles was immediately turned into a co-ordinated effort of double urgency. The food was funnelled into the relief committee's stores and the lorries then incorporated into nationalist Belfast's growing rescue mission.

Word was coming in of terrified families fleeing the Grosvenor Road, Donegall Road, Tiger's Bay, York Street, Sandy Row, Highfield and Greenisland areas. Ardoyne was facing a mass evacuation of women and children. The men were the only ones staying, forming themselves into a defence force against the loyalist threat of 'coming back to finish the job'. Buses were hijacked to augment the supply of trucks, and squads of young Ballymurphy men drove across the city, through burning streets and hails of loyalist gunfire, to snatch families from blazing homes, or to grab what they could if they were lucky enough to arrive one jump ahead of the loyalists. Jimmy Burns spent the whole of that Saturday evacuating people out of Ardoyne.

> I had a wee blue Volkswagon at the time. I was able to take four or five at a time. I was the first into Ardoyne, that end at least. All you seen was the cage-cars full of RUC and 'B' Specials. They'd been shooting at the nationalists all night along with the loyalists. Attacking Ardoyne and the old Glenard Estate. There was a bus depot up there and our ones got all the buses and blocked as many entrances as they could with them – used them for barricades.
> There was a committee in Ardoyne and one of them says to me that evening. 'This reminds me of Jerusalem. There's too many leaving; and the more that leave, the more the rest is starting to panic.' Me and the other drivers told them that all they had to do was tell us to leave and we'd go, but first check if anyone was really desperate. So they did that and we got one more load apiece, and that was the end of that operation ...

There were all sorts of rumours too that they were mobilising to invade Ballymurphy. Sensible men were talking like this. The 'B' Specials were supposed to be coming from Hastings Street Barracks – 22 cage-cars and tenders – and they were going to shoot their way up the Falls. At the same time all of Highfield was supposed to be up in arms.[2]

Similar rumours were running the opposite direction. Davie McCafferty and a few others had taken a bus to Ardoyne. On the way back across the West Circular, they were arrested by 'B' Specials and the RUC, and brought to Tennent Street Barracks. Later, as they were being released, an RUC sergeant who reluctantly provided them with an escort through a mob of rampaging loyalists told them, 'We're not going anywhere near Ballymurphy. We believe there are 500 riflemen in the area.'

Belfast was by then in total anarchy, while all the time, the areas under siege – the Falls, Ardoyne, Short Strand (6,000 nationalists, cut off from the city by the River Lagan, and surrounded by 60,000 loyalists), Ballymurphy, Turf Lodge and Andersonstown – pleaded with the IRA in Dublin to release the much-needed weapons; and the promise was always 'tomorrow'.

People from Ballymurphy went to see the staff officers of what existed of the Belfast Battalion, now all based in Andersonstown, and were again told 'tomorrow'. They were also told that the remnants of the Battalion were being organised into one big flying column that would be ready to rush off to any area that came under all-out attack. Ballymurphy wasn't too impressed by the practicalities of the flying column idea, or the fact that 'tomorrow' never came. It became increasingly clear that, if it came to the crunch, Ballymurphy's defence would be in the hands of its own hastily recruited vigilante corps, the three super-mobile shotguns and the boxes of petrol bombs being manufactured at a steady rate in 'factories' throughout the district.

The vigilantes were already in control of the policing of the area, bringing a marked decline in vandalism and petty crime, partly as a result of the efficiency of the vigilantes and partly because there was a new outlet for youthful frustrations. Young people, long-time victims of unemployment and institutionalised violence, were overnight placed in a role in which the lives and property of others depended on their performance. Most responded with a dedication that was a harbinger of times to come.

Many years later, Frank Cahill who was co-ordinating relief in St Bernadette's, would comment: 'Something that's got to be said about the young people: they slept in the schools, they were out doing the rescue work, always available, and they were afraid of nothing.' In St Thomas' School, youths, who would not, in the past, have been averse to putting a stone or two through the school's windows, were protecting the salvaged belongings of refugee families. Jimmy Burns, beaming with pride, said afterwards, 'The families dossed down in the classrooms. The desks were shifted. The hall and stage were kept for furniture. A square was marked off in chalk to show each family's possessions, and nothing was misplaced. Not one item went missing in all those months.'

The RUC had now been completely rejected by nationalists and the concept of community policing was born. Today, 20 years on, the lineal descendants of those early community police forces that sprang up in August 1969 are still called on by nationalists to contain crime and anti-social behaviour within the working-class districts.

For the first few days of the Ballymurphy rescue mission, all aspects of relief in the area were in the hands of groups of the estate's residents. These were mostly the people who had been the prominent community/political activists of previous years, who were now drawing to themselves the great pool of ability that, in the previously predestined course of events, would have gone unnoticed. They also had as an ally the unfailing generosity of the people. As Jimmy Burns would recall:

I had taken a fortnight's holidays. We only slept a couple of hours through the day, then we were going all night in the school. It's hard to describe what the pressure was like. But the people were great. All sorts flooded in to work on a voluntary basis. We had one ex-army cook and several professional chefs. And the people gave everything they had in their homes ... Some of the refugee women were really on the point of cracking up. We put them into houses, even for a few days. It eased their nerves. Some of our people even gave families their own homes and moved out themselves.[3]

Among the young men who came forward in those early days was 21-year-old Gerry Adams, a prominent Ballymurphy republican who would soon be O/C of the Provisional IRA's Belfast Brigade, and President of Sinn Fein within 15 years. (Ironically, as the future commander of the Belfast Brigade threw in his lot with the St Bernadette's relief committee, Andy Tyrie, future commander of the loyalist Ulster Defence Association, was among those co-ordinating events on the New Barnsley side of the Springfield Road.)

Together the Ballymurphy community leaders and the pool of energy that flocked from the overcrowded impoverished homes of the area ran an operation that would have done any relief agency proud. They accommodated, fed and comforted hundreds of incoming families; kept a detailed register of all refugee movements through the area, so that families could be kept in touch; commandeered food, bedding, clothing and transport; set up field hospitals stocked by the local chemists; established telephone and courier links with all other nationalist areas; and set up a 24-hour link with their opposites in New Barnsley, who included Andy Tyrie, to avert the escalation of rumours, agreeing that each area contain its own people – which worked until Easter 1970.

Throughout, Hughes', McErleans' and Kennedy's bakeries supplied bread and petrol, while Kennedy's Dairy donated milk. Simultaneously, the Knights of Malta staffed a 24-hour post at St Thomas', and the area's two GPs, Doctors Bunting and Beirne, volunteered their services, attending the sick and those in shock, and advising on vital health matters. Frank Cahill could never praise them enough:

There were the kind of things we weren't aware of, like burning stuff. Damien Beirne came in and told us we should put up incinerators. When we said we didn't know how, he replied that it was as simple as getting a 40-gallon drum and punching holes in it ... There were also the dangers of infectious diseases such as dysentery or whooping cough, and the doctors advised on the opening of an isolation unit at St Louise's.[4]

Meanwhile, during this whole period of catastrophe, as the biggest population movement in Europe since the Second World War got under way, and emergencies were declared in the protected corridor of West Belfast, the statutory bodies failed totally to respond. Ten days had passed before they made their first discredited appearance in Ballymurphy. They were greeted with a catalogue of human misery that would linger in the collective psyche of Ballymurphy. One story, later recounted by Jimmy Burns, would encompass much of the haplessness of the refugees:

One of the most harrowing sights I remember was up in St Aiden's. I went up there to find out where we could get provisions. There was an old man and an old woman in the school and they were in shock. They couldn't speak. In their lifetime it was the fifth time they had been burned out of their home by loyalists. If there had been a photographer to take a picture of yon grey-haired old woman ... She had been burned out as a child; she had been burned out along with her own children; and she was now burned out again after her children had their children.
This was her whole life.[5]

In another response to the August pogroms, the Central Citizens' Defence Committee (CCDC) was established in Leeson Street, in the Falls, as a co-ordinating body for nationalist districts; and Radio Free Belfast, staffed by People's Democracy, went on the air.

Mick Clarke, a member of the BTA and the St Bernadette's relief committee, and a resident of Ballymurphy since 1953, was one of the estate's representatives on the CCDC. He recalled how Ballymurphy began to close ranks against the state and its forces immediately after the barricades went up. The loyalist state, the enemy during almost two decades of institutionalised violence, was now showing its true hand. The deprivation and scapegoating that had been carried to such lengths in the past were now being pushed to their logical conclusion. Nationalists were under armed attack by the Orange state. Henceforth, that state, its armed forces and its agents were not welcome in Ballymurphy.

At the CCDC meetings everyone was told that we didn't want any of them in – there was none of them any good to us. And no way was the army or the RUC getting in. The RUC would only get in if there was serious crime – rape or murder. Then they'd be allowed in to investigate.
One night the RUC came in under cover, and a crowd of young fellows playing football in the Bullring spotted them. They ran down a hill and escaped out through one of the entries. Johnny McCullough and I fol-

lowed them, and we saw them go into the barracks which used to be in a house on the Springfield Road. We went in and saw Sergeant Curry and said, 'You very near had a riot on your hands.' We told him that if they did this they could expect an awful lot of trouble because our people were definitely not going to have it. Nobody wanted to know the RUC. It's still the same today, but they come in now in force with the British army.[6]

As the days went by, the community behind the barricades of Ballymurphy was gradually transformed. There was a pride in how the area had coped with the refugees. There was a new neighbourliness, almost a comradeship, born of the threat of invasion and the need for full co-operation of all residents in maintaining the massive relief operation and the staffing of schools and barricades. There were also the stories of heroic deeds carried out by Ballymurphy's rescue squads. And always the intermittent anecdote, like the time Packie McHugh and three or four others were shot at in Mountcollier Street down the Shore Road:

> They went down to remove that family twice. Twice they asked to be removed and twice they refused when the squad turned up. There was a dispute between the husband and the wife. It was a home they had bought and reared a family in and she was reluctant to go. On the third occasion, when Packie and the others went down, the whole lot were shot at. At that stage the wife decided that the Shore Road was no longer a wise place to be in.[7]

Eventually, as alternative accommodation was found for the homeless families, the emergency, the immediate emergency at least, eased off, but despite the apparent return to 'normality', Ballymurphy would never be the same again. The experience had cemented the whole community into a single highly-motivated machine that could, it transpired, be called upon again at a moment's notice. In the emotive highlights of those ten days the people had had nobody but themselves, but they had triumphed none the less. 'It was an amazing time', Mick Clarke said later, 'It was great to have been part of it. All the people were so much together at that time. But there were various things that happened afterwards that spoiled a lot of it.'

After ten days of hectic organisation and frenetic activity, the statutory bodies, discredited and redundant, began to make an appearance in Ballymurphy, and the schools closed down. The Relief Committee sat back to take stock and wondered what was coming next. Many of its members then went home for their first full night's sleep since August 15th.

The streets returned to their old selves except for the barricades that stayed on the outer perimeters and the three faithful shotguns that still did the rounds. But despite Ballymurphy's new-found togetherness there was, in the background of all the self-esteem and confidence, the gnawing unease that cropped up every time the locally emerging defence force looked at the three shotguns and the RUC/loyalist arsenal that might soon be stacked against them.

Fortunately, most of the area's residents were blissfully unaware of their vulnerability.

> The people in the area, they never panicked, they were never scared. I don't think most people ever thought, what are we going to do if there's an attack from New Barnsley or if there's an attack from anywhere else? They more or less thought that this was a fortress, our own people thought the same as the people in New Barnsley – that if the loyalists invaded Ballymurphy they'd probably get the ribbons cut out of them.
>   Well, as everybody knows, there wasn't a catapult here. It was pure bluffstakes. They walked about the top of that road on one side, and we walked about on the other side. They walked about armed and we walked about with hurley sticks. But still and all, even the army thought at that particular time that all the guns were on this side. And our people thought the same way; and that eased the tension, so long as you didn't know.
>   Our own people were under the impression that there was men and stuff in the area. It wasn't until afterwards, when the people moved out of New Barnsley, that it became known that we had nothing at all, and they realised how bad a position we were in. Although that was a good way to be. Had panic started at that time, it would have been a bad job.[8]

Within months, despite assurances from the statutory bodies that contingency plans would be drawn up so that no community would ever have to bear such a burden again, Ballymurphy was once more upended by a second major relief operation. On the morning of Sunday June 28th 1970, as the violence in Belfast spiralled into new heights, a young man rushed into the estate to say that Highfield and Springmartin were being cleared of nationalist families. Loyalists were burning homes, and 40 families were under immediate threat. They needed 40 trucks *now*! Frank Cahill rang Harry Mason, chief of the Welfare Department, who had promised transport and asked for the trucks: there were none to be had. In desperation, two available trucks were dispatched to Highfield. The first returned with a family: the second was overturned by loyalists on Highfield's West Circular Road. The British army was contacted and informed of the situation. They arrived with one truck; and later, after much argument, agreed to supply a second. That particular evacuation lasted from 9 am that day until 7 pm, and reinforced Ballymurphy's distrust of those from outside who were offering help. Isolated, along with the other nationalist pockets of Belfast, defence became an issue of paramount importance as trouble began to flare between one side of the Springfield Road and the other, and the attacks on nationalists continued across the city.

During the weeks of the Ballymurphy relief operation, and the overall Belfast rescue mission, other people in nationalist areas were also furiously and urgently discussing this very topic. Groups of men and women, the old guard and the young uninitiated, were meeting clandestinely in one another's homes and in community halls. In the 26 Counties similar meetings were taking place.

The IRA was reborn and mobilising.

The turbulent history of the Ballymurphy community had collided, at a cataclysmic crossroads, with the history of Irish republicanism. During the struggles of the past two decades deeply-seated anti-authoritarian feelings had implanted themselves in the area. At times there had been high hopes of improvement – and the BTA had achieved the seemingly impossible, but, by late 1969 the pot had been simmering a long time. The community in general were aware that their plight was no accident, that it resulted from being part of a political minority with no chance of ever assuming power. The problems of the area were therefore seen in a political context.

The onslaught of August 1969 had crystallised this perception. It was clear that the state was willing to do all in its power to maintain the oppression of nationalists. The solution of the Ballymurphy problem therefore lay in the final solution of the constitutional struggle and the dismantling of the Orange state.

Though the IRA had failed the nationalists in August, it had been partially redeemed by the handful of activists who had engaged the invading loyalist forces, and was still seen as the only organisation that might provide defence for Ballymurphy, now being menaced by the armed loyalist presence across the road. The IRA also embodied a political ideology that fulfilled the long-term aspirations of people who might now be considering that the state should, and could, be dismantled.

This was a decisive shift in Ballymurphy's politics. Just a few months earlier, in the Stormont elections of February, the area had returned Paddy Devlin, of the pro-Union Northern Ireland Labour Party, indicating little real urge to campaign outside the established framework. There was, however, a very strong political consciousness present, and the shift was but a short step that had been inevitable since the very moment the RUC cracked the first nationalist skulls on Derry's Craigavon Bridge, in October 1968.

Although the surge of recruits to the reborn IRA were primarily concerned with defence, they were also conscious that they were joining an organisation committed to the overthrow of British rule in Ireland. The unionist monolith was under severe strain, and there was a new possibility of escape from the social and economic problems of Ballymurphy and the state that had created them. Many years later Gerry Adams would say, 'If anyone was ever to ask me what makes a revolution, how does it happen, and what are the ideal conditions, I would say, "go take a look at what happened in Ballymurphy".'[9]

At the same time, Jimmy Burns would be telling how: 'All the men who worked at the relief around in St Thomas' are all dead now, bar me: Billy Lynch, John Maguire, Mr Irvine, John Conlon, Paddy Joe McGuinness and poor oul' Sean Fagan. They were the men that organised the younger ones.'[10]

Then the younger ones went on to organise themselves.

References

1. Jimmy Burns, formerly of Ballymurphy estate (1987 Interview).
2. Ibid.

3. Ibid.
4. Frank Cahill of Ballymurphy (1987 Interview).
5. Jimmy Burns (1987 Interview).
6. Mick Clarke of Ballymurphy (1985 Interview).
7. Frank Cahill (1987 Interview).
8. Mick Clarke (1985 Interview).
9. Gerry Adams, formerly of Ballymurphy (1986 Interview).
10. Jimmy Burns (1987 Interview).

5

Pursuing the Republic

Apart from its role in rescuing and accommodating fleeing nationalist families, Ballymurphy, on the surface, was reasonably quiet between August 1969 and Easter 1970. The liaison with New Barnsley prevented any inter-communal strife: rumours were nipped in the bud, and the Springfield Joint Committee ensured that no provocative action occurred on either side of the Springfield Road. However, the events of the summer had reached tendrils into every corner of the North, and those tendrils were ultimately all linked back to forces that were beyond the control of individual communities.

The British army was now deployed along what later became known as the 'Peaceline' between the Falls and Shankill roads. On the Falls they were being viewed by many as a more favourable alternative than the RUC machine-gunners who had killed their kith and kin in August – soldiers were being offered tea by many residents – but the nationalist community was not about to depend on pro-Stormont British troops for protection. The myth, that the British army had gone into Derry to protect nationalists, hadn't yet been forged. Nationalists were only too aware that they had gone in to prop up the crumbling power of the Stormont regime. As James Callaghan, Home Secretary of the time had explained:

> The government of Northern Ireland has informed the United Kingdom government that as a result of the severe and prolonged rioting in Londonderry it has no alternative but to ask for the assistance of troops at present stationed in Northern Ireland to prevent a breakdown of law and order.[1]

Nationalists in Belfast therefore put their trust in the CCDC which quickly built up its membership until 95 delegates represented some 75,000 people across the city. The CCDC was responsible for co-ordinating the defence of nationalist areas, organising foot and mobile patrols in the more tense neighbourhoods. This role had traditionally been the IRA's, but the Belfast IRA had been in disarray during the August crisis when the CCDC was born. (It later became known that there were no more than 50 to 60 active IRA personnel in the city during the time of the pogroms.) However, as the rejuvenated IRA began to grow, the CCDC was already in trouble, a victim of the class divisions that would eventually render it impotent.

The first major rift in the CCDC came in mid-September 1969, when the Catholic hierarchy in Belfast, who as usual had thrown in their lot with the ruling classes, coerced the people of the Falls into taking down

33

their barricades, prompting the immediate arson of three nationalist homes. The gradual takeover of the CCDC leadership by the Church, and its subsequent pandering to British interests, alienated it totally from much of the nationalist working class until the organisation became irrelevant.

Meanwhile, the Republican Movement was filling the gap. By the time the first barricades came down this process was well under way in Ballymurphy.

During the early 1960s Ballymurphy had formed part of an IRA company area that reached from the Grosvenor Road in the Falls, up through Ballymurphy and Turf Lodge and down into Andersonstown, all under the overall command of the Belfast Battalion. This macroscopic structure, in reality, boiled down to two or three Volunteers in Ballymurphy, two or three in Turf Lodge, maybe one in Springhill, and so on. In the wake of the Divis Street riots of 1964[*] and the 1966 commemoration to mark the fiftieth anniversary of the Easter Rising in Dublin, a handful of new recruits had come forward.

As a result the army had restructured itself a little so that Ballymurphy and Turf Lodge constituted a separate area. When the Republican Clubs were organised in the middle of the decade to circumvent an existing ban on Sinn Fein, Ballymurphy became part of the Andersonstown Republican Club area, whose PRO was the youthful Gerry Adams. Adams had joined Sinn Fein after the Divis Street riots and had already, through his involvement in housing agitation, become a well known figure in the Lower Falls.

At that time the Republican Movement consisted of older members from previous campaigns and a spattering of younger people who came from families in which the father or mother, or both, had been active in the 1930s or 1940s. Volunteer activity was generally confined to rudimentary arms training in homes within the area. They had the odd dump here and there, and their support was limited to a close circle of people in each area.

As the civil rights agitation, and the accompanying RUC/loyalist violence, developed during late 1968 and early 1969, the IRA numbers grew steadily. By August 1969 its strength in the Ballymurphy area was, relatively speaking, quite respectable: there were eight or nine people involved. Republican political activity, through the Republican Clubs, was also steadily advancing within Ballymurphy though it met with some strong opposition from the fiercely independent BTA, who were

*During the Westminster election campaign of Autumn 1964 Sinn Fein displayed an Irish Tricolour in the window of its headquarters in Divis Street. This was a violation of the Flags and Emblems Bill of 1954 which gave the RUC power to remove any display they considered to endanger 'public order'. When Paisley and his followers threatened to march on Divis Street to remove the flag, the RUC raided the Sinn Fein offices on orders from the Stormont Minister of Home Affairs, Brian McConnell. As soon as the RUC arrived, the people of the Lower Falls confronted them. The riots that spanned the next four days were described by the *Belfast Telegraph* as 'the worst outbreak of disorder for 30 years'.

deeply suspicious of all politicians and saw the republican interest in local issues as a possibly opportunistic move aimed at climbing on their bandwagon.

One of the issues in which republicans were involved in those days was a campaign to have safety rails erected at the Springfield/Whiterock junction after a New Barnsley child had been knocked down. Nationalists from Ballymurphy and loyalists from New Barnsley worked together for weeks on the issue and were eventually successful. But news of the combined effort had filtered up through unionist circles and an envoy of Paisley's turned up in New Barnsley to sow discontent among the loyalists.

Gerry Adams would later cite this experience as an example of the impractical nature of the 'stages theory' then being expounded in Dublin. 'If the state would not allow Catholics and Protestants to get a pedestrian crossing built together, it would hardly sit back and watch them organise the revolution together.'[2]

However, despite the early inspiration provided by Adams, it would take almost 15 years before community politics and the activities of a local political party would reach some kind of general common direction within the Upper Springfield. The party would again be Sinn Fein, but revamped and radicalised under the leadership of young republicans led by the man who so long ago had fought for that safety rail on the Springfield Road.

By August 1969, Gerry Adams was in a leadership position in Ballymurphy. In the immediate aftermath of the August crisis, he was involved in organisational work in the Falls, Ardoyne and Andersonstown areas, which took him away for three or four weeks. When he returned, he found an area that had been totally transfigured.

Ballymurphy had performed a very useful relief operation. The area was also barricaded. It was a difficult area to barricade because of the stretch along the front of the Springfield Road – not like down the Falls where you just had wee streets to be sealed off, or Andersonstown which was more of a closed estate. There was also the added difficulty of Springmartin being on the higher ground. The area was swept by rumours as well – of armed men in the windows of New Barnsley – although the relationship between the two estates was not bad. There weren't the same problems as in Ardoyne or Bombay Street, although the potential was there: there were the same circumstances.[3]

Commenting on the strength of leadership that was so obvious in every street, he attributed much of it to:

Some fine work done locally over the years by the Tenants' Association and others. You had the foundations being laid for the knitwear group, the Whiterock Enterprises, the survey ... that was all feeding into the accelerating politicisation of people. One major advantage that this area had over any other area, except for maybe the Bogside, was that you had that sort

of a background, you had a core of people who were in there and who
had been responsible for those developments.[4]

A number of the people who formed this core of leadership were old
republicans, no longer involved directly in the Movement, but fiercely
loyal to its principles. About them, they now saw a virtually unrecognis-
able community begin to mobilise, around the Republican Movement,
with a militancy that would have been unthinkable a few weeks before.
(It should perhaps be mentioned at this point that the Republican
Movement, though relatively small, was still the largest political organisation in nationalist Belfast in 1969. The politicians of the day – people
like Harry Diamond, Gerry Fitt and Paddy Devlin – did not have any substantial political machinery, and could in fact often be found courting
the 'republican vote' at election times.)

These new converts were now quite surprised to discover that the area
actually had eight or nine IRA Volunteers already in position – and a
Fianna Eireann (republican scout movement) group of some 25 youths
who had a reasonable grounding in republicanism, Irish history and
organisation. However, despite the surge towards militant republicanism,
six weeks were to pass before the relief operation would lose its urgency,
and the IRA would begin to organise on a large scale within Ballymurphy.

Towards the end of September a meeting was convened in one of the
local schools. Several hundred people from the now solidly bonded
Ballymurphy community heard speaker after speaker discuss the immediate problems of the area in relation to the continuing refugee influx,
the organisation of the vigilantes, the role of the CCDC, and the detailed
planning of an organisational network that would have threads into
every street and every home in the estate.

At the end of the meeting a man addressed the hall. He was a representative of Oglaigh na hEireann,* and he was inviting people to come
forward and volunteer for the Republican Army. The response was so
great, the volunteers came in such numbers, that a full-bodied IRA unit
came into being almost immediately.

Local republicans were astounded by the sheer number of recruits they
now had on their hands, and, as the weeks passed and these mainly
young men and women began to assume positions of responsibility on
the streets of Ballymurphy, local people were surprised at the quality of
leadership that had been spawned in their own streets, and by the calibre
of the individuals within the emerging republican organisation.

Men and women who, in another society, might have been highly
skilled members of the community, were turning their entire store of
creative energy into forceful opposition to the state, a fact not lost on
their future enemies, as was evidenced in a secret British military report
intercepted by the IRA in 1978. In it, Brigadier J.M. Glover of the

*Oglaigh na hEireann was the Gaelic name of the 1916 Irish Volunteers. It has
been retained to this day by the IRA.

Defence Intelligence Staff (who seemed to have a problem reconciling intelligence with the working class) described the IRA as: 'Essentially a working class organisation based in the ghetto areas of the cities and in the poorer rural areas ... Nevertheless there is a strata of intelligent, astute and experienced terrorists who provide the backbone of the organisation.'[5]

And, despite years of public denouncement of the IRA as a group of self-interested 'criminals' without popular support, Glover would go on to make a number of points that would prove extremely embarrassing to this official British propaganda line: 'Our evidence of the calibre of rank and file terrorists does not support the view that they are mindless hooligans drawn from the ranks of the unemployed and unemployable.'[6] And that the IRA would, in the coming years:

> probably continue to recruit the men it needs. They will still be able to attract enough people with leadership talent, good education and manual skills to continue to enhance their all round professionalism. The Movement will retain popular support sufficient to maintain secure bases in the traditional republican areas .[7]

This latter point was made at a time when it had become obvious that the IRA was devastatingly efficient in the manufacture of highly sophisticated weapons and intelligence technology.

Just as September 1969 would be remembered in Ballymurphy as the month when the IRA set down deep roots within the community, it would be remembered by the Republican Movement as the month that presaged the biggest upheaval in its history since the Civil War. On the evening of September 22nd, as growing tensions over the question of defence began to surface, the Ruling Council (Battalion Staff and O/Cs) of the IRA's Belfast Battalion were to meet at their headquarters in Leeson Street off the Falls Road.

Prior to that meeting, another IRA meeting was held in North Queen Street. It was attended by all the Belfast Company commanders except 'D' Company in the Leeson Street area. (The Battalion had now grown from five companies to 16.) Two dissident members of the Battalion Staff, who had decided that the pro-Goulding elements controlling the Battalion would have to be overthrown, were also present. Discussion revolved around the lack of arms in the city, the obvious intention of Goulding's Dublin Command – and his Belfast allies – of continuing with the 'stages theory', and the drive to end the Republican Movement's policy of abstentionism in relation to the Dail, Stormont and Westminster – all of which were interrelated.

The angry mood of the meeting was further amplified by a document entitled *Resistance* that had come up from Dublin in the wake of the burning of the Falls and Ardoyne. While the Northerners were clamouring for guns, Dublin was polishing up on its revolutionary rhetoric. It was decided to go on to the Cyprus Street meeting and stage a coup d'état.

The coup failed. According to one of the dissidents who burst in on the Cyprus Street meeting, the principal reason was that 'Jimmy Steele seemed the only one who was really serious about it, or at least had thought the thing out and may have been fairly ruthless about it.'

However, the dissidents were serious enough: when Billy McMillan, the Battalion commander, attempted to leave, a gun was produced and he was told to sit tight. There then followed a lengthy meeting at which a compromise was pieced together. The Belfast Command was increased from six to eleven for a period of three months, allowing all shades of opinion to be represented. If this trial period did not work to everyone's satisfaction, four steps would be taken. First, four members of the IRA's Army Council, including Goulding, would be removed; secondly, the Northern Command would become autonomous; thirdly, all political programmes would be abandoned in favour of a military build-up; and fourthly, the dissidents would not attend the IRA Army Convention in Dublin in December.

It was also decided that there should be no contact with GHQ in Dublin until the weapons issue was sorted out. Although, ostensibly, the Cyprus Street confrontation was about defence, it was also an attempt by the dissidents to stake out Belfast as their territory, knowing that whoever controlled Belfast would hold much sway in the broader political discussions coming up at the Army Convention. The old-time militarists and the young revolutionaries, politicised through the Republican Clubs and the civil rights agitation, were squaring up for the decisive showdown with Goulding's constitutionalists. The outcome would determine the future of the Republican Movement.

Between the Cyprus Street meeting and the IRA Army Convention, relationships further deteriorated between the pro and anti-Goulding factions, the dissidents accusing McMillan of welching on the September compromise. At December's Convention the Belfast IRA was therefore not represented, so that a compromise on a national level was no longer possible. And while the Bogside and the Falls braced themselves for further loyalist violence, the chief item on the Convention agenda was not the defence of Northern nationalists, but the unresolved issue of abstentionism.

The IRA delegates, heavily weighted with Gouldingites, voted 39 to 12 to end absentionism. Henceforth they would recognise the two Irish governments and Westminster. This was a crucial victory for the constitutionalists. All that remained for this to become the official republican position was for Sinn Fein to ratify the decision at its Ard Fheis in January.

The Army dissidents, feeling that the vote was a result of ongoing manoeuvreing that had put the Gouldingites into power, withdrew and formed a Provisional Army Council. Sean Mac Stiofain, Director of Intelligence of the Dublin Command, was elected Provisional Chief of Staff. The Northern Command was taken over by a number of the older republicans who had made the token stand against the RUC/loyalist invasion of the Falls in August 1969. Outlining their position, the dissidents issued a statement in which they said:

> We declare our allegiance to the 32-County Irish Republic proclaimed at Easter 1916, established by the first Dail Eireann in 1919, overthrown by force of arms in 1922 and suppressed to this day by the existing British-imposed Six-County and 26-County partition states.[8]

Meanwhile, events in the North continued to escalate. By the middle of September 7,500 British troops were stationed in the Six Counties and the British were effectively in control of the working-class areas of the cities and towns. Initially the military had shown a willingness to assault all sections of the Irish working class with absolute impartiality.

At the end of September they had clashed with Shankill loyalists who were attempting to attack the nationalist Unity Flats. In the ensuing riot the army fired 654 cartridges and 66 grenades of CS gas, equally affecting the loyalist attackers and the nationalists living in the flats. During a second night of rioting, shots were fired at the troops as they moved into the Shankill with heavy armour. Such confrontations between loyalists and the state caused consternation in unionist circles, with unionist politicians accusing the army of taking the nationalists' side. There were more clashes between loyalists and British troops in late September and early October, but the most catastrophic was to occur the weekend following the publication of the Hunt Report.

Back in August the British government had set up a committee headed by Lord Hunt to look at all aspects of policing in the North. Its findings and recommendations were published on Friday, October 10th 1969. Among other things, the Hunt Report urged that the RUC be disarmed in a cosmetic move to make the force more acceptable in nationalist areas and – the real crunch – that the notoriously partisan 'B' Specials be disbanded and replaced by a military regiment, locally recruited but under the control of the British army.

In loyalist eyes, the British government was caving in to nationalist demands: the armed forces of unionism were to be killed off at the stroke of a pen. The fact that the new force proposed by Hunt – the Ulster Defence Regiment (UDR)* – would be little more than a name and uniform change for the 'B' Specials was lost in the feeling of betrayal that swept loyalist areas.

On Saturday, October 11th, as partial disarming of the RUC began, young people began to gather at street corners on the Shankill Road. As the pubs closed that night, serious rioting broke out. The army came under attack as vehicles were hijacked and burned. The RUC came to the assistance of the military and they too were attacked. During the night

---

*Since its foundation, members of the UDR have carried out innumerable attacks against nationalists. These have included murder, maimings, bombings, kidnappings and serious assault. Many UDR members are also involved with loyalist killer squads responsible for the indiscriminate murders of 560 nationalists (up to February 1989).

the rioting worsened and eventually developed into a raging gun-battle in which two loyalists and RUC Constable Victor Arbuckle were killed. Thirty-seven others – 14 soldiers, three RUC men and 20 civilians – suffered gunshot wounds. Scores of others on both sides were injured in the rioting.

Three days after the Shankill riots, with unionist pressure growing on the British government, Robert Porter, Stormont Minister of Home Affairs, announced that the RUC were going back into the Falls, with military backing if necessary. Against this backdrop of loyalist firepower, and the threat of another invasion of the Falls, the IRA voted at the December Convention against arming the nationalists in the North.

When Sinn Fein met in January for its annual conference, the divisions within the Republican Movement were a running sore. There was an angry debate between those who favoured the stages theory and the abandonment of armed struggle, and those who argued that Sinn Fein should work as a propaganda arm for the IRA which should be fighting to destroy, not reform, the Six-County state.

Eventually the vote on the motion to scrap abstentionism was carried by a clear majority. However, as non-recognition of the three parliaments was enshrined in Sinn Fein's constitution, a two-thirds majority was required to effect change. The vote fell 19 short. It looked as if abstentionism would hold. At that point it was proposed from the hall that the Ard Fheis endorse the policies of the IRA Army Convention – which had already agreed to drop abstentionism. As this motion raised no constitutional questions a simple majority would suffice.

But, before the vote could be taken, the hundred or so pro-abstention, pro-armed struggle delegates walked out and reassembled at a hall in Parnell Square in the centre of Dublin. There, they gave their allegiance to the Provisional Army Council and created a Caretaker Executive of Sinn Fein.

In the North the schism convulsed through the nationalist communities. Families and neighbourhoods were split as the 'Officials' and 'Provisionals' consolidated their positions and attempted to win new ground. In Belfast, seven of the eleven old Battalion Staff remained loyal to Goulding's Official IRA (OIRA), whereas the officers and the majority of Volunteers from 15 of the Battalion's 16 Companies (all but Leeson Street) went over to the Provisionals. Initially, Ballymurphy adopted a unique position. Gerry Adams, who was a key member of the Northern Provisionals, later recalled that:

What happened in most areas was that Volunteers tended to follow the leaders. In Ballymurphy they held a meeting and invited the Battalion Staff – the Goulding element – to the meeting; and they had a debate. Sullivan put his case, and the local O/C put his; and the unit sat down and thrashed it out. Then some went with the Officials, while the rest stayed where they were. In fact what actually happened was that the Ballymurphy unit stayed semi-autonomous for a while.[9]

The future allegiance of the bulk of the Ballymurphy Volunteers had already been long predictable, even before the debate. The O/C of the unit had been suspended by the pro-Goulding element some weeks earlier as the anti-abstentionists attempted to manoeuvre as many as possible of their own people into senior positions. The Ballymurphy unit had refused to recognise the suspension, the only effect of which was to make the individual Volunteers more aware of the issues in the pipeline.

The day after the Ballymurphy debate an attempt was made by the Officials to arrest the IRA quartermaster for the area to gain control of the substantial weapons dumps in Ballymurphy. The attempt failed, and shortly afterwards the semi-autonomous Ballymurphy unit commandeered the entire dump. One of the men responsible for that operation described how they had lifted 'a massive Stickie* dump which caused palpitations for months. It was absolutely massive. It took six or seven big vans to cart it all away, and it just caused hysteria everywhere.'

The odd relationship between the Ballymurphy Volunteers and the remainder of the Belfast Brigade of the Provisionals was to last for six weeks and would flare up again a few months later in an unspoken disagreement on tactics and timing during the Ballymurphy riots. Structurally, the area was now part of the operational patch of the Second Battalion of the Belfast Brigade, Provisional IRA. The Officials, whose support in the city was mainly confined to the Lower Falls and Turf Lodge, had some following in the lower end of Ballymurphy estate; but this greatly diminished over the years, as did their support throughout the North.

Many of those who had stayed with the Officials after the split did so, not because they thought Goulding and McMillan were right, but because they felt uneasy with the sudden change. In late 1970 the Northerners forced Goulding to concede to 'defensive' armed action by the Official IRA in the Six Counties. When the Officials split again in 1974, two years after the leadership had declared a unilateral ceasefire, many of the Northerners joined the new Irish Republican Socialist Party (IRSP) whose military equivalent, the People's Liberation Army (PLA) (later the Irish National Liberation Army (INLA)) was to join in the armed offensive against the British presence in Ireland.

As 1970 began, with inter-communal clashes dominating the first three months, both IRAs steadily mushroomed in the working-class and rural parts of the North. Few of the young men and women flocking to the republican banner could have guessed that they would soon be at war with the British army. As far as most recruits were concerned, defence against loyalist attack was the primary concern. 'It was a gut reaction', a Volunteer in Ballymurphy would later explain. 'The loyalists were attacking our ones, and we knew that sooner or later it would come

*Shortly after the split the Officials brought out their own version of the Easter Lily, which commemorates the dead of the Easter Rising of 1916. Instead of the traditional pin-on lily, the Officials had theirs backed with adhesive, earning them the nickname 'Stickybacks', which was later abbreviated to 'Stickies' or 'Sticks'.

to the Murph. The Brits didn't really figure in those days. They just didn't belong in the fight .'

Then along came the Easter riots of 1970.

References
1. *Irish Times*, Dublin, August 15th, 1969.
2. Gerry Adams, *The Politics of Irish Freedom* (Brandon, Dingle, Co. Kerry, 1986), p. 15.
3. Gerry Adams of Ballymurphy (1985 Interview).
4. Ibid.
5. Brigadier J.M. Glover, *Northern Ireland Future Terrorist Trends* (internal report, November 1978).
6. Ibid.
7. Ibid.
8. *Irish Times*, Dublin, December 29th 1969.
9. Gerry Adams (1985 Interview).

6

The Battle of Ballymurphy

During the early months of 1970, as the Six Counties convulsed with regular spates of inter-communal rioting, the BTA maintained its local campaign for better living conditions. Its members also worked with other community organisations across the city, campaigning alongside them or helping them organise around their own issues.

On February 6th they joined tenants' groups from all the Corporation estates of Belfast in a takeover of the City Hall's public gallery. The Amalgamated Corporation Tenants' Association, protesting against a recent rent increase, had organised 50 per cent of Corporation tenants into a rent strike, and had decided on the takeover to highlight their demands. The action forced the City Council to abandon its meeting as the RUC carried the protestors – loyalists and nationalists united – from the Council chambers.

Housing issues had been brought to the fore at that particular time by the announcement on November 17th, by the Medical Officer for Belfast that, of 2,500 dwellings in the Lower Falls/Grosvenor Road area alone, only 40 were officially fit to be lived in.[1] Other inner-city housing was of an equally indefensible standard. The rent increases had added insult to injury, sparking off the city-wide protest in which the BTA played a prominent part. Of an executive of five on the Amalgamated Tenants' Association, the Ballymurphy people held two places.

At the same time, however, some members of the BTA, along with other community leaders in the area, were gradually being dragged deeper and deeper into the more perilous political process developing around them. The Springfield Joint Committee, comprising representatives of Ballymurphy Turf Lodge, Moyard, New Barnsley and Highfield, had managed to keep the peace between both sides of the Springfield Road since the previous August. Some of its Ballymurphy members had actually been caught in the middle – along with the IRA units that came in to quell the disturbances – on the third night of the Easter riots.

After the riots the Joint Committee had continued to strive for peace on the Springfield Road though it had been badly shaken by the events of Easter. But the spiral of escalating violence would soon push Ballymurphy's programme of social development, the Springfield Joint Committee and the Amalgamated Corporation Tenants' Association to one side as the community became engulfed in a war that would no longer keep its distance.

Throughout the latter half of 1969 attacks on civil rights demonstrators by loyalist and RUC forces had continued unabated, prompting sporadic spontaneous attacks by nationalist civilians on RUC barracks across the North. However, as yet – other than a gelignite and gun attack on Crossmaglen Barracks in South Armagh during the August trouble – the IRA had not been involved in the attacks. Military activity by republicans, though increasing, was still on a small scale. By the end of March, 16 explosions had been recorded for 1970, most consisting of small charges or incendiaries, many being the work of loyalists. Generally, these were free of casualties, the exception being a bomb at the Corporation Electrical Workers' Social Club on February 25th.

Following Ballymurphy's Easter riots there was a slight increase in bomb attacks. By June 25th, the day before the next disastrous weekend, 44 explosions were recorded. None the less, the overall situation had changed dramatically. During April, May and June, fierce rioting occurred on a regular basis in nationalist areas of North Belfast, following the pattern established in Ballymurphy over Easter.

Invariably these riots began with loyalist attacks on isolated nationalist pockets, often accompanied by the burning of homes and sniper fire. The British army would then arrive, turn their backs to the loyalists and, in a haze of CS gas, lay siege to the nationalist areas. Barbed wire barricades and mass house searches became a feature of everyday life in these areas. Those arrested by troops during street fighting (often passers-by who just happened to be in the wrong place at the wrong time) were taken away and systematically beaten in army barracks before being charged with riotous behaviour. During this period the Provisionals became increasingly active in engaging loyalist gunmen in sniping exchanges.

On April 18th loyalist attacks on nationalists took on a new form. Patrick McAuley of Ardoyne had just left a pub in Pilot Street and was on his way home when he was wounded by gunfire. It was the first attack of its kind when an individual nationalist had been picked at random for assassination.

Three days later Patrick Doyle of Colligan Street, off the Falls Road, was shot under similar circumstances as he left the Celtic Bar. Both men were lucky and recovered. The day after Patrick Doyle's attempted assassination, the British army came under gun attack in Ballymurphy for the first time. Shots were fired from a passing car at a sentry outside a temporary military base in a New Barnsley house.

A week later the area was momentarily reminded of the old days as Paddy Devlin MP came to its defence, lashing out at an article by Stephen Preston in the *Daily Telegraph*. Preston had stated, among other things, that Ballymurphy had the highest incidence of VD in the British Isles. Written corrections to his assertions were later released by Queen's University and the VD clinic in Belfast. The latter pointed out that there could be no foundation to Preston's VD slur as statistics were only available on a city-to-city basis.

Preston, however, was seeking nomination by the Unionist Party in Armagh for the coming Westminster elections. What better road to prominence than the time-honoured pastime of scapegoating Ballymurphy, especially in the aftermath of the Easter riots? A month later the tide was reversed a little when the media told of a visit on May 26th by Community Relations Commission chairperson, Maurice Hayes, to Ballymurphy Community Centre, where the first stage of the building was nearing completion.

On June 15th, in a continuing clarification of political divisions, the RUC and British army sent in a massive force to push 1,500 parading Orangemen through the nationalist town of Dungiven, County Derry.* Simultaneously, 5,000 republicans, led by a 1,500-strong Northern contingent, were gathering at Wolfe Tone's grave in Bodenstown, County Kildare. There, Ballymurphy's young recruits heard IRA leader, Daithi O Conaill, issue a ringing warning to the British:

> You never had any right to be in our country and you never will ... The more your troops impose their will, the nearer you bring the day of open confrontation. If you sincerely desire peace, then withdraw your armed force and the weapons of destruction you so lavishly supplied to the Stormont junta over the last fifty years. In a nutshell, get to hell [sic] out of our country.[2]

O Conaill also attacked the Dublin government for its attitude to the North. Then, in an unusual break from tradition, he indirectly forwarded sympathy to Charles Haughey and Neil Blaney, both ex-ministers in the ruling Fianna Fail party, who had been arrested, on May 28th, for allegedly conspiring to run guns into the country for use in the North.

O Conaill's oration came during the final days of the Westminster election campaign, a campaign punctuated by loyalist attacks on nationalist 'Unity' candidates at rallies throughout the North. Four days later the Tories came to power under Edward Heath. In the Six Counties, nationalists returned Bernadette Devlin (socialist Mid-Ulster MP since a by-election in April 1969), Gerry Fitt and Frank McManus.

At the time, Bernadette Devlin was facing a prison sentence arising out of her role during the defence of the Bogside the previous August. A week after her election, on June 26th, she was on her way to Derry to address a rally before giving herself up to the RUC when she was arrested in Drumahoe just outside the city. News of her 'kidnap' sparked off a riot in Derry and angered people throughout Ireland. Meanwhile, another riot, triggered off by an Orange parade along the Crumlin Road, blew up in Belfast as the city jerked towards its next major showdown.

Control of the Central Citizens' Defence Committee was now firmly in the hands of the nationalist middle class and the Catholic Church who, despite all the evidence, still believed that the RUC could be reformed and that British soldiers would protect the nationalist working class. It

---

*Each year, the North of Ireland, with its population of 1.5 million and an area the size of Yorkshire, is venue to some 2,000–2,500 parades (2,069 in 1987 according to the RUC Chief Constable's Annual Report, published April 12th 1988). All but a handful are Orange parades, many of which are highly provocative, often passing through staunch nationalist areas to remind the 'Taigs' of loyalist supremacy.

was with horror therefore that they learned on Tuesday, June 23rd, that, among the many Orange marches organised for the following Saturday, one was to pass through the rebuilt Bombay Street and Clonard, another was to pass Ardoyne where many families had been burned out, and a third was to come out of New Barnsley and pass along the Springfield Road – the very route taken by the Junior Orangemen at Easter.

Unable to believe that such obvious provocation could have been sanctioned by the state, Tom Conaty, a produce broker from Andersonstown, who was chairperson of the CCDC, spoke on Wednesday to Brigadier Hudson, military commander for Belfast, and the Chief Constable of the RUC, Sir Arthur Young, outlining the dangers of allowing those three particular marches to go ahead. He then hand-delivered a letter to Ronald Burroughs, British government representative in the North, in which the CCDC proposed that the Cupar Street and Ardoyne marches be re-routed, and that 'the march on the Springfield Road towards Ballymurphy be terminated no nearer to Catholic homes than the Orange Hall on the Springfield Road.'[3]

On Thursday the Joint Security Committee met at Stormont, with the Saturday marches top of the agenda. Despite the opposition of Hudson, Young and Burroughs, all marches were approved. By now the Stormont government of James Chichester-Clark, cousin of Terence O'Neill, who had taken over as Prime Minister on May 1st 1969, following O'Neill's resignation, was under severe pressure from the right wing within the Unionist Party and from the Reverend Ian Paisley's Protestant Unionists. There had been a serious crisis on March 18th, when Desmond Boal, John McQuade, William Craig, Harry West and Dr Norman Laird, five unionist MPs, had refused to support the government in a motion of support. The five were expelled – the first expulsions ever from the Unionist Party – the following day.

As recently as June 15th, Paisley had again been snapping at Chichester-Clark's heels, taunting him about pacts his Protestant Unionists had made with the Unionist Party in Derry, Armagh and South Down constituencies, and claiming these as evidence of a crumbling Unionist Party. Now, just a few days after an election that had shown Paisley's growing support among the loyalist working class, Chichester-Clark was not about to be party to any banning or re-routing of Orange parades.

Freeland, the GOC, went along with this line, as did the other political figures, believing that it would be 'easier to push them (the Orange parades) through the Ardoyne than to control the Shankill'.[4] Freeland's sentiments would have been coloured by his memories of the Shankill riots of June 3rd and 4th that followed the re-routing of an Orange parade along the Crumlin Road, as well as the British desire to prop up Chichester-Clark.

That evening the CCDC again approached Burroughs, asking that the Ardoyne march at least be re-routed or banned. On Friday Burroughs told them that the position remained unchanged. As a last resort a telex was sent by the CCDC to the British Home Office in London, requesting

Reginald Maudling, Home Secretary, to take action. Early Friday evening, the Home Office telephoned Conaty, saying that nothing could be done. As late as 7.30 that evening, the CCDC were back with Burroughs, asking that some small concession be made – it was suggested that the nationalists could be told that, after Saturday, no more provocative marches would take place; but no concessions were forthcoming.

In New Barnsley, the arrangements for Saturday were that Orange Lodge No. 9 District would march out of the estate and down the Springfield Road. In a last ditch effort to avert trouble, the military offered to take the band and their banner past the danger area to their assembly point. When this was refused, they offered to provide taxis rather than military transport; but this was also turned down. At 12.45pm Colonel Dodson, Paddy Devlin, Tom Conaty and the Rev. C. Courtney of the Springfield Joint Committee were informed by the parade committee that they would agree to march without music; but this time, the band refused to co-operate.

Finally, Rev. Courtney managed to get an agreement from the band that they would play hymns instead of party tunes. *Abide With Me* would be the tune. A half hour later, at 1.30pm the band appeared on the Springfield Road, hammering out *The Sash My Father Wore* – the Orange anthem. Marie Vallelly, who was 15 years old at the time, recalled how:

> I heard someone saying, 'The Orangemen are going to march through Ballymurphy'. There were Union Jacks out in New Barnsley and British soldiers on the Whiterock Road. A small crowd had gathered at the top of the Rock. Then the Orangemen came out of New Barnsley playing *The Sash* and jeering at by-standers. A row started and in no time the crowd tripled and the rioting started. Before we knew what was happening, all hell had broken loose.[5]

Within minutes, hundreds of youths had gathered on the Whiterock and Springfield roads. Battle-hardened by the Easter riots, and angry at the constant loyalist attacks on nationalists, the young people of Ballymurphy needed no further encouragement. They launched straight into the offending parade. After a brief, but savage, running battle, the musical Orangemen were chased down the Springfield Road.

The angry crowd then turned on the RUC barracks, based in a house on the New Barnsley side of the road. Eyewitness accounts are unanimous that, as the TV came hurtling out through the front window, the RUC men dashed out through the back door, never to be seen again. The barracks was wrecked – no more to be occupied by the RUC – and hats and batons were collected as trophies. Further down the road, another section of the crowd was already locked in combat with the soldiers from the Henry Taggart base. The Battle of Ballymurphy had begun.

During the next ten minutes, as Ballymurphy steeled itself for a second major confrontation with the British army, hundreds of troops, supported by Land Rovers and armoured cars, poured into the area. The advance was accompanied by so much CS gas that even the soldiers with their gas-masks were overcome. Although the gas again had a terrifying effect on families with young children, the Ballymurphy line was undaunted.

A section of the crowd actually swept forward, rushing into the Taggart and forcing the military to temporarily abandon the base. After wrecking the place and scattering army equipment to the four winds, they commandeered two jeeps, drove them up the Springfield and sent them careering driverless through the military lines. The success of this tactic prompted follow-up attacks with a blazing furniture van, a bull-dozer and a mechanical digger, which ended up embedded in the back of the post office.

Meanwhile, a number of youths went up the Springfield Road to the Alverno Hotel, asking that all bottles be handed over as ammunition. The management refused and as a result the hotel was later attacked. Subsequently it was petrol bombed. The battle then moved into Ballymurphy estate, and the Easter pattern of retreats and advances got under way, with casualty centres again opening up in the Taggart and St Bernadette's School.

By mid afternoon smoke was billowing from burning vehicles, from the Corporation yard at the top of the Whiterock, and from bales of hay scattered along the Springfield to delay the military advance. A bus blazed at the Whiterock/Springfield junction and a section of the Alverno was in flames. Twenty yards from the burning bus, however, in the Neptune Cafe, it was business as usual, but with a slight difference. The young people had taken over the cafe; and in the kind of peculiar quirk that would hallmark the Battle of Ballymurphy, they were making chips for the rioters.

> The Neptune, where the butcher's is now, there were people in there, in the middle of all this rioting, with CS gas everywhere and the whole place burning – and they were having fish and chips! Then some fellas came in and started serving chips to the guys outside. At that point the staff left and the fellas started making pasties to go with the chips. This went on for quite a while, with the young people coming into the place in relays for their chips. Then the guys making the chips let the pan overheat and blue smoke started rising. As soon as the smoke started everyone ran out. Next thing was the place went up in flames.[6]

As darkness fell, the streets, strewn with debris, were lit by burning vehicles and exploding petrol bombs that continued to rain down on the military and their armour until well after dawn when everyone finally went home to bed. The Alverno Hotel was by then a blackened ruin; and most of the remaining loyalists had fled New Barnsley, wrecking and booby-trapping their houses as they went, and leaving behind a chilling stillness. Gerry Adams later described going in there the next morning:

> People from here went over to deal with some primitive devices that had been left behind. It was one of the eeriest experiences you could imagine –

the back streets with their red, white and blue pavements, the odd flut-tering curtain, a door left open, somebody's cat that was left behind. And the total absolute silence. Empty, empty silence.[7]

Meanwhile, on the other side of town, the last shots had been fired in a night-long gunfight that tested the mettle of the reorganised IRA[*] for the first time, and re-established them as the defenders of the nationalist community.

As feared by the CCDC, the Orange parade in Ardoyne had also devel-oped into rioting along the edges of the small enclave; and as loyalist sniping broke out, the IRA's Third Belfast Battalion returned fire. In the next 30 minutes three loyalists were shot dead. As news of the killings spread, loyalists in the East decided to take revenge on Short Strand, a nationalist pocket of 6,000, cut off from the city by the river and sur-rounded by some 60,000 loyalists. When local people asked the British army for protection they were told by an officer to 'stew in your own fat'.

At the same time troops sealed off Albert Bridge, cutting off all retreat. Later, the military would claim that they sent no troops because they were stretched too thin, with 108 fires in Belfast that day. Whatever the explanation, the defence of the area was left to the IRA and Short Strand's vigilantes. That evening, as over a thousand loyalists closed in, a small group of Volunteers, along with a local man, Henry McIlhone, took up positions in St Matthew's churchyard and opened up with guns. During the night-long battle, Henry McIlhone and three loyalists were shot dead.

For the second time in 24 hours the IRA had shown that there would be no repeats of August 1969. Nationalist areas would henceforth be ruthlessly protected against sectarian attack.

The weekend after the Ardoyne and Short Strand engagements in which seven people had died and 54 others had suffered gunshot wounds, the new Tory government in Whitehall decided to move against the IRA. The area chosen was the Lower Falls – an Official strong-hold – despite the fact that the Provisionals had carried out both of the previous weekend's operations.

At 4.30pm on Friday, July 3rd 1970, the British army, reportedly acting on a tip-off, roared into Balkan Street on an arms raid. Stones were thrown and CS gas was fired in return. As the situation became uglier some soldiers were trapped and reinforcements were called in. Finally, 3,000 troops, supported by armour and helicopters, were concentrated in the narrow streets of the Lower Falls. CS gas was poured into the area, and in the end Freeland, the army GOC, placed the district under an illegal curfew.

Over the next two days, the residents of the Lower Falls, confined to their homes under threat of being shot, were systematically terrorised by

*Unless otherwise stated, the terms 'IRA' and 'Sinn Fein' in the remainder of this narrative will describe the Provisionals.

the British army in what became known as 'The Rape of the Falls'. Hundreds of homes were destroyed while four civilians were killed, more than a dozen wounded by gunfire, hundreds battered, and over 300 arrested.

At the same time, gun-battles echoed throughout the curfew area as the Official IRA, whose arms had been stored in Balkan Street, and then the Provisionals who came to their assistance, took on the British army. As the situation worsened, nationalists across the city united in revulsion at what was happening and decided to go in and break the curfew. On Sunday morning, July 5th, it was announced that the curfew would be temporarily slackened so people could go to Mass. By then, Freeland was under intense pressure from outraged nationalist opinion throughout Ireland.

By midday it became clear to everybody in the restricted area that the half-completed search operation had been abandoned, though the curfew had not been lifted. Then, at 12.45pm came the event that put paid to any thoughts Freeland might have had of continuing his operations.

In a long column, a thousand women carrying food and milk came marching down the Falls and into Leeson Street, barging through the military blockade. They had formed up just outside the curfew area and were heading for a food distribution centre in Raglan Street. But by the time they got to Raglan Street, all the food and milk had been given away to the people who had already rushed from their homes to embrace them. Sean Og O Fearghail described what happened next:

> Word got back to Andersonstown, Turf Lodge, Ballymurphy and all the other estates where there is scarcely a family without a Falls connection, and the response was equally spontaneous and magnificent. Three thousand women mustered at half past five at Casement Park and with protest banners as well as more supplies of food the long column of angry women and girls marched on the British lines ... No attempt was made to impede the marchers, and the world's journalists photographed General Sir Ian Freeland's final humiliation of the weekend. The legends on the banners and placards told their own story.[8]

One of the placards read: 'Remember Dunkirk and Ballymurphy!' Frank Cahill's wife, Tess, and her neighbour, Kate McCullough, were among the Ballymurphy women who marched on the Falls that Sunday. Tess Cahill later recalled:

> Word had been coming in that the people had no food. They wouldn't let bread or milk or lorries in. And of course there were stories about what they were doing to the houses. Word went around that the women were going to march from all the areas to bring supplies in. So me and Kate left the house, and on the way we met with Maggie Arbuckle, Josie Dixon, Bridie Adams, Lilly Hall, and a lot of others.
>
> We all gathered from the Greater Ballymurphy area at the bottom of the Whiterock Road, waiting on the march coming down from

Andersonstown. And it was the same all the way down – at Iveagh, at Beechmount and so on – the women joined the march until there was thousands of us. The Brits had all the streets sealed off, all the side streets, Leeson Street, Clonard and the like. First, they tried to stop us getting through; but there was that many that the women just forced their way through, pushed them aside.

We went down Leeson Street first, then did a tour of the whole area, handing out food and milk. The people there were overjoyed to see us. They ran out of their homes and threw their arms around us. But I'll never forget my own feelings. I was devastated – we were all devastated – when we seen the houses. People on the march were standing crying their eyes out at the destruction. Stairs ripped out. Statues smashed to bits. Toilets just wrecked. It was really terrible. I'll never forget that feeling.[9]

That night, when the stories of the Falls Curfew were brought back to Ballymurphy, the young men and women who had been engaging the troops resolved that the British army would indeed remember Dunkirk and Ballymurphy.

The Battle of Ballymurphy was to last until January 1971. For seven months the fighting continued, almost without respite, despite the IRA's best efforts to quell it. The IRA leadership later explained:

The full truth about this rioting, particularly in the Ballymurphy area of Belfast, was that it was most dangerous and embarrassing for the IRA.

Not only was there always the danger of a repeat of the Falls Road Curfew of July, and of a direct confrontation with the British army being forced on the IRA, but the Ballymurphy rioting was bringing large scale British forces into the area where the major part of the training of hundreds of new recruits was going on.[10]

However, Ballymurphy was undeterred. The struggle against the British had taken off on a conscious level, and the semi-autonomous Ballymurphy republicans were central to it, deciding that fighting the British was what they were there for. It was a fierce and bloody confrontation with many casualties; but it is a period remembered with dignity and pride by the people who lived it. It must also rank as one of the most extraordinary confrontations ever between a civilian population and a modern army. Gerry Adams later described how:

Every man, woman and child was involved. They didn't fire a shot, but for months, the British army had the hell beaten out of them. The women were humiliating and demoralising them. The kids were hammering them. You had the whole community organised right down into street committees, so that you had a sort of spider's web of regular co-ordination.[11]

One of the most striking features of the early riots was the level of organisation achieved in such a short time. The area was now one solid unit of operation with a role for all. Those too old, slow or inhibited to join the combatants provided the escape routes, warning systems, cups of tea and ammunition. RUC messages were being picked up on the radio and British army messages from the TV, while front gardens had buckets of vinegar and water, and rags, to counteract the gas.

Lily Quinn of Divismore Park was so enthusiastic that she would actually throw the water and vinegar over the rioters to speed up the process. Front and back doors were also left open as escape routes, while the women provided First Aid, many having availed of the rash of courses specialising in the effects of the gas, cuts, broken limbs and – just in case – gunshot wounds.

Innovation, meanwhile, played a large part in the tactics of the combatants. The ammunition advanced to blast bombs and nail bombs as the violence of the military intensified, particularly after the introduction of rubber bullets. Gardens were booby-trapped with low-lying clothes lines, tripwires and cheesewire. Wire was also stretched between telegraph poles to catch soldiers standing up in speeding jeeps or running through blacked-out streets at night. Dustbin lids were used to cover cannisters of gas and to carry ammunition to the front line. (This led to night forays by the troops, during which they confiscated as many bin lids as they could.)

There were also incursions into the field of psychological warfare. After all, what could be more disconcerting to a bunch of squaddies weaned on British invincibility than four or five hundred teenagers tossing bin lids over smoking cannisters of gas, or batting them back with hurleys, while chanting in unison, 'we want more gas'? This response, also found in Derry over the same period, prompted a captain of the Scottish Borderers to assert on August 6th 1970 that, 'the Irishman is absolutely immune to CS gas'[12] as he introduced the killer rubber bullet to the media.* There was also an element of psychological warfare in the bottle-clinking – borrowed from the troops' own shield-thumping – that accompanied advances on the soldiers' lines. Two or three hundred young people, all clinking two empty bottles together, is by all accounts a sound to put the shivers up any spine.

At about this time, the dogs of Ballymurphy also joined the war. Not only did they howl and snap at the soldiers, but the individual howl of each dog (all called 'Rebel' in those days) could pinpoint a military incursion with the accuracy of a radar screen. In later days, the dogs would prove invaluable early-warning systems to men and women on the run, whose ears would become very finely attuned to the howls of dogs.

The British army too had its secret weapons. Dyed CS gas enabled the soldiers to return to the area during periods of calm and arrest those of

---

*The rubber bullet – 6 inches long, 1.5 inches across, and 5 ounces in weight – was complemented in 1973 by the plastic bullet, which has replaced it since 1975. The 4-inch plastic bullet, weighing 4.75 ounces, has a muzzle velocity of 200 mph. The authorities admit having fired over 100,000 rubber and plastic bullets. The real figure may be twice as high. The results are 16 dead (seven of them children), 70 maimed (blinding etc.) and hundreds seriously injured. Many of the dead were killed in non-riot situations by revenge-seeking troops and RUC personnel. All but one of the dead have been nationalists.[13]

unusual hue. They also brought in soldiers originally from the area to identify combatants during riots. They had the snatch-squads and water cannon too, but pride of place must have gone to the man known in Ballymurphy's annals as 'The Big Black Brit'.

This man, described as having been 'like a giant Zulu', was at least '14 feet tall' and the most awesome thing since the Colossus of Rhodes. He would square up to several dozen Ballymurphy warriors, strip off his shirt, roar like a demented bull, and charge – and all before him would scatter. Or, in the peculiar intimacy that grew out of the prolonged confrontation, he would 'do a war dance', as it is still described in Ballymurphy, in front of hordes of stone-throwers, and engage in 20-minute sessions of banter and abuse.

As time passes, the chronology becomes a little blurred; but the totality of the experience is deeply carved into the psyche of Ballymurphy. The slightest mention of the riots unleashes a deluge of memories. Like the day Geordie Stanton went up to the commander of the troops lined up on the Springfield Road and said, 'Here, I'm a community worker. Gimme that loudhailer and I'll tell these 'uns to go home.' He then turned and bellowed into the loudhailer, 'OK boys. That's it now! Knock it on the head!' Next thing, Geordie had swung back to roars from the crowd, who were all in on the act. 'Go on ya bloody oul' eejit, giving me a loudhailer ... up the Murph!'

Or the night the searchlights were beaming out from the Henry Taggart down on to Divismore Park, along the gable walls of the houses, back across the tarmac square, when ... out of nowhere three 'minstrels' appeared in the middle of the square, imaginary hats in hand, doing a quick expert sideways shuffle to the rhythm of their straining voices singing *Are you from Dixie?*!

Then there was the Divismore Park woman who admonished a group of children for throwing stones at the Taggart on their way home from primary school. 'Away home outta that!', she shouted as she chased them, 'I've been putting up with this now for the past week, and I'm fed up with the racket!' 'Missus,' one of the children shouted back, 'we've been putting up with it for 800 years!'

And everyone remembers Herbo Gibson and his portable siren that had to be plugged into a light socket in whatever house Herbo happened to be passing when it was time to raise the alarm. Herbo was also excellent at imitating bugle sounds, so that Ballymurphy could always rely on attacks and retreats being accompanied by appropriate military notes. But of all the stories of those seven months of riots, the saga of 'Dunne's Guerrillas' and the sad end that befell Herbo's dog remain most repeated.

Dunne's Guerrillas have been described as 'bloody wild', 'impossible to control', and 'between ten and two dozen wilders, depending on whether or not their mothers let them out'. Led by Shamie Dunne, they were said to have fought like tigers, to have had a specially outrageous rapport with the troops, to have been super-inventive in tactics and weaponry, and completely unpredictable. In the middle of a raging riot, after 'clodding' everything movable at troops for eight or nine hours,

Shamie Dunne might suddenly shout 'Halt!', and to the amazement of the squaddies, the opposition would stop dead. 'Right boys,' Shamie would call to the soldiers, 'we're away home now. That's it for tonight. See youse all in the morning.'

During one particularly nasty affray, Dunne's Guerrillas declared that they were off home to watch a match on TV and would be back in two hours. So the riot was called off, hundreds of young people from Ballymurphy – and their allies from beyond – went home to watch the match, and two hours later, the battle was on again, with the gas, rubber bullets, nail bombs and paving stones flying in all directions as if there had been no interlude. Herbo's dog was one of Dunne's Guerrillas.

> He was a pup from one of Dunne's dogs. They called him 'Bo' because one day someone gave him Strongbow and he got drunk. Then I got him. He was a real loving dog. The only people he ever went for was the Brits, the 'Peelers' and my brother-in-law. And army dogs. He was just an oul' mongrel, but he hated the army dogs, and no matter what size they were, he'd go for them.
>
> We had him from before my Da died; and, see when he died, Bo wouldn't leave the grave; we had to drag him away. And he was in every riot. You know the way, over here, dogs get their proper name; so he was 'Bo Gibson'. And you never seen a riot on TV except Bo Gibson was in the middle of it. He used to chase stones that were thrown at the Brits and bring them back again. Then one day there was a riot down at Divismore Park, near Murphy's entry, and somebody chucked a nail bomb – I think it was maybe the first nail bomb ever thrown – and Bo went after it.[14]

What happened next has been described by a hundred witnesses and several thousand people who heard it second hand. Herbo's dog caught up with the nail bomb just as it landed at the edge of the military line, and turned back for the Ballymurphy ranks, tail wagging and fuse sputtering away. As it trotted towards its master with the trophy, everybody started to scatter, diving over walls and in through hedges; and Herbo took off at a gallop. The last thing most people remember was the dog breaking into a run, and the fleeing Herbo, casting furtive glances over his shoulder, doing the four-minute mile up towards Glenalina Road. Lucky for Herbo, the nail bomb blew up before Bo caught up with him. That evening Dunne's Guerrillas gave Bo a military funeral. The cortege was accompanied by a guard of honour in black berets and dark glasses, followed by a large crowd of youngsters. The *Last Post* was played and Bo was laid to rest in Herbo's back garden 'You know what happened then?' Herbo says, 'the Brits came along that night and dug him up for forensics!'

It was, by any standards, an incredible period of history.

While all this was going on in Ballymurphy, serious rioting was also taking place in other centres across the North. In July, over the 'Twelfth' marching season, 1,500 nationalist refugees had fled south of the border to be accommodated in Irish army camps. On July 31st, during a riot on the New Lodge Road, rubber bullets were fired for the first time, and the

British army implemented Freeland's shoot-to-kill promise by murdering 19-year-old Danny O'Hagan. During the riots that followed, shots were again fired at the military in the Upper Springfield. On August 4th, the day after Danny O'Hagan was buried, 1,000 Ballymurphy women marched in protest from McCrory Park to the military base on the Springfield Road as yet another riot broke out.

From then until the end of 1970 the war gradually intensified. Rioting was as often as not accompanied by gun-battles. Ambushes on troops and RUC personnel were carried out whenever the opportunity arose. Arms searches, with their attendant brutality, were a matter of form, as were hijackings, arson, bank robberies and the explosions that now rocked the Six Counties on a nightly basis. By the end of the year there had been 154 explosions and 18 people had been killed.

Other signs of the acceleration into war could be seen as the British 'spiked' unapproved roads and blew up bridges along the South Armagh border. This was to continue until most of the small roads between the North and the rest of Ireland had been severed. There had also been indications that the Official IRA was feeling pressure from the North to engage the troops. Cathal Goulding stated on a Tyne/Tees broadcast on October 18th, that 'the establishment' would not allow the IRA (Officials) to attain their goals without the use of violence, 'guns, bombs or any other method you may use'.[15]

On the political front, future nationalist trends were beginning to take form. A new political party, the Social Democratic and Labour Party, had been launched on August 21st. The SDLP included many of the 'Unity' candidates who had fought the Westminster elections in June, and many of those already elected to Stormont and local government on nationalist tickets. Its formation signalled the end of the old atrophied Nationalist Party which had maintained a base in the North after partition, and the beginning of a power-struggle within nationalist areas between the reformist, liberal politics of the nationalist middle class and the revolutionary republican politics of Sinn Fein, though the latter in 1970 was as yet devoid of any really coherent policies.

An example of the type of confusion that then existed within Sinn Fein was seen on December 19th, in Ardoyne. While urging local people to join the Republican Movement to strike for a free, socialist, Gaelic Ireland, they were also condemning the 'infiltration of the district by communist elements'.[16] The SDLP, meanwhile, was the updated face of constitutional nationalism. It was there to provide an opposition to Sinn Fein, which was then the only organised party with support in all nationalist areas, and to push for a new political framework – either a united Ireland or a reformed Northern Ireland – where the middle-class nationalists would get a bigger slice of the cake.

Meanwhile, as the riots continued in Ballymurphy, and more sporadically in other areas, with the RUC no longer present and the British army now equally unacceptable, the Provisionals and Officials were forced to play an increasing role in policing the area. To avoid friction between the two organisations, it was agreed that each should police its own supporters, an agreement that lasted for as long as the Officials maintained significant support.

One of the first problems faced by the two IRAs was that of organised crime, considered anti-people and therefore intolerable as it brought additional hardships on an already hard-pressed community. A number of people were tarred-and-feathered; others were forced to carry out community service; while those suspected of being informers were ordered to leave the country. The Provisionals even had their own 'jail' in a small electricity sub-station in Springhill.

However, despite many warnings of harsher punishment, Ballymurphy was shocked when, on Monday, November 16th, Arthur McKenna and Alexander McVicker were shot dead on Ballymurphy Road. It was one of the handful of times the IRA took such severe action against alleged criminals; and, as with all the others, it attracted widespread criticism.

The McKenna and McVicker killings also brought Arthur McKenna's brother, Jimmy, back from Australia on a vengeance mission. Undeterred by the fact that the IRA had carried out the killings, Jimmy McKenna got himself a gun and publicly threatened to get even with those who had shot his brother. His declaration that he knew who was responsible earned him a visit from the RUC, but proved to be without substance. Otherwise, there would undoubtedly have been other corpses around Ballymurphy, as Jimmy McKenna was a wild and impulsive man unused to the concept of superior force.

A former acquaintance would later describe the armed vigilante prowling the Upper Springfield in late 1970 as 'a header'.

> The story was that Jimmy had been in the merchant navy during the war, and that he was torpedoed and had a steel plate in his head. He was built like a bull and would've gone right through you. At one time he was going out with this woman who lived with her mother down in Bow Street. He renovated the mother's house and put furniture in, with the intention of marrying the daughter. Then your woman jilted him. So Jimmy arrived down with an axe, demolished the front door, chopped up all the furniture, and decapitated the family's Alsatian dog.

However, Jimmy McKenna's vengeance mission came to an abrupt halt some months after his return from Australia when he was arrested on the Springfield Road while in possession of his gun and a Special Intelligence Branch pass. He was charged and brought before the courts where the judge ordered him back to Australia, where he died of a heart attack in 1986.

The New Year of 1971 was heralded in Ballymurphy by an upsurge in the recurrent rioting that had gone on since June. The incidents which led to the final (and some of the most bloody) riots in the Battle of Ballymurphy were later angrily described by the IRA (still trying to quell the upheaval) as 'the asinine tactics of the British soldiers'.[17] There had been a lull of some weeks in the riots by the second week in January, but local anger was again mounting at the behaviour of the military. As well as driving at speed through the area, endangering the many children playing in the streets, soldiers had been verbally and physically abusing individual young people whenever the opportunity cropped up.

They had also, early in December, opened up a disco at the Taggart, now occupied by the Second Royal Anglians, which was being attended by some young girls from the area. Local women were furious when it was discovered that the girls had to show their birth certificates to prove that they were above the age of consent. Ballymurphy's young women were not going to become objects for the sexual gratification of the British army. There was talk of drink and drugs been supplied to the girls, so that by Christmas local women had nightly pickets on the base. The disco was closed down; but some of the girls continued to attend film shows at the Taggart; and rumours were rife that the soldiers were using the ongoing contact as a means of intelligence gathering. The pickets remained.

On Sunday, January 10th, a larger than usual group gathered at the Taggart. Earlier in the day the soldiers had stoned a group of boys playing football, and this had raised the general level of tension in the area. As some girls arrived at the base, heckling broke out. A soldier shouted back that the protestors were 'Irish bastards', whereupon stone-throwing developed between the soldiers and a crowd of youths. Shortly after midnight, when the trouble had died down, a young man on his way home through Ballymurphy suddenly found himself surrounded by eight soldiers. He was attacked and badly beaten, one of the soldiers breaking a baton over his head.

The next day wholesale rioting broke out in Ballymurphy, spreading to other parts of Belfast during the week. At this point the Belfast command of the IRA and the local Ballymurphy republicans ended their unspoken disagreement about the tactical value of the rioting. The IRA command still viewed the riots as 'patently *not* in the interests of the IRA'.[18] The Ballymurphy republicans felt that they had served their purpose: the people were cemented together; the British army was humiliated and demoralised; alienation between the people and the state was complete and irreversible; and self-confidence and an efficient infrastructure of organisation had been developed within the area.

On the night of January 12th, the IRA managed to scale down the level of rioting by placing some of the more ebullient combatants under armed arrest, a fact that did not go unnoticed by the British army. Once again, what was happening in Ballymurphy was about to have far-reaching effects on the rest of the Six Counties as new contortions were brought to the wider political process.

First, the January riots themselves had triggered off a double response on the part of Chichester-Clark: disenchantment with reforms, and an increasing reliance on repressive measures. The latter was articulated by John Taylor, Minister of State for Home Affairs, on February 4th. 'We are going to shoot it out with them,' Taylor said, 'it is as simple as that.'[19] Secondly, the IRA's intervention on the night of January 12th set off a chain of events that would finally weld the British army to the loyalist cause, bringing about an all-out IRA offensive against British forces in the North.

On January 13th the British army contacted the IRA. Already, the Royal Anglians' commander, Colonel Dick Gerrard Wright, had had ongoing communication with the Provisionals in Ballymurphy through two members of the Belfast Brigade staff and a staff officer of the 2nd Battalion in control of Clonard and Ballymurphy. Both sides appear to have seen the contact as a fairly simple intelligence operation.

Now, however, the military were appealing to the IRA for help in controlling Ballymurphy. They began by inviting one of the IRA men to the army base in North Howard Street to tell him of a rumoured threat against his life. The subject of the Ballymurphy riots was then raised. At a second meeting in a Falls Road house, the military were told: 'If you get out of Ballymurphy, we can control it without your assistance.'[20]

At a further meeting attended by another senior member of the Belfast Brigade, the IRA rejected outright the suggestion that the RUC be allowed back into the district. By the end of that meeting, the British army seemed happy enough to allow the IRA to keep order in Ballymurphy. This fitted perfectly with IRA designs. But, as the deal was struck, the meeting was ended prematurely by renewed rioting in the area.

The next morning, January 14th, 700 troops acting on 'higher orders', invaded Ballymurphy to begin a brutal house-to-house search of the estate. Paddy Devlin MP described it as 'bashing left, right and centre'. The occupants of houses were methodically beaten up as furniture and fittings were destroyed. In the streets, passers-by were savagely and indiscriminately attacked by troops. By early afternoon Ballymurphy was in the throes of another fierce riot. An RUC Land Rover was overturned in Ballymurphy Road by women hurling stones and bin lids. Its occupants took refuge in the nearest house, holding the Martin family hostage, while one RUC man fired a shot over the women's heads from an upstairs window. It was the last time the RUC would patrol Ballymurphy for many years to come.

That night the riot became a gun-battle as the IRA hit back. At 2am the following morning, January 15th, a soldier was shot in the leg as the British force withdrew. The war had come at last to Ballymurphy.

Nevertheless, the IRA went on to quell the riots by the evening of Sunday, January 17th, and the policing deal with the British army was resumed. On the same day, in Corpus Christi Church in the heart of Ballymurphy, Dr William Philbin, Catholic Bishop of Down and Connor, condemned the Ballymurphy combatants from the pulpit, claiming they were being directed by 'immoral orders'. The community was furious. On Thursday, January 21st, 15 women crossed the city to the Bishop's residence in upper-class Somerton Road to hand-deliver a letter of rebuke. A most unusual step for the Catholic working class.

Condemning the Bishop's sermon, the letter went on to say:

The men you spoke of last Sunday are needed here to keep our estate free from crime, protect our homes and keep us from being trodden into the ground ... peace protests carry no weight in this city. No one seems to care and so we rely on our own men and boys and back them in their efforts. God guide them all – they are doing a great job.[21]

The letter was signed by Tess Cahill on behalf of 'the mothers of Ballymurphy'. On the same day, the women also sent a letter to Freeland, telling him to 'call off your mad dogs before you push Ballymurphy over the brink'. But the situation was already out of control. The finale of the Ballymurphy riots had almost been a signal for the opening up of the IRA's offensive, an offensive accelerated by one final British botch-up.

On January 18th, the besieged Chichester-Clark visited Reginald Maudling, British Home Secretary, in London. He was looking for some straw to prop up his crumbling political standing. All he got was a declaration – repeated on his return to the North – that the troops 'may now take the offensive' against the IRA. It was a feeble effort that earned little redemption. Inside a week 170 of the 900-strong Unionist Council were calling for Chichester-Clark's resignation. Meanwhile, the British army was doing its best to help the Stormont Prime Minister stay in power – by liaising with the Provisionals to maintain peace on the streets. But this was to backfire badly.

On January 27th Ian Paisley revealed in Stormont that *their* army and the IRA had developed a relationship of *co-operation*! Paisley told of two RUC men who had been patrolling in the Clonard area of the Falls when they were approached by two Provisionals. The Provos told them to get out of the area if they valued their lives. The RUC men approached a military patrol, only to have this advice confirmed. There was uproar in Stormont where most unionists were unaware that Clonard had long been a 'no-go' area for the RUC and that the real cause for surprise was that they were there in the first place. In the ensuing consternation, nobody bothered to ask how Paisley had come to know about this odd incident even before news of it reached senior RUC personnel in Belfast.

To circumvent the gathering storm and ease the pressure on Chichester-Clark, the military decided to put the boot into Clonard. Ballymurphy and Clonard were both covered by the IRA's 2nd Battalion, and part of the deal between the British army and the IRA was that both areas would be immune to military activity while policing talks lasted.

On Wednesday, February 3rd, the deal was broken. The 2nd Royal Anglians cordoned off and invaded Clonard.

After a punitive house-to-house search, and the general thrashing of the community, the troops remained in the area, sparking off the predictable riot. They were joined at lunchtime by loyalist workers from nearby Mackie's engineering works, who pelted the nationalists with bolts, ball-bearings and other metal debris from the workshops. The trouble died down a little in the afternoon, until shortly before the loyalists from Mackie's were due out. At this point the military moved in to clear the streets of Clonard. They roared up and down in their jeeps, and viciously assaulted anyone who came their way. The idea was to soften up the IRA in Clonard: the effect was to spark off city-wide riots.

During the next two days of rioting, gun-battles erupted across Belfast. On the New Lodge Road five soldiers were wounded by sub-machine-gun fire. A gelignite bomb broke another's thigh. On February 5th the British army, in an attempt to counter unionist claims that they had no idea who the Provisionals were, named the five IRA leaders with whom they had been liaising. The talking was over.

The following night, on the New Lodge Road, Gunner Robert Curtis became the first British soldier to die in combat in the present 'Troubles'. Four of his comrades were wounded. On the same night, three other soldiers were wounded; and a civilian and an IRA officer were shot dead by the army. Next morning Chichester-Clark announced on television that: 'Northern Ireland is at war with the Irish Republican Army Provisionals.'

References

1. *Belfast Telegraph*, November 17th 1969.
2. *Freedom Struggle – The Provisional IRA* (1973), p.18.
3. *Irish News*, Belfast, November 29th 1970.
4. *Sunday Times* Insight Team, *Ulster* (Penguin, 1972), p. 206.
5. Marie Vallelly of Ballymurphy (1985 Interview).
6. Pat Mullan of Ballymurphy (1985 Interview).
7. Gerry Adams (1987 Interview).
8. Sean Og O Fearghail, *Law? And Orders* (Central Citizens' Defence Committee, Belfast, 1970), p. 21.
9. Tess Cahill of Ballymurphy (1985 Interview).
10. *Freedom Struggle*, p. 25.
11. Gerry Adams (1985 Interview).
12. *Irish News*, Belfast, August 7th 1970.
13. Fr Denis Faul and Fr Raymond Murray, *Plastic Bullets – Plastic Government* (1982).
14. 'Herbo' Gibson of Ballymurphy (1985 Interview).
15. *Belfast Telegraph*, October 19th 1970.
16. Richard Deutsh and Vivien Magowan, *Northern Ireland 1968–73, a Chronology of Events, Volume 1, 1968–71* (Blackstaff Press, Belfast, 1973), p. 85.
17. *Freedom Struggle*, p. 26.
18. Ibid.
19. *The Times*, London, February 5th 1971.
20. *Sunday Times* Insight Team, *Ulster*, p. 238.
21. *Irish News*, Belfast, January 22nd 1971.

7

'Is There Life Before Death?'

The latter months of 1970 brought definitive proof that the community leaders in Ballymurphy, particularly those involved with the BTA, did not give up easily.

The first stage of the community centre, completed in the early summer, had no sooner been opened than, riots or no riots, it became the venue for a summer playscheme run by Irish Quaker Workcamps. The play-leaders, who lived at the community centre, became a second dominant feature of that turbulent summer as they went about the area, accompanied everywhere by droves of children. Many were students, and the label was to stick. Henceforth, everyone who came to work in voluntary youth or community work was a 'student' whether they were 18 or 80. Over the next twelve years the 'students' and their summer playschemes became an integral part of summer, providing a release for much youthful energy, introducing all sorts of ideas and personalities to the area, and providing the British with at least one opportunity to slip an undercover agent into Greater Ballymurphy.

In the autumn the BTA, still concentrating on attempts to improve local conditions, and coping with the additional burden of riots and refugees, decided to go ahead with the appointment of a youth worker. Other youth work initiatives were taking place at the same time in St Thomas' School under the auspices of the lower Ballymurphy CDC. This section of the Ballymurphy CDC was aligned with the Officials and still affiliated to the Central Citizens' Defence Committee with its clerical and middle class leadership. The youth club – Corpus Christi – was controlled by the Church and its activities and philosophy reflected the traditional controlling influences of youth work.

The BTA, while wishing to see improvement in the anti-social behaviour of some of Ballymurphy's youth, also placed a strong emphasis on individual development. Many of the more prominent members of the organisation argued that the imposition of middle-class culture and values through the education system had simply resulted in a counter-culture of rejection. They pointed out that the vast majority of Ballymurphy's youth was totally alienated from the school system and had come to associate the word 'education' with coercion. They also argued that the purpose of this system was to ultimately deny working-class people entry into the structures of power. Since youth work originated in the same quarters as the education system, they would have to be very wary of its traditional values and ideology. With this mixed bag of ideas, they appointed Paddy McCarthy to the daunting task of being Ballymurphy's first professional youth worker.

61

Paddy McCarthy, a 43-year-old portly Londoner, who had spent eight years in the British army, arrived in Ballymurphy on November 17th 1970, the day after the McVicker and McKenna killings. He was a seasoned youth worker who saw Ballymurphy as a personal challenge. However, despite his enthusiasm and a work-philosophy closely matching the BTA's, his first progress report was an illustration of how easily idealism can be dented by hard reality.

> Within a week or two of opening the membership lists, I had over 1,100 applications for membership. I had totally failed to realise the sheer volume of the need represented by the huge number of children in the under 14 age group on the estate ... I settled for a policy of containment of the maximum possible numbers.
>   In practice, this meant mounting up to four sessions per day for the different age groups ... accepting a primitive level of activity; and initially at least, any standard of behaviour not actually lethal.[1]

Paddy McCarthy was soon to become a central figure in many of the other developments taking place in the local social field, and was twice involved in defusing unexploded nail bombs – the legacy of the night before's rioting – before children could get to them in the morning. And, in a shorter time than he could possibly have imagined, he was to die on the streets of Ballymurphy.

In the autumn of 1970 the BTA also contacted Queen's University to explore the possibility of a joint survey of the estate. After meeting with the entire Social Studies Department, at St Aidan's School, they committed themselves to the project, to be planned and reported on by the Department but carried out by the residents. It was hoped that the publication of such a report would: 'Stimulate statutory and voluntary bodies to take "from the outside" action that would improve conditions on the estate. And second, to help and encourage the residents themselves to take corrective action "from the inside".'[2]

This period, beginning in the summer of 1970, marked the opening up of Ballymurphy to a wider world than it had ever known. This was a direct result of the riots. In the past some philanthropic outsiders had shown occasional interest, and the area had been the subject of the *Study of Unsatisfactory Tenants*, undertaken by Dorita Field for the Belfast Council of Social Welfare (1957–9). But much of this interest had quickly waned or come to nought. Other than the exceptional contributions of people like Sean Mackle – the BTA's architect who hailed originally from Whiterock – and Nick Ragg of the Child Poverty Action Group, the kind of outside support required was not forthcoming.

This, however, now began to change dramatically. The Quaker playscheme had been followed by further contacts by individual Quakers who would make invaluable contributions to the area over the next six or seven years. Next came Tony Spencer and his team from Queen's University. Then Paddy McCarthy and his wife Jan. And Paddy was soon joined in the BTA's youth club by Felicity McCartney, a young woman who, along with her colleague of the time, Fred Bass, had been central to the success of the summer playscheme.

By the beginning of 1971 the Northern Ireland Community Relations Commission was also operating in Greater Ballymurphy through Sheila Barry, Community Development Officer for the area. (Initially, people were extremely suspicious of the Commission. However, this was overcome as time passed by the quality of the work carried out by individual workers. Eventually, the Commission produced much valuable documentation, some of it highly critical of government policies. It was therefore not surprising when the government finally axed its embarrassing offspring in the summer of 1974.) But perhaps the most significant entry into the mainstream of Ballymurphy life in 1971 was made by Fr Desmond Wilson, a 46-year-old local curate who was then beginning a personal journey of his own. It was a journey that would culminate in a head-on clash with the Irish Catholic Church.

Des Wilson, a Belfastman by birth, was living in St John's Parochial House on the Falls Road when the pogroms broke out in August 1969. Already thoroughly sickened by the state's cumulative response to the demands of the civil rights movement – ultimately climaxing in the killings and burnings of August – he was soon to find himself almost as disturbed by the response of the Catholic Church. Many years later he recalled how, in the wake of the pogroms, the Church first showed itself to be impotent, and later underhand and devious, in its relationship with the nationalist working class of Belfast. For the Falls Road priest, they were days that would shape the rest of his life.

> We were so remote there in the Parochial House. It's amazing even though you're only about a mile or so away. I got the lesson of my life that 15th of August – after the burnings. The people of the Falls were going up the road, going up in lorries with whatever they had managed to salvage – God, it was desperate – and I knew, we all knew, that the people of Ballymurphy had opened their doors. Over-crowded houses here that had opened their doors and let those people in.
>
> In the Parochial House, there was no way we could have done that. The whole ecclesiastical conventions, customs, and models of authority would have prevented us. We were probably the only people in the parish who couldn't open our doors freely to the refugees. And in fact there was very deep clerical resistance to opening the schools in some of the districts. In some instances, people just booted the doors in. Although people saw this thing coming and had been trying to prepare for it for a couple of days – more than that, but intensively for a couple of days to make sure that the places would be open – we couldn't. It was events like that that made Hugh Mullan and myself feel that we needed to move out of the Parochial House and in among the people.[3]

Although the inactivity of the Parochial House in the face of the suffering of the Falls Road may have been the catalyst, Des Wilson had for some time been considering his position in relation to the structures of the Catholic Church as they were to be found in the diocese of Down and Connor. Both he and Fr Hugh Mullan had their own very definite, and separate, ideas on how they would like to see the Church relate to the people. They both felt that there was much practical work to be done on the ground and that the Church had to be seen to be a caring institution if it was to remain relevant to the people. Against monumental odds, they decided that they should make a small start in that direction.

Hugh Mullan felt that, as a beginning, he would like to develop systems whereby financial hardship might be alleviated. One of the initial ventures he planned was the opening of a second-hand furniture depot, and a strike against the moneylenders who were bleeding families to death. Des Wilson wanted to develop a programme of adult education and social action. They had also talked about the idea of establishing a credit union. But always, they faced the same recurring problem – no accommodation.

Despite the fact that the Catholic Church owned numerous buildings – schools, halls and the Parochial House – they could never get the uninhibited use of such property for any of their proposed developments. They therefore concluded that their first priority was to find themselves some kind of independent space out among the community, however small that space was. Other developments too were playing on Des Wilson's mind in particular, and bringing him increasingly into conflict with the Church hierarchy in Down and Connor.

In 1968, in the early days of the civil rights agitation, Bishop William Philbin had issued strict instructions to his clergy that no members of the executive of the Northern Ireland Civil Rights Association were to be given any space for meetings in either Church or school properties, which effectively meant most of the public buildings in nationalist areas. Some time later, Michael Farrell of People's Democracy addressed a meeting in St Bernadette's School in Ballymurphy; and the whole question again came up for discussion at the next clerical 'briefing session' at the Bishop's house. Monsignor Mullally, Vicar-General and the Bishop's second-in-command, made reference to 'such people as Michael Farrell being allowed into Church property in some parts'; whereupon Des Wilson, at whom the jibe was aimed, replied angrily that Farrell had not been *allowed* in: he had been *invited* in. From then on, as the saying goes, promotion was not going to be easy.

The next clash between the Ballymurphy curate and the hierarchy came immediately after the relief operation of August 1969. Welfare committees, similar to the one that had organised the mammoth operation in Ballymurphy, had sprung up throughout nationalist Belfast. Once the initial pressure relaxed, a number of the Ballymurphy people, and some others from other centres, felt that the lull should be used to develop a central co-ordinating body so that maximum use could be made of all resources in the event of a recurrence of the emergency.

All the relief committees were contacted, and all agreed to attend a meeting towards that end – until contact was made with the Catholic-run St Joseph's Training College in Stewartstown Road. There, the organisers were told that they were duplicating work already in hand by the clergy, and to hold off for a day or two. This they did, only to learn that no such work had been under way. The story was pure fabrication, and was simply designed to sabotage the working-class development that was taking shape.

The clergy and particularly the hierarchy, already dismayed by the more radical elements of the civil rights movement and the alarming growth of republicanism, apparently saw the liaison of the welfare committees as yet another example of the unruly working classes running out of control. Another threat to their own power-base. This one, however, might yet be nipped in the bud. The Bishop was contacted; and he quickly arranged a meeting to be held at St Kevin's School on the Falls Road. It was a very different meeting from that envisaged by people like Des Wilson and Frank Cahill.

Ever after, Frank Cahill would recollect that meeting as one of the supremely distasteful experiences of a long life in community politics:

Dessie had decided to go along, after being invited by Fr Toner, the Bishop's secretary, but only to make a protest. None of the groups who had been doing the work were invited. The only people there from the working-class communities were the few representatives who went along to support Dessie's protest. When we got there, the hall was full of clergy, representatives of statutory bodies, and hand-picked people of middle-class background. First of all, Philbin insisted that he should chair the meeting. He then stated that the reason for setting up his proposed committee (which was seen by the working-class representatives as a deliberate attempt to create an alternative 'safe' base – away from working class control – for the channelling of resources) was so that people could get all the benefits they were entitled to.

After some time he introduced Fr Lowry, one of the priests with him on the platform. He said that Fr Lowry, who had been brought home from England especially for the job, should chair this committee because he had been trained in welfare benefits. He also introduced another of his followers as a historian who was going to write everything down for posterity. It was fairly unbelievable to us that a man who had been in England through the whole of the emergency was now being put forward by the Bishop as an 'expert'!

There was a heated discussion; then one of the working-class representatives proposed Dessie as an alternative chairperson. Philbin began to argue strongly against this. At that stage, Dessie got to his feet and made a strong protest about the way in which the whole thing was being stage-managed. Then he walked out. It was while he was out that a compromise was proposed – there would be two chairpersons for the committee, Dessie and Fr Lowry. The rest of them were middle-class people who were more or less chosen by the Bishop.

You'll remember that by then there was overt liaison between the hierarchy and the Brits. Philbin had been instrumental in the early attempts to get the barricades down, and had worked directly, and through the clergy, on this. They were afraid, you see, of the developing working-class skills – of the direct challenge posed to their own position – and felt that they had better get out and take control. And this – the meeting in St Kevin's – was how they did it.

There was another interesting suggestion at that time too. After the initial problems had died down, and families were being sorted out with alternative accommodation, the numbers in the schools dropped. So you had five or six families in St Thomas'; another five or six in St Bernadette's and so on. The clergy then suggested that all should be centred in one place; and they proposed that St Aidan's be the place. This was just a ploy to get control of the schools back from the people. In St Aidan's the Christian Brothers had run the relief operation, and had therefore maintained control of the school. And Philbin, of course, controlled the Christian Brothers.[4]

The clerical behaviour at St Kevin's was the classic Church tactic that was to surface over and over again. Working-class radicalisation and organisation, which were always perceived by the middle-class clergy – and the middle classes generally – as a threat, had to be undermined at all costs. The method was always the same: first, infiltration; second, expansion of influence; third, isolate or overthrow opposition. From the moment the co-ordinating committee was established, there was never a single occasion when anybody from the Bishop's camp made any further reference to Des Wilson. He was completely excluded, as if he had vanished in a puff of conjuring smoke. From then on, all funds coming in, all contacts with welfare services and all resources were directed through, and monopolised by, the Church, until the committee – now operating from the safe confines of St Joseph's College – became little more than a clerical vehicle. Des Wilson extricated himself in disgust as quickly as decency would allow. Later, when discussing those early days of working-class organisation, he would roundly condemn the hierarchy.

They were afraid of the republicans, they were afraid of the civil rights people, and they were afraid of the welfare committees. Every initiative the people took – civil rights, citizens' defence committees, welfare committees, everything – these people stepped in. Either took it over or else paralleled it. Rather than supporting the people's initiatives, they attempted – successfully in many cases – to subvert them.[5]

After the debacle of the St Kevin's meeting, the Catholic Church's next contribution to the undermining of working-class politics in Belfast was the takeover of the Citizens' Defence Committees. At yet another briefing session at the Bishop's house, attended by Dr Philbin, Monsignor Mullally and Fr Toner, and priests from all nationalist working-class areas it was stated very clearly that part of the clergy's task in their respective areas was to take over the CDCs.

Against a background of assenting silence, Des Wilson once more surfaced as the burr in the ecclesiastical buttock. He first argued against the principle, and then pointed out that there was a certain difficulty that had, perchance, been overlooked. What would happen, he asked, if in the future CDCs were shown to be arms-procuring bodies? This would in fact mean that the clergy would have taken control of arms-procuring organisations. He believed that this would be disastrous; that if people felt they had to defend their areas, that was for people other than clergy to decide. Mullally interrupted to tell him that if he didn't do it, somebody else would do it for him. By the end of the briefing, Des Wilson's was the only dissenting voice; it was otherwise agreed that the clergy would take over the CDCs.

And so it was. Either clergy, or those whom they caused to be introduced into positions of power – the nationalist middle class – took control of the working-class defence organisation, eventually rendering it impotent. As the Ballymurphy curate points out, the fate of the Central Citizens' Defence Committee was probably the most interesting case-study of them all:

> When they moved the whole centre of gravity to that house on the Falls Road, that was a highly political move. It was a move into property that was Church property. Then they gave them typewriters, staff and money, further increasing their hold. The Church's desire was to move the CCDC away from what they saw as left-wing republican territory into a more conservative and controllable setting, in which the CCDC was using Church premises, typewriters, secretarial help, and money. They then introduced their own people and pushed them up the ranks, and in this way removed the organisation from the clutches of the left-wing movement into the more safe and conservative section.[6]

By early 1971 Des Wilson and Hugh Mullan had decided that it was high time to move to saner pastures. They approached the parish priest and got his approval to move into the Ballymurphy area. They applied to Belfast Corporation for a house in Springhill, which was given over without hesitation. The two priests were all set to move when the minutes of the Corporation's meeting, containing a reference to the house, were published as was normal – and the news reached the attentive ears of Bishop Philbin. Immediately, word came back that the move was not to be. Des Wilson heard from a curate who heard from the parish priest who heard from Philbin.

They were not to move into Springhill. Hugh Mullan accepted this, deciding that if there was no permission, he would draw back. Des Wilson decided to hang on to the house and see what happened. A move into the area of sorts was eventually sanctioned: Hugh Mullan was permitted to set up residence in Springfield Park, one of the few owner-occupied areas in the parish, where a house was bought for the purpose. A few months later he was to leave that house to meet a sudden and violent death in a hail of British bullets.

Meanwhile, Des Wilson, who had no sanction from the Church to move into Ballymurphy, continued to use the Springhill house as a base from which he was beginning to develop his own ideas. In order to establish residence he would also sleep in the house every now and then. The end result, after a change of address prompted by his giving over of the original house to Mother Teresa of Calcutta, was Springhill Community House.

It was from there that the rows between the Ballymurphy priest and the Bishop of Down and Connor continued to simmer until the final rupture in June 1975 when Des Wilson resigned from a position which was no longer tenable.

The new Community House in Springhill Avenue became a third focal point – along with the BTA Community Centre and the Cahills' house in Ballymurphy – for the growing influx of those aligning themselves with the many-faceted struggle of the area.

The arrival of Des Wilson in Springhill coincided with another notable development in Ballymurphy – the setting up of Ballymurphy Enterprises, and the start of a bold attempt to tackle the local unemployment abyss from the inside. Early in 1971, Catherine Reynolds from Ballymurphy Road, a voluntary helper with Ballymurphy Handicapped Association, had a simple idea:

> I had a daughter myself who was disabled through deafness. I felt at the time that the physically handicapped and the mildly mentally handicapped could be taught various skills such as basket making, embroidery, knitting. I talked to a doctor from Fleming Fulton who introduced me to Daphne Robinson, a Quaker woman.
>
> That Sunday I was at the Community Centre, when Daphne Robinson and a man called John Mee arrived in. I told them my ideas, and we went on talking about other possibilities of bringing employment to the area. John Mee knew a man who wanted to start a fireplace-making business. He had been interested in the old Corporation yard as a possible base. However, that fell through because the man's wife was afraid to put money into the area, with all the trouble and so on. Then Daphne said 'Why not start up a cottage industry?' So we decided to call a meeting.[7]

The meeting, held shortly afterwards, was attended by a number of residents and non-residents, including some of the people who had recently completed the reconstruction of Bombay Street. Bombay Street, burned to the ground during August 1969, had in many ways become a symbol of the violence meted out to the nationalists during the pogroms. The residents had vowed to return, and in defiance decided to rebuild the street themselves. Towards this end, they brought in professional help – all of whom agreed to contribute freely and without payment. Now this same body of professionals, their work in Bombay Street completed, moved into Ballymurphy. They included Sean Mackle, a solicitor named Christopher Napier, and Ciarán O'Kane from the Department of Business Studies at Queen's University.

Catherine Reynolds and Daphne Robinson put their ideas to the meeting, and it was agreed to investigate the possibilities of setting up a home knitting industry in the area. Catherine Reynolds was asked to collect the names of local women who might be interested. Although she had only moved to Ballymurphy the previous year, and was still a relative stranger to the neighbourhood, she managed to quickly round up two dozen willing participants. At the next meeting of the steering committee, she recalls how:

> I brought along the list of names, but explained that the women could only afford to buy a little wool at a time, and this would slow down production. I told the meeting that we could be talking forever and get nowhere. What we needed was money to get started. If we had that, I would do the selling (which later succeeded in getting orders for Arans from Canada, Sweden, America and Germany). At that point, Daphne Robinson opened her handbag and gave me £20. 'Look,' she said, 'will you get the wool and co-ordinate with the women?' And that was the start of Ballymurphy Enterprises.[8]

The initial venture, which began production in May 1971, was a very modest affair, employing some two dozen women on a part-time basis. But it opened the door for one of the most daring social experiments ever conducted in Belfast – an attempt to industrialise Ballymurphy, while at the same time introducing revolutionary concepts of management and industrial organisation.

By December the committee had purchased some second-hand machinery and set up a unit in a house in Springhill Avenue; and full-time employment commenced. For the next two years Ballymurphy Enterprises would be plagued by financial difficulties; but the committee – none of whom had any background in industry – would struggle on. Meanwhile, they would gradually introduce their own ideas of management to what must have been a fairly bewildered staff.

> Ballymurphy Enterprises was not set up to be simply an ordinary commercial concern. It is non-profit-distributing, i.e. no individual or group may be paid dividends, but this does not mean that it aims to be non-profit-making. It is also envisaged that the Enterprises will become a workers' controlled co-operative in a true sense. Employees, it is hoped, will not regard the organisation as something supplying them with a job, but rather they will think of it as their enterprise. At present there exists a management committee which consists of three employees of the Enterprise plus a number of people who have some necessary expertise to offer. It is hoped that, as the pay-roll grows and the employees become more familiar with the details of running a business, they will replace the non-employees on the committee.[9]

In September 1971 many of those involved in the Ballymurphy Enterprises experiment, along with a number of others interested in the ideas being pioneered in the Upper Springfield formed a co-operative called Whiterock Industrial Estates Ltd. Their plan was an ambitious one – to develop a 12-acre site on the Upper Springfield Road into 40 factory units that would eventually, it was hoped, provide 1,000 jobs. It was envisaged that the new industrial estate would incorporate both capitalist and co-operative ventures. With this goal, Whiterock Industrial

Estates Ltd went about the task of raising funds towards an estimated total cost in excess of £1 million.[10] It was as well that there was a strong outside interest in the scheme because, by September 1971, Ballymurphy had had its innards ripped out.

*   *   *

The IRA's response to Chichester-Clark's declaration of war had been immediate. On February 9th 1971, five civilians, travelling in a jeep, were killed by a landmine on Brougher Mountain in County Tyrone. It had been intended for the British army. On February 15th another soldier died of gunshot wounds received in Ardoyne the previous week. On February 26th two RUC men were shot dead, again in Ardoyne. And on March 10th three Scottish soldiers were found assassinated on the outskirts of Belfast. They had been shot by an IRA unit from North Belfast in reprisal for military repression in Ardoyne. Meanwhile, sniping exchanges, gun battles and commercial bombings increased.

Loyalists, outraged by the escalating IRA campaign, began to stage marches, demanding the internment of republicans and Chichester-Clark's resignation. On March 16th Chichester-Clark flew to London. His demands and those of the Stormont government, already aired to the British government in January, were: more troops, more arrests, total curfews of nationalist areas, an extended role for the loyalist Ulster Defence Regiment, and massive reprisal raids against nationalist areas. At this point the Heath government did not wish to add any further fuel to the nationalist insurrection, and realised that satisfying Chichester-Clark's demands would do just that.

The British, having abandoned all attempts to force token reforms on the unionist state, were carrying out a policy of containment. Ironically, by sending Chichester-Clark home empty-handed, they had lost round one. On March 20th the unionist leader resigned, and was replaced three days later by Brian Faulkner, representing the caveman element of the Unionist Party.

Faulkner was a firm believer in internment, having operated it himself as Minister of Home Affairs, during the Border Campaign of the 1950s. He met with Heath on April 1st and demanded its introduction. The British, not wishing to lose yet another unionist prime minister, made a deal.

Over the next three months, IRA activity was intensified throughout the North. Gunbattles, bombings, military raids, bank-robberies, road-blocks, and military funerals for IRA dead became a way of life. In May, after a pub bombing on the loyalist Shankill Road, in which several people were injured, Faulkner stated that henceforth: 'Any soldier seeing a person with a weapon or acting suspiciously may, depending on the circumstances, fire to warn or with effect without waiting for orders'.

'Acting suspiciously' now merited summary execution. But, being an astute politician, Faulkner realised that repression, as the only approach to the nationalists, would not be enough. He therefore tried to neutralise the nationalist middle class by offering them some crumbs from the unionist table. On June 22nd he announced a plan for the formation of three new parliamentary committees to advise on social, industrial and environmental issues. These committees would have in-built unionist majorities, but two would have Opposition chairpersons.

It was a meaningless gesture; but the SDLP loved the idea. John Hume, deputy leader of the party, commented: 'It should be made clear to all people today who say that no change has taken place, that this is simply not true. There have been changes in this community.'[11] The IRA, realising that the destruction of the Stormont parliament – one of their prime objectives – would be so much more difficult to achieve if it was being propped up by the SDLP, stepped up their bombing campaign. But other events overtook them.

On July 7th, the day the SDLP attended its first Stormont 'all-party' discussion, the British army put substance to Faulkner's shoot-for-effect policy. That night, they shot dead Seamus Cusack in Derry's Bogside. Rioting, which had already gone on for three days, intensified the next day. The British then shot Desmond Beattie dead. Both youths had been unarmed.

That weekend, as Sinn Fein president Ruairi O Bradaigh and vice president Maire Drumm addressed a huge rally in Derry, and young people queued up to join the IRA, Hume met with a number of his SDLP colleagues in Derry. Realising that they were grossly out of touch with feeling in the nationalist areas, they agreed to call for a public inquiry into the Derry killings. If it was not granted, they would pull out of Stormont. Gerry Fitt, leader of the party, had refused to attend the Derry meeting. He heard the story on the news. His reaction was to rush off to London to try to do a deal with Maudling. But Maudling would not deal, so that Fitt, reluctantly, had to lead his party out of Stormont on July 15th. In *The Orange State*, Michael Farrell points out that: 'The SDLP had been forced into the same path as the nationalists in 1921, 1932 and 1938, though none of their predecessors had ever somersaulted quite so completely – from fulsome praise of the government to abstention, in three weeks.'[12]

The Derry killings were, in one sense, a blessing for the SDLP. For by now internment was on the cards, and preparations were already being laid. Had the SDLP not been forced out of Stormont, they might have found themselves an unwilling party to its introduction. On July 23rd, as the violence continued unabated throughout the North, 2,000 troops took part in a series of dawn raids in nationalist areas across the Six Counties. Further dummy runs took place on August 1st and 2nd, as sectarian clashes flared on a wide front.

On August 5th Faulkner met with Heath and General Tuzo, GOC Northern Ireland, in London. No statement was issued, but 1,000 extra troops were dispatched to the North, bringing the military presence excluding the UDR, to 11,900. Over the next three days, the cycle of riots, gun battles, killings, bombings, hijackings, arson and intimidation continued.

Finally, at 4.30am on August 9th, British troops, supported by heavy armour, swept into nationalist areas to lift the first 342 internees. In Ballymurphy, with good reason, somebody went onto the Whiterock Road two days later, and daubed along the cemetery wall, 'Is There Life Before Death?'

References

1. Paddy McCarthy, *Youth Work Progress Report*, May 18th 1971 (Ballymurphy).
2. Spencer, AECW, *A Tale of Two Surveys* (Queen's University of Belfast, 1973), p. 9.
3. Fr Desmond Wilson (1985 Interview).
4. Frank Cahill (1986 Interview).
5. Fr Desmond Wilson (1985 Interview).
6. Ibid.
7. Catherine Reynolds, founder member of Ballymurphy Enterprises (1985 Interview).
8. Ibid.
9. Ciaran O'Kane, 'Co-operative Self-Help in Belfast', in *Co-operative Self-help and Local Economic Development and Some Contributions*, edited by John Darby and Geoffrey Morris (Northern Ireland Community Relations Commission, 1974).
10. *Whiterock Industrial Estates Ltd – 224,000 Sq. ft of Factories* (Promotional Brochure, 1973).
11. Henry Kelly, *How Stormont Fell* (Gill and Macmillan, Dublin, 1972), p. 40.
12. Michael Farrell, *Northern Ireland: The Orange State* (Pluto Press, London, 1976), p. 281.

8

The Internment Killings

Right through the Tan War* and Civil War, there were pogroms against the nationalist areas in Belfast. Much IRA energy in the North was spent in defending nationalist areas. That was when they first used internment here.

As soon as the state took full control in 1922, Sir Richard Dawson Bates, Minister for Home Affairs, introduced the Special Powers Act. One of the provisions of the Act was the power to intern people without trial. This power was used by the Stormont government every time it felt the slightest threat from the nationalist community.

The first period of internment in the North was from 1922 to 1924. At that time the Civil War was going on in the South and republicans were being interned – and executed – there as well. My own first experience of internment came about six or seven weeks before the end of the Civil War. I was caught by Free State forces in Athlone, and held until the ceasefire. I was about 19 or 20 then ...

After the Civil War, when the order had come to 'dump arms and scatter' I came back up North like a lot of others from here, while we waited to see what would happen next. Then in 1926 a taxi-driver named Woods from the Short Strand was shot dead by the IRA for being an informer. Dozens of men were immediately rounded up and 'detained' without trial for three to four months in Crumlin Road Prison. This 'detention ' was to be a regular occurrence, used on the slightest pretext. I was in five or six times on 'detention' – in 1926, 1929, 1932, 1933 and 1934. During one of these periods the Branchman interrogating me said 'Billy, we're going to fingerprint you'. I said 'No, you're not', and started quoting my rights to him. He said, 'Billy, under the Special Powers Act, we can take your fucking life'. We were all held for about three weeks that time. We were released just as they were about to charge us under the Questioning Act. They had made it an offence to refuse to answer their questions ...

During the 1920s and 1930s the state also used internal exile against us. People were deported to hostile rural areas where they couldn't get a house or a job. This was a way of forcing people over the border. Then they couldn't come back without being jailed. It was a way of banishing people from the North ...

*During the 1919–21 War the IRA's campaign brought about a sharp drop in recruitment to the Royal Irish Constabulary. To fill the gap, recruits were imported from Britain. Such was the haste of the operation that insufficient uniforms were available for the new force so that they arrived in Ireland wearing an assortment of black and khaki uniforms, earning them the name 'Black and Tans'. Even after the uniform situation had been sorted out, the new paramilitary force, in its police uniforms, still retained the name. It was to become a notoriously indisciplined terror organisation, and the IRA's most sought-after target until the Treaty.

Internment on a large scale was brought in again just before Christmas 1938 and lasted until 1945, through the whole period of the Second World War. In 1938 the IRA gave an ultimatum to the British government, giving them to the middle of January to leave Ireland. If not, the IRA would embark on a bombing campaign in Britain. But the Stormont government in the North decided to move first, although this didn't prevent the campaign from getting under way. About 30 or 40 republicans were interned in the first swoop. They were held first in Crumlin Road, then the ground floor of Derry Prison where the criminal lunatics had been held (as there was no asylum in Derry). Conditions were bad in Derry and there was a mutiny on Christmas Day 1939. The republican prisoners barricaded the corridors and cells and chased the warders. But the Specials and firemen came in and hosed them and beat the hell out of them. A fellow called John McArdle was O/C and they left him for dead ...

I had been in Britain in 1939, and came home on holidays in 1940, but ended up being interned – first in Crumlin Road, then on the *Al Rawdah*. By the beginning of the war there were 207 men on the *Al Rawadh*. They were brought on board handcuffed to 'B' Specials, with crowds of loyalist women shouting, 'Drown the bastards'. It was an old Indian boat, full of cockroaches. We used to chase them to fill in the time. And at night we slept on hammocks. (Paddy Grimley, who had only one leg, had a hell of a time getting to bed at night.) The boat was staffed by Indians who used to hold religious meetings on the second deck.

The governor was Taylor who had been a chief warder in the Crum. But Taylor took very little to do with the internees; he left that to 'Daddy' Holmes who was the chief warder. The internees were on two decks; but a hole was cut between the two so that men could pass up and down. This nearly drove Daddy Holmes mad. He'd count the men who should number, say, 50 in each mess, only to find that there were 70, which added up to a total of about 80 more than there were on the boat! Before going to Killyleagh the *Al Rawdah* was at the head of Strangford Lough; but it was moved after the Germans dropped bombs around Newtownards ...

Internment was introduced again during the 1956–61 period, the time of the Border Campaign. Again the reaction of the Stormont government was to intern all the republicans they could get their hands on. As with the 1940s period, the South simultaneously introduced the same measures to help crush any opposition to British rule in the North. I was lifted in August 1957 and held until the end of 1960. I had been a Corporation employee, but had lost my job and never got it back. I had 14 or 15 years' service, but was left with no pension, nothing.[1]

Liam 'Billy' Mulholland was almost 70 years old when they came for him again at 4.30am on Monday, August 9th 1971. Internment had been expected. The arrival of the extra 1,000 troops in itself, on top of the mock swoops, had been enough to tip the government's hand. But the Provisional IRA had also received other more direct information 48 hours in advance of the military raids. Joe Cahill, O/C of the Provos' Belfast Brigade, was to explain a few days later that 'after Brian Faulkner had arrived back from London, we got a tip-off from a political contact on the unionist side'. Orders went out to all Volunteers to find safe billets away from home. The two officers and 30 Provisional Volunteers who were included in the 342 men arrested on August 9th, had ignored the warning. The other 310 were either Officials, political and community activists or old-time republicans no longer active in the Movement.

It was an illustration of how ineffective and incompetent British intelligence was. The army had relied on old Special Branch files and their own observations, which had netted them a mixed bag of community leaders and political activists who would soon prove much more a political embarrassment than the great coup being claimed on the morning of August 9th. It was precisely because these men were *not* IRA Volunteers that they had been so readily available for arrest.

In Ballymurphy, as in other nationalist areas throughout the North, the first clear indication that internment had arrived came in the persons of the raiding parties. Families in every street woke up to the sound of splintering wood and glass as their front doors were kicked in. Whole families were assaulted and clubbed as arrested men were dragged, half dressed, into the street. Outside, the district was swamped with soldiers, all on foot so as not to arouse the community with the sound of invading military vehicles. However, within minutes of the first arrests, the area was in uproar. Large numbers of people, mainly women, poured out of their homes, confused and frightened by the intensity of the operation which was clearly designed to terrorise the entire community. But there was little they could do as the prisoners were kicked and beaten through the streets towards the Taggart. (In some cases men were dragged from their homes with sacks over their heads and cotton wool in their mouths.)

Over in Springhill the young Gerry Adams, and his brother Paddy, watched from a distance as their family home was torn apart by the British army. The house had, since the 1970 riots, been a regular target for CS gas attacks and military raids, while Gerry Adams (Senior), one of the Ballymurphy relief committee activists, had been beaten on a number of occasions. Now, he and his son, Liam, were among those being arrested. (Liam, who was a minor, was later released barefooted to make his own way home across the city.)

Following the arrests the remainder of the Adams family were ejected from their home, which was then occupied by the military. When Annie Adams was finally allowed to return, she found the house uninhabitable: furniture had been destroyed, ceilings ripped down, the fireplace torn out; and as a parting gesture, the soldiers had urinated and defecated in the beds.

Once inside the Taggart the prisoners were again assaulted by baton-wielding soldiers who punched, kicked and clubbed them until many lay semi-conscious on the ground. Liam Mulholland who, it will be recalled, was almost 70 years old, was spared the introductory assault. Instead, he was brought into a room in the base where:

A sergeant came in and said 'I don't like you, and because I don't like you, take that!' A slap in the head. He then worked himself into a temper and slapped me across the room. On the side of the head, on the ears, bouncing me off the walls. He kept this up for about 15 to 20 minutes. Then I was taken outside and thrown bodily into a lorry where I landed on top of somebody else. I tried to get up and in the dark a soldier sunk his boot into me.[2]

By the time all those arrested in Ballymurphy and Turf Lodge had been brought to the Taggart, several lorries were full of men. As the convoy sped off, the last sounds the men heard were the stones raining down on the tins surrounding the base and the crescendo of binlids banging on the streets of every nationalist area of Belfast. Meanwhile the troops who had boarded the trucks by walking over the men on the floor, sang songs, stamping time with their boots on the bodies beneath them. Anybody who moved was clubbed with batons. Edward Campbell (19), from Springfield Road, had been arrested along with a friend when the soldiers raided the house looking for someone called 'Fox'. When told that nobody of that name lived there, they decided that 'you'll do'. At the Taggart he was thrown into one of the trucks and batoned. His subsequent ill-treatment was fairly typical:

The lorry moved out and we were raised to our feet and placed against the canvas side of the lorry. One soldier was heard to say 'If any of your mates throw stones, you're the ones will get it'. After we got through the crowd we were thrown to the floor again. While the lorry was still travelling I was pulled up by the hair and told to sing *God Save the Queen*. I refused and was hit across the head with a baton and thrown to the floor. I was hit on the head again and told to keep it down. The soldiers began to sing *The Sash*, beating time to it on our heads with their batons ...

A soldier told me he did not like the shape of my nose and hit me across the face with his baton. I was lying face up, and was again hit on the back of the head ... Another soldier shouted 'There's the two bastards who play the guitars' (myself and Raymond). At this stage a number of soldiers pulled Raymond's shirt up and spat all over his back. The soldier nearest to me commenced to hit me across the fingers with his baton. He then removed a bullet from his magazine. 'What was this doing in your pocket?' He put the bullet into my pocket and took it out again. Next he grabbed two fingers on my right hand and bent them backwards, saying 'I'm going to break these two fingers, you little bastard. You're going to enjoy this, aren't you?'[3]

The trucks brought the men across the city to a military camp which they later learned to be Girdwood Barracks on the Antrim Road. Getting out of the trucks, each man had again to run the gauntlet of clubs, boots and rifle-butts. Inside the camp, the men from Ballymurphy and Turf Lodge were herded into a room to join those already in from other areas of the city, many of whom were injured and bleeding. Frank Cahill, who had been lifted along with most of Ballymurphy's prominent community leaders, described how:

The redcaps were in charge of that operation in Girdwood. We were brought into an assembly hall where all our personal belongings were taken away, if you had any at all – very few people had. In fact I had a watch that was broken, deliberately broken, while I was in the back of the lorry. The soldier who took it from me put it on his knee, smashed it, and then put it back on my wrist. Anyway, in the assembly hall we were made to squat on the floor. Nobody got a chair. It didn't matter whether you had an ailment or not. Then there was this intense noise there. We didn't know what it was at the time; it was only later on that we realised it was part of the whole process.

Right from we went into the place there was brutality, and that lasted all the time we were there. They took one young fellow out and shaved every hair on his body, saying that he was 'lousy'. This was simply an attempt to humiliate him and show us how powerless we were ... You weren't allowed to talk. You had to raise your hand like a schoolboy if you wanted to go to the toilet. And even then they mightn't allow it for half an hour. We got nothing to eat that day, and were subjected all day to taunting, provocation and random attacks. I think if people had taken action, we might have come out of it feeling better, but it was a very difficult situation. You had redcaps walking about the perimeter of the men with Sterling sub-machine-guns crooked in their arms.

The next day, they came in and gave everyone who hadn't shoes slippers. Later on they allowed us to take a shower, which was nothing more than further brutality. You were simply booted through the shower by soldiers. Then they gave us something to eat, and it was absolute swill. Nevertheless some people ate it. Later in the evening they gave us all a camp bed. It was all wrapped up, and we were told to assemble it. Most of us hadn't a notion as to how we should go about this. Anyway, eventually everybody got sorted out and went to bed. Twenty minutes later, as soon as the men were settled, the Brits raced in and turned everybody out of the beds.[4]

Throughout the first two days, the men at Girdwood Barracks – all the Belfast detainees – were systematically interrogated, refused sleep, and subjected to indiscriminate brutality. Along with the beatings and degradation taking place in the assembly hall and the interrogation rooms, groups of men were taken away at random for further ill-treatment outside in the football field. Here, groups of six men at a time were forced to run distances of 50 to 100 yards over cinders, barbed wire and broken glass in their bare feet, while two lines of soldiers smashed at them with clubs and boots and others jeered from beyond. They were then blindfolded and taken into helicopters where further beatings were administered as the helicopters rose into the sky. Believing themselves to be high in the air, they were pushed backwards from the helicopters to fall six feet to the ground — a terrifying experience that can only be appreciated by those who went through it. Within 48 hours 105 of the 342 men arrested across the North, on August 9th, were released to bring harrowing tales back to their neighbourhoods.[5]

Fr Denis Faul and Fr Raymond Murray, who have campaigned extensively against British infringements of human rights, listed 30 methods of torture used against prisoners at Girdwood, Ballykelly and the infamous Palace Barracks in Holywood. They included: severe beatings; kicking; batoning and hand squeezing of the testicles; insertion of instruments into the anal passage; injections of hallucinagenic drugs; electric shocks; burning with matches, candles and electric fires; Russian roulette; firing of blanks in prisoners' mouths; urinating on prisoners; hooding; forced 'exercises' for long periods; deprivation of sleep; and forced staring at pegboard walls for periods of twelve hours or more.[6]

There were also twelve 'guinea pigs' who were secretly taken away and held incommunicado from August 11th to 17th. Spreadeagled against a wall for days on end without food or sleep, they were hooded, refused toilet facilities and subjected to 'white noise' and horrific assaults. Two more subjects were added to the experiment a few days later. After a public outcry, the British government was forced to conduct an inquiry into the allegations of torture. The result – *The Compton Report* – was considered a disgraceful whitewash by outraged nationalist opinion throughout Ireland.

A month after its publication, in December 1971, the Dublin government brought a case against Britain to the European Commission on Human Rights. After lengthy and complex legal wranglings, the Commission would find Britain guilty of 'torture' and 'inhuman or degrading treatment' of Irish political prisoners. On appeal in 1978, the European Court of Human Rights would drop the 'torture' finding on a technicality, whereupon the British government, to its further and eternal shame, would attempt to claim exoneration.

On their third night in detention, the last of the Girdwood detainees were transferred through a specially prepared hole in the wall to neighbouring Crumlin Road Jail. From there they would later be taken to Long Kesh and Magilligan concentration camps and to the *Maidstone* prison ship in Belfast Lough. Meanwhile, as they looked across the city from their cells in Crumlin Road, they could see the glow of fires in every direction as the city trembled with explosions and the crackle of gunfire.

Reaction to internment had been immediate. Rioting and gun-battles had broken out in every town in the North. Trees were felled in rural areas. Military and RUC bases were placed under siege by enraged crowds. Condemnation flowed from every shade of Irish political opinion other than unionism, while human rights and civil liberties groups in Ireland and Britain called for an immediate end to the new policy. Belfast, Derry and Newry were in a state of open warfare. The Provisional and Official IRAs had abandoned ideological differences and the bitterness remaining from their brief feud in March[*] and combined

---

*On March 8th, a feud between the Official and Provisional IRAs broke out in Belfast. Charlie Hughes, a Provisional, was shot dead from a shop in Cyprus Street by the Officials, and several men on both sides were wounded. That evening a truce was declared. Several hours later a Ballymurphy Provisional was shot while delivering milk on the Springfield Road. As he lay slumped over the wheel of his milkvan, his would-be assassin put the gun to his shoulder and pulled the trigger, leaving him paralysed down one side of his body.

forces to fight the British army. Not since the Rising of 1916 had Irish and British forces engaged one another on such a scale.

Troops ran amok in nationalist areas, shooting wildly, firing rubber bullets and CS gas, wrecking houses, and assaulting and gunning down civilians in the streets and in their homes. Factories and shops were set alight in many centres. Buses and cars were hijacked and burned. Barricades were erected in all nationalist areas. In Dublin 26-County Prime Minister Jack Lynch, though not condemning internment as such, described its introduction as 'deplorable evidence of the political poverty of the policies which have been pursued there for some time, and which I condemned publicly last week'. Lynch's refusal to bow to British pressure for the introduction of internment in the South caused a severe Dublin–London diplomatic clash, although London recognised that Lynch's political position, following the North's recent history, made the introduction of internment in the 26 Counties impossible. At the same time Lynch announced the opening of five army camps to receive refugees and the dependants of those interned. (Within two days, the camps were dealing with 6,000 refugees.)

In Dungannon, at an emergency meeting attended by the SDLP, NICRA, the Nationalist Party and the Republican Labour Party, a statement was issued calling for a withdrawal from public positions and a campaign of civil disobedience by nationalists. In Belfast, the city came to a virtual standstill. Bus services were cancelled. Public houses closed under instruction from the Licensed Vintners Association. Whole areas of the city were battlegrounds.

In North Belfast, loyalist families fled their homes in Farrington Gardens, Velsheda Park and Cranbrook Gardens, burning houses as they left so that they could not be occupied by nationalists. In loyalist areas across the city, nationalist families were being burned out by mobs of loyalists who roamed the streets in lorries, armed with sledgehammers, axes and guns. There had been increasing sectarian conflict in the week leading up to internment, but nothing on the scale that followed. The Central Citizens' Defence Committee and the Association for Legal Justice logged endless examples of wholesale intimidation in the immediate aftermath of internment. In most cases, the RUC and the British army did nothing to intervene, the British army in fact stating on August 10th that it could not intervene in communal strife!

In the three weeks following the introduction of internment 2,069 forced evacuations were recorded, though the true figure was probably closer to 2,500.[7] The effect on Belfast was:

> the re-sorting of mixed areas into segregated areas, the continuation of the patterns of 1969 and 1970. Also observable was the stability of the militarily enforced 'peace' line between the Shankill and Falls roads, and the differences between Catholic and Protestant movements. Protestants who left their homes tended to move to 'safe' estates on the outskirts of the city ... Catholics crowded into the already over-populated Catholic areas, especially West Belfast and the Short Strand.[8]

Despite the loyalist intimidation and arson, and the nightly gun attacks on nationalist areas, not one loyalist was interned in the August swoops. On August 9th the London region of NICRA observed: 'For the last two years we've been told of warring factions in Northern Ireland. Last night 300 people have been arrested and not a single one of these is associated with voting for Brian Faulkner.'⁹

The death toll for the four days, August 9th to 13th, was 22 dead, 19 of them civilians. In Derry, by the end of the week, the IRA had succeeded in sealing off the Bogside and Creggan, and for the next year Free Derry was a veritable fortress, with its barricades protected by armed IRA personnel and the British forces fully excluded. The civil disobedience campaign, officially launched at a meeting of Stormont opposition MPs on Monday, August 16th, had already taken root in all working-class areas, with people ceasing to pay rent, rates, gas and electricity.*

In Belfast, bus services remained cancelled, giving the black taxi shuttle service its kiss of life. And in Ballymurphy they were mourning the dead. Of the 19 civilians killed in the whole of the North, seven had been killed in Greater Ballymurphy. Paddy McCarthy was also dead. Three other Ballymurphy men were mortally wounded and would die in the coming weeks, bringing the district's death toll to eleven. Scores of others had been injured by gunfire.

In the immediate aftermath of the internment swoop, crowds from every street in Ballymurphy had converged on the most obvious focus of their confusion and anger: the Taggart. There they laid siege to the base while their husbands, sons, fathers and brothers were being brutalised inside. Kate McCullough, a 42-year-old mother of eleven, was among those who marched on the Taggart. A small laughing woman with a heart of gold, Kate was a fearless protector of her neighbours no matter what the odds or how rough the treatment. She remembers how:

There was nothing but confusion. They were lifted in their stockinged soles. It was a terrible frightening experience. We went out to the front of the road – all the crowds of women and children. It didn't do us much good; but we let them see there was still fight in us anyway. We went up to the Taggart, and as we got onto the Springfield Road, the Saracens – the big six-wheelers – were coming down from Turf Lodge with more men that were lifted. We threw everything at the Taggart: stones, bits of wood, binlids. Anything that was liftable. I remember throwing a binlid, and whatever way it went, it caught one of the soldiers as it rolled along the road. He tripped, but he was far faster at getting up than we were ... We stayed there until the lorries came out. Once they had left there was nothing else we could do so we went on home and started to organise. A couple of nights later, the women had set up the hen patrols.¹⁰

---

*Among the SDLP MPs who 'officially' launched the civil disobedience campaign on August 16th, was Austin Currie. On April 3rd 1974, as Minister for Housing in the short-lived British-imposed power-sharing Executive at Stormont, Currie levied a punitive weekly collection fee on those still on rent and rates strike.

The 'hen patrols' were the women's first response to internment. They decided on their return from the Taggart that surprise would not be on the British army's side in the coming nights. The raiding parties, with their blackened faces and silent boots, were called 'duck patrols'. The women would counter with their own hen patrols. Armed with whistles, football crackers, bells and rattling binlids, and calling 'Quack! Quack!', they would follow the invading troops from street to street, handing over from one hen patrol to the next. Not alone did they deprive the soldiers of the element of surprise; but between themselves and the dogs, life for a foot patrol in Ballymurphy became a recipe for incurable jitters.

The hen patrol to which Kate McCullough was attached had perhaps the most formidable vanguard of all, Big Alice Franklin, who, in Kate's words, 'made the air blue with the names she called the Brits'. Big Alice was another fearless opponent of repression, and a great woman for spurning convention. In the summertime she would organise bingo sessions with the neighbours: a line of women sitting on their doorsteps with books supplied by Alice while the big woman herself called the numbers. When trouble broke – no matter where in Ballymurphy – Alice had the knack of being there, terrorising the massed forces of Perfidious Albion with the scientific use of a very colourful tongue projected from an almighty larynx.

In more recent years, Alice's health wasn't the best and she settled back into running a little house-shop from her home in Glenalina Gardens – an illegal practice as far as the Housing Executive was concerned. The Executive heard about the shop and duly sent one of its officers to investigate. 'Shop!' Alice bellowed as she scowled over the top of her glasses at the man from Murray Street, 'Just you have a good look there and you tell me if you see a shop!' Her visitor followed Alice's gesture to the neatly stacked table of cigarettes, bread, milk, sweets and other goodies, and the boxes stacked in the hallway and swore that, for the life of him, he couldn't see a shop.

After Alice's death in 1985, the hen patrols and Big Alice's crusade against all forms of authority were the topic of conversation for a month. In August 1971, however, their inception marked the beginning of the most violent week in the history of the Upper Springfield.

By then Greater Ballymurphy – encompassing the estates of Whiterock, Westrock, Springhill, Ballymurphy, Moyard, New Barnsley, Dermott Hill and Springfield Park – had become one clearly-defined unit of organisation, cemented by the riots, the relief operations and the ongoing programme of community action. Ballymurphy estate was its epicentre. On its eastern flank, curling up a small ridge to front up against loyalist Springmartin, was Springfield Park, a small enclave of some 90 owner-occupied houses. As the women in the different estates discussed the idea of the hen patrols, trouble was already brewing in a big way in Springfield Park.

It began mid-morning of August 9th, when a crowd gathered on the ridge at Springmartin chanting 'Where's your daddy gone?' Behind them were the low flats of the loyalist estate and a row of houses that swept down Springmartin Road to the Springfield Road, terminating behind Glenravel Special Care School, a short distance from the entrance to Springhill. Shortly, several groups of loyalists began hurling rocks from the flats down onto the houses in Springfield Park. Others moved down towards Springhill. There was no retaliation from Springfield Park. Father Hugh Mullan, the 37-year-old resident curate, saw to that. He also rang the RUC and the military. The latter sent one armoured car into Springmartin on a brief excursion. Its effect was minimal and very temporary. Neither the military nor the RUC made any further appearance as the scenes at the Springfield Park/Springmartin front grew uglier by the hour.

At 4pm Hugh Mullan climbed the ridge and attempted to reason with the Springmartin crowd, now jeering wildly as the rocks and bottles showered down onto the unprotected houses below. He attempted to plead for the 100 children under twelve living in Springfield Park. He was told to 'Fuck off you Fenian bastard', and the bombardment continued. Shortly afterwards, the first reinforcements began to pour in to Springfield Park from the other estates of Ballymurphy. By 7pm a pitched battle was raging along the entire interface between the nationalist and loyalist strongholds, while Hugh Mullan tried in vain to telephone for some kind of official protection.

Just after 8pm the first shots rang out. The consensus among both loyalists and nationalists was that they came from the loyalist-held ridge.[11] The IRA had been preparing for such a contingency.

Since early morning the Republican Movement, practically untouched by the internment swoop, had been taking stock of its resources. Unknown to the British, some of the IRA's most senior officers, including the Belfast commander, were billeted in Ballymurphy. Since morning all units had been on full alert. Now, as the shooting from Springmartin intensified, Volunteers began to fire back from the flats in Moyard. Immediately, the troops in the Taggart opened up on the entire nationalist area, firing at anything that moved. Soldiers also moved into Springmartin, *taking up positions alongside loyalist gunmen*, to fire into Moyard and Ballymurphy.

Once the shooting started, the evacuation of families began from the upper end of Springfield Park where the danger was most immediate. Moving through back gardens, they made their way down to the lower end of the road, then headed instinctively for the community centre in Moyard, where a team of local people were already preparing emergency facilities for the expected influx from other parts of the city. To get to Moyard, however, the evacuees had to cross a strip of open ground in front of Hugh Mullan's house. The exodus had prompted lulls in the gunfire as the children were escorted to safety. But there were more children than adults in the Park, so some of the men had to run a ferry service, which meant returning across the open field without the immunity of a child in arms, and risking a fusillade of loyalist and British bullets.

At about 8.30pm 19-year-old Bobby Clarke went back to collect another child and was shot in the back from the Taggart. Father Mullan saw him fall. Waving a white handkerchief, he left his house in Springfield Park with the intention of administering the Last Rites to the wounded youth. When he realised that Clarke was not dying, the priest rose to go back home to 'phone an ambulance. He was shot twice, once through the leg and once through the heart, in a hail of fire from the Taggart. Almost immediately, another young man, Frank Quinn from Moyard, came to the rescue. He too was shot dead by the British army.

Up at Moyard Community Centre, Brian McLaughlin, a local community activist, Steve Pittam, an English Quaker who had stayed in Ballymurphy after the summer playscheme, and Ali Keeli, a Jordanian student doctor, were among those who watched in horror as the three men were shot and word came in of others who had been killed or wounded. Brian McLaughlin recounted how:

> The bodies lay there for hours. Every time anyone made a move towards them, they were shot at. Eventually Ali Keeli went out waving a white helmet. He got to the three bodies and dragged them, one at a time, clear of the field. Once he got them to the paths, the rest of us took over. Hugh Mullan's body was brought into Eddie and Kate Spence's house, Frank Quinn into McAlorum's in Moyard Parade, and the other lad was treated in the community centre before being taken down to the First Aid centre in St Bernadette's school.[12]

In an interesting example of how the British media distorts reality in order to portray the best possible British image, the *Sunday Times* Insight Team reported on Sunday, August 15th, that: 'The Special Branch is now investigating the denomination of the bullets that killed Father Mullan: were they Protestant or Catholic or perhaps even military?'[13]

The suggestion – heaven forbid – that they might have been 'military' (not 'British') comes almost as an afterthought, just to be fair you see. Yet, late on the night of August 9th, Major-General R.C. Ford, British Commander of Land Forces, stated in a press release that the British army was responsible for at least six of the day's deaths, including 'the two men shot dead' in what his own fiction described as 'an attack on the Henry Taggart Memorial Hall'.

On Friday, August 13th, two days before the *Sunday Times* article appeared, Brigadier Marston Tickell, Chief of Staff for Northern Ireland, further stated at a press conference in Belfast that the British army had taken a great toll of 'gunmen', '20 to 30 of whom have been killed'. As there were only 19 civilian deaths, the British army was clearly claiming responsibility for the full total, justifiably, as they had in fact killed all but one. It is inconceivable that this information was not available to the *Sunday Times* team. When we further consider that the Insight Team was among the few sections of the British media to look critically at British policies in the North when such sedition was still permissible, we can surmise that little of value to students of modern Irish history will be found in the pages and newsreels of the British media.

Fifteen minutes before the shooting broke out, Daniel Teggart of New

Barnsley Crescent decided to call down to his brother in the lower end of Moyard, close to the rioting. He asked his wife, Belle, to keep the children inside so they wouldn't get into any trouble. Ten minutes later, down in Ballymurphy, he met with two of his friends, Dan Breen and Willie Ward. All three decided to go for a pint. They went down the Springfield Road towards Springhill Avenue. Directly across from Springfield Park, within 30 yards of the Taggart, they stopped to talk to Dessie Crone who had gone out to look for his son. With Dessie Crone were Joseph Murphy, Davie Callaghan, Dan Delaney and 14-year-old Tommy Morgan, all of them gathered at two stone pillars forming the gateway to 'The Manse', an old house between Ballymurphy and Springhill. They could see the rioting at the upper end of Springfield Park.

Joan Connolly also left her home in Ballymurphy Road at about 7.15pm. Fearing for the safety of her children, she went out to round them up. She arrived up at the Springfield Road and turned down towards Springhill, passing the group at 'The Manse' gates and bidding them the time of day. She never made it to Springhill. Dessie Crone heard the shooting from Springmartin. Then:

> The Paras opened up from the Taggart, just blasting in every direction. Murphy and I ran to one of the pillars for protection. But Murphy was hit in the leg. He said, 'I don't know if this is blood or wine' – him being so fond of the drink. There wasn't that much room behind the pillar so Delaney, young Morgan and I threw ourselves into a hedge behind. There were so many rounds being fired that my knuckles were cut by the flying gravel. I looked over to the other pillar where Davie Callaghan was and I thought he was dead. He had been hit in the forehead by a piece of flying masonry and was just lying there. Then we heard a woman saying 'I'm hit', and found out later that it was Mrs Connolly. She was hit once, got up to get away, and they blew her head away. The force lifted her and threw her into the field so that her body wasn't found till the early morning.
>
> After what seemed like hours, a loudspeaker called from the Taggart 'Ceasefire. You have a couple of minutes to get your wounded out.' Then a Saladin came out from the Taggart and backed right into where we were. I put my hand over young Morgan's mouth and we just lay where we were. If we had said anything they would've blown us to pieces. They trailed Davie Callaghan into the back of the Saladin by the feet and threw him there like a piece of meat. Dan Breen, Joesie Murphy, Danny Teggart and Willie Ward ran off across the fields and that was the last we seen of them until the Brits came in with another Saladin and trailed Joesie out, saying: 'Here's another of the bastards'. They were so close that time that we could've pulled the legs from under them. Then the shooting started again and went on and on; if they fired one round, they fired a thousand.
>
> At about ten o'clock the loudspeaker came on again, and said, 'You have two minutes to get the wounded out', that a civilian ambulance was coming. So Dan Delaney and me, we lifted Tommy Morgan as if he was shot and went over across the field to Divismore Park. A woman called us into a house, and we found Willie Ward and Dan Breen there. They told us

that Danny Teggart had been shot. He had 13 bullets in him. Willie's coat was torn and he had a burn on his shoulder from a bullet. Afterwards, the Brits claimed that Danny Teggart had 30 odd bullets in his pocket. That was a load of shit![14]

(Later on the soldiers would claim that Danny Teggart was searched and found to be 'clean', but that an hour later a soldier 'accidentally' kicked him and heard the rattle of the cleverly hidden bullets.)

Early on the morning of August 10th, Joan Connolly's body was found. Later on that day Noel Phillips of Ballymurphy was found face down in the stream between Ballymurphy and Springhill. He had been shot dead the night before from the Taggart, bringing the area's death toll for August 9th, to five. Joseph Murphy would die on August 22nd from injuries received that night – injuries which mostly resulted from the treatment dished out to the wounded in the Taggart. Afterwards in hospital he told his wife, Mary, that he was laid out along with the dead and that every time soldiers passed, they booted the living and the dead.

They fired rubber bullets into my husband from point blank range. He was wounded in the leg, but when he got to hospital it was the internal injuries that were the worst. They had to put him on a kidney machine, his liver and kidneys were destroyed, and there was all sorts of other injuries. The doctor told us that his leg needed amputation that night; but because of the damage from the beatings, he couldn't operate. Over the next few days gangrene set in, and he died 13 days later ...

Our men were murdered, you know, they were shot down in the streets like dogs; and there wasn't one, not one, to get up and say.[15]

In 1977, the families bereaved by the 'Manse' killings had their cases heard in Crumlin Road Court in Belfast. Mrs Murphy was offered the princely sum of £250 to compensate herself and her nine children for the loss of a husband and father. She told them to keep it. Mrs Teggart, who was jeered outside the courtroom by the soldiers who had killed her husband, received not a penny for herself and her ten children.

The brutality that killed Joesie Murphy was also meeted out to Davie Callaghan, a 59-year old retired postal engineer who suffered from chronic asthma. Grazed by the piece of flying masonry, he had lain prone, praying that that would save his life. He was still praying as he was dragged to the armoured car, beaten with a rifle, and thrown in. Inside the base, he was discovered to be alive and kicking – or at least kickable. He was viciously beaten by soldiers who at one stage held his legs apart and repeatedly kicked him in the testicles. Davie Callaghan spent the next ten days in hospital with his injuries. He was then subjected to a six-day interrogation at Castlereagh where he was further brutalised.

Another casualty of August 9th, was eleven-year-old Eddie Butler who was shot from the Taggart as he tried to climb through a hedge. As he lay screaming on the ground between Springhill and Ballymurphy the soldiers continued to fire at him. Only the courage of Sean McStravick saved his life. McStravick, who had one artificial leg – so that people often got the impression he was 'walking about with a gun down his trousers' – pulled a door from a shed behind his own house. He then crawled over to where young Butler lay, rolled him onto the door, attached a rope and returned. He and some neighbours were thus able to haul the boy to safety from the cover of McStravick's gable wall.

On the morning of August 10th, with the smoke from the previous day's fires hanging over the city, homeless families again poured into West Belfast from 'mixed' areas. They brought with them endless stories of beatings, burnings and widespread looting of nationalist property by both the loyalist arsonists and the British army. When they arrived in Ballymurphy they were greeted by stunned relatives and friends, still trying to understand the events of the past 24 hours. This time around Ballymurphy was anything but a safe corridor. In the community centre, behind heavily fortified barricades, Paddy McCarthy and BTA chairperson, Frances McMullan, were co-ordinating a massive exodus of terrified and uncomprehending children, fleeing south to the 26-County army's refugee camps.

At the Taggart the military were still firing rubber bullets, CS gas and live rounds as groups of youths attacked the base with petrol bombs and nail bombs. News bulletins, meanwhile, reported that Belfast city centre lay eerie and deserted with less than 25 per cent of workers appearing for work. The Upper Springfield was equally eerie, with every street entrance sealed and patrolled, and four homes and the Parish in mourning. Simultaneously, like Nero of old, British Prime Minister Ted Heath, was out sailing his yacht, soon to pass within four miles of the Irish coast.

As morning passed to afternoon, rumours mounted that another loyalist/British attack was imminent. All available weapons had been mobilised, and sentries posted in strategic positions. Many of these were young men and women who, until quite recently had been the ordinary, boy and girl down the street. Now, with very little military training, they found themselves in the front line against loyalist snipers and the British army's shock troops. Nervously, many of them wondered if they would live to see the morrow. With the same nervousness they fired their guns whenever they thought they spotted the first signs of enemy attack. Early in the afternoon, Joe Cahill, the 51-year-old commander of the Belfast Brigade, Provisional IRA, almost became the first 'enemy' casualty. Cahill, a soft-spoken gentle man with a penchant for tweed caps, had been making his way back into the area along with Gerry Adams and another republican leader. They had come up through the disused brickyards in Beechmount, and were crossing the playground in St Peter's School when they were fired on.

> We had to hit the dust and the bullets were flying around us. Luckily, your man was a bad shot. When we got up to the house in the Whiterock where I was set to meet a newspaper reporter, one of the fellows who was

on armed guard at that particular spot came running in and said that they had got three UVF men down in St Peter's School![16]

A couple of hours later an attack was launched on the area by the British army. Soldiers arrived in force at the bottom of the Whiterock Road to attempt to remove a barricade close to McCrory Park, a playing field belonging to St Peter's. Eddie Doherty (28) was making his way home to Iveagh on the Falls Road when the troops came into view. Danny McGuinness, a 22-year-old Ballymurphy man, who knew Eddie Doherty, was on patrol at the barricades:

When the Brits came on the scene, we tried to set fire to the barricade with diesel, but it wouldn't catch. Then the bulldozer attacked the barricade; and one of them big Saladins behind opened up with a Browning machine-gun. Everyone ran across the field until the machine-gun stopped firing. Most of the crowd were kids. Then a single shot came from behind the digger and killed Eddie Doherty.[17]

It was as chillingly simple as that. Later on that evening a particularly brutal killing took place at the junction of Whiterock and Springfield Roads. Some time after dark, the military had made a sortie into Whiterock and converged on the Springfield Road. Expecting a second internment swoop, people had come out on to the streets to bang binlids and blow whistles. Over in Turf Lodge John Lavery (19) and his brother Terence (17), who had been visiting their sister, heard the commotion. Worried for their family in Ballymurphy, they set off for home, Terence sticking to the main roads while John took a short cut through the waste ground separating the two estates.

At the top of Whiterock Road, Terence Lavery ran into a patrol of paratroopers in the blacked-out street. They tied him to some railings outside the launderette at the Whiterock Road side of the junction, then broke into the butcher's shop further down, returned with the knives used for cutting the meat, and commenced to cut Terence Lavery's clothes and boots to shreds. Unknown to the terrified Ballymurphy man, his brother was at that moment lying dead 50 yards away in what used to be the Corporation Yard. He had been abducted on his way home, brought into the derelict yard, beaten up, and coldly executed. Mrs Julia Grego, the boys' aunt, recalled how:

We had no idea where John was. He vanished on the 10th of August and was missing for nearly 24 hours. It was only the following day, when Tom Farrell of the BTA went down to the morgue to identify Pat McCarthy, that he saw our John there too ... Then Terence was given six months in jail on a bum charge![18]

Like all the others, the killing of John Lavery was claimed by the British army as yet another glorious victory against 'terrorism'.

An hour or two later, Joe Cahill had a narrow escape in Whiterock.

Not realising that the military had moved in, he was on his way home to his billet for a wash, a change and a few hours' sleep.

> I was walking towards the door of the house when I tripped over a Brit who was lying in the garden. He let a grunt out of him, and his mates who were in the other gardens jumped up and trained their rifles on that particular house. I apologised to the Brit as the others shouted 'Who is it?' So he shouted back at them to hold their fire, that it was a friend.[19]

And as the soldiers resumed their vigil for 'gunmen', the most prestigious catch in Belfast bade them a very good night and went on in to his bed.

In the early hours of Monday, August 11th, a major assault was launched on Ballymurphy by the British army. Margaret Keenan, who lived in New Barnsley Grove overlooking Dermott Hill, was at home listening to RUC and military messages on the radio when she glanced out towards the mountain. She immediately knew that the expected second raid was about to commence:

> They were coming down the mountain loney. A line of Saracens and soldiers. They had no lights on and no engines running. They must have come over the Ballygomartin Road. I ran out into the street and shouted 'They're coming!' I ran around to my sister's; but the Brits were there before me. A short while afterwards the shooting started.[20]

Once the paratroopers reached the first houses they began to shoot indiscriminately. The indiscipline and blanket fire of the British gunmen brought many in the area to initially conclude that the loyalists were invading. One of these was 43-year-old Joseph Corr, who left his home in Divismore Crescent along with his young son Joe to try and gauge the nature of the attack and the threat immediately posed to his family and neighbours. Father and son made their way to the top of the Crescent where it joined the Springfield Road. They were spotted by the troops who fired on them, wounding the father. Young Joe later told how his father was taken away and interrogated by the soldiers despite his wounds, and how the family spent three days trying to track him down, not knowing if he was alive or dead.

> We searched every hospital, rang every military and police barracks. And nobody would tell us where he was. In the end, after three days, we found him in the military wing of Musgrave Park Hospital. He was badly wounded and had been beaten up by the Brits. He died 15 days later.[21]

Word of Joseph Corr's fate spread quickly, adding to the general confusion and panic as people took cover behind walls and on the floors of their homes. But this time the IRA was ready. As the soldiers raked the houses with gunfire, shooting the very dogs in the streets, contingents of Volunteers fired back from blacked-out alleys and gardens. Immediately people unlocked their front and back doors and impromptu First Aid centres were set up. Maureen McGuinness (23) was attached to one of those centres:

> Around midnight or a little after, heavy shooting started. I ran to Kate Pollock's house in Glenalina which was used as one of the First Aid centres. There were five of us based there. That was the worst night of all – the real nightmare night. It never stopped all night. There were fellas running everywhere with guns. In and out of every house. They were engaging the Brits in running battles. It was just chaos.
>
> All you could hear was screaming, shouting and shooting. Then about 5 o'clock the Brits started kicking in doors. At this stage the gun-battles had died down, and the Paras were just moving along the street, kicking in doors and shooting. You could hear their voices screaming 'There's one! Shoot the bastard!' or 'Halt!' then heavy firing. We thought the place was literally covered in bodies. We couldn't look out the window. When we had, they fired on us. A wee fella Quinn across the street was grazed when he tried to look out.[22]

Jean Campbell, a young domestic science teacher, lived in Glenalina Park along with her three sisters and three brothers. At 21, she was the eldest of the family, and had acted as guardian to the others since the death of their parents. During the morning of August 11th, she lay on the landing floor of her home along with the rest of the family and Lizzie Maguire from Beechmount who was their home help.

> There was shooting going on non-stop. There had been heavy shooting on Monday night when Fr Mullan was killed, and there had been sporadic gunfire all day Tuesday, but this was continuous. By now there were no supplies left in the area. The Brits came in shooting from every direction, and we could only assume that some of the shooting was the IRA trying to hold them off. They systematically moved through every street. They tore down the fences, smashed in the doors, and just wrecked the houses. They were totally destructive. Any male over 14 found in the house was dragged out and taken off. You could hear it getting closer and closer and closer. There were a few dogs shot in the street, and people screaming ...
>
> When they got to our house, they burst in the front door, and all you could hear was Lizzie saying 'Oh Sacred Heart of Jesus! Oh Sacred Heart of Jesus!' Lizzie had been stranded in the house since Monday morning, and couldn't get out of the area. They stayed downstairs for about 15 minutes, but for some reason, they never came up. But you can imagine the hysterics going on upstairs.[23]

Eileen Brennan (18) was at home with her parents, her friend Rosie McCabe, and two younger sisters, Geraldine and Betty, when the soldiers reached their house in Divismore Crescent.

> Two soldiers moved along the gardens, smashing all the windows with their rifle butts, and firing plastic bullets into the houses. They seen the people in our house and one of the Paras said 'Get them bastards!' They fired at us, and a bullet passed through my mother's hair, showering her

hair with glass. And they shot my father in the chin. They knew they'd hit somebody; but they didn't come in. They went into Collins' next door and wrecked the house. They drank everything in the fridge. They had already broken into Kelly's Bar and stolen drink. They were full ... They shot someone's chickens up in New Barnsley.[24]

Every house in Greater Ballymurphy had its own tale to tell by morning.

On the Whiterock Road, soldiers had put Bernard Vallelly up against the bedroom window of his own home, while they fired from both sides of him at a sniper in Turf Lodge.

In Ballymurphy Parade, Mary Murphy, whose husband had been shot two days earlier, had her home destroyed, while soldiers fired from her back window at a neighbour's dog.

In Divismore Crescent, Anne Collins and her two daughters were punched about the house, while the Paras threatened to shoot her husband. They then broke every stick of furniture in the house.

Anne McLaughlin of Dermott Hill Road was kicked and beaten with a binlid.

In Ballymurphy Road, Jimmy Burns pulled his daughter, Peggy, into the house as the soldiers threatened to shoot her. He then watched as they moved up the street, smashing windows and firing rubber bullets, CS gas and live rounds into the houses.

In every street, men were taken from their homes, beaten savagely, and handcuffed to fences and railings until military vehicles arrived to take them away. Others were tied spreadeagled to the doors and sides of Saracens, acting as hostages and shields for the occupants as they drove through the area. In every street people were wounded by army gunfire, though the actual numbers will never be known as most were treated in secret 'surgeries' in West Belfast or in hospitals over the border. By 8am the area was fully occupied and under military curfew, while the IRA for the most part, had vanished. Paddy McCarthy, the BTA youth worker, was dead.

When the gunfire started in the early hours, there had been some 30 people gathered in the BTA community centre, many of them young children. At about 3am the paratroopers opened fire on the building from three points, maintaining their fire for two hours. In an attempt to evacuate the children, Paddy McCarthy, who had been in the centre since the previous morning, tried to obtain a ceasefire from the army commander. He stepped out with a Red Cross flag tied to a broomstick, only to have it shot out of his hand, a splinter tearing his wrist in the process. He zig-zagged back to the centre exhausted from fatigue and loss of blood, and commenting wryly that 'Even the Jerries respected that flag'.

Some time after dawn Daphne Robinson, the Quaker woman involved with Ballymurphy Enterprises, learned about the plight of the Ballymurphy people. Supplies were out; no traders had been able to get into the area for two days; and there was no milk for the children. She left her home on the other side of town, loaded her car with milk, and drove across to the Falls. Unable to go up the Whiterock Road because of the barricades and gunfire, she took her car through the City Cemetery to the wall of the community centre, and passed the crates of milk over to Paddy McCarthy.

The youth worker loaded a trolley, wheeled it out of the community centre, and crossed Whiterock Road to Ballymurphy estate, calling out 'milk for babies'. The whole area was at this stage under curfew, with the troops ransacking homes and assaulting men, women and children. Two paratroopers accosted McCarthy, one aiming a rifle at his head, and the other kicking over a crate of milk, smashing several bottles. McCarthy replaced the crate and backed off, telling the soldiers that they would not get the opportunity to shoot him in the back. He then began calling at houses where he knew there were young children.

In Whitecliff Drive, a small entry with a double row of houses, Paddy McCarthy collapsed, the victim of a heart attack. He was carried into a house while the paratroopers smashed every remaining bottle of milk on the trolley, taunting the women standing nearby. Paddy McCarthy was dead on arrival at hospital, the eighth person to die in Ballymurphy in less than 50 hours.

A few hours later, as the military pulled back to the perimeters of the estates, women from the Falls arrived into Ballymurphy with bread, milk and other supplies, and brought an end to the unofficial curfew. However, the killing was not over yet. At 11am, as a funeral cortege made its way out of Corpus Christi Church in Whiterock Drive, a single shot rang out from Corry's timberyard, overlooking Westrock. John McKerr from Andersonstown fell to the ground with a bullet through his forehead. He died nine days later.

Unbelievably, 54 residents of Greater Ballymurphy were charged with 'riotous behaviour' as a result of the Paras' invasion of August 11th. Not one soldier was ever charged with murder or unlawful shooting.

On August 13th, Ballymurphy's dead were being proudly claimed by Brigadier Marston Tickell as eliminated 'terrorists'. Internment, according to Tickell, had been a resounding success. The only unfortunate side effects had been 'a great deal of mess from these barricades' and 'intimidation leading to ... a number of families leaving their homes.'[25] As for the IRA? In the first of many such British delusions, Tickell announced that, 'we have undoubtedly inflicted a major defeat on the IRA'. Brian Faulkner, in his assessment of the internment shambles, was a little more realistic. He simply claimed that internment was 'exposing the gunmen'. To which the *Sunday Times* would reply: 'It was a remarkable statement – internments, by their nature, are not usually supposed to expose gunmen. The idea is to lock them up.'[26]

And as Tickell gave his press conference in Tyrone House in Belfast his analysis and credibility were being torpedoed in Ballymurphy. Right under the noses of the British army, Joe Cahill was holding another press conference at St Peter's School.

We felt the need to go on the air to counteract British propaganda. They were claiming that all the dead were IRA personnel, whereas we had only lost two Volunteers. And they were claiming that the IRA was defunct. So we took advantage of the press conference being called in St Peter's by the defence people. Towards the end of the conference, one of the media men asked, 'If the IRA are not defeated, where are they?' At that point, Paddy Kennedy, the MP, said, 'Well, you'd better ask the commander of the Belfast Brigade'. The atmosphere was electric after that ...

Afterwards, when we were leaving, the Brits were closing in on the school, and I actually ended up walking right past them.[27]

After the press conference, Joe Cahill moved out of Whiterock and left Belfast for Dublin, where he took up the position of Quartermaster General of the IRA.

By the end of internment week it was clear that, far from destroying the IRA, the British initiative had merely unleashed an IRA offensive. It also gave a massive boost to recruitment. Young men and women who had seen their relatives and neighbours being dragged away, and had later learned of the treatment inflicted on the detainees, flocked to join. Others, who might have been part-time Volunteers, were now on the run and unable to return to their normal affairs, so that their participation in the Movement became full-time. The Officials also launched a full offensive.

The nationalists had a new cause, a new set of martyrs in the 'men behind the wire'. There was a rash of street ballads, one of which became the personal property of every child in the Upper Springfield on the merits of one stanza referring to the night of August 10th/11th:

On that black day in August when Faulkner showed his hand,
He thought that with internment he could smash that gallant band,
But the boys of Ballymurphy, they led the way that night,
When they showed those English soldiers how Irishmen could fight.

Throughout August there were mass marches of workers and women in every nationalist centre in the North. In the South the establishment was eventually forced to issue an outright condemnation of internment and, on August 19th, Lynch called for its termination. Three days later the North's middle-class nationalists – now forced into open confrontation with the state – dropped out of public office; 130 councillors quit from local government; and, as international condemnation poured in, the IRA and the Officials continued a concentrated assault on the state.

By the end of the month, over a hundred explosions had occurred, some of them enormous; rifle fire was general in urban areas; rural areas had become a death-trap for the RUC and British army; and 35 people were dead. From the secure bases of Free Derry, and the republican strongholds of Belfast, and along the border, the guerrillas were reducing the loyalist state to tatters. Meanwhile, the state forces were striking back blindly with random mass arrests, beatings, torture, internment, and a 'shoot-on-sight' policy.

In Ballymurphy the attacks continued on the Taggart; and on August 19th two British soldiers, home on leave, and a civilian were wounded when men with revolvers burst into a house in Westrock Drive. British military personnel, regardless of their origin, were no longer safe in the area.

Between August and the end of 1971 events continued in a similar vein. In September there were also three new organisations formed. On the nationalist side ex-servicemen created the Catholic Ex-Servicemen's Association (CESA) while, on the loyalist side, a number of local defence associations banded together in the Ulster Defence Association (UDA). Whereas CESA would eventually fade away into the misty realms of tavern-ownership, the UDA would embark on a campaign of random assassinations against nationalists, joining the UVF as an indiscriminate loyalist terror force which, despite its record, would remain a legal organisation. The third development occurred on September 14th, when Desmond Boal and Johnnie McQuade combined forces with Ian Paisley and the Rev. William Beattie to launch the Democratic Unionist Party which would soon become the Six-County forum for right-wing discontent.

On the same day a sentry was shot in the neck and seriously wounded at the Taggart as the game of cat-and-mouse between the troops and the IRA maintained its intensity. Also on the 14th, soldiers in Ballymurphy displayed an amazing gullibility by coming out into the open to investigate a parcel left in Divismore Way and labelled 'bomb'. Inevitably they were shot at and the 'bomb' was found to be a brick. By now the Taggart was used by the IRA for target practice, to test new weapons, and to train recruits.

Gunfire was constant in its vicinity; but, remarkably, there were very few casualties in the Taggart shoot-outs. Then on October 17th Scots Guardsman George Hamilton (21), the second soldier to be killed in the Upper Springfield, was shot dead in Ballymurphy estate.* On November 4th another Scots Guardsman, Stephen Maguire (20), the soldier wounded at the Taggart on September 14th, died of his wounds to become the British army's third Ballymurphy fatality.

On October 13th, the military began the cratering of 200 minor roads along the border. On the 17th, the Northern Resistance Movement was founded. Supported by People's Democracy and the Provisionals, the NRM differed from NICRA (now controlled by the Officials) in that one of its aims was the destruction of Stormont, which now seemed an attainable goal.

A week later Ballymurphy was struck a double blow. On October 23rd Dorothy Maguire and her married sister, Maura Meehan, two unarmed Ballymurphy women, were killed by troops in the Lower Falls as they drove through the streets with a siren blaring, to warn of a British raid.

---

*On September 26th 1970 Peter Taunton of the Scots Guards was found shot dead at the Vere Foster military base in Moyard. The death was either an accident or suicide.

Both women were republican Volunteers. Their deaths brought the total of Ballymurphy's IRA dead to four. (Liam McParland had been injured in a car accident on October 19th 1969 while on active service. He died on November 6th. Michael Kane was killed in a premature explosion in New Forge Lane on September 4th 1970.) On the same day as the Maguire and Meehan killings, three unarmed men were shot dead in Newry by the army while engaged in a petty robbery.

Three days later, the nationalist middle class, in an attempt to regain some of their battered credibility, convened an 'Alternative Assembly' of SDLP and Nationalist MPs, senators and councillors at Dungiven. John Hume, the SDLP deputy-leader, was elected president. (It was a purely symbolic move. The 'Dungiven Parliament' had only one further sitting.) By now there were 14,000 British troops concentrated in the nationalist areas of the North.

Meanwhile, unionism took another lurch to the right. On October 23rd 1971 William Craig was elected chairperson of a steering committee of hardliners from 43 of the 52 unionist constituency parties. The influence of the extreme right manifested itself on November 11th, when James Callaghan, former British Home Secretary, visited Belfast. Almost 20,000 loyalist workers came out onto the streets in protest, and marched to a rally in the city centre. Michael Farrell points out:

> Protestant industrial workers, especially in the big, almost exclusively Protestant engineering works, were now becoming a significant factor in loyalist politics. Unemployment was relatively low, and as the 'aristocrats of labour' with secure jobs in heavily subsidised industries dependent on the British markets, they were the staunchest opponents of a united Ireland. It was not for nothing that the Stormont and Westminster governments had pumped money into the Belfast shipyard over the years. (£64 million in subsidies was paid to Harland & Wolff between 1969 and 1974.)[28]

While the loyalists were marching in Belfast, the Payment of Debt Act, introduced in mid-October to counter the civil disobedience campaign, was being debated at Westminster. The Act allowed for the recoupment of rent and rates arrears from wages or social security payments. It was described by Professor Peter Townsend, Chairperson of the Child Poverty Action Group, as 'a candidate for the worst piece of social legislation passed in the United Kingdom in this century'. The Payment of Debt Act was to become a scourge in areas like Ballymurphy.

At the end of November, the IRA, in response to yet another claim that it was decimated, launched a two-day bomb blitz across the North, involving the co-ordination of over 200 Active Service Units in setting off 30 explosions.

December 1971 began with the second IRA escape from Crumlin Road Prison in just over two weeks. On November 16th an entire football team of nine men had scaled the walls on a rope ladder thrown over from the outside, earning them the nickname 'The Crumlin Kangaroos'. On December 2nd this embarrassment was iced and decorated with a further break. Three men, including Martin Meehan and Anthony 'Dutch' Doherty – two almost legendary figures from North Belfast – disappeared, and were over the border before the escape was detected.

Two nights afterwards, loyalist bombers struck at McGurk's Bar in the New Lodge Road, leaving 15 nationalists dead in a mound of rubble. The attack was seen by many as a reprisal for a bomb attack that had killed two men at the Four Step Inn on the Shankill Road two months earlier, an attack later attributed to British 'dirty tricks' operatives. At the time both the Provisionals and Officials had denied responsibility, the Provos pointing out that it would be virtually impossible for a group of strangers to carry out the operation and escape undetected in an area patrolled by loyalist vigilantes. None the less, the bombing of McGurk's Bar was carried out in apparent reprisal, heralding the start of a campaign of assassinations against nationalists, which, the loyalists hoped, would terrorise people away from supporting the IRA.

On December 8th, as the riots, gun battles and bombings continued across the Six Counties, Sean Russell, a soldier of the Ulster Defence Regiment, was shot dead in his New Barnsley home by a masked IRA Volunteer. His 10-year-old daughter, Geraldine, was also hit in the thigh. On the 15th, Reginald Maudling said that he could see a situation in which the IRA would 'not be defeated, not completely eliminated, but have their violence reduced to an acceptable level'. Another cliché – the 'acceptable level of violence' – was added to the language of the Northern conflict.

Meanwhile, protest marches against internment continued, with nationalist women to the fore in the new phase of the Irish struggle against British imperialism. On Christmas Day a march from Belfast to Long Kesh was undertaken by the Northern Resistance Movement. All marches had been banned since August 9th, and the protestors were stopped a few miles along the M1 Motorway by the RUC and military. Bernadette Devlin and Frank McManus, both MPs, took part in the Christmas Day march; and between then and the end of January, there were six more 'illegal' marches, in which NICRA and the SDLP also participated.

By the end of 1971, Faulkner's grip on power was slowly beginning to slip. His security policies, and particularly internment, had failed. He was under pressure from Craig and Paisley, while the British government, dismayed at his misreading of the general situation, began to pull away from him. The international campaign being organised around internment was proving an embarrassment to the British. Embassies were being picketed worldwide as civil libertarian groups and supporters of the Irish cause lobbied for an end to this blatantly undemocratic approach to a political problem.

At the same time, the Provos were bombing on unhindered, and the casualty toll was rising. In the first seven months of 1971, from January 1st to August 8th, there were 34 deaths in the North: eleven British soldiers, four members of the RUC, and 19 civilians. Between August 9th and December 31st, 139 people died: 37 British soldiers (five were UDR soldiers), seven members of the RUC and 95 civilians. Internment had clearly been a disaster.

The year of 1972 began in Ballymurphy with the deaths of two IRA Volunteers. On January 11th 16-year-old Michael Sloan was accidentally shot dead at an arms training lecture in a house in New Barnsley. Five days later, 18-year-old Eamonn McCormick died of injuries he had received the previous Halloween when he was shot by the British army. A dance at St Peter's School, with a large number of Volunteers present, had been surrounded by the military earlier in the evening. The Fianna had been mobilised immediately to draw off the army with diversionary tactics should the need arise. However, the Volunteers managed to slip through the military cordon, and they in turn took up stand-by positions (with ready access to weapons) throughout the area in case of further military action. Some time after midnight the order was given to disperse, and Eamonn McCormick took off alone and unarmed along Westrock Drive. He was mortally wounded by a British army sniper, firing from the roof of St Peter's School.

Then on January 17th the area had some good news. Seven internees, including two Ballymurphy men, had escaped from the *Maidstone* prison-ship in Belfast Lough. By feeding a visiting seal, they had been able to determine that no sonar equipment was being used on the boat and the plan was hatched. Covered in grease and butter, they sawed through a bar in the window, slipped into the icy water, and swam to the shore. There they hijacked a bus and drove to the Markets, where local people were astounded to see a group of men, dressed in their underpants, disembarking from the bus. Despite a huge British dragnet the seven made good their escape and appeared at a press conference in Dublin a few days later.

Three days after the *Maidstone* escape, troops launched a face-saving search operation at Long Kesh, only to discover that holes were already being tunnelled under the floors of two of the camp's Nissen huts. In a tribute to the ingenuity of the prison population, they also unearthed wire cutters, a hacksaw, a chisel, a file, a jemmy, a knife, a model of a Thompson submachine-gun, military-style clothing, counterfeit coins, dies – and a poteen still!

After a brief stay down south, the two Ballymurphy members of the *Maidstone*'s 'Magnificent Seven' – 23-year-old Jim Bryson and 25-year-old Tommy Tolan – returned to Belfast to rejoin 'B' Coy, 2nd Battalion of the IRA's Belfast Brigade, covering their home ground in Ballymurphy. Bryson took over as O/C and 'Todler' Tolan, his life-long friend, became a kind of unofficial joint O/C. And both became a joint legend, under whose leadership the local Volunteers would become a deadly efficient urban guerrilla force who made life hell for British forces in the Upper Springfield.

Stories about the daring and courage of the two men are legion: Bryson, the 'terrible nice fellow despite the hard outer shell', the clinical operator who always put the lives of his men before his own; and Tolan, 'a man who knew no fear', the fearless soldier who would take on an armoured car while standing in the middle of the street. To the younger Ballymurphy Volunteers the expertise of their two heroes was beyond question, which gave rise to some wildly dangerous escapades before it was realised that courage alone is not sufficient. One Volunteer who fought in Ballymurphy in the early 1970s recalled how:

At the time the Brits seldom came in, but these two Saracens had been making forays into the estate. So Todler decided to chase them out. Me and him went out together. We had a Sten and a Garand with armour-piercing bullets. As we were going down the street another fellow came along and says 'Hang on a minute, and I'll come too'. So away with him to a house where he knew he could get some gear, and he comes back with an Armalite. The idea was that we'd hit the second Saracen. Todler says: 'I'll blow the doors off their hinges with the Garand; then the two of youse shoot into the back'. So, being wee lads at the time, we never questioned the wisdom of this. If Todler said that was the way to do it, then that was the way to do it.

The Saracens eventually came along, and when they'd passed, all three of us stepped out into the middle of the street and aimed our guns at the back doors, and Todler started to fire to blow the hinges off. And there was the other two of us, standing there, wondering why the doors weren't falling off! It was a crazy idea, but at the same time the audacity of it shook the Brits, along with the fact that several of them were wounded inside the Saracen where they might have thought they were safe. You could hear the squeals of them as they drove away.[29]

The position of the IRA in Ballymurphy was further strengthened by events in Derry on January 30th 1972. On that day a huge anti-internment march was planned for the city, beginning in Creggan and proceeding down through the Bogside to the Guildhall. It was to be a mass show of defiance against Faulkner's ban on parades, with every civil rights and nationalist organisation pledging support. Westminster MPs Bernadette Devlin and Frank McManus, and Stormont MPs John Hume and Ivan Cooper, were among the 20,000-strong crowd that set off for the city centre on the unseasonally bright Sunday afternoon that became known as Bloody Sunday.

On January 27th the Democratic Unionist Association of Derry had given notice to the RUC that they planned a 'religious rally' at Guildhall Square for 2pm on the same day as the anti-internment march. This familiar tactic to force confrontation was nothing new, but the cancellation two days later was unusual. The Rev James McClelland, a Minister with Derry Free Presbyterian Church and Vice-President of the Derry and Foyle Democratic Unionist Association, gave the reason in an interview that appeared in most of the British newspapers on the morning of the march. 'We were approached by the government', he said, 'and given assurances that the civil rights march will be halted – by force if necessary.'

A front-page report in the *Observer* carried much of the McClelland interview, along with an ominous joint military/RUC statement, which was also carried in the *Sunday Mirror*.

We choose the time and place to intervene and this policy, which is clearly in the public interest, allows the possibility that marchers may in some cases proceed for some distance before being stopped.

This does not mean however that they will be allowed to break the law with impunity. Experience this year has already shown that attempted marches often end in violence, and that must have been clearly foreseen by the organisers.

Clearly the responsibility for this violence and the consequences of it must rest fairly and squarely on the shoulders of those who encourage people to break the law.[30]

In advance of any trouble breaking out at a march which would be heavily stewarded, the British were preparing their public's mind for the massacre about to be perpetrated in Derry. The army was going to crush street politics with a vengeance. The paratroopers – shock troops – were to be deployed against the large column of largely working-class nationalists winding their way down from Bishop's Field in Creggan. At about 3.40pm the massive crowd had made its way through Bogside and was approaching the city centre when the first soldiers were seen. Saracens and foot patrols had sealed off a number of streets. Most of the crowd were diverted away from the barriers, but a small group of teenagers engaged the Paras in a ritualistic mini-riot. The soldiers took their cue, opening up first with CS gas, rubber bullets and a watercannon spraying dye. The civil rights march began to disperse towards the rallying point at Free Derry Corner, when the second volley of rubber bullets was accompanied by army gunfire. In front of a shocked world media, the paratroopers opened up with high velocity SLRs on the fleeing crowd, killing 13 people and wounding another 29, one of whom would later die in hospital. Fulvio Grimaldi, an Italian journalist, described to Radio Eireann what he saw:

It was the most unbelievable ... I have travelled many countries, I have seen many civil wars and revolutions and wars, I have never seen such a cold-blooded murder, organised, disciplined murder, planned murder. The army jumped out and started shooting in all directions. I took pictures of this, I took recordings of this, and there is no doubt whatsoever that there wasn't the slightest provocation.

I saw a young fellow who had been wounded, crouching against the wall. He was shouting 'Don't shoot, don't shoot'. A paratrooper approached and shot him from about one yard. I saw a young boy of 15 protecting his girlfriend against the wall and then proceeding to try and rescue her by going out with a handkerchief and with the other hand on his hat. A Paratrooper approached, shot him from about one yard into the stomach and shot the girl into the arm. I myself got shot at five times.[31]

For his day's work, Colonel Derek Wilford, commander of the Paras in Derry, was awarded the Order of the British Empire in the Queen's honours list for 1973, while on February 1st 1972, two days after the massacre, Brigadier F.P. Barclay, the Royal Norfolk Regiment, dropped

Wilford a few lines commending the paratroopers' action 'against those blighters last Sunday. They looked splendid and, as usual, bang on the ball'.[32] And from a tape recording of snatches of army conversation on Bloody Sunday:

> 'Your mother's been killed by the Armee, Doo da, doo da' ... (singing) ... static. 'Return fire ... aim pistol lower regions ... Roger, Wilco, Out' ... static ... (sound of shot) ... 'Yoo-hoo! Well done. Keep it up' ... static ... 'I said shoot for lower regions ... the balls ... Over.'[33]

Bloody Sunday was the crowning, final alienation of the nationalist people. The politics of peaceful struggle had been shot to bits on the edge of the Bogside. The final great show of strength on the streets of the North for many years to come took place in Newry on Sunday, February 6th 1972, when upwards of 100,000 people marched to demonstrate to the British government that murder in the streets would not deter them. Then many went home to join the IRA. Meanwhile, John Hume, signalling the extent of middle-class nationalist outrage, had declared, 'It's a united Ireland now or nothing!' In the South, 30,000 people marched on the British Embassy in Dublin and burnt it to the ground, while the besieged Lynch declared February 2nd, the day of most of the Derry funerals, a day of national mourning. Derry's city coroner, in his report, would describe the events of January 30th 1972, as 'sheer unadulterated murder'.

In the North, Bloody Sunday was followed by rioting, strikes, hijacking and gunbattles. The Catholic hierarchy was thrown into confusion in its attempt to find a comfortable position for itself, being temporarily muzzled in its anti-republican tirade. In Westminster, Bernadette Devlin attacked Maudling and punched him in the face when he tried to justify the killings. The IRA stepped up its campaign as the anti-internment marches dwindled. NICRA would later bemoan the fact that:

> Bloody Sunday was a British government success in that it immobilised NICRA from returning to the streets, not through imposing fear in the ranks of the marchers, but in finally driving a large section of the apolitical masses away from the concept of civil rights and into the arms of the men of violence.[34]

The assertion by the Official-dominated NICRA that they were dealing with 'the apolitical masses' was in fact an elitist sour grapes slur against a people who had been embittered – and quite politicised – by more than three years of the state's violent onslaught on a just cause. It was this that had driven the mass of the nationalist working class – and a fringe of the middle class – away from the gradual reformist policies of NICRA and the Officials to the militant position of the IRA, who were now bent on the destruction of Stormont and the withdrawal of British forces from the north-east of Ireland.

Bloody Sunday had finally convinced the nationalist people that Stormont was beyond reform and had to be brought down. It had also, ironically, pushed the British government towards the same conclusion, mainly as a result of the political backlash.

The international outcry against the Derry massacre was deafening. In the United States, Senator Edward Kennedy was urging Britain to make way for a united Ireland, while sponsoring a congressional resolution demanding an end to internment, the withdrawal of British troops, and the abolition of Stormont. Newspapers throughout Europe and North America loudly condemned Heath and his government.

At the same time, the IRA campaign went on unobstructed. Money, guns and recruits were flooding in. Westminster was beginning to realise that it could no longer ignore the Provisionals and continue responding to nationalist grievances with repression. The military solution was failing.

The more astute among the loyalist leadership also realised that Stormont was running into trouble. Among the loyalist paramilitary groups, the danger lights were the signal to step up the assassination campaign against nationalists. On February 3rd Bernard Rice of Ardoyne was shot dead from a passing car which drove off into loyalist Woodvale.

As far as the IRA was concerned, the war was against British imperialism, whereas to loyalists, the IRA, and the nationalist community that supported and sheltered the Volunteers, were one. Therefore all nationalists were 'legitimate targets'. Gun and bomb attacks on pubs, homes and community centres soon became commonplace. Eventually, republican groups began to hit back on a smaller scale.

By the end of 1972 a total of 42 nationalists and seven loyalists had been killed by loyalists, and 13 loyalists had been killed by nationalists. Although the IRA has a policy of never participating in sectarian killings unless it is absolutely unavoidable, there is no doubt but that republican units, with or without official sanction, were involved to some degree in sectarian attacks in the early 1970s.

Less than a week after the assassination of Bernard Rice, the right wing of unionism had formed itself into a potential parliamentary block which looked certain to topple Faulkner. On February 9th 1972, William Craig announced the formation of Vanguard, a new party supported by Billy Hull of the Loyalist Association of Workers, Rev. Martin Smith, Grand Master of the Orange Order in Belfast, and Captain Austin Ardill, former Stormont MP for Carrick. Vanguard opposed outright any further reforms.

At its first rally in Lisburn on February 12th, 7,000 loyalists watched Craig drive up in a motorcycle sidecar, protected by uniformed bodyguards. He then inspected a body of 500 men in military formation before addressing his audience. He told them that he was their man, and for each to raise his right hand and shout 'I do!' three times in unison as an endorsement of his message. The spectacle, with its echoes of earlier times in Europe, was not lost on the media. On March 18th, as Stormont teetered at the chasm, Craig told a 60,000-strong rally at Belfast's Ormeau Park:

> We must build up dossiers on those men and women in this country who are a menace to this country because one of these days, if and when the politicians fail us, it may be our job to liquidate the enemy.[35]

Meanwhile, as Craig and Paisley competed for control of the extreme right, both IRAs were pounding at economic, military and political targets, and the loyalists were picking off soft civilian targets. On February 22nd, in reprisal for Derry, the Officials bombed the regimental headquarters of the Parachute Regiment in Aldershot. An officer-priest, based in Ballymurphy during internment, and six civilians, were killed. Four days later, two more nationalists were shot by loyalists. Both survived, but a new fear began to discourage people from wandering too far from home, especially at night.

In the Upper Springfield, Bloody Sunday had triggered off an even greater assault on British forces. As well as the almost constant shooting at the Taggart, IRA Volunteers from the area were now heavily involved in city-centre bombings and gun-battles with military patrols. And the area was taking more casualties. On February 2nd Thomas McIlroy (29) was working on a car outside his Divismore Park home when he was murdered by soldiers shooting from the Taggart. On the 7th, a soldier accidentally shot himself in the head in the district. Two days later troops in the Taggart opened up on 14-year-old Patrick McVicker, shooting him in the stomach, then claiming their victim as another 'gunman'. On the same day Dr Maurice Hayes resigned as chairperson of the Community Relations Commission, saying that reconciliation was nonsense given the present security policies. In Ballymurphy community centre they were wondering how it could take a man so long to come to such a perfectly rational conclusion.

On March 4th a bomb at the Abercorn restaurant in central Belfast killed two people and injured 136 others. Both IRAs denied involvement; but the political fallout against republicanism was nevertheless overwhelming. On March 9th four IRA Volunteers were killed in a premature IRA explosion in Clonard Street, adding further to the pressure on republicans. Initially believing the Clonard bomb to have been planted by loyalists, the Ballymurphy IRA immediately opened up on loyalist sniping positions in Springmartin. A fierce day-long gun-battle followed.

The next day, the Provisionals called an unexpected three-day ceasefire. They gave the British three conditions for a continuing halt to hostilities: withdrawal of the military from the North; the abolition of Stormont; and an amnesty for all those arrested as a result of the Troubles. The effectiveness of the ceasefire ended all speculation that the IRA had no central control structure, which was one of the reasons for calling it. It also prompted an unofficial British response. On March 13th Harold Wilson, leader of the British Opposition, enraged the Dublin government when he used a brief official visit as cover for a three-hour secret meeting with the IRA. Wilson returned to London with a first-hand assessment of the IRA leadership's position as the campaign was resumed in the North. But the Heath government had already decided to act.

The rise of the extreme right, and the definitive threat it posed to Faulkner's ailing regime, left London under no illusion as to how the British image was about to progress. On March 22nd, Faulkner and his deputy, Jack Andrews, went to Downing Street to see Heath, Maudling, the Defence Secretary Lord Carrington and William Whitelaw who was leader of the House of Commons. Heath explained that Westminster was taking over control of security, realising that Faulkner could never agree to accepting a toothless Stormont. Faulkner threatened to resign. Heath told him that if he did, London would suspend Stormont and impose direct colonial rule.

On March 24th Heath announced to the world that Faulkner and his cabinet were resigning. Stormont was to be prorogued for one year, and William Whitelaw was taking over as Secretary of State for the Six Counties. Loyalists were stunned. There were marches, violent speeches, pledges and recriminations. And quietly in the background, the gunmen began to prepare for an escalation of the loyalist war.

On the nationalist side, the middle classes, the clergy and Dublin all welcomed the fall of Stormont. Meanwhile, People's Democracy, Northern Resistance and NICRA announced that political agitation would go on. The IRA, through Chief of Staff Sean Mac Stiofain, promised that the war would continue, regardless.

The following day, March 25th, Patrick Campbell of Oglaigh na hEireann was accidentally shot dead during an IRA stand-by at the top of Springhill Avenue. He was 16 years old.

References

1. Liam Mulholland of New Barnsley (1986 Interview).
2. Ibid.
3. Danny Kennally, *Belfast, August 1971 – A Case to Be Answered* (Eric Preston, Independent Labour Party, National Labour Press, London, 1971), pp. 79–80.
4. Frank Cahill (1986 Interview).
5. *Report of the Enquiry into Allegations Against the Security Forces of Physical Brutality in Northern Ireland Arising Out of Events on the 9th August 1971*, Chairman Sir Edward Compton (HMSO, London, November 1971), p. 9.
6. Fr Denis Faul and Fr Raymond Murray, *Violations of Human Rights in Northern Ireland 1968–1978*, pp. 4–5.
7. *Flight* (Community Relations Commission Research Unit, Belfast, 1971).
8. *Intimidation in Housing* (The Northern Ireland Community Relations Commission, 1974), p. 2.
9. *Irish Times*, Dublin, August 10th 1971.
10. Kate McCullough of Ballymurphy (1986 Interview).
11. *Sunday Times*, London, August 15th 1971.
12. Brian McLaughlin of Springfield Park, formerly of Moyard (1986 Interview).
13. *Sunday Times*, London, August 15th 1971.
14. Dessie Crone of Ballymurphy (1986 Interview).
15. Mary Murphy of Ballymurphy (1986 Interview).
16. Joe Cahill, formerly of Whiterock (1986 Interview).
17. Danny McGuinness of Whiterock (1986 Interview).
18. Julia Grego of Ballymurphy (1986 Interview).

19. Joe Cahill (1986 Interview).
20. Margaret Keenan of Moyard (1986 Inteview).
21. Joe Corr of Dermott Hill (1986 Interview).
22. Maureen McGuinness Tolan of Ballymurphy (1986 Interview).
23. Jean Campbell, formerly of Ballymurphy (1986 Interview).
24. Eileen Brennan Hay of Moyard (1986 Interview).
25. *Irish Times*, Dublin, August 14th 1971.
26. *Sunday Times*, London, August 15th 1971.
27. Joe Cahill (1986 Interview).
28. Michael Farrell, *Northern Ireland: The Orange State* (Pluto Press, London, 1976), pp. 291–2.
29. Interview with the author.
30. *Observer*, London, January 30th 1972.
31. Radio Eireann, January 31st 1972.
32. *Sunday Press*, Dublin, February 6th 1972.
33. *Massacre at Derry* (Northern Ireland Civil Rights Association, Belfast, 1972), p. 48.
34. *We Shall Overcome – The History of the Struggle for Civil Rights in Northern Ireland 1968–1978* (Northern Ireland Civil Rights Association, Belfast, 1978), p. 36.
35. *Newsletter*, Belfast, March 20th 1972.

9

A Peculiar Kind of War

By the spring of 1972, Ballymurphy was for all practical purposes a No-Go area. The RUC never ventured in except hastily to deliver the odd summons under British army protection. The military, on the other hand, made occasional sorties from the Taggart during daylight hours; night adventures were less frequent. Sometimes, people were arrested and taken off for interrogation. Other times, people were simply lifted and beaten up. But on most occasions military moves against the area were short-lived and ended in retreat under the encouragement of IRA gunfire.

At night the blacked-out streets were patrolled by the IRA whereas the military generally stuck to the main roads. Shooting was almost continuous. During the day the Taggart was under constant attack and ambushes were taking place all the time, while at night the British bases were under siege and gun-battles developed in the open spaces around the City Cemetery and the BTA centre.

There were two fascinating elements to those gun-battles: first, although thousands of rounds were fired, there were very few casualties on either side; and secondly, the British army displayed a remarkably fertile collective imagination. Had a third of the 'hits' claimed by the military actually occurred, Ballymurphy would have been entirely depopulated.

The campaign of civil disobedience was also firmly established. In fact, the Upper Springfield had done it more than justice. Not only were people withholding rent, rates, gas and electricity payments, but also control of housing, 'licensing' of drinking establishments, the conversion of Housing Executive property into community facilities, and the development of local industry had all passed into the community's hands. This had brought many blanket changes. For example, full gas meters had to be broken open so that a single shilling provided every family with an unending supply of gas. Nobody from the gas company or electricity service ever even considered coming to read meters or cut off supply. When the gas company finally made an appearance in Ballymurphy estate in March 1975, the meter-readers arrived in a mini-bus with a heavy military escort. Streets were sealed by armoured cars and families held at gunpoint while the meter was read by the nervous gasman![1]

Even if meters had been read in 1972, it is doubtful if bills could have been issued anyway as nobody could possibly have known who lived in which house. A great number of families had swapped houses. Others had been vacated by people whose nerves couldn't take any more, and these had been occupied by squatters. There were also many derelict houses, some wrecked by the military because they had belonged to suspected IRA Volunteers, others that had lain idle until they fell into disrepair. These were used for IRA ambushes one day and were torn apart in arms searches the next. The flats above the Bullring were empty except for a welfare office.

In Moyard whole blocks of maisonettes – popular battle positions – had been deserted as had many houses in Springhill. Steve Pittam had a block of flats to himself in Moyard Parade; next block was home to Moyard Working Men's Club, one of the many 'shebeens' in the area. Needless to say, the outdated records of the Housing Executive were about as useful as a blank map of the Amazon Basin.

Despite the fact that the Upper Springfield was in the front line of the war, life went on regardless. People got up and went to work or signed on the dole as they always had. Dinners were eaten as gun-battles flared outside in the street. The clubs were full to capacity at night and the BTA still ran its bingo. Instead of battering the community – though internment was taking its toll – the war seemed to have given new life. There was a proliferation of community groups and children's schemes while the adults broke the record for the largest number of social clubs in one square mile. One of the old huts used as emergency accommodation after the pogroms of 1969 had been planted in Maggie Smith's back garden down in Divismore Park to become 'Maggie's Tavern', providing a swashbuckling atmosphere where Dick Turpin would have felt at home. Other than St John's GAA Club, none of the clubs had a licence, leading to all sorts of misunderstandings with the RUC in later days. Then there was the odd beer lorry commandeered for a special occasion, and the liberation of stocks from lorries about to become burning barricades. Other such liberated commodities included food, coal, clothing and a £60,000 consignment of stainless steel sinks that revolutionised the kitchens of Ballymurphy.

At the same time an elephant's graveyard of wreckage steadily built up beside the BTA community centre. The skeletons of vehicles used on barricades, or burned to destroy forensic evidence after IRA operations, lay scattered over a wide area bordering the Whiterock Road. On the far side lay the IRA's 'firing range' where Volunteers could be seen firing rifles at stand-up targets. Others in the cemetery fired handguns at tin cans, the military presence in the Taggart causing not the slightest concern. In Moyard and Turf Lodge, firing-slits, painted white by the military, cut gashes in the gable walls of the flats. All this in the familiar streets where everybody grew up.

The streets that could suddenly produce an ambush or bomb attack as you made your way home. The author lived in Ballymurphy from 1972 to 1976, spending many an hour lying in the gutter dodging bullets, or waiting for a lull to cross the street for a loaf of bread. And in the shops would be the women of Ballymurphy, buying the 'rations' and passing the time of day, with hardly a reference to the rattle of gunfire outside. The war had become part of life, and you simply worked around it. Guns were noisy; but it was the subtle nuances you had to watch. A street without children, or a parcel marked 'bomb', would be clear signals for a quick spurt in the opposite direction.

Such was life in Ballymurphy in 1972, where children with stones launched themselves against the British military machine, the ice-cream van still did the rounds, and Larry Sloan, as always, sold fish from a barrow on Fridays.

The BTA, however, had been thrown into turmoil by the internment of Frank Cahill and the other community leaders. The survey and other projects were suspended as many of the remaining community activists went over to the IRA auxiliaries who had taken over local policing and some elements of defence. None the less the association employed three youth workers in 1972 to continue Paddy McCarthy's line-of-containment strategy. The job was made no easier by the simmering feud between the Provisionals and Officials, which continued to spill into the youth centre, as sympathisers of both sides furiously defended the honour of their adopted guerrilla army. Given the fact that a young person in the Upper Springfield, who did not align him- or herself with one or other IRA, was almost stateless, virgin fields were being discovered in youth work. Asking teenagers to go home and remove the pistol from their belt was not an uncommon feature.

Eventually, in May 1973, the inevitable happened. The youth workers, along with the author's wife, Cora, and Big Alice Franklin, found themselves trying to quell a youth riot – successfully at first, then very unsuccessfully. One lad's life was saved when Donal Fagan, one of the workers, threw himself between him and the iron bars raining down from a dozen pairs of hands. Later that night running gunfights blew up between the two groups and the same youth was grazed in the head. Shortly afterwards the three youth workers resigned, partly due to the impossible situation created by the feuding and partly due to the in-fighting then plaguing the BTA. As an alternative, they set up shop at 42 Ballymurphy Road, soon to become the base of a major community development initiative.

Meanwhile, Des Wilson's community house had taken off in Springhill, with the priest now firmly identified with Ballymurphy and continuing to rankle the hierarchy with his outspoken support for 'unde-sirable' causes and his opposition to clerical oligarchies. Two doors away the little community set up recently by Mother Teresa was attracting large numbers of children and adults to a varied programme of commu-nity activities. The four Indian women in their strange white habits had been wholeheartedly embraced by the community. Not so, however, by the hierarchy, as would be illustrated in an ugly manner a year hence. But in early 1972 the hierarchy was lying low in Ballymurphy, its reputa-tion still caked in the mud of the Vere Foster affair of 1971.

The loyalist flight from New Barnsley and Moyard during the riots of 1970 had overnight stripped the Henry Taggart Memorial Hall and Vere Foster state school of their clientele. The Taggart immediately became a military base whereas the school became the obvious focus for new families seeking an education for their young children. On September 1st 1970 the first nationalist parents arrived at Vere Foster to enrol their children. In the Six-County context this was an unusual move. Education is strictly segregated in Northern schools, the state providing for Protestant children, and the Catholic Church, through its 'maintained' schools system, providing for Catholics.

Bernadette Savage, one of the first six mothers to put their children into the state school in Moyard, explained that the two Catholic-run primary schools in the area were already full. Besides, they were on the far side of the busy Springfield Road whereas Vere Foster was on her doorstep. She was also interested in the opportunity of taking her children out of the mould of a sectarian education system. The Savage family, who had been intimidated out of their Donegall Road home, saw in Vere Foster the possibility of an experiment in integrated education. They felt that if children of different cultures could be educated together, they might grow up with a less warped view of their opposite numbers. As it transpired, the violence of internment week was to denude the area of the last of its Protestant families, but that was still eleven months into the future.

What Mrs Savage and her co-travellers failed to realise in September 1970 was that their desire to provide an education for their children according to their religious and political beliefs – a liberty enshrined by the European Convention of Human Rights – was, in clerical eyes, an alarming assault on the Bastille of the Catholic school principle. The Catholic position on education is that religion should permeate the entire atmosphere of the school, not simply be another subject as would be the case in a state school. This constant indoctrination from an early age ensures the permanence of the flock, and the continued flow of revenue into the coffers. It also ensures the dominance of the Catholic ideology in wider political life.

The women who turned up at Vere Foster on September 1st were therefore treading heavily on the territorial instincts of the Catholic Church. The following day, Bernadette Savage had a visitor:

> Father Fitzpatrick came to my door and asked if we could come to an emergency meeting at 8 o'clock in St Bernadette's School. Altogether about 20 parents were down. We were told that if the children remained at Vere Foster they would not be allowed to make their Confirmation or Holy Communion.[2]

To traditional Catholic parents this threat of partial excommunication of their children was serious stuff. Some withdrew their children. But the majority – the parents of 218 children – decided to fight the issue. The pretext for refusing the Catholic sacraments was that proper religious instruction would not be provided at Vere Foster. If the Church was concerned by the lack of Catholic instruction and the 'loss of souls', the parents argued, then surely it was the duty of the clergy, who drew their sustenance from the community, to make good the shortfall. They felt that a Catholic teacher should be sent into Vere Foster by the Down and Connor Maintained Schools Committee.

In November the parents approached the local clergy to put their case. They were told that the solution lay in their own hands: transfer the children. If they refused they would have to live with the consequences and their consciences. Acquiescence by the parents would have automatically meant the closure of Vere Foster and its probable sale to the Catholic Church. The alternative being suggested would create a dangerous precedent when it came to the broader debate on integrated education. By December the parents began to drift towards defeat. Then Bill Rolston, a 24-year-old ex-seminarian who had returned from New Hampshire in November, heard of the parents' plight. He wrote to the school, offering to give the children religious instruction. The principal put him in touch with the parents' committee. Margaret McErlane, a young mother from Dermot Hill, later admitted:

> When Bill arrived we had almost reached the bottom. We had approached several retired teachers and asked them to take the kids for religion, but they said they would lose their pensions. If it had gone on much longer we would probably have given in.[3]

As Bill Rolston was not qualified to teach, he could not be employed by the school authorities. However, although he was prepared to work for nothing, the parents decided that *they* would employ him, raising the money by means of a weekly collection.

When the new term began in mid January 1971, the Catholic hierarchy's position had been severely weakened. An ex-seminarian was in charge of religious education in Vere Foster; and the community, militant from the civil rights struggle and united by the riots, was no longer willing to listen to obstinate clerics pursuing illogical arguments. Despite the Bishop's refusal to meet the parents – Philbin claiming that he did not feel there was anything to discuss! – it was clear that the Church was losing the battle. Its tactics had badly misfired: not only was religious education now being supplied – but it was also being done completely outside of the sphere of hierarchical influence.

On March 10th the parents of children due to be confirmed were asked to bring their children along to Corpus Christi Church that evening. To their surprise, Fr Kelly, the Diocesan Inspector, was waiting to examine the children. Bill Rolston was not invited, but he turned up anyway. He was completely ignored. However, the Church had conceded. Five days later it was announced that a Ms McKenna was being seconded from St Bernadette's to teach religion at Vere Foster. It was only at this point – when the Church was back in control – that the Vere Foster children were deemed ready for Confirmation.

Immediately after Easter, in a final show of ham-fisted arrogance, a delegation of three clergymen, including the Diocesan Inspector, turned up at the school to establish Rome's position, and to sack Bill Rolston, who had to explain patiently that they could hardly fire when they hadn't hired in the first place.

On the economic front, Ballymurphy Enterprises and Whiterock Industrial Estate were both moving along optimistically. The Enterprises, though not yet making a profit, were expanding their market and continuing to develop the concept of workers' control of the unit.

Whiterock Industrial Estate, meanwhile, had launched an appeal for subscriptions on December 1st 1971 – the response was highly encouraging. It had already been established through a survey carried out by St Thomas' School that the unemployment rate for the 'heads of household' in Ballymurphy was 47 per cent, the same figure arrived at by Tony Spencer in his *Tale of Two Surveys*. It was also suspected that the figure was somewhere around 40 per cent in Turf Lodge, which lay directly across the Springfield Road from the Industrial Estate site. This was confirmed at 38 per cent in November 1972. The corresponding figure for Belfast County Borough was 5.8 per cent.[4]

In their press release, the Industrial Estate management pointed out that 30,000 people lived in their catchment area, 57 per cent of whom were below the age of 20. If the area was extended to bring in Andersonstown, you were talking about a population of 55,000 – greater than Bangor, Lisburn or Newtownabbey – where there were 'little or no social or recreational facilities, no shopping facilities, and most important, no employment opportunities'.[5] They further pointed out that 45 per cent of all jobs attracted to the North between 1945 and 1966 went to the Belfast urban area. The nationalist enclave of West Belfast – the most densely populated part of the city – had only been allocated 4.9 per cent of the total employment figure on a locality basis.[6]

The Industrial Estate would, they hoped, help redress the balance a little by providing 1,000 jobs. They outlined a ten-year development plan for the building of 40 units, and announced that the first unit, a candle factory in the old byre they had inherited, would begin production in the spring. It was hoped that, initially, industrialists could be encouraged in to set up business on a capitalist basis. Later, when sufficient income was being generated, it was envisaged that co-operatives could be established to co-exist alongside the capitalist ventures. The government had agreed to pay for security at the estate, and to build a training unit where young people could become skilled in various trades. The impossible was becoming a reality.

Another remarkable venture being undertaken in those days was the Lazy Acre. It had begun as the Riverbed Landscaping Scheme under the Borough of Belfast Urban and Rural Improvement Campaign, but nobody ever called it that again. The idea was to pipe the Clowney stream that ran between Springhill and Ballymurphy, and convert the surrounding area into playing fields and a children's playground. The scheme would employ local labour.

It was a fine idea, the management of which had been briefly considered by the BTA before they shied away from it inexplicably. And a fine idea it would remain. It may have had something to do with the war, or the roughness of the terrain, or the continual arrests of the workers, or the loaning of the JCB for various community ventures (which at one point included the assault upon, and demolition of, an army sangar at Corry's timberyard), or the easy conversion of Springhill Avenue's gable walls into a permanent handball alley; but whatever it was, it worked, and the scheme didn't. Until the Lazy Acre became a legend. Years later, when the scheme finally folded, it was widely rumoured that the greatest burst of activity to ever strike the site occurred one Tuesday morning when the present writer's motorbike backfired loudly in Ballymurphy Road and the boys thought they were being shot at. Why, heaven only knows!

Just as the Ballymurphy community was continuing to expand its activities during the early months of 1972, so too were the republicans, the loyalists and the British army. Hardly a day passed without the smoke from burning buildings billowing into the skies over Belfast. Flying glass had become known as 'Belfast confetti', as IRA carbombs, introduced in March, reduced the city centre to a flattened blitz zone. Nationalist areas were armed camps under siege by the British army, and increasingly by the loyalists who were stepping up their assassination campaign. By May, the Ulster Defence Association (UDA), claiming 50,000 members, was drilling openly, without interference from the British army, while the victims of UDA, UVF and loyalist Tartan Gang killings were found in their homes, streets, pubs and places of work.

Soon, Belfast city centre was a ghost town after 6pm as people stayed in their own areas. The main city arteries were virtually devoid of pedestrians at night. Every passing car was a potential gun-attack. Every parked car was a potential bomb. Units of the British army's Special Air Service (SAS) were also now prowling the streets looking for victims. The number of 'sectarian' killings carried out by plainclothes units of this regiment, or by agents trained and deployed by them, will probably never be known. But it is an indisputable fact that they have been operating in the North since at least April 15th, 1972, the day the Conway brothers were shot in Ballymurphy.

The SAS had been deployed in the North as early as July 1970, when the Heath Cabinet sent 45 men from the counter-insurgency regiment to Belfast for specialist training on the local situation. After further training in Britain, these men returned to Belfast at the end of the year, and were placed with the 39th Infantry Brigade under the command of Brigadier Frank Kitson.

Kitson, who had a long history of involvement with British military intelligence and covert operations in several colonial situations, was the author of *Low Intensity Operations – Subversion, Counter-Insurgency and Peacekeeping*, a blueprint for a new concept of political-military counter-insurgency. In a changing political world, in which the European ruling classes feared the internal enemy as much as any, Kitson's theories were of special interest. Covering the control of populations, psychological warfare, the containment and destruction of all expressions of civil disobedience, methods of surveillance, the infiltration and manipulation of political groups, and the creation of an administration that is subservient to the military need, Kitson was offering a means whereby the ruling classes could prepare in advance 'to make the army ready to deal with subversion, insurrection, and peace-keeping operations during the second half of the 1970s'.[7] He was given Ireland as his experimental laboratory and the SAS as his vanguard.

The 22nd SAS is the dirty tricks unit of the Secret Intelligence Service (SIS) of the British Foreign Office. Established in 1950, its mission orders include information-gathering, surveillance and 'community relations', 'the ambush and harassment of insurgents' and 'liaison with, and organisation of, friendly guerrilla forces operating against the common enemy'.[8] In line with Kitson's principles, members of this secret regiment had attached themselves to regular units, building up intelligence on nationalist areas; others were co-opted on to the vital centres of the counter-insurgency machine – communications, propaganda, the military intelligence units of the Defence Intelligence Staff in liaison with the MI5 security service, and psychological operations (Psyops). They had also formed semi-autonomous hit-squads and were infiltrating loyalist organisations at the same time. Operating as the Military Reconnaissance Force (MRF), the SAS claimed its first victims, the Conway brothers, at the junction of Whiterock and Ballymurphy roads in April 1972.

Gerry and John Conway were about to set off for the city centre where they ran a fruit and vegetable stall. When they reached the gates of St Thomas' School a car drew up in front of them and three armed men jumped out. The brothers turned and ran as the men opened fire. The incident was later graphically described by one of the three gunmen:

> We had a death list with names and photos, with the orders 'shoot on sight'. One of the soldiers saw James Bryson, a man on the list, and another whose name I forget.* We swerved our car in front of them, and leapt out, drawing our pistols, and opened fire. They tried to run down an alley. We ran after them and the patrol commander gave the order 'bullets'. I scored several hits myself, both men were severely wounded. We radioed for a uniformed patrol. When it turned up, their commander said to ours, 'You stupid bastards, you've shot the wrong fuckers'. The army issued a statement alleging that the men had shot at us and that the army had a pistol to prove it. This was a lie.[9]

A month later CESA (Catholic Ex-Servicemen's Association) vigilante, Patrick McVeigh, was murdered, and four others wounded, by a mobile SAS patrol at a barricade in Andersonstown. Nobody at the barricade had been armed. On June 22nd, in a similar incident, three Black Taxi drivers and a nearby resident were cut down by Thompson sub-machine-gun bullets fired from a passing car on the Glen Road. Subsequently, two soldiers were charged. They were later acquitted, but an illuminating feature of the trial was the assertion by one of them that the ammunition used in the attack 'belongs to the police at Castlereagh and was issued by the

*Gerry and John Conway had been mistaken for Jim Bryson and Tommy Tolan, the two most wanted IRA Volunteers in Ballymurphy.

Special Branch'.[10] This attack was nothing more than a crude attempt to discredit the IRA for whom the Thompson sub-machine-gun was a standard weapon at the time.

As time passed the MRF/SAS would also take their share of casualties in gun-battles and as a result of IRA intelligence work. They had a particularly bad day on October 2nd 1972, when a Ballymurphy connection put the Four Square Laundry and the Gemini Health Studios out of business.

On the morning in question, the Four Square van was in Twinbrook estate when two men sprang from a car and sprayed it with sub-machine-gun fire. The driver, 'Bobby Jones', pulled out a Browning automatic pistol, then slumped over the wheel dead. His 'sister' who was collecting laundry, became hysterical as the Volunteers drove off. The IRA claimed to have also killed two other agents in a hidden observation compartment in the roof. Along with the direct information gained by chatting casually to people in the street and taking photographs, the laundry had been an ideal cover for the surreptitious forensic testing of clothing.

The Gemini Health Studios, on the other hand, was part of a network of massage parlours and prostitutes used to blackmail people into spying on the IRA. There, the IRA attack cost the British two more agents. In desperation, army headquarters attempted to deny the loss of the Gemini agents, or that the massage parlour had anything to do with their operations. But later on, after the IRA had given detailed information of the attack, a large body of soldiers arrived to remove equipment from the Antrim Road 'health studios'. In the veil of secrecy that followed, the two bodies, presumably, were also removed.

The IRA's success was a direct result of a stroke of luck. Since the beginning the MRF had actively recruited IRA renegades into its ranks to become key operatives. One was a Belfast man who 'disappeared', along with a number of others, around Christmas 1971 after being arrested by the British army. Some months later, he turned up unexpectedly in Ballymurphy and fell into the hands of the local Volunteers. He was carrying an army-issue Browning pistol. Under questioning, he told the IRA that he had been living in Palace Barracks along with several other 'missing' people and had been trained as an MRF operative. The Volunteers listened in astonishment as he outlined the extent of military undercover operations – including the Four Square Laundry and the Gemini Health Studios. He was afterwards executed by the IRA and his body was buried secretly. He is still officially listed as 'missing'.

The more subtle side of Kitson's blueprint for repression – intelligence work, the militarisation of the courts and media, and psychological operations (Psyops) – were well under way in 1972. On the intelligence front the IRA was keeping pace, causing acute embarrassment from time to time by their own disclosures and the evidence turning up in many raids. In May 1974 the British discovered the IRA's Director of Operations in a house in the upper-class Malone area of Belfast. They also found a store of telephone recordings going back to 1971. Despite sophisticated scrambling devices, the Provisionals had been successfully tapping British telephones for years.

As regards the militarisation of the media, the BBC has, since 1941, been strongly influenced by British intelligence, its External Services supervised and funded by the Foreign Office. In her investigation of media treatment of the Northern conflict, Liz Curtis lays bare the web of censorship and political jackbooting that produces the garbled nonsense posing as 'news' and general coverage of the Irish war. She lists 45 TV programmes on the North that were banned or tampered with between 1968 and 1983.[11]

In its psychological war, the British army had, since 1969, been attempting to isolate the republican guerrillas from their communities by every means at their disposal, from outright terror to 'community relations'. In several cases youth clubs and social centres were erected by the military as a 'gesture of goodwill', to be promptly demolished by republicans in recognition of the spirit from which they had emanated. So ludicrous did the 'community relations' illusion become that, in early 1973, at a meeting convened by the Community and Youth Service Association, Major Howard James of Psyops headquarters in Lisburn saw fit to announce that he had '15,000 community relations officers in the field'. Pity about the corpses left in their wake.

In later years the British army's 'community relations' role would extend to the planning of housing and roads, the erection of a 'Berlin wall' in Belfast, and the redevelopment of whole areas to suit British operational needs. The RUC also jumped on the community relations bandwagon, employing 60 Community Relations Officers by 1977 and operating 'Blue Lamp' discos, in loyalist areas. Direct 'community relations', however, proved an abject failure in nationalist areas. But the upheaval of academic interest in what was happening in the working class areas provided an alternative source of intelligence material, while the massive influx of voluntary workers during summer schemes opened up a neat avenue of infiltration into close-knit communities. This was used at least once in Ballymurphy by British intelligence, and once, it is believed, by the CIA.

Since the abolition of Stormont in March the war had continued without respite; but some dissension was beginning to appear in nationalist ranks. On March 20th, in Lower Donegall Street, an IRA bomb had killed two RUC men and four civilians, and injured scores of others. The scale of the civilian casualties rebounded badly on the IRA despite their accusation that people had deliberately been moved from an adjoining street by British forces, who had been warned of the bomb's actual location.

On March 30th an Andersonstown woman was killed in crossfire during a gun-battle between troops and the IRA, prompting the development of a small peace movement in the area. Over the following weeks, the SDLP, the clergy and the media orchestrated a peace campaign which was to find a degree of ambiguous support among the more war-weary of the nationalist community. Others, however, fiercely opposed the stop-the-war meetings, agreeing with the IRA line that the British were politically bankrupt, that they knew they were losing the war, and all that was needed was one final heave.

Although there were also those in the IRA who felt that a breather might be in order for the Volunteers, the idea of a ceasefire, as advocated by the nationalist middle class and the peace women, was firmly rejected. In Ballymurphy the Volunteers endorsed that position on April 6th, when they wounded an RUC man in yet another gun-attack on the Taggart. The next day, as Whitelaw released 73 internees, the Taggart and an army post at Vere Foster School came under sustained attack. Peter Sime (22), of the King's Own Scottish Borderers, was shot dead. In the evening, bonfires burned throughout the Upper Springfield to welcome home the released internees.

May was a bad month in Ballymurphy. It began with a riot, sparked off when soldiers in armoured cars fired rubber bullets at a group of toddlers playing in a sand-pit.

On May 2nd the IRA decided to move against Corry's timberyard which had repeatedly been used by the military and by loyalists for sniping attacks on the area. Overlooking Springhill and Westrock, it also afforded the British an ideal surveillance platform. The yard was attacked with a deluge of petrol bombs tossed over the high wall and blast bombs were hurled in for added effect. The timberyard survived, but a major gun-battle broke out in Springhill and Ballymurphy between the troops and the IRA. A soldier was wounded in Corry's, as was 17-year-old William Robinson, an employee at the yard; and in Ballymurphy Drive 14-year-old John Armstrong was shot in the back by a stray bullet.

Much of the afternoon's gunfire centred around Des Wilson's community house, where a meeting was in progress. The author, who was not long in Ballymurphy at the time, attended that meeting along with Jenny Quigley, one of the voluntary workers at the BTA youth club. To the newly initiated novice it was quite beyond belief: as the military and the IRA alternately occupied the front garden, as rifles and sub-machine-guns blazed and blast bombs exploded, the people in the house continued their discourse with an imperturbability that would have done the Buddha proud. It was only when a bomb landed directly outside the window that the meeting rushed for the back door with Jim Donnelly from Westrock muttering in disgust at having to endure 'such a Laurel and Hardy act'. Then, to crown the farce, a young boy ran in through the back door saying, 'It's OK. It's only a wee bomb!'

The next day another attempt was made to burn down Corry's. This time a truck was driven into the wall and set alight. In the subsequent gun-battle a soldier was wounded. There was also a sectarian clash at the Springhill/Springmartin flashpoint on the Springfield Road. To separate the combatants the RUC talked the loyalists back up the Springmartin Road while the British army blasted the nationalists with rubber bullets. At 9.30pm a second soldier was wounded when a patrol raced into Kelly's Bar at the Whiterock/Springfield junction in search of a wanted man. All they found was the usual quota of bar philosophers; and when they came out they were shot at from Dermott Hill. The sectarian trouble, small-scale rioting and gun-battles went on for the next ten days.

On May 5th a sniper wounded a soldier near St Bernadette's school in an action that was typical of the period. The British army came in; the IRA engaged them; a soldier was wounded; and the army retreated. Two days later the troops again made a lightning raid into Ballymurphy estate, this time to the Bullring where a young man was tied to a lamp post. Leaping from their Pigs, they charged to the rescue only to discover that the victim, plastered in flour, lipstick and tomato ketchup, was merely undergoing a traditional Belfast pre-nuptial ceremony. (On April 1st 1971 the military had descended on another such incident in Ballymurphy. The tarred-and-feathered victim on that occasion was a tailor's dummy adorned with a placard that read 'April Fool!')

On May 11th two buses were hijacked and burned at the waste ground beside the BTA community centre. The army arrived in two Pigs to investigate. They drove in between the buses and the community centre, stopped with the backs of their vehicles facing Ballymurphy estate, and piled out – straight into an ambush. Six soldiers were wounded before they managed to withdraw, the two Pigs speeding down the Whiterock Road towards the Royal Victoria Hospital.

This particular regiment, the King's Own, was eventually withdrawn from Ballymurphy owing to its casualty rate. The local IRA described them as being 'so amateurish that you'd have pity on them'. One Volunteer recalled that 'Todler' Tolan used them for a while as an alternative to the stand-up targets at the IRA 'firing range' when training new recruits:

> There was a patrol of them in Springhill one day, and Todler had all the young lads over in Divismore Park lined up against the gable end of a house, waiting their turn to have a go at them with a Sten. Between digs, he'd show the next one how to use the gun – without any fear of the Brits doing any damage.[12]

Throughout this period gunfire in Ballymurphy was no longer reported by the media, as was the case in other republican areas of the North where resistance was also fierce; but, during the week-end of May 13th and 14th 1972, the Upper Springfield again made banner headlines.

At 5.17pm on Saturday, May 13th, Kelly's Bar at the Whiterock/ Springfield junction was bombed. The pub had been crowded with customers watching the England v Germany football match and listening to the racing results from the Curragh when a loyalist bomb exploded at the front door. Sixty-three people were injured. John Moran, who worked in the bar, would later die from his injuries. Mick Clarke of the BTA was sitting in the back room along with Charlie Tolan and Barney Vallelly when a 'whoof' sound brought the windows in on top of them. (To this day Mick Clarke is grateful to fellow customer Sammy McHugh who, in the face of much jocular derision, had cross-taped the glass a few days earlier so that it wouldn't become lethal shrapnel in such an eventuality.) At another table Hugh McCormick, former secretary of the BTA, was being bowled over by what he remembers as 'the strongest drink of my life. I had just put the glass to my lips when the world went up around me!'

Once the initial shock had subsided those who had been in the back rooms rushed into the front of the bar where most of the damage had been done. Mick Clarke and the others began to work with the wounded in the chaos and rubble of the explosion.

> One man, Matt Cassidy, looked pretty bad. I got out through the front door to the street, where a young lad was lying – young John Moran, a student from Turf Lodge, who worked part-time at the bar. By then a big crowd had gathered and the ambulances were starting to arrive. We got the wounded into the ambulances, but had a terrible job with John Moran who was badly injured. Then one of the ambulance men said to me 'I think you should come along too'. I had a nick in the head and was bleeding heavily but hadn't noticed. Before getting in, I called back to see if my 16-year-old son Gerard, who also worked in the bar, was OK. Gerard McGlade, who thought I was calling to him, answered 'yes'. But, unknown to me, my Gerard was lying outside at the Whiterock end of Kelly's with a blazing motorbike on top of him. As we made our way down the Springfield Road in the ambulance, the shooting started.[13]

As the first casualties of the explosion were being whisked off to hospital, loyalist gunmen opened up from the flats on the ridge in Springmartin, scattering rescue workers and ambulance personnel, wounding a number of people, and sending two army Pigs scurrying for the safety of the Taggart. Within minutes Jim Bryson, Tommy Tolan, Micky Clarke (whose brother had just been badly injured) and a number of other IRA Volunteers left the top of the Whiterock Road in a taxi and headed for the centre of Ballymurphy. After a quick muster of Volunteers and weapons, the IRA began to return fire into Springmartin. Immediately, the military at the Taggart opened up on Ballymurphy.

Meanwhile, three buses had been commandeered and thrown across the Springfield Road to obscure the view from Springmartin so that rescue work could continue with some modicum of protection. At the same time, a young Volunteer, who had been accidentally shot during an arms training session in a local house shortly before the bomb went off, had to be taken to safety. At Kelly's itself the remaining bar staff and customers were busy mopping up the debris and boarding up the windows – and drink was stoically still being served!

Gerry McGlade, who was the manager at Kelly's at the time, had been blown off his feet by the explosion, but was otherwise uninjured. Later he recalled two incidents, which to his mind were significant:

> The night before, we had been sitting at a table near the window having a staff drink – it was about half twelve – when a shot came through the glass and buried itself in a mirror at the other side of the bar. We immediately turned off the lights, which, with hindsight, was probably a bad mistake. I

reckon that they [the loyalists] were just finding their range for the next day, and us turning off the light gave them their clue. Then, on the day of the bomb, an odd thing happened: shortly before the explosion a stranger of about fifty odd turned up at the door and said that there was trouble down the Kashmir and we should get on down there. It was a very strange thing for someone to do, and to this day I think that he was probably a scout for the bombers.[14]

Gerry McGlade was still in the bar as Tommy McIlroy, the 50-year-old barperson, served up the drinks to those who had cleared up the mess:

Tommy had his hand to the optic when a bullet came through the window and shot him through the heart. We knew straight away that he was dead; but, just in case, we rushed him to the hospital anyway. The Brits had sealed off the bottom of the Whiterock and they wouldn't let us through at first. And on the way home we had to come up through Turf Lodge.[15]

For the remainder of Saturday the British army made no attempt to move further up the Whiterock Road than its junction with Britton's Parade. Throughout the night they maintained their position, pinned down by sniper fire from several directions, including Turf Lodge, as the gun-battle raged along the base of the mountain. At the same time news came in of heavy gunfire in the Grosvenor Road, Rodney and Oldpark areas of the city, with isolated incidents elsewhere, along with confirmation that two more local people had been killed. Thirty-two-year-old Robert McMullan of Moyard Parade had been shot, either by the British army or the loyalists in Springmartin, while 16-year-old Michael Magee, a member of Fianna Eireann, was hit by a stray IRA bullet in New Barnsley Parade.

An attempt by neighbours to get young Magee to hospital in time to save his life proved futile, and ended in a prolonged assault on the two men who accompanied him. Eamonn Logan, who lived at the bottom of New Barnsley Parade, had run from his house to where Geraldine Brennan and 'Bimbo' O'Rawe, two friends of the wounded youth, were trying to carry him to safety. He and another neighbour, Joe Slavin, took over, lifting the youth into a car that had arrived on the scene. When they got to the Royal Victoria Hospital, the car left, Michael Magee was wheeled off by hospital staff, and Logan and Slavin were arrested. They were brought downstairs in a lift to the basement to a secret military post:

An ordinary corridor, sandbagged and full of troops. After a while one of the Brits brought in a combat unit in a plastic bag and said that a soldier named Buckley had been shot dead near Kellys'. They then started kicking us and generally abusing us and this went on for hours.[16]

Later they were brought to Springfield Road Barracks where they were made to stand nose to the wall for hour after hour of 'kickings, mock executions and whacking with the rifles'. They were released at 5am, battered and bloodied, to make their own way home through the gunfire of the Falls. The soldier who had been killed, Corporal Alan Buckley (22), of the 1st Battalion of the King's Own Regiment, had been shot while behind the Browning machine-gun of a Ferret armoured car. Another had been wounded.

On Sunday morning, the IRA mounted a Lewis gun on a coalshed close to the rear entrance of St Bernadette's School and later moved it to another coalshed in Ballymurphy Drive. This added tremendously to the firepower of the Volunteers who were still blasting away at Springmartin and the Taggart and Vere Foster posts from positions in Moyard, New Barnsley, Ballymurphy and Springhill. Bryson was operating the Lewis gun while a teenage girl changed the ammunition pans.

As the gun moved about the area, large groups of children followed, singing some song about having Bryson elected King of the World. At one stage the children became such a danger to themselves that Bryson had to take drastic action to clear them out of Springmartin's line of fire. Some 50 of them had gathered on a wall behind the Lewis, all cheering wildly each time it let off a burst, and refusing point blank to go home. In desperation, Bryson eventually swung the gun around and roared that anyone not off the wall in two seconds was a goner. It worked admirably.

In the early afternoon the British army made an attempt to come up the Whiterock Road. The leading armoured car, however, was cut to ribbons by rifle fire and the soldiers who had been moving under its cover were forced to take shelter in the cemetery. They, and the armoured car, had to be rescued and the army retreated. At about 6pm 17-year-old John Pedlow was shot dead in Springmartin by the IRA, who claimed to have hit several loyalist gunmen. Three hours later 13-year-old Martha Campbell was shot dead in Springhill. Tommy Ramsey (28), who lived with his wife, Kate, and their four children at the top of Springhill Crescent, saw the young girl trapped along with a friend at McStravick's gable wall.

There was heavy firing from the Springmartin flats Then there was a lull of about 15 to 20 seconds. They knew that if they could make it to the next alley they'd have a clear run through to Des Wilson's house and on into Ballymurphy. They started to run and the wee girl Campbell lost her shoe. Just as she stopped to pick it up there was a blatter of gunfire and she was hit in the neck. I picked her up and carried her to the nearest house and sent in for Kate. Some of the First Aid people who were based at the bottom of Springhill Avenue came up, but she was dead when they got there.[17]

By then British reinforcements had begun to arrive. Some 300 paratroopers under Colonel Derek Wilford (who had presided over the Bloody Sunday massacre) began to move in from the Springfield Road direction and from the mountain to support the besieged members of the King's Regiment. For the next hour the IRA fought a fierce rearguard action back through Moyard, New Barnsley and Ballymurphy. Then shortly after dark, as the Paras moved forward under a screen of coloured smoke (and were shot at by some of their colleagues who had moved into Springmartin) the IRA melted off quietly into the night. By Monday morning nothing was left but the cartridge cases, the burnt out cars, the bullet-holes and the broken barricades. The Paras were dug in on the mountain and at St Peter's and St Thomas' schools, and the area was swamped by military vehicles.

After a couple of days the Paras left and the area returned to 'normal', but not before the pride of the British army had ploughed their armoured cars through the mourners at Michael Magee's funeral.

Three days after the bombing of Kelly's Bar, the war against the British shifted its focus to the prisons. Forty republicans in Crumlin Road prison embarked on a hunger strike for political status. Led by Billy McKee, former commander of Belfast's Third Battalion, the Volunteers said they would fast until death unless their demands were met. This move began the politicisation of the war. Up until then the IRA had relied completely on gut reaction for its support. No real effort had been made to build up a political base, either in the North or in the 26 Counties. This non-policy had proven disastrous in the recent EEC referendum in the South. While the Provisionals and Officials both campaigned against Ireland joining the European Common Market, politically they did not have the ears of the people.

The EEC victory was seen by Lynch and his government as a green light to move against republicans. Already, in a glaring illustration of the South's willingness to support the British war effort, more than a hundred republicans had been jailed for their activities in the 26 Counties. Despite occasional 'republican' rhetoric, Fianna Fail felt threatened by the real republicans who had become such a powerful force throughout the country, and were once again challenging the colonial and neo-colonial regimes in Ireland. The first opportunity to increase anti-republican repression was therefore fully exploited .

It came on May 26th, when Provisional prisoners in Mountjoy Jail, who were also campaigning for political status, rioted in protest against attempts to enforce prison regulations. Lynch opened up the military detention camp at the Curragh and transferred all those who had participated in the riot into military custody, while political courts were set up in Dublin to fight republicanism. The republicans, however, were undeterred; and the campaign for political status continued.

Meanwhile, in Derry, the pressure for a ceasefire mounted. On May 19th, the British army had killed a 15-year-old boy in the Bogside. The next day the Official IRA shot dead 19-year-old William Best of the Royal Irish Rangers in retaliation. But Best was no ordinary British soldier. A Catholic from Creggan, he was home on leave from a posting in Germany, and his regiment, along with the other two Irish regiments in the British army, had never served in the North. There was bitter reaction in the nationalist areas of Derry: 2,000 people marched in protest and the Officials' Derry headquarters were taken over. Nine days later, on May 29th 1972, the Officials, dismayed by the slackening of support for the organisation, called an indefinite ceasefire. In *The Secret Army* Bowyer Bell points out that: 'In part, in large part, as a result of the fallout from their ruthless and inept military operations and in part in fear of a Protestant backlash, the Officials announced a ceasefire.'[18]

To the Official leadership, it was the end of a long period of tortured confusion. They could now resume their strategy of gradualist reform. In the South it was pretended that the Official IRA no longer existed, and even in the North, where their obvious presence, and their participation in future feuds, made this notion more difficult to foster, similar claims were made. By the end of the 1970s, the Officials, having changed their name to The Workers' Party, were announcing that they had no political prisoners, thus disclaiming those still doing time for activities carried out under orders from the same Dublin leadership that now, in a strange case of political lobotomy, condemned 'acts of mindless violence' and 'terrorism'.

The loyalist backlash feared by the Officials, and long encouraged by the British media, was in fact already well under way. The assassination campaign, the pub bombings, the sectarian gun-battles and the sniping were daily occurrences throughout the Six Counties.

Loyalist tactics were also turning another corner in May with the declaration of No-Go areas in East Belfast and the Shankill. On May 13th barricades had gone up in these areas with the announcement that token barricades would be erected every week-end of the coming five weeks. If the British refused to move against the nationalist No-Go areas, the UDA warned, then the loyalist barricades would become permanent. On May 20th the loyalist barricades went up again. This time the British army tried to bulldoze them away in the East of the city, but the attempt sparked off a week-end of rioting, after which the British made no further attempt to interfere with the loyalist No-Go areas. Behind the barricades, nationalist families were attacked, intimidated and driven out, while the British army and the RUC maintained cordial relationships with the masked vigilantes of the UDA. Despite the organisation's involvement in robberies, intimidation and assassinations, UDA leaders were freely issued with gun licences by the authorities during this period.

On May 21st, as the riots continued in East Belfast, loyalist snipers again opened fire on Ballymurphy. Twenty young members of the Liam McParland Accordion Band had gathered at the steps of St Bernadette's School when the shots rang out, wounding 17-year-old Ann McBride in the stomach and Liam Thornton, also 17, in the left hand. (Sniping from Springmartin was so common during early 1972 that few people ventured out onto the Springfield Road unless it was absolutely necessary.) Two days later Private Eustace Handley (20), of the King's Regiment, was shot dead in Springhill Avenue, and 19-year-old John Moran of Turf Lodge died in hospital from injuries received at Kelly's Bar.

By the beginning of June the Provisionals were under increasing pressure to call a halt to hostilities. The day before the Officials' ceasefire, a premature explosion in the Short Strand had killed four IRA Volunteers and four civilians and had blown away half of Anderson Street. At the same time, the South was hammering out a deluge of anti-republican propaganda, and stepping up its harassment of republicans. Special criminal courts had been established in May to deal with political cases without juries.

Although the South was still a relatively safe haven for republicans, the ground was being laid for a very different scenario in the future. The fact that the IRA and Sinn Fein had made no serious attempt to build up a political base in the South again militated against them. The Dublin establishment was able to present the fall of Stormont as a victory for nationalists, and the Provos as mad bombers bent on jeopardising that victory. The fact that the SDLP – the most publicised spokespersons of Northern nationalists – were pushing the exact same line – helped Dublin enormously. Whitelaw, meanwhile had met the UDA – masks and uniforms being no deterrent – at the beginning of June to try to persuade them not to erect permanent No-Go areas. They agreed to postpone their action for the time being. By June 6th, when yet another soldier, George Lee (22), of the Duke of Wellington Regiment, was shot dead in Ballymurphy, rumours of an IRA ceasefire were rampant, as the media and clergy argued that no support remained for the armed struggle.

On June 13th the Provisionals held a referendum in Derry. The people of the Bogside, Creggan and Brandywell were asked to give their verdict on the IRA campaign. The response was overwhelmingly in favour of continued hostilities – 87 per cent of the total poll. But, despite the non-compromising exterior of the republican position, peace feelers were already out, the Derry referendum being simply an indicator to the British that the IRA was negotiating from a position of strength.

At the beginning of June, at a press conference in Free Derry Sean Mac Stiofain, Daithi O Conaill and Seamus Twomey (the IRA Chief of Staff, the Vice-President of Sinn Fein, and the Belfast IRA commander), offered William Whitelaw, the British Secretary of State for Northern Ireland, safe passage into the IRA-controlled section of the city to discuss the terms of a truce. Whitelaw refused the offer.

John Hume of the SDLP then intervened. He asked if the IRA would allow him to carry out further negotiations on the issue with Whitelaw. The republicans agreed, and discussions began between Hume and the Northern Ireland Office at Stormont. Hume told Whitelaw that negotiations towards peace were possible if the British agreed to two preconditions: first, the demands of the hunger strikers for political status would have to be met; and secondly, Gerry Adams, already a key member of the Republican Movement, would have to be released from internment before any negotiations could commence.

The release of Adams presented no real problem for Whitelaw. The British, who were unhappy with the publicity surrounding internment, had already released 550 internees, more than half of the total held, while they worked out an alternative method of achieving the same ends. The release of one more internee would not create any undue ripples.

However, the granting of political status, even in the face of a politically devastating hunger strike, was anathema to the colonial administration in London. The granting of prisoner-of-war status to the IRA prisoners (a status automatically granted to the internees in the Long Kesh cages) would have long-term consequences on the international stage of world opinion, a fact only too well understood by a country steeped in a history of colonial wars. But Whitelaw and Maudling, the Home Secretary, argued that the only way forward was to negotiate with the IRA. Political status was accordingly granted to both republican and loyalist prisoners on June 20th 1972.

By then, the death toll from the beginning of the year was 171; 115 civilians, 47 British soldiers (including nine members of the UDR), seven members of the RUC, one RUC reservist and one Garda killed in an explosion in the South. Hundreds of others had been injured.

On June 22nd the IRA announced that a ceasefire would take effect at midnight on June 26th. In the 24 hours leading up to the truce, the North was rocked by IRA attacks: bombings, gun-attacks, hijackings, and bank robberies (one in which three 'nuns' robbed the Allied Irish Bank in Castle Street, Belfast). An RUC man was killed in Newry, a soldier was killed in Derry, and at a minute to midnight, a second soldier was killed in Belfast. Then midnight, and silence, as both sides sat back to study their position in relation to the coming negotiations.

References

1. *Spotlight Community Newspaper* (Ballymurphy Detached Project, March 1975.
2. *Irish Times*, Dublin, June 17th, 1971.
3. Ibid.
4. *Report on Employment Survey* (Turf Lodge Development Association, November 1972), p. 3.
5. *Irish News*, Belfast, December 2nd 1971.
6. Ibid.
7. Frank Kitson, *Low Intensity Operations – Subversion, Insurgency and Counter Insurgency* (Faber and Faber, London, 1971), p. 2.
8. 'Counter-revolutionary Operations, 1st Part, Principles and General Aspects', *Land Operations, Vol. III* (Ministry of Defence, August 29th 1969).
9. *Troops Out!*, Troops Out Movement, London, July 1978.
10. *Belfast Telegraph*, February 27th 1973.
11. Liz Curtis, *Ireland: the Propaganda War* (Pluto Press, London, 1984).
12. Interview with author.
13. Mick Clarke of Ballymurphy (1986 Interview).
14. Gerry McGlade, former manager of Kelly's Bar (1986 Interview).
15. Ibid.
16. Eamonn Logan of New Barnsley (1986 Interview).
17. Tommy Ramsey, formerly of Springhill (1986 Interview).
18. J. Bowyer Bell, *The Secret Army, the IRA* (The Academy Press, Dublin, 1970) p. 388.

10

The Westrock Massacre

There was a carnival atmosphere in Ballymurphy. The British had agreed to stay out of nationalist areas, travelling only on the main roads. The arms raids and swoops for wanted guerrillas were over. The beatings, riots and gun-battles were no longer the norm. You could go to the shops, let the children play in the street, hang out the washing, sit in the front garden in the sun, without fear of finding yourself in the middle of a gunfight or surrounded by belligerent troops.

The barricades went up on the perimeters of the estates, but they were more a symbol of victory than fear, although there was still the unknown element of loyalist response to the truce. Even the children got in on the act, erecting their own little barricades on the pavement or at the street corner. A special effort to clean up the streets was co-ordinated by the BTA youth workers and the glass and rubble of two years' conflict was swept up, exposing once more the long forgotten tarmac. Plans for a summer camp on the Leslie Estate in Glaslough, County Monaghan forged ahead. Fred Bass was back in the area to organise the summer's playscheme to be run by the Voluntary Service Bureau.

The Upper Springfield estates were being patrolled by armed IRA Volunteers. Sentry posts were built at each entrance from the Whiterock and Springfield roads. Owenie Meehan, a mentally retarded young man, who none the less was a reasonably integrated member of the community, was seen at the barricades, complete with mask and toy pistol. The Provisionals had set up headquarters in one of the empty flats above the Bullring shops. Jim Bryson and some of his comrades toured the area in a jeep, 'liberated' from some forgotten source, and now neatly emblazoned with a republican logo and the words 'Oglaigh na hEireann'. A single car-seat was welded to the roof, where the famed Lewis gun was mounted. The Republic seemed all but won in Greater Ballymurphy.

To the British ruling classes, abysmally ignorant of the politics of the Irish conflict, the truce was a desperately-sought breakthrough in the deadlock that had existed since the introduction of internment, a deadlock compounded by the fall of Stormont. With the loyalists unco-operative and the SDLP and NICRA still refusing to talk until internment was ended, Whitelaw had argued that private negotiations with the Provisionals might open the way to further political development. Already Whitelaw had hinted at such negotiations when he announced in parliament plans for a conference on the North's future to which 'all shades of opinion' would be invited.[1]

The Northern Ireland Secretary's analysis that such a truce could be achieved at little real cost, and that a lengthy cessation of hostilities would make the IRA's return to armed resistance all the more difficult, was accepted by the British Cabinet. The IRA also felt that dialogue was desirable: if nothing else, it would show that they were reasonable people; and there was always the possibility that the British might actually be ready to accede to republican demands.

The central demand was British recognition of the right of the Irish people as a whole to self-determination. In other words, the loyalist veto, granted by the Government of Ireland Act 1949, would have to be abolished.* There would also have to be a date for British withdrawal, and a general amnesty for political prisoners in British and Irish jails.

These demands, however, were now tabled as long-term objectives to be considered as the subject of future negotiations that would eventually lead to the reunification of Ireland. In the interim, to make the truce viable, the British government was offered five conditions: the release of all internees; the repeal of the Special Powers Act; the removal of the ban on Sinn Fein in the North; the elimination of oaths of allegiance to the Crown, which were required of certain public office-holders and election candidates; and the confirmation of the proportional representation system for Northern elections.

The republican demands brought no immediate public response from

*On May 11th 1946, Sean McCaughey of Belfast, a former IRA Chief of Staff, died in Portlaoise Prison after 23 days on hunger and thirst strike. After his death, horrific details of Fianna Fail's treatment of republican prisoners emerged: because McCaughey and his comrades had refused to wear prison uniforms, they had been kept naked in their cells since 1941, and McCaughey himself had been allowed no visitors in all that time. In the resultant climate of public outrage, a new political party, Clann na Poblachta, was formed by Sean MacBride, a lawyer who was himself a former IRA Chief of Staff and the son of an IRA guerrilla executed after the 1916 Rising.

In October 1947 Clann na Poblachta won two by-elections, putting MacBride and one of his colleagues into the Dail. Alarmed by this threat, Fianna Fail leader, Eamonn de Valera, called a general election, which misfired. Clann Na Poblachta won ten seats, tipping the balance of power. By joining with the Irish Labour Party and the anti-republican Fine Gael they ousted the 14-year-old government of Fianna Fail. The pay-off was the release of republican prisoners in the South, and the declaration in Canada on September 7th 1948, by Taoiseach John A. Costello that his government intended to declare the South a Republic and take it out of the Commonwealth.

Unionist reaction in the North was one of hysteria. Perceiving a political onslaught on the loyalist position, Prime Minister Basil Brooke called an election for February 10th 1949. The campaign that followed was the most violent since 1921 with widespread attacks on anti-partition meetings. The election result, giving the Unionists a mandate to remain part of Great Britain, was a foregone conclusion. But the violence shook the British. On May 3rd 1949, the Labour government introduced the Ireland Bill, giving the loyalists their veto:

Parliament hereby declares that Northern Ireland remains part of His Majesty's Dominions and of the United Kingdom and affirms that in no event will Northern Ireland or any part thereof cease to be part of his Majesty's Dominions and of the United Kingdom without the consent of the Parliament of Northern Ireland. (Clause 1(1)B) the British; but Whitelaw indicated privately that some of the points appeared reasonable and would be carefully considered. However, given British and NATO interests in maintaining a military presence in Ireland, and the North's further strategic role in the testing of Kitson's theories, there was little or no chance of the IRA's key demands being granted. Instead, while playing for time, the British appeared to believe they might be able to sway the IRA away from those demands, and bring it around to a more sympathetic view of the British position. There was also a possibility that the Provisionals were 'turning political' and would be willing to bargain.

The 'discovery' by the British that the IRA was actually possessed of a coherent political ideology came as a great surprise in Whitehall circles, and was soon being acknowledged by some sections of the British media. As the ceasefire continued to hold, *The Times* wrote:

> The Provisionals, who are now under able political leadership, are bent upon having a say in any Northern Ireland settlement proportionate to their power. And that power has not been extinguished. The concessions that Mr Whitelaw is making to the IRA in particular and the Catholic community in general are not yet complete.[2]

Impressed by the IRA's sincerity in relation to the ceasefire and its presentation of a political prospectus, the British government decided to sit at the bargaining table with the republicans. Their rationale was simple: nothing would be lost by talking; and, if the whole affair collapsed, word of the talks would be leaked to Dublin, where Lynch, having again been upstaged by the Provos, might be prompted to crack down on republicanism with renewed vigour.

On July 7th the Provo delegation was flown to London by the RAF for a secret meeting at the exclusive Chelsea home of Junior Minister and Guinness heir Paul Channon. The IRA participants were Sean Mac Stiofain, Daithi O Conaill, Seamus Twomey, Martin McGuinness (O/C of the Derry Brigade), Gerry Adams and Ivor Bell (O/C of the First Battalion, Belfast Brigade). Myles Shevlin of Provisional Sinn Fein was the seventh member of the delegation.

The Provos placed on the table their demands for a permanent peace settlement – the right of the Irish people as a whole to self-determination, a British withdrawal, and an amnesty for political prisoners – along with their five interim points. Whitelaw made no promises other than that the British government would consider all the demands and meet again with the IRA in a week's time. In the meantime, it was agreed, the IRA and the British army would both have freedom of the streets in the North; the IRA could bear arms as long as open displays were limited to republican areas; and searches of individuals, vehicles and homes would cease.

The IRA delegation returned home disappointed that no concessions had been made on their demands and conscious of the feeling among many Volunteers that the British were not to be trusted and should be bombed and shot into submission. But the truce was still holding, and in a week's time they hoped there might be some more positive British response. They were never to find out what the response might have been.

Ever since the ceasefire had been announced the loyalist community had been incensed. The extreme right, which had long been clamouring for a full onslaught by British troops on nationalist areas, was outraged at what it saw as an IRA victory. Republicans – the avowed enemies of their state – were now openly carrying arms on the streets of Belfast and Derry, and the British army was pulling back from nationalist areas. (In Derry, three of the Bogside's barricades came down to allow environmental work to take place, and in response the British vacated the Brandywell army post.) On June 27th, the first day of the ceasefire, the *Belfast News Letter*, organ of unionist opinion, articulated the general loyalist attitude to the ceasefire in its leader: 'A prospect of still further relaxation of the powers required to deal with terrorism is, perhaps, the most blatant example yet of the degree and the nature of the capitulation we have seen.[3]

On the same day a leaflet distributed in Ballymurphy and parts of Andersonstown by the IRA declared that they were now assuming full control of 'law and order' in republican areas, basing their authority on 'an administration reaching back to the Provisional Government (1916) of the Irish people'. Choking on such blasphemies, Ian Paisley was furiously and simultaneously demanding that IRA Volunteers should be hunted down wherever they existed. He bluntly warned the British government that: 'If they fail in this matter they are only inviting an enraged Protestant community to take the law into its own hands and to execute vengeance.'[4]

The Ulster Protestant Volunteers, closely associated with Paisley in those days, reacted to the ceasefire by promising to 'resist with force if necessary any effort by the IRA to police these areas with the consent of the present administration'.[5] It was also announced that all organisations associated with William Craig's Vanguard – the Loyalist Association (former 'B' Specials), the UDA and the Orange Volunteers – had been placed 'on general alert'. Craig described the truce as 'a certain recipe for civil war', and went on to echo Paisley's sentiments: 'If the security forces do not discharge their duty in apprehending the IRA terrorists the loyalists will have no option but to clean them out themselves and take such action as is necessary against the republican community.'[6] The loyalist assassination squads agreed with these sentiments.

During the next two weeks sectarian attacks increased dramatically. Gun-attacks on nationalist areas, riots, mass intimidation of nationalists out of all remaining 'mixed' neighbourhoods, and a string of assassinations punctuated the truce. Worst affected was Belfast where huge sections of the city were barricaded off and patrolled by armed vigilantes. At night, with great parts of the city blacked out, few people travelled abroad, and those who did stuck to the main arteries, where guerrilla road-blocks and checks were less likely.

Nevertheless, beginning with the seven killings which took place during the week-end of June 30th–July 3rd, 15 people died in sectarian killings between June 27th and July 9th, while three others were shot dead as they crashed through IRA roadblocks. (The first death of the truce was that of 38-year-old Bernard Norney of New Barnsley Crescent, shot on the morning of June 27th, on the Whiterock Road at an IRA checkpoint which, ironically, was designed to protect the area from loyalist assassins.) Nine of these killings – including the murder of two Protestant brothers because they had Catholic girlfriends – were carried out by loyalist gunmen; whereas the others were the work of IRA or other republican cells, operating on their own initiative.

For the first time, nationalists were hitting back. Although sectarian attacks by republican elements were never to assume substantial proportions, they continued intermittently until the mid 1970s when they were finally stamped out by the republican leadership.

After the week-end killings that heralded the opening of the new loyalist onslaught, and the advent of republican gunmen into the arena of sectarian killings, the North – and Belfast in particular – was engulfed in a new kind of fear. Nobody was safe anywhere anymore. This was especially true for nationalists who were now under attack in their homes, streets, bars, clubs and places of work. It was also clear that the loyalists, particularly the UDA, were determined to force the British into renewing the war.

On June 28th UDA leaders had told Whitelaw that their position remained unchanged on the republican No-Go areas: unless the British moved against them, more barricades would go up in loyalist districts at the week-end. In Belfast on the same day 1,000 khaki-clad, bush-hatted UDA members marched at the funeral of John Brown, a UDA member killed during the previous week-end's disturbances. The following day, June 29th, 2,000 loyalists, including four battalions of masked UDA men, marched through Armagh; while 500 other members attended the funeral of 32-year-old John Black, shot by troops during an attempt to remove loyalist barricades in East Belfast on May 31st.

On Friday, June 30th, the UDA barricades went up in Belfast, Bangor, Ballymena, Lisburn and Derry as the week-end of killing got under way. By early Monday morning seven people were dead, and many working-class areas were pinned down by inter-communal sniper fire. Six days on, and the fragile truce was already buckling under pressure from the extreme right.

In Ballymurphy the optimism of the first days of the truce had been severely dented: by Monday, July 3rd, the BTA community centre was again evacuating children to the refugee trains that would take them across the border. The area was extremely tense, as was the case in all frontline nationalist areas, as rumours of imminent loyalist invasions were fuelled by the mass mobilisation of the UDA and the week-long deluge of anti-nationalist threats.

Late on Monday afternoon the invasion became real. A car drove into Ballymurphy with word that the UDA was massing on the Springfield

Road for a sweep into West Belfast. Somebody had been monitoring a loyalist pirate radio station, broadcasting from Wilton Street in the Shankill area, and had heard the order go out to UDA units across the city to converge on the junction of Springfield Road and Ainsworth Avenue. The invasion of West Belfast by loyalists intent on penetrating the No-Go areas was, apparently, about to begin.

But, though a number of nationalist families living in 'mixed' streets between the Springfield and Shankill were under immediate threat, the real reason for the UDA call-up was a confrontation that had developed between some of its units and the British army. Earlier in the day, an attempt had been made to seal off another loyalist-controlled No-Go area, which included the 'mixed' streets. This time, however, the area was of strategic interest to the military, and hundreds of troops, supported by a heavy convoy of armoured vehicles and Browning machine-guns, were sent out to prevent the barricades from going up.

The UDA called up its reinforcements and by 7pm 8,000 uniformed men had gathered on the Springfield Road, having been ferried across the city in hijacked trucks, buses and cars. Armed with guns, cudgels, iron bars, riot shields and dustbin lids, and backed up by truckloads of bricks, bottles and other missiles, they sang *The Sash* and rattled their sabres at the line of British troops. Unknown to the UDA and the troops, IRA units had also moved into the area.

Prompted by the unsavoury prospects on the Springfield Road, Whitelaw and General Robert Ford, GOC Land Forces, in talks lasting four hours, agreed a deal with UDA leaders. At 11pm it was announced that joint UDA/British army patrols would be conducted in the Lower Springfield, and checkpoints between the Springfield and Shankill would be similarly controlled. The British army and the UDA both hailed the outcome as a victory. As the late news told of further attacks on nationalists in Bangor and Carrickfergus, republicans were beginning to wonder how many more UDA/British army victories the truce would withstand.

Over the next week, in a build-up to the 'Twelfth', hooded and masked members of the UDA, UVF and Tartan gangs attacked homes and business premises while assassinations, attempted assassinations and sniping attacks were stepped up. In the Upper Springfield, two men were shot from Springmartin. The IRA returned fire, carefully avoiding the Taggart, and claimed one hit.

At about the same time, 'Todler' Tolan decided to strike back directly at the UDA by hitting their club in Springmartin. He and another Volunteer drove across from Ballymurphy with rifles, ran from the car to the UDA club and kicked the door in. As they did, two hands inside the door grabbed Tolan's rifle, wrenched it out of his arms, and kicked the door shut. Both Volunteers had to run for their lives and bee-line back to the safety of Ballymurphy.

Armed loyalists also invaded nationalist homes in South Belfast on July 5th, and told their occupants that they would be eliminated by July 12th. 'Intimidation,' Whitelaw said, 'is an abhorrent and despicable activity', and as nationalist homes burned, and 200 families fled loyalist

Rathcoole, he announced the formation of the Public Protection Agency, which by some unfathomable means was going to counter intimidation. Meanwhile the British army and RUC colluded openly with the masked khaki-clad organisations responsible for the bulk of that intimidation.*

On July 7th, at Tobermore, William Craig addressed a crowd of several thousand, including 400 UDA members and 800 Orange Volunteers. If loyalists could not have their 'democratic rights', he told them, they would take up arms in the tradition of their forefathers. Meanwhile, in Belfast, another confrontation between the UDA and the British army had ended in compromise.

It was now becoming increasingly clear that the balancing act being played by the British could not last. Sooner or later the scales would have to tip one way or the other: either the British faced up to the mushrooming loyalist challenge, which meant armed conflict with the 'loyal' settler population; or, to placate the loyalists, they resumed the war against the IRA. The Springfield Road encounter had embodied a significant shift in the latter direction. On Sunday July 9th the UDA in East Belfast declared a sixth 'permanent' No-Go area. The British army casually watched from a distance as Dee Street ceded from the state.

The prospect of a war with the loyalists had by then evaporated: the truce was breaking down on the other side of Belfast, only two days after the Chelsea meeting between Whitelaw and the IRA.

Again a confrontation had been engineered by the UDA, this time in a situation in which the British army was forced to finally declare its hand. A number of nationalist families, intimidated out of other parts of the city and subsequently granted tenancies in Lenadoon, had arrived with their furniture in the 'mixed' estate on Friday afternoon. A contingent of the UDA had also arrived to prevent them from occupying the homes. The situation had been one of stalemate until Sunday, when the British army decided on a show of force – against the nationalists. As tension rose in Lenadoon, young men from many parts of West Belfast began to converge on the estate. Several trucks left Ballymurphy with dozens of men – including most of the area's Volunteers – on board.

In the afternoon the British army and UDA blocked a furniture van that was attempting to unload in front of one of the vacant units in Lenadoon. A Saracen rammed the truck and triggered off a riot. CS gas and rubber bullets were fired at the nationalists. Seamus Twomey on the spot, and Daithi O Conaill in Dublin, attempted to have the troops called off. O Conaill managed to get Whitelaw, who was in London, on the telephone.

Whitelaw told him he would confer with his aides and ring back. The call is yet to come.

At about 5pm as the Lenadoon riot continued, the first shots were fired. The truce was over, the British firmly realigned with the extreme right of Irish politics. At 9pm the IRA Army Council made it official: 'The

---

*The newspapers of July 1972, particularly the loyalist *Belfast News Letter*, contained a striking photographic record of the extent of the collusion between state forces and irregular loyalist forces.

truce between the IRA and British occupation forces was broken without warning by British forces ... Accordingly, all IRA units have been instructed to resume offensive action.'[7]

Fifty minutes later a new round of killings descended on Ballymurphy, this time at the aluminium huts in Westrock. At 9.50pm a sniper in Corry's timber yard opened up on two cars sitting in Westrock. One reversed immediately, the other moved forward seeking cover. The bungalows, built as a temporary provision after the Second World War, provided little real cover as bullets simply sliced through the aluminium walls and roofs.

As the occupants of the cars tumbled out, the sniper fired a burst of approximately 14 shots, hitting 19-year-old Martin Dudley in the back of the head and leaving him seriously wounded. The other passengers were pinned down for the next 90 minutes. At 9.35pm Paddy Butler, a 38-year-old married man with five children, ran to get a priest for Martin Dudley. At 9.55pm Brian Pettigrew (17) and John Dougal (17) ran towards the wounded youth. No sooner had they broken cover than a second sniper opened fire, killing John Dougal, a member of Fianna Eireann, and hitting Brian Pettigrew several times in the chest. Sixteen-year-old Micky Vallelly had been in nearby Springhill when the shooting started he recalled a quiet evening suddenly shattered by gunfire.

> When I came down the car was lying in the middle of the road, but no one could get near it. People pinned down in the entries were saying that ones were lying dead. Then a priest, Fr Fitzpatrick, came along in his car and got out at the chapel. He started to head towards the dead and wounded. People were shouting at him not to go, to stay in the alleys if he wanted to make his way over to Westrock Drive. He was only away about 30 seconds when someone came down and said that the priest was dead.[8]

Fr Noel Fitzpatrick – the second priest to be shot dead in Ballymurphy – had arrived on the scene at 9.57pm along with Paddy Butler and 14-year-old David 'Dean' McCafferty. Someone then shouted that a young girl had been shot and a priest was needed. She was 13-year-old Margaret Gargan who died in a fusillade of bullets fired by a third sniper positioned further down in Corry's yard. Fr Fitzpatrick and Paddy Butler ran from the cover of a house. The first sniper opened up and shot the priest, the same bullet passing through him and killing Paddy Butler. Young McCafferty attempted to drag the bodies clear of the line of fire. He was shot to pieces by the same sniper.

In just under ten minutes five people had been murdered in Westrock. The perpetrators were, beyond a shadow of doubt, British army marksmen. One of the few senior IRA Volunteers still in the area at the time of the shooting recalled how:

> Our own intelligence reports had confirmed that the Brits had a sandbagged observation post in one of the wood piles in Corry's. Even without that, the shooting was far too precise to be ordinary. They never missed.

They just had to be highly practised marksmen. Nothing else could explain the accuracy. They were hitting people who were pinned down in alleys by ricocheting bullets off walls and lamp posts. And the next day, when we took some bricks out of the wall at Corrigan Park facing Corry's, the sniping was so accurate that every time something moved on our side a hail of bullets came through the gap.[9]

Although the British army claimed later that night to have hit a number of 'gunmen' during a prolonged gun-battle with the IRA, they did not officially accept responsibility for the Westrock killings, and suggested that loyalists might have been responsible – that they could have sneaked into the yard during 'the general din'. However, along with the sandbagged hide in the timber, reported by IRA intelligence, there was another military observation post in Corry's. It was therefore highly unlikely that loyalist gunmen, without the acquiescence of the military, would have climbed into the timber yard (closed for the week-end) and operated against Westrock so openly. Besides, since all the shooting that night occurred in the vicinity of Corry's, where else could the British army have notched up its Ballymurphy 'hits'?

The IRA Volunteer previously mentioned went on to describe the panic and confusion that followed the slaughter at Westrock:

It took a while for the Volunteers to get organised. Most of them had to get back from Lenadoon. As well as that people were seeing snipers everywhere. Not alone did we have to engage the snipers at Westrock, but we had to follow up all sorts of reports of firing coming from other directions. At one point me and Jim Logue went up by the riverbed and fired some flares to light up Corry's wall. Then Jim jumped up with a carbine, but the bloody thing had dud rounds and never fired. It's just as well there was no one to fire back or Jim would have been a dead man.[10]

In Westrock it had taken the IRA some 15 minutes to get into defensive positions. Ann Maguire (26), who had been visiting her mother-in-law, Bridget Maguire, in the bungalows, was among those trying to assist the wounded during those 15 minutes.

People were pinned down everywhere, in all the alleyways. If there was a target, they [the Corry's snipers] shot at it; if not, they just shot into the houses. The priest was brought into May Donnelly's brick house in Westrock Drive. He was dead; but two of Mother Teresa's nuns, who were in a state of shock, continued to bathe his wounds. Then Canon Murphy and Fr McCaul arrived – McCaul was nearly shot too – and the Canon brought the nuns back to their own house while the priest heard everyone's confession, including the Volunteers who were beginning to come into the area with weapons. Then the ambulances came, and they were shot at too.[11]

At this point, with the ambulances unable to reach the wounded, Tommy Ramsey of Springhill Crescent jumped in a car and set off under fire for St Peter's School where an impromptu field hospital had been set up by a local volunteer First Aid corps. For most of his journey he was fully exposed to the snipers in the timber yard. At the school he was joined by one of the men in attendance, who lay on the floor of the car as they turned back for Westrock. Tommy Ramsey remembers turning into Westrock Drive, advising his passenger that, 'If we hit the lamp, get into the nearest house, because no way am I going to slow down on this bend.'

By the time the two men got back to the scene of the killings the IRA was returning heavy fire into Corry's. Under its cover the dead and wounded were being taken to ambulances, some of which had come to the perimeters of the estate, others which waited further away. But, despite the IRA fire, it was still impossible to move openly in Westrock. Young Dean McCafferty's body had to be carried through a house and hoisted out through a back window, while it took over half an hour to get John Dougal's body and the wounded Brian Pettigrew out of Pettigrew's garden where they had lain since they were hit. Kate Campbell, a grandmother in her early fifties, who had lived in the bungalows for 20 years, was the Pettigrews' next-door neighbour:

> The house was riddled with bullets. When the priest came I was lying on a mattress with my one-year-old granddaughter, and a spent bullet was lying right beside her head. No one could get out. We had to cut a hole between our house and Pettigrews' to get the bodies through. First they were dragged into Pettigrews', then brought through the hole into our back bedroom. Then they were carried under cover of the bungalow to a hole in the wall of Corrigan Park, and over on to the Whiterock Road to an ambulance ... It was terrible. It went on for days. Even the very cats were shot at. We had to get out through the hole in Corrigan Park to go to St Thomas' School for bread and milk ... Two other men – Bob Nesbitt and someone else – were also carried into my house as well to have their wounds treated. And the next day, when Gargans were having the wake for their wee girl, another man was shot coming out of the house, and he was brought to our house too.[12]

On Monday, July 10th, as the newspapers reported widespread violence across the North, the gun-battle at Corry's continued. There was also a continuous shoot-out between the IRA and loyalists in Springmartin, and the Taggart was again under siege. During the course of the day several civilians and soldiers were wounded, but the snipers in Corry's could not be dislodged.

> We fired thousands of rounds at them. We tried to hit them from the houses in Whiterock, from Corrigan Park, from Westrock and from Springhill. Bryson brought the Lewis gun up to the verandah of the flat above Mary's Shop in Springhill Avenue. He stood up on two bins with the Lewis mounted on a piece of wood held by pigeon-holes in the brickwork, and raked Corry's; but they were still there.[13]

And through it all, there were the inevitable quirks that made Ballymurphy's war so eternally bizarre. There was Bridget Maguire for whom no cigarette would suffice but Gallahers' Greens. On Monday morning, as the battle raged around her home, Bridget ran out of Greens. Some time later, after heated debate in Maguires', Bridget's son, Martin, who was engaging the snipers in Corry's, heard his name being called from behind. He looked around in astonishment to see his sister-in-law, Ann, gesticulating frantically as she ran from the cover of one bungalow to the next. 'Martin,' the awful request came, 'would you ever give us some cover? Yer ma wants 20 Greens!'

By all accounts, Bridget Maguire was not a woman easily swayed. Later that night, young Susie Roberts was around in the house when Bridget began to put on her scarf and coat, boldly announcing that she was off to bingo. 'You'll be killed!' Susie tried to warn, but Bridget would have none of it. 'But, sure I go to bingo every night,' Bridget replied, 'they'll see me and say "There's Bridget Maguire going off to bingo, don't shoot her!"' In a similar example of Ballymurphy fatalism, Micky Vallelly recalled another anecdote:

> You remember how there was always spectators at every gun-battle? Well, I ended up back down in Westrock the next day (Monday). And some time in the afternoon, with the bullets knocking lumps out of the walls, this woman with a pram comes sauntering along the path between the bungalows and Corry's wall. At this stage anything that moved was shot at. We all started screaming at the woman to get back, but she just walked right through the middle of it as if nothing was happening at all.[14]

On Monday, July 10th, as the guns blazed around the Upper Springfield, the undertakers refused to enter Westrock so that the IRA had to bring in the hearses. 'It was the eeriest thing I've ever seen,' one of the Volunteers later recalled, 'Just a single black hearse coming down a totally deserted street, Bryson driving and Todler riding guard with a rifle.'

Meanwhile, the IRA in Dublin released a statement spilling the beans on Whitelaw and the London talks, thus saving the British the bother. Lynch and the Dublin government were enraged; the *Irish Times* expressed shock that the IRA's status had been elevated to that of 'national negotiators'; and London, having been caught talking to 'terrorists', was in no mood for reconciliation. From now on, in both directions, force would be met with force.

Over the next six days the IRA, angry over the breakdown of the truce and the Westrock murders, hit back hard, killing eight soldiers and an RUC man and wounding many others. Cities and towns were blitzed while massive landmines exploded in rural areas. Resumption of the war with such ferocity was taken as a cue by the loyalist assassins. Over the coming weeks and months hooded bodies were turning up on an almost daily basis. Many nationalist victims – who constituted the vast majority – were slowly tortured to death and horribly mutilated, the purpose being to terrorise the whole nationalist community with the horror of the killings.

To protect nationalist areas, barricades continued to go up. At the same time sniping and inter-communal gun-battles went on as before, sometimes bordering on civil war proportions. And as the military carried out massive punitive raids, destroying nationalist homes, beating up residents, and arresting and torturing suspects, the flood of refugees to the South increased. By July 16th, 5,000 people had crossed the border.

Two days later, in an attempt to combat the car-bombing of Belfast, Whitelaw announced a traffic ban in the city centre. Belfast, the British army declared, was now 'bomb-proof'. On Friday, July 21st, the IRA set out to demonstrate that it was not. In the space of 75 minutes – between 2.15 and 3.30pm – the Provisionals detonated 21 bombs in the city centre. In line with their policy of avoiding civilian casualties, warnings for each bomb were telephoned to the Public Protection Agency (Whitelaw's anti-intimidation body), which had come to be a reliable means of relaying bomb warnings to the British army and RUC.

In 19 cases the warnings were acted upon and there were no casualties as the bombs went off. However, at Oxford Street bus station and at Cavehill Road Shopping Centre the military and RUC chose to ignore the warnings. The Public Protection Agency would subsequently confirm that it had received and transmitted warnings of those two bombs to the RUC 30 minutes and 73 minutes respectively, before the blasts.[15] Yet, at Oxford Street, four civilians and two British soldiers were killed, while three civilians were killed at Cavehill Road.

'Bloody Friday', as it became known, did irreparable damage to the IRA cause, giving the British a huge propaganda coup. The British decision to let the bombs go off succeeded in discrediting the IRA, handing the state a long-awaited opening. Immediately, British war plans were given a major boost, and Whitelaw had his excuse for an invasion of the No-Go areas, which would temporarily get the loyalists off his back.

Throughout this period the war went on unabated in the Upper Springfield. After the Westrock killings the IRA engaged the British army and the loyalists in Springmartin on a continuous basis, while local Volunteers carried out countless bombing missions in the city and its environs. There were seldom moments, day or night, without the rattle of gunfire or the sound of exploding blast bombs, nail bombs or grenades. Unless the shooting was directly outside the window, people became as indifferent to it as city-dwellers are to the sound of passing cars.

And through it all, the ice-cream van still did the rounds, Larry Sloan sold his fish, Geordie Stanton rode up and down the Whiterock Road on his horse, and Micky Marley – a famous Belfast character – wheeled his horse-drawn roundabout to wherever children could be found. There was even an owl living in a wrecked house in Springhill. And the scrap-man called, as illustrated by one of the area's many hidden tales.

Sometime in July explosives in transit through New Barnsley were hidden in an old cooker. Shortly afterwards two IRA Volunteers called to collect them, and were told they were outside in the hiding place. They went off, only to return a few minutes later saying, 'What cooker?' There was instant panic as a child with some conspicuous balloons, similar to those given out by the scrap-man, was spotted in the street.

Some Volunteers, including a woman who pretended to be pregnant, raced in a taxi to the Royal Victoria Hospital to take a short-cut that would get them to the scrap-yard at Cullingtree Road before the scrap-man with his horse and cart, and dubious load, arrived. No sign of the scrap-man, so they doubled back to New Barnsley, and a comb-out of the district began.

Eventually, much to the IRA's relief, the scrap-man was found making his merry way through Westrock, still handing out balloons for scrap. 'Excuse me,' one of the Volunteers ventured, 'I think that's our cooker.' The scrap-man, keen on the maxim that possession is nine-tenths of the law, hotly refuted this counter-claim, pointing out that good balloons had changed hands. 'Well mister,' the IRA man smiled, 'there's something in your oven, and it isn't a friggin' chicken.' Apparently the matter was settled there and then. On another occasion a whole binload of explosives was innocently tipped into their wagon and carted off by the binmen.

On July 18th the IRA struck again at Corry's, using a Roman-style catapult to lob containers of petrol over the wall. As 60-foot flames lit up the sky, causing £250,000 worth of damage – and accidentally gutting two bungalows and a community hall in Westrock – the military came under fire throughout the area. At Vere Foster, 18-year-old James Jones of the King's Regiment was shot dead, bringing the official British army death toll in the North to 100. A second soldier was wounded on the Whiterock Road. Over the next week three more soldiers were shot in the area. One of them, Brian Thomas (20), was killed, also at Vere Foster. The observation post on the roof of the school could be clearly seen from the Bullring flats, where the IRA would wait, sometimes for hours, to get a shot at the guards.

Elsewhere, the pace of events was quickening. On July 26th the SDLP agreed to meet Whitelaw, who had recently announced plans for a conference on the political future of the Six Counties. The IRA ceasefire talks with the British had taken them off the hook of no talks until internment ends, and the middle class of nationalism wanted desperately to get out of the political wilderness to a position from which they could pull support away from the militant republicans and present themselves as the voice of nationalism.

The next day, as the war raged on, 4,000 extra troops and heavy military equipment arrived in the North; and in Belfast the dead became embroiled in the Troubles. A Corporation spokesperson announced that the City Cemetery, bordering on Ballymurphy, was to close temporarily as the gravediggers were refusing to work without danger money. However, people who owned plots there would be offered new plots at Roselawn on the opposite side of the city – at half price.

Four days later, at 4am on Monday, July 31st 1972, Operation Motorman began. 21,000 British troops, supported by Centurion tanks, helicopters and hundreds of armoured cars, invaded the No-Go areas of Belfast and Derry. In the Bogside and Creggan alone, 1,600 troops and 300 military vehicles were used to smash through the barricades. On Creggan Heights, 'Moaning Minnie', Free Derry's early warning system, wailed out over the city, heralding the end of one phase of the republican war and the beginning of another.

The 2nd Battalion of the Parachute Regiment had invaded Ballymurphy.

References

1. *The Times*, London, June 16th 1972.
2. Ibid., June 28th 1972.
3. *Belfast News Letter*, June 27th 1972.
4. Ibid., June 28th 1972.
5. Ibid.
6. Ibid.
7. *Irish Times*, Dublin, July 10th 1972.
8. Micky Vallelly of Ballymurphy (1986 Interview).
9. Interview with the author.
10. Ibid.
11. Ann Maguire of Ballymurphy (1986 Interview).
12. Kate Campbell, formerly of Westrock (1986 Interview).
13. Interview with the author.
14. Micky Vallelly of Ballymurphy (1986 Interview).
15. Kevin Kelley, *The Longest War* (Brandon Publishers, Dingle, 1982), p. 183.

11

Motorman

Motorman heralded a turning point in British policy. Whitelaw's previous attempts to divide the masses from the Provisionals had been ditched in favour of stepped-up repression. Since Easter 1970 the British army's terror campaign against nationalists had run unchecked. Hundreds of civilians had been shot, many of them killed, by trigger-happy troops acting under cover of 'the law'. Whole areas had been subjected to months of CS gas saturation. Thousands of people had been viciously assaulted in punitive raids against riot areas, or simply because they were on the spot when soldiers decided to bash a few more natives. The Association of Legal Justice had logged countless cases of severe injuries resulting from the brutal military attempts to bludgeon or shoot all opposition off the streets (tactics later used by the Israelis in the Middle East, and sanctimoniously condemned by the British government!). Motorman, however, was to be the pinnacle.

Whereas in the past military brutality had been random, and interspersed with political fumblings, it now became the single British approach. In pursuit of a military solution in the North, the army was cut loose without restraint to be a law unto itself.

The 2nd Battalion of the Parachute Regiment, and a company of the 1st Battalion, were sent in to wrest the Upper Springfield back from the IRA and place it under full military occupation. At 4am on July 31st, they swarmed into the district in heavy armoured cars to set up bases in St Peter's and Vere Foster schools, the Taggart, a block of Moyard's maisonettes – abandoned because of its dangerous proximity to the Taggart – and McCrory Park where they erected a massive corrugated iron 'Wild West' style fort.

Elsewhere in West Belfast, people woke up to find schools, community halls, flats and Belfast's main Gaelic football ground, Casement Park in Andersonstown, occupied by the military and being fortified for an extended stay. There were also three other forts, similar to McCrory Park's 'Fort Pegasus', covering most of what little green space there was in the Greater Andersonstown/Ballymurphy/Turf Lodge area. The Para invasion of Ballymurphy had swept away the barricades and IRA sentry posts, and the Provo jeep was gone. There had been little opposition, the IRA having discreetly withdrawn. To understand what the military occupation of an urban area by British paratroopers actually means, it is helpful to read the memoirs of Lieutenant A.F.N. Clarke of 3 Para who completed a tour of duty in Belfast in early 1973. Clarke's account gives an illuminating picture of undisciplined, racist thugs, spoiling for blood, unleashed on a defenceless civilian population. Describing his 'peace-keeping' role, he writes:

The whole camp is praying for a contact. For an opportunity to shoot at anything in the street, pump lead into any living thing and watch the blood flow. Toms sitting in their overcrowded rooms putting more powder into baton rounds to give them more poke; some insert pins and broken razor blades into the rubber rounds. Buckshee rounds have had the heads filed down for a dum-dum effect, naughty, naughty, but who's to know when there are so many spare rounds of ammunition floating about? Lead-filled truncheons, Magnum revolvers, one bloke has even got a Bowie knife ... We have spent months and years training, learning from pamphlets called *Shoot to Kill, Fighting in Built-up Areas* and others. So now we're let loose on the streets trained to the eyeballs, waiting for a suitable opportunity to let everything rip.

A few kills would be nice at this stage, good for morale, good to inject some new life into the jaded senses of the company.[1]

Clarke was describing Belfast nine months after Motorman, when the natal vigour of the operation had subsidised a little. In August 1972 it was in its initial frenzy, bringing a reign of terror unknown in Ireland since the days of the Black and Tans. The savagery of the paratroopers in the Upper Springfield would later cause an officer of the Coldstream Guards to state that, as a British soldier, he was ashamed of the parachute Regiment.[2] (We are reminded of the Auxiliaries of the 1920s – an earlier 'superforce' recruited from ex-British army officers to terrorise anti-British resistance out of Ireland – whose commanding officer, Brigadier F.P. Crozier, resigned in disgust at his men's behaviour.)

What happened after Motorman can be best understood in the context of Kitson's counter-insurgency theories:

In attempting to counter subversion it is necessary to take account of three separate elements. The first two constitute the target proper, that is to say the Party or Front and its cells and committees on the one hand, and the armed groups who are supporting them on the other. They may be said to constitute the head and body of the fish. The third element is the population and this represents the water in which the fish swims. If a fish has got to be destroyed it can be attacked directly by rod or net, providing it is in the sort of position which gives these methods a chance of success. But if rod and net cannot succeed by themselves, it may be necessary to do something to the water which will force the fish into a position where it can be caught. Conceivably it might be necessary to kill the fish by polluting the water.[3]

All attempts to separate the IRA fish from the water had failed. Whitehall decided that it was time to pollute the water, to flatten and disorientate the population until every individual's sole concern was personal survival.

Greater Ballymurphy was placed under 24-hour military occupation by the paratroopers. Patrols of 15 to 20 soldiers, keeping mainly to back-gardens, would race from one position to the next, so that troops were constantly appearing out of entries to search, question, assault and arrest passers-by. The streets were patrolled by Saracen armoured cars,

Browning machine-guns trained on any visible resident, along with smaller Ferrets and the heavy Saladins – small six-wheeled tanks sporting machine-guns and 76mm cannon. Any male leaving the house now risked beatings and humiliation from the patrols that passed at a daytime average of one every five minutes.*

People were dragged up entries or taken off in armoured cars to be subjected to interrogation and grievous assault. It became common for women to walk men through the district in the hope that their presence might have a restraining influence on the troops. More often than not, however, it only added another dimension to their capacity to degrade.

An 18-year-old youth from Ballymurphy Crescent, who was stopped along with his girlfriend at the Bullring, was spreadeagled against a wall for 20 minutes while the soldiers twisted and squeezed his testicles, goading the young woman with lewd remarks about her boyfriend's future virility. Another youth was forced to go on his hands and knees in a patch of mud with the Paras calling him a dog and ordering him to bark at his girlfriend. Resistance of any form to this treatment would have resulted in beatings and arrest – and a charge of assault from which there would be no escape in the courts.

Mass arrests became an hourly occurrence: lines of men and boys, and sometimes women, were frog-marched off under a barrage of boots and rifle-butts to waiting Saracens for 'screening' at military bases. Beatings, burning with cigarettes and matches, mock executions, partial drowning and psychological experiments were an inherent part of this screening. Seventeen-year-old Frankie Cahill described how:

Some time around midnight I was arrested at home and taken to Black Mountain army base ... I was made to stand for an hour with my nose pressed against a wall. Soldiers walking past would kick me or jab me in the ribs with batons or rifles. I was in one of the screening cubicles and two six-foot-six Brits were on guard. The interrogation started off with a Branchman who was notorious – he had previously broken the arms and legs of three boys with an iron bar (one of them later ended up in an asylum). He asked me questions about the IRA. He then said, 'Put your hand behind your back', which I did; and he placed a pistol in it. 'Right,' he said, 'your prints are on that. You're getting done with that.' He then said, 'Go! Make a break for it!'

Next thing was I was placed against the wall and spreadeagled. The Branchman who was wearing big shiny army boots, then came behind me and started systematically kicking me between the legs until I collapsed. And as I collapsed, the two Brits trailed me up again and I was kicked till I collapsed again. This went on for I don't know how long. Eventually, when this produced nothing, a third Brit came in. One of them then took me in a full nelson, folding me in two and sticking my head between my legs until I couldn't breathe any more. My neck and back felt broken; and they held me like this until I became unconscious, then dropped me on the

---

*During a visit to Ballymurphy estate in September 1972 the secretary of the Cork-based Association for Human Rights in the North counted an average of 14 patrols an hour over a period of three days.

floor. As soon as I became conscious again I was beaten back against the wall with batons. And the kicking would start again.

In between they wrapped a towel around my head and poured water over it. As it filled up with water I felt like I was drowning and suffocating until I fell on the floor unconscious. Once I was conscious, they would beat me again with the batons until I was on my feet, and repeat the process again. I lost a stone in weight in seven hours and my clothes were ripped to shreds.

Finally an army officer came in – I had met him before – and said he believed I wasn't involved; but that he felt I could get him information on the IRA, and would give me one week to do it. They drove me back to the Springfield Road and threw me out. When I got home my mother was still waiting up for me and I could feel the tears running down my face, but other than that I was in a state of complete shock. When I took off my clothes my stomach, thighs, everything, were black, not just black and blue, but black from the kicking I'd got.[4]

On one of the other occasions when the same youth was arrested, the soldiers stopped the Saracen after a short distance and told him to get out. He refused. Had he complied, he most likely would have been shot. In September 1974 21-year-old John Walsh of Newtownhamilton brought a case of attempted murder against the British army after he had survived being shot in similar circumstances. In court he told how he had been ordered to climb over a fence, and was shot in the back of the head as he did so. Ex-British army major and Lord Chief Justice, Sir Robert Lowry, refused to believe his story, preferring the army's 'shot while trying to escape' version. In Ballymurphy nobody doubted his story.

All those arrested for screening, most of whom were never charged, were photographed and put on file until Lisburn had files on 500,000 people – one in three of the North's population. The intensity of the operation can be judged by looking at the BTA youth centre with its 1,100 members, where every male over twelve years of age was beaten up and 'screened' during the first few months of Motorman. At times people would disappear for days, with relatives unable to learn anything about their whereabouts from the military. Often those lifted were dropped off after screening in hostile areas to accompanying shouts of 'Here's a fucking Fenian!' Just how many victims of the North's sectarian assassins were delivered to their killers in this way will never be known.

People's cars, homes and family possessions became another target of the Paras in the Upper Springfield. Armoured cars deliberately rammed parked vehicles; furniture, fittings, floors, ceilings and panelling were destroyed during searches, while money and valuables were often stolen; fences were ripped down; clothes lines were snipped at night and clothes trampled, all the women's underwear having first been stolen, leading to much local speculation as to how the Paras entertained themselves back at base; windows were broken by marbles fired from catapults; and air-guns were used as a matter of form against the area's children.

Families were also subjected to continuous night searches and 'head-counts' by face-blackened soldiers, during which details of furniture, the colour of doors and wallpaper, even the make of the TV, were taken. These could later be used to cross-check the ID of persons stopped in the street or taken away for interrogation and screening. But the central purpose of the 'head-counts' was to wear down the community, to expose people to their individual vulnerability, and to break down the IRA's network of safe houses by terrorising people away from providing billets for guerrillas. Random attacks on houses were also carried out.

Approximately 7.45pm on Wednesday, October 25th, I was upstairs running the bath for the children when I heard a commotion. On going downstairs I found my husband and three daughters in the back garden; someone had smashed the dining room window. My daughter, Ann, called for a lantern as it was too dark outside to see anyone.* I saw shadows going up and across the back garden of the derelict house, number 13, towards Glenalina Road. I ran up the side path of number 13 towards the back garden. I met a paratrooper who was coming towards me.

I pointed at him and was going to accuse him of the broken window, when he swore and shoved me bodily away. I struck my head against the gable wall of number 13 and as I bounced back he hit me with the butt of his gun on the head. I fell into a hole left by the electricity men and struck my head for the third time. I blacked out. When I came to I was lying on the settee ... my husband had been beaten up with rifles. I was taken by ambulance to the City Hospital.[5]

As well as the physical controls of forts, ramps, steel and concrete barriers, and spot checkpoints, tight control of information was maintained by the military until the Upper Springfield was effectively cut off from the rest of the world. The Catholic hierarchy, which had opposed the use of schools as First Aid and relief centres during the previous three years, and had banned the civil rights people from church property, were now conspicuous by their silence. Although schools and the grounds of a college of education were under occupation, not a peep was heard, suggesting acquiescence at least, and prior knowledge, on the part of the hierarchy. The media, relying almost exclusively on British army press handouts, further cemented the isolation of the Upper Springfield.

In an effort to destroy all social interaction the Paras complemented their other activities with nightly raids on pubs and social clubs, using the occasions to further terrorise the community. Eighteen-year-old Vera Stone recounted a typical experience:

After the social every week the military wait outside the community centre to arrest the men and abuse the women. They spit at the women and use abusive language. Last night, Saturday, November 4th, we were leaving the centre at 12.30am. The soldiers were there as usual. They waited

*The whole of West Belfast was blacked out at the time. Porch lights were installed by some families, but these were all smashed by the military and people warned that they would be shot if the lights were replaced.

outside until the bulk of the crowd were gone. We were last out. About 35 of us left together. As we were heading home they stopped us and told the boys to get spreadeagled against the wall. They then started to kick them. They then let the fellows go; but as they left they grabbed two of them by the hair.

The girls turned around to protest at this. The soldiers then just took a charge at us, like a riot squad. They swung the butts of their rifles and kicked us and trailed us by the hair. They laughed as they did this, and called us 'Irish whores' and 'Fenian bastards' and said we were 'the type who took 30 bob a turn'. I was kicked to the ground and beaten by a rifle butt. I was then dragged by the hair along the street and my clothes were ruined. My boyfriend shielded me from one blow and he himself received a broken arm and eight stitches in his head. Later on, while walking down Ballymurphy Crescent, a mobile patrol followed us, calling us names. They then stopped us and pulled the fellows into the Saracen and beat them up.[6]

Along with the general campaign of mass intimidation, the military used every presented pretence to shoot up the neighbourhood. A visiting Italian sociologist, who studied the Para campaign from an academic point of view (and was beaten up for his pains), concluded that it was an attempt to arrive at a situation in which 'the pressure of repression becomes so overwhelming as to crack the whole structure of social intercourse within the community'. His conclusions confirmed what many in the Upper Springfield had already guessed:

When community cohesion itself is identified as the main obstacle of the military aim of controlling the civilian population, repression is manipulated to achieve [its destruction], to break the social group into a mere aggregate. The intimidatory techniques of mass disorientation employed by the 1st and 2nd Parachute Regiments [battalions] in the Upper Springfield area fit into this pattern, and seriously impair the ability of the residents to function as a community.

By physically isolating Ballymurphy from the rest of the Catholic community, by isolating areas within the estate itself, by reducing the amount of sociability and disrupting normal patterns of interaction, by constantly threatening residents and by humiliating and degrading individuals and groups, the paratroopers are endeavouring to disintegrate the community.[7]

However, despite threats and assaults on those who protested, community cohesion was not destroyed. On the contrary, a vigorous opposition to the Para campaign, initiated by the BTA's youth workers, was mounted. It was supported by the Belfast-based Association for Legal Justice and the Cork-based Association for Human Rights in the North.

At the outset an attempt was made to get the Catholic Church to raise its voice in defence of those being bludgeoned in the ghettoes. A delegation went to see Cardinal William Conway, Archbishop of Armagh and Primate of All Ireland. It consisted of Sean McCann, chairperson of the Association for Legal Justice and a teacher at St Thomas' School; Sean

Quigley, a young teacher living in Ballymurphy; Lily Quinn of Divismore Park, who had recently been shot in the wrist while lying in her own bed and hospitalised for 24 hours after a Para attack on her home; Anna Andrews, a quiet woman who gave much of her time to the charitable works of the St Vincent de Paul Society; and the author, whom the paratroopers had attempted to crush against a wall with a Saracen after finding documentation of their actions – copies of statements witnessed by the author – during a raid on his lodgings.

The Cardinal's response was to summon to his aid Canon Padraig Murphy, Parish Priest of Greater Ballymurphy, and tell the delegation that he could not speak out against the documented violence and brutality presented by the group for fear of appearing 'sectarian'! He then attempted to dismiss what was happening in Ballymurphy on the grounds that 'I know of far worse cases in other places'. It was a response that left the delegation in a state of disbelief, both of the women in tears, and the gentle Anna Andrews afterwards commenting that 'For the first time in my life I felt like saying "f—" to another human being'. None the less the campaign against the Paras was a sufficient thorn in the British side to warrant a mention in David Barzilay's *The British Army in Ulster*.[8]

With the approach of the winter of 1972 Greater Ballymurphy and neighbouring Turf Lodge, cowed but vengeful, looked every bit a sullen battleground. The streets, littered with the debris of the weeks prior to Motorman, were now also home to the wrecked secondhand cars, smashed by Para vehicles. Whole blocks of flats in Turf Lodge and Moyard lay derelict. (In Moyard 250 of 450 maisonettes were empty shells.) Half of Springhill was wrecked; 20 houses in Ballymurphy estate were uninhabitable, along with several more in New Barnsley and Springfield Park; and several bungalows and the community centre lay gutted in Westrock. Hardly a house was free of bullet-holes. The general atmosphere was one of simmering rage and loathing of the occupying paratroopers. And every now and again the community struck back. Sometimes from the most unlikely quarters.

On a Sunday afternoon in late October one such attack took place at the bottom end of Glenalina Park. Ten soldiers and a Saracen had just turned into the street when a boy of about eight appeared at the corner, ten yards behind the patrol, with an empty whiskey bottle in his hand. He let fly and the bottle shattered on the Saracen. Immediately, the soldiers gave chase, cursing their diminutive assailant who had instantly vanished. Having failed in a search of the gardens and entries, the patrol returned to the Saracen and proceeded to climb aboard.

Just as the last man reached the rear of the vehicle, the same boy appeared, with a second whiskey bottle, which shattered off the Saracen door closest to the retreating soldier. After another angry and thoroughly futile search, the soldiers again arrived back at the Saracen. This time one of them kept a rubber bullet gun trained on the corner as the others, swearing loudly at the entire street, climbed aboard. The rubber bullet man then backed up to the armoured car, closed one of the doors, and gingerly worked his way backwards into the vehicle. Then he dropped the gun to close the door.

And there, lo and behold, was the self same lad with yet another empty whiskey bottle, which, this time round, shattered inside the Saracen. The Paras drove off at speed; and little Goliath went off to where his mother was calling him for his dinner.

The story was added to the communal store of 'Para-stories' and absorbed into the area's collective heritage. By then everybody had their own individual stories, both of events witnessed and personal traumas. And the community had built up a remarkable defence mechanism against the degradations and violence of the military: they somehow laughed it off. People who had suffered the most horrendous brutality could later turn the story into a burlesque of black comedy, so that instead of weakening the community's ties, the violence of the troops was adding yet another hitherto undiscovered fount of strength, against which the Paras had no weapons.

The dogs, too, came out shining. Although many were shot dead by the military, they never gave up. Frothing Beelzebubs, disguised as dozy old mongrels, would spring into howling dementia at the first whiff of khaki, hurling themselves at the Paras and harrying them from one street to the next. Once, the army mounted a special military operation to shoot a particular dog in Whitecliff Crescent. The street was sealed with armoured cars as an officer with a Browning pistol walked up to the snarling enemy and shot it from close range. Unfortunately for the Paras, the dog survived and never forgave.

At a later stage, Harriet Kelly from the Springfield Road had to send her dog underground to save it from a similar fate. The dog, named after a famous IRA guerrilla of the 1920s, was, according to Harriet, high on the shoot-to-kill list:

> If you ask any of the fellas about Dan Breen, they'll tell you. Because he always barked and warned the Boys when the Brits was in. We had no call for nobody so long as there was me and Dan Breen. There's not another dog led the people like he did, day and night, night and day ... Sometimes he'd come in white as a ghost with the vengeance in him. If there was internment camps for dogs, he'd be there ... Dan Breen was on the run from the Paras. He used to follow me out on the binlids and they said they were going to get him. So I went down and got him a licence under a different name – so they wouldn't know it was him ... He gave the Brits hell. Then, one night he never came home and we thought they'd got him. But where was he? He was out with the rest of them vigilanteing – and getting the best of food![9]

Although repression in nationalist areas was acute, with the civilian population taking a bashing, Operation Motorman did little to curb the IRA campaign. Within hours of the disruption of their bases – with the loss of a considerable amount of military hardware – the guerrillas were back on the streets.

Despite the military saturation of cities and towns, and the heavy patrolling of rural areas, the bombing and shooting went on. Although bombings were down (393 explosions in the four months following Motorman as opposed to 500 in the four months prior), the harassment and arrests by the British were merely causing the IRA to change tactics. Instead of prolonged assaults in urban areas, they switched to single-shot sniping and quick ambushes, although lengthy gun-battles would occur from time to time.* In the country, however, the campaign was intensified so that military and RUC bases were under permanent siege.

Meanwhile, the much-lauded British 'hits' were more often than not proving to be either innocent civilians or phantoms. (In one earlier incident in Ballymurphy, in which one Volunteer's ankle was grazed by a bullet, the British claimed eleven hits; in another in which no Volunteers were injured, they claimed that 'several men were seen to fall'. A Volunteer later commented, 'so would you if some bugger was shooting at you'.) Resentment at the brutality, and the killing of many innocent civilians, that accompanied Motorman had also created an increased 'waiting list' of potential Volunteers so that those arrested were quickly replaced.

In the Upper Springfield the intensity of the Para operation forced a temporary scaling down of the campaign – with many of the more well-known Volunteers being transferred to the Falls area – but sporadic sniping attacks went on. On September 17th paratrooper Francis Bell (18) was fatally wounded in Springhill Avenue. He died three days later. Ballymurphy Volunteers also continued to bomb targets across the city. And to suffer casualties.

Of the eleven IRA fatalities in Belfast between August 1st and December 31st 1972, three came from Greater Ballymurphy units.[10] On August 3rd Robert McCrudden (20) was shot dead during a gun-battle with troops in Ardoyne. Eight days later Micky Clarke (22) and Anne Parker (18) of Cumann na mBan, were killed in an explosion in North Howard Street. They had gone to bomb Kernohan's Cash & Carry, but apparently aborted the mission because of the probability of civilian casualties. As they left Kernohan's – directly across the narrow street from a large military base in an old mill – they had to negotiate some ramps, and the bomb exploded. And on September 29th Jimmy Quigley (18), who had Ballymurphy connections, was shot dead in the Lower Falls. He had been waiting in an attic above the chemist's shop to ambush a patrol, when he was taken unawares by troops who came in on his blind side, then threw his body from the attic into the street.

The IRA funerals from Corpus Christi church to Milltown Cemetery became communal shows of defiance against the paratroopers. Uniformed guards of honour, answering to commands in Irish, flanked the coffins, while large crowds marched behind, ignoring the troop satu-

---

*On the night of August 28th, the British army and IRA were engaged in a gun-battle over a one mile and a quarter front in the Upper Falls area of Belfast. During the four-hour battle loyalists, operating from the 'Village', and using rifles and a Bren gun, were also firing on the nationalist area.

ration and intimidation. Women lining the route held up sheets tied between poles and unfolded umbrellas to obscure the view of army photographers. Similar displays of support for the republicans were taking place at other IRA funerals.

However, the British, and other anti-republican forces had been given a major propaganda coup by Bloody Friday, and this was to be followed by a number of other botched IRA operations. On July 31st three car bombs had been driven into the village of Claudy in County Derry. They exploded without warning, claiming nine civilian lives, while on August 22nd a premature explosion at Newry customs killed two IRA Volunteers and seven civilians. (In 1972 IRA-manufactured explosives were proving disastrously unstable. In August alone, there were two further premature blasts, in which another three Volunteers lost their lives.)

The breakdown of the truce and the civilian deaths in subsequent bombings had given the SDLP their opportunity to move. Already the British/IRA negotiations had taken them off the no-talks hook; and they were now anxious for some kind of political development that would deflect support away from the IRA's revolutionary campaign. Lynch in Dublin, horrified at Whitelaw's talks with the Provos, was becoming desperate. With the spectre of republicanism hanging over Leinster House, Dublin needed some radical gesture by the British that would favour the middle-class constitutional nationalists and justify strong repression of the Provisionals in the 26 Counties. That required talking, and to emphasise his government's concern, Lynch sent a helicopter north to ferry SDLP leaders to Dublin to press them with the urgency of a more positive response to Britain.[11] On August 7th, after the Dublin talks, the SDLP met with Whitelaw.

On September 4th Lynch and Heath met at the Munich Olympic Games. Both were anxious that the SDLP should take part in Whitelaw's conference for 'all shades of opinion', due to take place at the end of the month in Darlington in England. However, although they were now openly talking to the British – meeting with Heath in London on September 11th – internment was still too emotive an issue for the SDLP to completely abandon their protest. They refused to participate at Darlington, and published their own publicity document, *Towards a New Ireland*, on September 20th. In it they called for a British declaration of intent to withdraw and, as a short-term measure, a local parliament that would be subordinate to an Anglo-Irish condominium.

The Darlington conference went ahead, boycotted not only by all shades of nationalist opinion but also by Paisley's Democratic Unionist Party, now determined to shine as the most uncompromising of the reactionaries. The three parties taking part – the Unionists, the moribund Northern Ireland Labour Party, and the small centrist Alliance Party – were all pro-Union, yet the conference ended after three days with no more than an agreement to disagree, poor consolation for the besieged Whitelaw.

Nevertheless the British announced their own programme: a plebiscite on the border to take place in early 1973; and local government elections in which all adults would be entitled to vote, using the proportional representation system. On October 30th 1972 Whitelaw published a Green Paper with three options for limited devolved government in the North: either a council with certain executive powers; a convention with given legislative powers; or an executive with a range of legislative responsibilities. The usual guarantees to the loyalist position were given, but there was also a proviso that any arrangements should involve the nationalists – meaning the SDLP – in some form of power-sharing. The Green Paper also stated that:

> A settlement must also recognise Northern Ireland's position within Ireland as a whole ... It is therefore clearly desirable that any new arrangements for Northern Ireland should, whilst meeting the wishes of Northern Ireland and Great Britain, be so far as possible, acceptable to and accepted by the Republic of Ireland.[12]

Lynch grabbed at this 'Irish dimension'. It gave his government another excuse to attack republicans who were a threat to such 'progress'. Already Provisional Sinn Fein's headquarters had been closed down; now the republican leadership came under attack. On November 19th Chief of Staff, Sean Mac Stiofain, was arrested and later jailed for six months for IRA membership. At the end of November the Dublin government, launching what would gradually become an outright assault on free speech and the free flow of information, dismissed the entire governing body of the state-controlled Radio Telefis Eireann broadcasting network for broadcasting a banned interview with Mac Stiofain.

The southern ruling class, wanting nothing but the quiet life and the perks of political and economic power, were keen to keep as much distance as possible between themselves and the North while simultaneously attacking every aspect of the threatening republican base in the South. The task of quelling the Northern uprising would be left to the British with the Dublin government mopping up anti-British (and anti-Irish-ruling-class) resistance south of the border.

Meanwhile, other events in the 26 Counties had enabled Fianna Fail to push a draconian amendment to the Offences Against the State Act through Leinster House. On September 21st and 22nd violent rioting had erupted in Dundalk. On September 23rd a bomb was defused at the local income tax office. On October 28th, three weeks after the closure of Provisional Sinn Fein's office, a bomb was discovered at Connolly Station in Dublin, while incendiaries exploded in four of the city's hotels. On November 1st the UDA carried out a cross-border raid into Donegal, warning the Dublin government to curb the Provisionals. By mid-November Dublin was more than willing to do so. Then came Mac Stiofain's arrest, and a subsequent hunger and thirst strike that threatened to bring open fighting onto the streets of Dublin. Although a wave of republicanism swept the country during the nine days of Mac Stiofain's protest, the government pressed ahead with its amendment.

In the lead-up to the crucial amendment vote it began to seem that the government would lose the vote and a general election would be forced on the country. On the day of the vote, December 1st 1972, two huge bombs exploded in the centre of Dublin. Two people were killed and 127 others injured. In the Dail the amendment passed 69 to 22. Lynch had his bill, tainted with the suspected hand of the British Secret Intelligence Service.

In the North the SDLP were also looking favourably at the proposals in Whitelaw's Green Paper. However, internment was still a thorny question. The British recognised this but were unwilling to discard such a useful weapon without first replacing it with an alternative system of arriving at the same end. Whitelaw's game of releasing small batches of internees, who were promptly replaced by others, was fooling nobody. There were still over 500 nationalists in Long Kesh.[13]

Then a 'solution' was found. On September 22nd it was announced that special Tribunals would be set up at Long Kesh to hear the cases of internees. The Tribunals would have the power to release those it considered 'not guilty'. It was a farcical procedure, designed as a stalling tactic until the system being perfected by the British in the background was ready. But its implementation in October had the desired effect of softening the SDLP's stance. The stage was set for a shift in SDLP policy. On November 24th Lynch met Heath in London to give his seal of approval to the Green Paper. The following day the SDLP Conference voted overwhelmingly to negotiate with the British, internment or not.

A month later, with the mechanics of an internal political debate safely in hand, the British added a new weapon to its repressive arsenal with the approval in Westminster of the Diplock Report. Lord Diplock, a prominent English jurist, had been given the task of devising an effective legal system that could deal 'with terrorist organisations by bringing to book, otherwise than by internment by the Executive, individuals involved in terrorist activities'.[14]

Diplock's proposals would result in a system of jury-less political courts, known since as Diplock Courts, in which British law would be turned on its head to facilitate the needs of the military, and where confessions induced by torture would be sufficient 'evidence' to secure convictions. This was again in line with Kitson's ideas that 'the law should be used as just another weapon in the government's arsenal, and in this case it becomes little more than a propaganda cover for the disposal of unwanted members of the public'.[15]

Diplock also recommended the ending of political status for prisoners of war. The 1973 legislation that followed Diplock's recommendations would mark the opening of Britain's policy of 'criminalising' the war in the North. Henceforth they would pretend to the world that they were no longer dealing with a war of liberation. The IRA campaign would be portrayed as a Mafia-type conspiracy, a problem of 'law and order' or part of the myth of 'international terrorism'. This move by the British would culminate in the republican hunger-strikes of 1980 and 1981.

Meanwhile, despite the best efforts of the British, the IRA was continuing its campaign with spectacular success. On November 27th, as Mac

Stiofain was moved from Dublin's Mater Hospital to military detention at the Curragh, units in the North had announced the arrival of a new weapon. In a series of co-ordinated attacks, Russian-made RPG-7 rockets were fired at British bases and patrols in several locations. In December there were 48 bombs along with further rocket attacks and the continuing sniping and ambushes. Maudling's 'acceptable level of violence' was still a long way off.

The assassinations, too, continued. From August onwards, with nationalist areas now opened up, the loyalists began to widen their campaign. Pubs and homes were bombed, while nationalists were machine-gunned in the streets from passing cars. On September 30th a carbomb exploded at Conlon's Bar in Smithfield, killing Patrick McKee (25) from Ballymurphy and injuring 17 others. Among the injured was Jimmy Gillen, also from Ballymurphy, who would later die from his injuries. By the end of 1972 the year's tally of sectarian killings was 121: 81 nationalists and 40 loyalists (some killed by loyalists for 'fraternising' with nationalists). Hundreds of others had been wounded, the vast majority of them nationalists.

There was also growing evidence of state forces being involved in the loyalists' terror campaign. Dossiers on nationalists and republicans, compiled by the British, were turning up in UDA and UVF hands. The Ulster Defence Regiment, ostensibly under the control of the British army, but in fact heavily infiltrated by the UDA and UVF, was simultaneously becoming intrinsically linked with the public image of loyalist violence. By the end of January 1973, over 130 members had been purged from the regiment – most of them suspected of having links with loyalist guerrilla groups.[16] However, members of the regiment would continue to embarrass the British by regularly surfacing in the Diplock Courts.* There would also be several 'raids' on UDR armouries, in which large numbers of weapons would be handed over to the UDA and UVF.

The sanctioned violence of state forces also continued. Civilians in nationalist areas were being shot at random by troops using the catch-all justification that they were shooting at 'gunmen', while the SAS went on with its covert operations, claiming two more casual victims in the early hours of September 27th. Daniel Rooney (19) and Brendan Brennan (18), were machine-gunned from a passing car in the Upper Falls. Daniel Rooney was killed. A week later the IRA hit back at the Four Square Laundry and the Antrim Road massage parlour.

The aftermath of Motorman also brought a cooling of relationships between the British and the loyalists. The paratroopers had provoked a riot on the Shankill Road on September 6th, demonstrating their antipathy towards all sections of the Irish working class, and a man had been shot. The next day, gun-battles broke out on the Shankill between the Paras and the loyalists. Two loyalists were shot dead – one a UDA man who was also a member of the UDR – and two others were wounded. The

*Members of the UDR, RUC and British army have been convicted of a wide range of anti-nationalist activities including murder, kidnapping, bombing, possession of arms and explosives, assault and attacks on places of religious worship.

trouble continued until the 9th, when the Paras were withdrawn to barracks to let things cool down.

But relationships worsened in October. On the 16th, troops in Saracens ran down and killed two civilians during rioting in East Belfast. Tommy Herron, the local UDA commander, declared war on the British army. For the next two nights, fierce gunfire rocked the east of the city, and the Shankill and Sandy Row areas, leaving two more loyalist civilians dead. Herron's two-day war was undoubtedly one of the factors leading to his assassination at the hands of British agents in September 1973. It also drew considerable middle-class support away from the UDA and put further pressure on the British to come up with a political initiative.

Herron's war was greeted in Ballymurphy with not a little hope. Perhaps the loyalist working class was beginning to realise that, whatever reason the British had for being in Ireland, it was patently not to promote their specific interests. It was a false hope, but it temporarily loosened the burden of repression, as did the local shows of defiance and the IRA's daring 'digs' at the Paras.

With the level of military saturation in the area, it seemed impossible that anyone would shoot at the troops, but shoot they did. Sniping operations, many in broad daylight, were invariably followed by chases through the district, with heavy fire directed from Para rifles and the machine-guns of the armoured cars. But when the 'Boys' got away it was all the more wonder, and morale went up a rung or two. It was even worth the savage house searches and mass arrests that followed. And besides, the British were still being hammered everywhere else.

The flares that lit up the Ballymurphy sky, as a lone night sniper darted through the City Cemetery under a hail of tracer bullets, symbolised the whole war. The 'Boys' had luck, local knowledge and a growing expertise on their side, whereas the British, with all their technology and military might, were the clumsy prisoners of the wrong kind of military tradition.

The situation on the streets of the Upper Springfield was also symbolic: the type of mass repression needed to put the lid on the IRA campaign was beginning to prove counter-productive, and the British were aware that there were more ways than one to lose a war. There was already the lobbying campaign and the publication by Amnesty International of the dossier compiled by the BTA youth workers.

There was also a strike in September by teachers at St Peter's against the military occupation of the school. On September 21st shots fired at a British position in the school hit the science block. The teachers walked out, refusing to continue while children were effectively used as hostages. The Irish National Teachers' Organisation called a strike while local parents simultaneously withdrew their children from the school. The political flak forced the British to announce on September 30th that they would quit the school before the end of term. Ballymurphy was again enraged that the hierarchy had not spoken out, that powerful political influences remained silent, leaving the teachers to protect the interests of working-class children. Joe McGlade of the BTA remarked acidly, 'It wouldn't take the bishops long to raise a howl if the Brits were in schools up the Malone Road' (a suburban district of Belfast populated by the upper middle class).

By then Joe McGlade's remark was a barometer of a wider resentment within the area. Not only were the people totally alienated from the British state and its paraphernalia, but they were also becoming increasingly disgusted by the behaviour of the nationalist middle class, the Catholic hierarchy and the Dublin government. Lynch's collaboration with the British was causing the nationalist working class – and a proportion of the middle class – to see Lynch and his followers as little more than a junior partner of the British. Young people from Ballymurphy, when they encountered Irish army patrols at the border, were now referring to them as 'Irish Brits'.

The nationalist working class was moving to the left. It may not have been an academically doctrinaire position; but it was real. The people of Ballymurphy could, without any qualms, proclaim in 1972 that their goal was a 32-County socialist republic. The Republican Movement, an inherent part of the community, was moving in the same direction. The earlier confusion, evidenced when people in Ardoyne were warned to watch out for 'communists' but work for socialism, was now giving way to a coherent developing political ideology which was coming from the bottom up.

Opposition to the paratroopers' presence in Ballymurphy, and to army brutality in general, continued to mount throughout October and November. On October 17th 1,000 people marched through the Upper Springfield in a rally organised by the Officials' Republican Clubs. On November 9th the community was further incensed by the random shooting of 15-year-old Micky O'Rawe and 51-year-old Ruby Mulholland on the waste ground below St Aiden's school. Ruby Mulholland, a mother of eleven, had been shopping at the Whiterock/Springfield junction and was on her way back to Turf Lodge, taking the short cut along 'Shepherd's Path'. Micky O'Rawe was coming along behind her, having just come from Whiterock post office. Ruby Mulholland remembered hearing a bang.

> I asked the wee lad was it shooting. I told him to keep his head down going over Shepherd's Path. We just got over Shepherd's Path when there was another bang and then another one. The wee lad said, 'Missus, I'm shot!' As I turned around, I seen the blood coming out of my hand and I realised I was hit too. The bullet went in my back and through my arm ... The Brits who shot us had been standing on the Whiterock Road when I came out of the Spar to cross the field.[17]

In a series of confused statements the military first claimed that a youth had aimed a pistol at them, so they'd shot him. A woman who had gone to his aid had picked up the fallen pistol, and they shot her too. When asked about the whereabouts of the pistol, they changed the story. Ruby Mulholland now became an innocent bystander, while the woman with the pistol, unnoticed by the soldiers, had managed to escape across the flat waste ground to Turf Lodge! Such shootings had now become so common that 65 Catholic priests issued a statement in Belfast on November 20th, roundly condemning the military for gunning down 'innocent and unarmed civilians, regardless of age or sex', while in and out of uniform.[18]

The groundswell of clerical protest, added to Ballymurphy's – and the Shankill's – campaign against the Para outrages, was a signal to the British that they were overstepping themselves. The blanket repression was becoming a liability and would have to be conducted with more subtlety. As a 'concession' it was announced on November 25th that, following the 'success of Motorman', 1,000 troops were to be withdrawn from the North. Among them would be 1st Para, who had caused so much bother on the Shankill. When they left at the end of the month 2nd Para were also pulled out of Ballymurphy.

The incoming regiment, the Coldstream Guards, found an angry and united community, more anti-British than ever, and only too willing to go on with the war, while the dogs that had survived the Para dog-shoots were just itching for revenge.

Motorman had failed to destroy the IRA. It had failed to break up the cohesion of the community, having been foiled by the earlier actions of the state, which had in fact cemented together one of the most fragmented communities in the North. Those earlier experiences of extreme stress had been the source of Ballymurphy's strength in the face of Motorman. Somewhere, the theoreticians of the British army had gotten it wrong. In a later study of Ardoyne after it too had been subjected to Para brutalisation, English sociologist Frank Burton noted the same communal resilience. Ardoyne, he concluded,

is capable of 'soaking up' the attempts that are made by both the Protestant and British military forces to break its own military activists. The community reaction to a number of serious confrontations has not produced a chaotic or anomic breakdown. Rather, it has resisted enough of the external pressure ... to make the continuation of the war a possibility.[19]

Phoenix-like, community life took a jolt forward as soon as the Paras left the Upper Springfield, and the IRA ambushes went on, with another British army fatality on December 8th. Two shots, fired through a rear door of a Saracen as it travelled along Westrock Drive on December 6th had wounded three members of the Royal Green Jackets. For Rifleman John Josebury (18), the wounds proved fatal.

Despite Motorman, 1972 had cost the British dearly: 149 members of the occupation forces, including 106 British soldiers (excluding UDR members), had been killed, hundreds of others had been wounded. At home and abroad, there was mounting pressure to get out of this war that had already left over 600 dead and another 10,000 wounded.

Whitelaw's assurances and 'success' statistics were lost in the face of the sustained attack on the state. As for his notions of a new Stormont? Those were greeted in the Upper Springfield as the gobbledegook of a man who didn't know what he was talking about.

References

1. A.F.N. Clarke, *Contact* (Secker & Warburg, London, 1983), p. 43.
2. Conversation with author during person check, 1973.
3. Frank Kitson, *Low Intensity Operations – Subversion, Insurgency and Counter-Insurgency* (Faber and Faber, London, 1971), p. 49.
4. Frankie Cahill (17) of Ballymurphy (statement taken by author in 1972).
5. Lily Quinn of Ballymurphy (statement taken by author in 1972).
6. Vera Stone of Ballymurphy (statement taken by author in 1972).
7. Dissertation by Paulo Pistoi.
8. David Barzilay, *The British Army in Ulster* (Century Services Ltd, Belfast, 1973), p. 215.
9. Harriet Kelly of Springfield Road (1987 Interview).
10. National Graves Association *Belfast Graves* (AP/RN Print, Dublin, 1985).
11. *Fortnight,* Belfast, August 2nd 1972.
12. *The Future of Northern Ireland* (Discussion Paper, Northern Ireland Office, HMSO, London, 1972), p. 33.
13. Kevin Kelley, *The Longest War* (Brandon, Dingle, 1982), p. 187.
14. Diplock Report, December 1972.
15. Kitson, *Low Intensity Operations,* p. 69.
16. *Sunday World,* Dublin, June 22nd 1980.
17. Ruby Mulholland of Turf Lodge (1988 Interview).
18. *Belfast Telegraph,* November 20th 1972.
19. Frank Burton, *The Politics of Legitimacy – Struggles in a Belfast Community* (London, 1978), p. 3.

12

Deadlock

In the north the New Year began with the killing of 31-year-old father of two, Jack Mooney from Whiterock Road. He had been travelling to work at the Rolls-Royce factory in Dundonald in the early hours of January 2nd, when the car was machine-gunned by loyalists. Five others, including the dead man's father, were lucky to escape. It seemed that the assassinations were set to continue at the 1972 level.

Then, out of the blue, as the Upper Springfield prepared to bury one more victim of the Troubles, Tommy Herron issued a statement announcing that the UDA had ordered the assassins 'on both sides' to stop. If they did not, he said, they would face 'the full wrath of the UDA'. And it worked. Between then and January 29th no more nationalists were assassinated. But why did the UDA call off its own killer-squads in mid strike? And then return to the offensive on January 29th?

The explanation lay in the tensions then rupturing within the UDA. Charles Harding-Smith, former UDA commander in Woodvale, had been imprisoned for some time in London awaiting trial on arms charges. In December he was acquitted in a surprise verdict, and returned to Belfast. He was aghast at the state in which he found the UDA. Not only were many of the local commanders extensively involved in racketeering, but the leadership had fallen into the hands of a group of men with extremely dangerous ideas. Whereas Jim Anderson was chairperson, the real power lay with Tommy Herron, East Belfast commander; Dave Fogel, commander in Woodvale; Ernest 'Duke' Elliot, Fogel's second in command; and a battery of local leaders put into position by the new leadership.

Herron, Fogel and Elliot had initiated contacts with both the Official IRA and a number of small left-wing groups in the 26 Counties and were talking about unity of the Northern working class in the context of a Six-County state – which fell in line with the Officials' 'stages theory', and was not too far off the Provisionals' *Eire Nua* policy which envisaged a nine-county regional parliament for the North where loyalists would not feel as threatened as they might by the concept of a united Ireland. The new direction of the UDA leadership was also anathema to the British secret service, which had already infiltrated several sections of the wider organisation. The distaste of both of these elements cost 'Duke' Elliot his life on December 7th, when he was shot by a UDA unit loyal to Harding-Smith.

Still, Herron, unaware of the extent of the danger, went ahead with his calling off of the assassins a month later, possibly believing that the IRA had killed Elliot. It was a gesture which he hoped would encourage the

154

Officials into taking on the Provisionals in the nationalist working-class areas. With the defeat of the Provos, both the UDA and the Officials could then work on building unity of the working class within the context of a Northern state.

It was all pie in the sky that could not possibly have worked for a number of reasons. First, the Officials were in no position to defeat the Provisionals. Secondly, the bulk of the nationalist working class did not see any future in a Six-County state that would still have its inbuilt loy-alist majority. Thirdly, Herron could never have sold his ideas to the loyalist working class and, fourthly, the designs of British intelligence were already turning against him in the person of Harding-Smith.

On January 10th 1973, a week into Herron's ceasefire, Harding-Smith nudged Anderson to one side by creating joint-chairpersonship of the UDA and assuming one of the positions himself. Three days later, Dave Fogel was taken before Harding-Smith by some of the supporters of the new boss. Realising how close he was to joining Elliot, Fogel fled to England on January 22nd and sold his story to the *Sunday Times*. He talked of a 'cruel and vicious' smear campaign being directed against Herron, and also of the leftward drift that had been Elliot's undoing.

> Ernie had helped me train the Woodvale men. He had been our press officer. He had been the man who always encouraged me to think in terms of politics. When I first met him I was a conservative, but he made me more left-wing. He used to walk around Woodvale with Che Guevara books stuffed in his pockets.[1]

Herron was now also the victim of a British Psyops smear campaign. But, whereas Harding-Smith was in full control of the West Belfast UDA, the commanders in the East still remained loyal to Herron. Eventually a compromise was reached. Herron would remain in control of East Belfast, but would accept Harding-Smith's overall command of the organisation and end his flirtation with the nationalists – which also meant abandoning his ceasefire. At the end of January, with Harding-Smith back at the helm, the assassins were let loose again, and five nationalists were killed in a few days, one in a grenade attack on a busload of nationalist workers.

The resumption of sectarian attacks by loyalists forced the British into making a token gesture. On February 3rd 1973 two loyalists were interned, the first in half a century. In the East, where Herron was in control, the UDA took on the British army in a wild gun-battle, and a further seven nationalists were assassinated over the coming week-end. Harding-Smith refused to sanction any action against the British in the West of the city. On February 7th, the UDA, Loyalist Association of Workers (LAW) and Craig's Vanguard sponsored a one-day strike which triggered off riots and more gun-battles in several loyalist areas. However, loyalists continued to be interned in a sop to the SDLP until eventually there were 60 in Long Kesh – along with 600 interned republicans!

At the same time Harding-Smith consolidated his position within the

UDA, his supporters setting up an alternative headquarters on the Shankill Road on June 7th 1973 in opposition to the existing one on the Newtownards Road in East Belfast. But the East still stayed with Herron. Eight days later, in the early morning, two gunmen turned up at Herron's home where they ran upstairs and shot dead Michael Wilson, Herron's brother-in-law and bodyguard, thinking they had got Herron himself. The two gunmen escaped on foot through the loyalist Braniel estate. The car that brought the assassins to Braniel had been hijacked on the Shankill Road. None the less the UDA gave Wilson a big funeral, the mourners being led by Harding-Smith himself, and Paisley presiding over the burial. Publicly the UDA blamed the IRA, but nobody took the claim seriously.

Then on Friday, September 14th, the East Belfast commander was kidnapped close to the Newtownards Road headquarters of the UDA. When his body was found at Drumbo two days later, a legally-held gun was still in its holster. Paisley and other loyalist leaders blamed British intelligence, correctly, although the evidence suggests that the actual killers were from the West Belfast UDA. British involvement in the killing, either direct or indirect, was confirmed by undercover agent Albert Baker in 1974. UDA leaders, he said, were untouchable provided they followed British orders, 'which was not the case with Tommy Herron whom the SAS have killed'.

Eventually, the UDA gunned down Harding-Smith in January, and again in February, 1975. On his release from hospital after the second attempt on his life, the UDA commander spent two days living at Tennent Street RUC Barracks before he and his family slipped unnoticed out of the country amid suggestions that he had been a British agent for over two years. Meanwhile, there would be no more talk in Woodvale or East Belfast of Che Guevara. And the assassinations would continue to serve their purpose – along with the overt and covert killings carried out by the British army – of terrorising the nationalist community. It was a terror that would hit Ballymurphy several times during 1973.

On February 18th, less than seven weeks after the murder of Jack Mooney, David McAleese (38) of Ballymurphy Parade was one of two postmen shot down within yards of a military observation post on the roof of a derelict mill on the Falls Road. The two men were on their way home from work when a car pulled out from Northumberland Street and stopped beside them. A man jumped out and fired on them with a Sterling sub-machine-gun. He then ran to the fallen men and fired several more bursts into their twisting bodies. The coolness with which the murders were carried out suggested that the killers were fully aware that the sentry in the overhead post was nothing more than a tailor's dummy, information that would have been available only to British forces.

The next Ballymurphy victim was 45-year-old David Glennon, whose hooded body was found dumped in a car in Summer Street in the Oldpark area on Thursday, March 8th, the day of the British government's plebiscite on the future of the North. As the predictable result –

57 per cent voting to remain British, and a general nationalist boycott of the affair – was announced, the Glennon family and their neighbours went into mourning.

Twelve weeks later, on May 31st, Gerard Barnes (31), of Springhill Crescent, was passing McGlade's pub in Donegall Street when a 20lb bomb was thrown from a passing car into the bar. The pub was extensively damaged, many people were injured, and Gerard Barnes was killed outright.

From then until August 10th, the Upper Springfield was spared from the hand of the assassins. But only to suffer a double blow that Friday night. Shortly after 8pm on August 10th, Joseph Murphy (30), and his pregnant wife Mary, were returning home along Kennedy Way after visiting a relative in hospital. Without warning a hijacked taxi with two young men in it pulled up alongside them, the passenger firing a pistol through the open window. Joseph Murphy fell wounded on the pavement, whereupon the taxi stopped, and the gunman got out to pump more bullets into his victim's head. When news of the killing reached Ballymurphy Joseph Murphy senior collapsed and died of a heart attack. The double funeral through the streets of Ballymurphy once again united the community in tragedy, stirring the emotions of even the most battle-hardened of a people long inured to the consequences of war.

* * *

Since the beginning of the year the IRA campaign had maintained a relentless ferocity, with the weeks punctuated by bombings, grenade, rocket and landmine attacks, ambushes, gun-battles and sniping. Although hampered by continuing arrests and the loss of the No-Go areas, the Volunteers were clearly far from being out of business. They were also improving their armoury and operational sophistication and proving that, no matter what efforts the British made, they were capable of coming up with an antidote.

In the border areas, particularly in South Armagh, the military travelled out from their bases at their grave peril, being mainly serviced by helicopter as they lay dug in behind fortifications of concrete, sandbags, rocket-wire and machine-gun posts. Despite painstaking searches of vehicles, perennial spot-checkpoints, control zones in cities and towns, and the presence of tens of thousands of armed men, the IRA slipped in and out to plant their bombs and incendiaries, rob banks and post offices, fight lengthy gun-battles with troops or loyalists, even visit other Volunteers in prison!

The quality of IRA explosives was also improving as was the reliability of timing and detonating systems. Premature explosions were gradually becoming a thing of the past, with a resultant reduction in civilian and Volunteer casualties. Inadequate warnings, however, caused six civilian deaths in an explosion in Coleraine on June 12th.

The IRA had also taken the war to Britain. On March 8th 1973, the day of the foregone conclusion of who wanted to remain British and who did not, Volunteers had set off a chain of bombs across the North, shot dead a soldier at a polling booth, and to emphasise their disgust at the British refusal to treat the Irish people as one entity in any such poll, they had hit London. One man died of a heart attack and 200 people were injured when the Old Bailey and Great Scotland Yard, both chosen as symbolic targets, were blasted by car-bombs.

When the bombing teams were picked up soon afterwards by British intelligence, 19-year-old Gerry Kelly and 29-year-old Joseph Armstrong from the Upper Springfield were found to be among them. So too were two young sisters from Andersonstown – Marion and Dolours Price – who would later embark on a 206-day force-feeding hunger-strike, along with Gerry Kelly and Hugh Feeney, to support their demand for repatriation to a prison in the North.

Nevertheless the British pushed ahead with their plans for an end to Direct Rule, which had simply exacerbated the problems they faced in attempting to govern the North. On March 20th they published a White Paper which opted for a new 78-seat single-chamber Assembly at Stormont with an Executive that would ensure power-sharing on a meaningful level. The Assembly would be elected by proportional representation; and it would form links with Leinster House through a Council of Ireland. Besides the overriding aim of defeating republicanism, the Council of Ireland would also be used as a means of securing 'the acceptance of the present status of Northern Ireland'.

The Alliance Party, who were expected to play a central role in the new developments, were the only group in the North to openly welcome the White Paper's proposals. The response of Brian Faulkner's Unionist Party, the SDLP and the (Officials') Republican Clubs was one of grudging acceptance. People's Democracy and the Provos unequivocally rejected the document, which was, after all, principally aimed at stabilising the very state they sought to overthrow.

But the most ominous signs for the British came from the far right. Paisley described the White Paper as 'an act of treachery', while Craig responded with the formation of the Vanguard Unionist Progressive Party, backed by the UDA and the Loyalist Association of Workers, which, he pledged, would oppose the proposals tooth and nail in alliance with Paisley's DUP. At the end of April, another dismal note for British policy was sounded by the Grand Orange Lodge who also came out against the White Paper. Whitelaw went ahead regardless. Elections for the Assembly would be held on June 28th.

In the South a new government was settling into office. In February Lynch, hoping to catch the potential Fine Gael/Labour alliance off guard, had called a snap general election for the 28th of the month. It misfired when the Coalition, with a narrow majority, pushed Fianna Fail out of government for the first time since 1954. Fine Gael, however, with its anti-republican Civil War background, was even more anxious than Lynch to ensure that the North's future lay within a context of British rule and reform, and keep unity well off the agenda. Unlike Fianna Fail, there were no ritualistic demands for a British declaration of intent to withdraw. The new Taoiseach, Liam Cosgrove, leaned in the opposite direction, insisting that any move towards ending partition would do nothing more than 'dangerously exacerbate tension and fears'.[2]

In the months prior to the Assembly elections the British made a concerted effort to cripple the IRA's military capacity so that the elections could take place as smoothly as possible. In March British intelligence scored a major coup when the gun-running ship *Claudia*, with Joe Cahill and five tons of Libyan arms aboard, was captured by the Irish navy. But, despite numerous claims of having the IRA on the run or on the verge of defeat, there were few other signs of a British victory. By election day on June 28th, IRA bombing operations for the first half of 1973 had involved the use of 48,000 lbs of explosives, while gun and rocket-attacks, and the introduction of mortars, were still pinning thousands of troops down across the whole of the North.

On June 28th the Six Counties went to the polls with the British hanging their hopes on the emergence of a strong middle ground. Shortly before the elections Provisional Sinn Fein supplemented their 1971 *Eire Nua* policy document with a further paper entitled *The Quality of Life in Ireland* covering environment and social welfare issues not previously covered in *Eire Nua*. At the same time they again drew attention to the proposals in the original document, which had been revised in June 1972, and called for a boycott of the Assembly elections.

Eire Nua had envisaged a single-chamber federal parliament for the whole of Ireland, with four provincial and reasonably autonomous parliaments based on the ancient provinces of Ireland. It also proposed a massive decentralisation of power through local community councils, public ownership of financial institutions and large industries, the large-scale development of co-operatives, and an end to foreign ownership of Irish farmland.

Gradually, in the intervening years, Sinn Fein has transformed the original *Eire Nua* into a strong left-wing political programme, always insisting however, that they move slowly 'to bring people along with us, because you cannot create a new society without mass support providing the muscle to do it'.[3] However, in the war-weary days leading up to the June elections of 1973 *Eire Nua* and the Provo/PD call for a boycott went generally unheeded. Internment, imprisonment, military saturation, the state of siege imposed by Motorman, and the prospects of an indefinite war had sapped the will of the ghettoes sufficiently to make the White Paper proposals – with their apparent promise of a peaceful step towards the national aspiration – at least worth a try.

Even in the staunchest of republican areas the boycott failed. But the election results provided little promise of a peaceful transition towards any future that would involve either power-sharing or a Council of Ireland. Of the 78 seats, unionists loyal to Faulkner won 23, the SDLP took 19, the Craig–Paisley alliance had 15, anti-White Paper unionists won two, and the Northern Ireland Labour Party had one seat. The Republican Clubs failed to have a single candidate elected. With a 27-seat bloc absolutely opposed to the White Paper, Faulkner would have to form a coalition with the SDLP and Alliance.

During the next two months, as the Orangemen marched throughout the North, and an angry nationalist population commemorated the second anniversary of internment, the Stormont Assembly made no progress, many of its sessions ending up in inter-unionist uproar. The IRA meanwhile planted a further 167 bombs. At the end of August an impatient Heath flew to Belfast to demand the establishment of an Executive. However, it took three more months of political wranglings before Whitelaw was in a position to announce the formation of an eleven-person executive-designate with six unionists, four SDLP and one Alliance. Faulkner was to be Chief Executive, and Gerry Fitt, the SDLP leader, would be his deputy.

Plans were also announced for a London–Dublin–Belfast conference to arrange the Council of Ireland. The ensuing four-day talks took place at Sunningdale in England, beginning on December 6th, and a vague deal was struck on the Council of Ireland. In it the status of the North was guaranteed; the British agreed to be guided in the future by the wishes of the Northern majority in relation to partition; and a commission was set up to study methods of combating the IRA. The components of the power-sharing Executive – the Faulknerites who had sworn never to share power with those bent on demolishing the state (which included the SDLP), and the SDLP who had vowed not to participate in Northern institutions until internment ended – returned to Belfast to sell their 'victories' to their respective electorates.

Meanwhile, prospects for the deal were already looking dismally bleak. On December 5th the RUC had to be called to put down an inter-unionist riot at Stormont. The following day, as the Sunningdale conference got under way, 600 delegates from the anti-White Paper unionists, Vanguard, the Orange Order and the DUP formed the United Ulster Unionist Council whose sole purpose was to destroy the power-sharing Stormont Assembly and the Council of Ireland. The IRA also continued to oppose the deal through its military campaign, once more extending its bombing operations to England over the Christmas period.

At the close of 1973 the British were nowhere near achieving their military solution despite the massive resources poured into the war since Motorman. All they had succeeded in doing, other than the short-term gain of several hundred arrests and internments, was to add to the bitterness, resentment and alienation of the nationalists. Politically the situation looked no better. The power-sharing experiment had produced a forced result that may have looked good on paper, but was already feeling the dead weight of the Neanderthals on its back. Meanwhile the bodies were mounting up. The toll by the end of the year was 250 people killed during 1973, with thousands of others injured. Of those killed 79 were members of the occupation forces.

* * *

The changes that had occurred in Greater Ballymurphy by the beginning of 1973 were phenomenal, and perhaps best illustrated by one small event. Towards the end of 1972 the Housing Executive had proposed that the area be renamed as this might help to remove the 'stigma' attached to 'Ballymurphy' over the previous two decades. As this would primarily affect Ballymurphy estate, the suggestion was put directly to the BTA, who found the notion quite incomprehensible. 'Stigma? What stigma?' they wanted to know: Ballymurphy was a name to be proud of. Long gone were the days when 12,000 families had passed through the estate in 14 years. Even in Moyard and Springhill, two estates still having serious teething problems, there was no question of wanting to belong to any entity other than Ballymurphy.

Along with the sense of community nurtured by the Troubles, many of the area's earlier problems were beginning to disappear. With housing allocation no longer under the control of the authorities, there was an end to the policy of dumping problem families in the area. Also, as it was now a case of first come first served, local knowledge played a major part in the acquisition of a house so that an extended family network began to spread through the area, adding to its stability. The younger families were simultaneously moving away from delivering to Ireland masses of sons and daughters, and this helped to alleviate the problem of over-crowding. Between 1971 and 1973 the average household in Ballymurphy estate had dropped from 6.5 to 5.7,[4] and this pattern was to continue, giving a 1983 average of 4.5.[5]

At the same time, partly due to the controlling effects of the extended families, partly due to the diversions offered by the Troubles, and partly due to the policing of the IRA, petty crime was virtually absent. With the area entrenched in a protracted guerrilla war, and outsiders terrified of its very name, Ballymurphy paradoxically offered its residents one of the safest urban environments in Europe. The war aside of course. It also offered a caring mantle of some 80 community groups which ensured to the best of their abilities that everyone's needs were accommodated.

None the less, the months of brutal repression had taken their toll. A number of older community groups, which had to weather the brunt of the hurricane since 1969, were beginning to show signs of strain. The BTA in particular had taken a severe battering, and would never recover its former dynamism. Plagued by in-fighting and the regular long absences of a chairperson through whom all business was transacted, the organisation had lost its direction and its morale was at an all-time low. Meetings had become irregular, and much of the administration had been passed over to Mark Duffy, one of its treasurers. Frank Cahill's release from Long Kesh in October 1972 had injected a fresh burst of life, but it was short-lived, although it did manage to revive the BTA's building programme and bring Spencer back to complete the Ballymurphy survey.

Motorman had also left a residue of other problems. Military repression was still rampant, but there was no longer any opportunity for the young people to vent their anger as they had during the riots of 1970. Instead, the anger became frustration and finally turned in on itself.

Although the pressure had eased a little,* the aftertaste was now running its own course, with gang warfare erupting between supporters of the Officials and Provisionals. Discos became major flashpoints, and in the Upper Springfield, that primarily meant trouble for the BTA.

The spring of 1973 became increasingly a time of guns about the youth centre. Then, on May 7th, a major riot left the place in a shambles and triggered off several days of gunfights before the youth workers managed to negotiate a ceasefire through the local leadership of the Provisionals and Officials. Meanwhile, two other discos in the area were closed for similar reasons: one in St Thomas' School when two sub-machine-guns, eight pistols and a nail bomb were discovered among the clientele; and a second in St Aidan's when young men from each side turned up with Armalite rifles and Thompsons. Deducing that the time was not right for the theoretical niceties of youth work, all three centres fled post haste from their duties to the youth of the Upper Springfield, one worker commenting drily that 'bored teenagers are better than dead teenagers'. Two months later the BTA youth workers resigned and moved to 42 Ballymurphy Road to establish the '42' project, which soon became a major focus for political and social action within the area. Frank Cahill, who had been central to most of Ballymurphy's earlier political struggles, became an integral part of the new project.**

At about the same time, Ballymurphy became embroiled in the reconciliation 'industry'. The passage of the Social Need (Grants) Bill of April 1970 had opened the way for the Community Relations Commission to fund 'get together' camps, organised on a 60:40 per cent ratio of loyalists and nationalists. It proved an irresistible incentive.

This is not to suggest that those engaged in the new industry were motivated simply by the availability of funds. Many firmly believed that there was some not too clearly defined intrinsic value in bringing people of opposing political beliefs together, especially if they were children, who, the theory went, were malleable and open to change. Among them were the Shankill and Ballymurphy youth workers, who spent the next several years discovering the improbability of the theory. Although many good relationships developed among the adults involved, and hundreds of children enjoyed the holidays, many of the early enthusiasts

*The easing of pressure did not bring about a lessening of the brutality meted out to those arrested. An example was the treatment that cost 16-year-old Joseph Duffy of Ballymurphy Crescent his life in May 1974. While being beaten and interrogated at the Oaks military base, the brother of the BTA treasurer was hung by the feet from some beams. He was kicked back and forth by a group of soldiers. Many of the blows landed on his head. He died of a brain haemorrhage a week later.

**In the early 1970s, Sinn Fein was little more than a propaganda voice for the IRA. It was not a sophisticated political force in itself, and certainly saw no point in involving itself in grassroots working class politics. Indeed, in the early part of the decade, the type of working class agitation being undertaken in Ballymurphy was described as 'counter-revolutionary' by the people who would later, as prominent members of Sinn Fein, become principal advocates of republican involvement in such work.

later concluded that when people are ready to talk, they will; that reconciliation is not something that happens in a vacuum, but relies on the appropriate political climate.

One memorable example of the short-livedness of children's camp reconciliation occurred in the summer of 1974. A party of Shankill Road children were dropped by coach in their home patch after spending a week in Donegal with the Ballymurphy children still on the coach. No sooner had they disembarked than the home environment swallowed them up complete. 'Fenians!' they screamed, sending the coach into a healthy retreat down the Shankill away from the hail of bricks and bottles that had materialised from nowhere.

On another occasion a mini-bus from Ballymurphy had just dropped two Shankill Road men home when it broke down across the main Shankill artery as the pubs were depositing their customers onto the streets. One of those on board, Jim Carlin from Whiterock, had recently survived a loyalist assassination attempt, and his immediate response was to grab a hurley (symbol of Irish nationalism) from the floor of the bus and, guided by the old refrain that attack is the best form of defence, head for the door. Hardly the reactions of a man who might have felt that his good intentions would be understood and appreciated on the Shankill Road. The other three on board, who included the present writer, had a hell of a job immobilising Jim (while still blocking one half of the Shankill Road) and convincing him to sit at the wheel while they 'casually' pushed the bus across the Peace Line to the Springfield Road. Straight into a conveniently-timed exchange of gunfire between the British army and the IRA.

However, in 1973 the idea was still novel, and a perfect site was apparently available outside Cootehill in County Cavan. Some old coach-houses and grooms' quarters, belonging to Dublin's Department of Lands, lay empty and disused. There was a great deal of local enthusiasm for a Shankill-Ballymurphy camp, and all that was required was a caretaker lease on the property. From a government whose rhetoric on reconciliation had been loud, that would surely be forthcoming. In fairness, the Department didn't refuse, it just ignored the request. The only sign of Dublin having ever received any correspondence was a token visit to the Shankill Road by Dr Garret FitzGerald, the Minister for Foreign Affairs. The camps were facilitated by a school in Donegal and by the Cork-based Association for Human Rights in the North.

Immediately after the camps, there was a neighbourhood ceasefire in the Upper Springfield. A community festival had been organised for August 12th–19th, to restore morale after the bleak months of Motorman. As a result of an evil collective sense of humour on the part of the organisers, Charlie Heath of Westrock, the committee chairperson, was despatched to the Taggart to make peace with the major. He returned railing at the iniquities of the state and how visits to the Taggart were 'bad for the bangers'.

'NAME!' the major had bawled as soon as Charlie walked into his office. 'Charlie Heath,' Charlie had replied, 'I'm here to see if there could be a ceasefire during our festival.' 'ADDRESS!' the major yelled; and the discussion continued in that vein. But in the end there was an unspoken agreement, and neither the IRA nor the British engaged in hostilities during festival week. A second spin-off of the festival was to bind together the 80-odd local community groups into a solid network that has since weathered well the test of time.

Springhill Community House used the festival to launch a community theatre. A month earlier Des Wilson, writing in the '42'-based community newspaper, *Spotlight*, had announced the formation of the company, which intended to bring theatre back to where it belonged – with the people who suffered the ills and injustices of society. 'Remember Sam Thompson,' he had written, 'some people were afraid of Sam Thompson ... and yet, all Sam did to frighten them was to write plays.'

During festival week the People's Theatre came on stage for the first time, delighting packed houses in St Bernadette's school with presentations that might well have had a similar effect on those who were intimidated by Sam Thompson. The Catholic hierarchy could only have been dismayed – that man Wilson had taken to the stage, accompanied and supported by none other than Noelle Ryan, another irritant they had vainly hoped to get shot of.

In 1971, after five years as a Parish Worker in Liverpool, Noelle Ryan had returned to Dublin where she assisted in a holiday scheme catering for Belfast children. Afterwards she wrote to Bishop Philbin, saying that she would like to work in Belfast if he could find a place for her. The Bishop suggested she go to Ballymurphy. The Parish Priest, 59-year-old Canon Padraig Murphy, who found all intrusions in his patch obnoxious, agreed under the circumstances to a month's 'trial period', although he could see no possible role for a parish worker, and a woman worker at that!

The month, however, became eight months, and by the time the PP got around to telling her she had to go, the Dublin woman was up to her neck in the activities of Des Wilson's Community House and loving it. So, in defiance of the PP, the Bishop and everybody else, she took a part-time job, dug in at 123, and stayed to become Des Wilson's alter ego and yet another hindrance to the grand designs of William Philbin and his Merry Men.

Coincidentally, no sooner was the festival over than the simmering conflict between Springhill Community House and Down and Connor bubbled to the surface again. On August 21st, the day Derry City Coroner Hubert O'Neill described the Bloody Sunday killings as 'sheer unadulterated murder', the Ballymurphy priest was in the news again. A few days earlier he had come out strongly against the role of British army padres, whom he accused of information-gathering on behalf of the forces repressing the nationalist community.

Now, Monsignor Patrick Mullally, Bishop Philbin's chief lieutenant, was rushing to the defence of 'our brother priests', as he described the soldier-priests of the occupation forces. Instead of investigating the claims made by Fr Wilson, Monsignor Mullally chose to launch a direct attack on the accusing priest's 'credibility' at a time when he might well have turned an eye to the 'credibility' of those whom he himself represented.

In an effort to capitalise on Mullally's stance, the British army convened a press conference at army headquarters in Lisburn on September 5th, to which they invited Bishop Gerard Tickle, Catholic mentor to the British army. The Bishop began by describing the Derry coroner's statement on Bloody Sunday as 'out of order', and continued with an affirmation that there was 'certainly no intention on the part of the soldiers to kill anyone'.[6] To which some far-sighted hack replied that an anti-killing stance was a strange one for soldiers in a war setting.

The Bishop was then asked if soldiers serving in the North should examine their conscience before firing if an officer ordered them to shoot someone. He replied that: 'If every soldier questioned himself before carrying out an order, where would we be?[7] When he was reminded that the defence of 'acting under orders' had not been acceptable at the Nuremberg trials of Nazi war criminals, he stated that he quite frankly knew nothing about that.

At this juncture, with the propaganda exercise crashing about his ears, Colonel Warren Stillitoe intervened, telling the assembled journalists not to ask such questions. When they refused to comply with his demands by asking further questions on the morality of army killings, Stillitoe brought the press conference to an abrupt end. The final scene was of a confused Bishop Tickle protesting his willingness to answer all questions while at the same time being hustled away by the angry and red-faced Stillitoe.

Twelve days after the Tickle press conference, the hierarchy struck back at Ballymurphy. On September 17th the four Asian nuns from Mother Teresa's Missionary Sisters Of Charity vacated their house in Springhill Avenue, which was immediately occupied by local nuns under the control of Down and Connor. Overseeing the evacuation and reoccupation were Canon Murphy and Fr George O'Hanlon. The following Sunday, September 23rd, an official statement from Mother Teresa was read out at all masses in St John's and Corpus Christi churches. In it she claimed that her nuns left Springhill because their presence elsewhere was 'very necessary ... No one has forced me'.

But despite this assurance nobody in the Upper Springfield was about to believe that the sudden visit by Mother Teresa all the way from Calcutta, the hurried consultation with the Bishop, and the unannounced departure of the nuns in the middle of many successful unfinished projects were unrelated. The day before departure, Mother Teresa herself had given weight to the belief that the evacuation was in fact an eviction when she told a Springhill woman over tea that she 'wouldn't put the blame on any one person'.[8]

Then a week later the most damning evidence of all turned up in a rubbish tip – a draft letter in Mother Teresa's own handwriting. In it she expressed anger and bitterness at being forced to leave Springhill. Whether or not Mother Teresa's actual letter to Bishop Philbin contained the same words, there was no doubting the sentiments in her heart as she turned home for Calcutta. In a last ditch effort to prevent the nuns' decampment, Des Wilson, who was abroad at the time, telephoned Mother Teresa from San Sebastian in Spain and asked that her sisters stay a little longer so as to minimise the hurt to the community. She replied that if her nuns were wanted in 32 places around the world, why should she stay a day more than necessary in a place where they were not?

Within five days of the loss of Mother Teresa's nuns, the Upper Springfield suffered a second blow at the hands of the hierarchy as Down and Connor continued its clearance of 'undesirables'. Two nuns from the Society of the Holy Child, Sisters Eileen and Elizabeth, had arrived in Ballymurphy with the Bishop's approval at the beginning of the year. Sister Eileen specialised in adult education and Sister Elizabeth was involved in family welfare, two services much in demand in the area. The two women, who had shed their habits to remove all barriers between themselves and the community, had moved into a house in Springfield Park, both finding paid work so that they might be self-supporting.

Already, prior to Mother Teresa's departure, they had been told by Canon Murphy that they were not wanted. Now, on September 22nd, Sister Eileen was called to the Canon's house on the Falls Road and told that she and Sister Elizabeth were to pack their bags at once and go.

Three days earlier, the Ballymurphy community, seething at the loss of the Asian nuns, had decided to confront the hierarchy on the new issue relating to Sisters Eileen and Elizabeth. On the afternoon of Wednesday, September 19th, a woman representing the residents telephoned Bishop Philbin's house and got through to Fr Thomas Toner, the Bishop's secretary. In 'explanation' of why the two nuns were told to leave the Upper Springfield, Fr Toner told the woman that 'we can't have Sisters roaming around the district on their own and setting up communities'.[9] When asked if the parish of St John's hadn't set some kind of world record in expelling two religious orders in five days, Fr Toner told the Ballymurphy woman that she should keep out of affairs of which she knew nothing. As the autumn of 1973 progressed, the showdown between the people of Ballymurphy and the Diocese of Down and Connor was entering a stage of bunker-building.

Alongside the Community Festival and the other summer reliables like the VSB Playscheme, the arrival of the foreign students, the holiday schemes, and the plague of frogs that annually descended from the mountain on Moyard, August 1973 was also marked by the publication of *A Tale of Two Surveys*. Tony Spencer's far-reaching report on social conditions in Ballymurphy estate provided the ailing BTA with the energy and weaponry for one last assault on the state, and a reference document for all who would continue Ballymurphy's original war down through the coming decade and beyond. In his introduction, the survey director paid tribute to the quality of leadership within the area:

I was deeply impressed at my first meeting in 1970 by the personal calibre of the officers of the BTA. I have many times reflected that in Great Britain they would have had extremely successful careers. The same thought was expressed by the late Paddy McCarthy who observed that it would be rare to find people of the same calibre on a working class housing estate in Britain. This high level of ability was not confined to the officers of the BTA. The operation to rescue the survey in May 1971 revealed among half a dozen unemployed men in Ballymurphy capabilities that would have got them into management outside of Northern Ireland.[10]

But Spencer also pointed out that the BTA, and many other existing organisations, reflected 'the near-monopoly of power that is enjoyed in rural Ireland by middle-aged and elderly men'. [11] This was partially the downfall of the BTA; as one had to be a tenant to qualify for membership, most young people, and their energies, were excluded. However, many of the new organisations that had come together to make the Community Festival such a success were weighted in the opposite direction as young people established their own avenue for addressing the problems created by state and Church for them and their families. As time went on, it would be these groups, further buttressed by the increasingly politicised prisoners returning from the jails and internment camps, who would become the backbone of working-class politics and community action in the Upper Springfield.

The BTA's final grand offensive, stimulated by the arrival of *A Tale of Two Surveys*, began in December 1973 with the formation of working parties to act on the various recommendations of the report. By the beginning of 1974 the community was again at loggerheads with both Church and state. Meanwhile, community activists from the area were also involved in a city-wide campaign against government plans to carve up Belfast with an urban motorway. By September 1973 the British had spent £9 million in buying and clearing land for the proposed development. Whole communities had been bulldozed away, as had hundreds of commercial premises. So widespread was opposition to the plan (not least from those whose neighbourhoods were being razed) that when the Belfast Urban Study Group (BUS) published its report in October it seemed that the public outcry was having an effect. BUS was in fact arguing that the motorway was 'stoppable' because the Ministry of Development had realised that: 'They have backed a loser, the second and third phase have been 'delayed'. This is nothing but a polite way of saying they have been abandoned. The crucial issue is now to stop the first phase.'[12]

But BUS and the city's community groups had missed the essential point: phase 2 and 3 were about road-building, and were most likely abandoned due to spiralling costs; phase 1 was about population control. Already, the combat zones had been compressed by the clearance of an entire nationalist community from the Docks area on the verge of the city centre. When the link between the M1 and M2 was eventually completed in 1983, the involvement of the British army and RUC in all aspects of urban planning was open knowledge – and clearly evident. The sealed streets, the cul-de-sacs of new housing projects, the 'walkways' with foundations to accommodate military armour, and the 20-foot 'environmental walls' perfectly complemented the new motorway which cut an impassable barrier between republican West Belfast and the city centre, simultaneously dividing the loyalist Village from nationalist Grosvenor Road, and the Shankill from Unity flats. Further 'road improvements' along the Springfield Road in 1986 completed the subtle 'Berlin Wall' of West Belfast.

As the autumn of 1973 turned to winter, the energy generated by the summer festival euphoria could be tracked down in many corners in the Upper Springfield. In a block of three houses adjacent to Springhill Community House, a craft centre had colonised the ground floor, while Richard Fox, an American who raised much local CIA-related suspicion, was busy with a sledgehammer converting the top floor into a youth club. Alas, the stress-bearing walls fell to Richard's alacrity, and the whole block had to come down. At '42' there was the chaotic children's library where the little borrowers practised mountain-climbing on the bookshelves.

And there was the 123 Mountaineering Club, run by a ruddy-jowled ex-British soldier, who attempted to open a mixed youth club at the Springhill/Springmartin interface. Thankfully, the building was wrecked before anyone had a chance to be killed. On another occasion, the same man, while working on plans to bring disabled children over the Mourne Mountains in sedan chairs, invited the British army to descend by helicopter on one of his weekend camps, which catered for Ballymurphy and Shankill children. The Englishman's naivete was unforgivable in Ballymurphy. Shortly afterwards, the club met its demise when some Shankill Road members burned its weekend cottage at Annalong to the ground. Community leaders in Ballymurphy mourned not its passing.

On the economic front 1973 was a year of unprecedented optimism in the Upper Springfield. Ballymurphy Enterprises, the knitwear operation, was forging ahead, with Ciaran O'Kane from its management announcing in June:

> A new factory is under construction and new plant has been ordered. Production has increased by more than 100 per cent over the past six months and sales, at the moment, are at a satisfactory level ... a reasonable profit is forecast when the new plant comes into operation.[13]

In October Sean Mackle, the BTA's architect and also a member of the Whiterock Industrial Estates' management, was explaining to the community that the organisation had managed to negotiate an interest-free loan of 30 per cent from the Ministry of Commerce on each factory built in the Industrial Estate at what used to be McAulfield's farm. By raising the remainder – 70 per cent of £2 million (double the original estimate) – through its own fund-raising efforts, they would preserve 'local co-operative ownership and management-control by the community itself'. He went on to say:

It is necessary that ... communities of individuals should have the right to contribute to the development of their own environment, to the development of all things that affect or in fact mould and condition their life ... It can only be achieved by sustained well-informed community collective action. All local organisations must co-operate to forge a new order ... A new magic is coming to the whole Whiterock/Springfield area ... where human needs and human values will be the main concern.[14]

A month later another co-operative, Whiterock Pictures Ltd, went into production, turning out block-mounted paper prints and photographs. This new enterprise had been funded by grants donated by a number of trusts and the remainder negotiated through the Local Enterprise Development Unit, a government scheme aimed at assisting small businesses to get off the ground. The person appointed to manage the unit was Frank Cahill. By December the co-operative was working flat out to keep pace with orders and in the New Year it was decided to employ two more workers. Gerry Finnegan, a Community Development Officer appointed to the area in 1972, had become its business adviser, a role he would maintain for the following decade.

The optimistic mood continued to gather momentum in early 1974. Ballymurphy Enterprises moved into its new factory on the site of the old Corporation yard at the top of Whiterock Road; Whiterock Pictures, despite a row with the manager of the Industrial Estate that prompted the group to declare 'UDI' in April, was still good news; and the management of the Industrial Estate was declaring success after success:

By creating small craft industries like Ballymurphy Enterprises and Whiterock Pictures it was possible to demonstrate to an internal apathetic community and an external uncaring society that local skills existed, that initiative and imagination were infectious commodities, they just required release ... Now Whiterock is an ever-growing centre of co-operative enterprise. There are already 64 full-time jobs ... Perhaps the biggest challenge ... assumed is the development of Whiterock Industrial Estate on Community Co-operative lines. This requires huge outlays. To date it has all services and roads ready to cater for factory building and two factories in occupation ... over £200,000 has been spent ... a new factory is beginning construction, a petrol filling station and shop whose profits will go to more factory building are officially open.[15]

What must be remembered about the above achievements is that they took place during a year in which the Upper Springfield continued to be one of the principal battlegrounds in the war between the IRA and British forces. Although Motorman had deprived the Ballymurphy guerrillas of much freedom of movement, they were still very much in business, beginning the New Year offensive with a gun attack on Vere Foster army post on January 10th, the day after the Coldstream Guards had ripped away the side of the Tutins' bungalow in Westrock Way with a Saracen armoured car.

For the next six weeks the IRA continued to mount sporadic attacks on the Taggart, Vere Foster and Fort Pegasus as well as sniping attacks on mobile and foot patrols. On occasions, such as the January 28th commemoration of Bloody Sunday and the early hours of February 4th, there were intense prolonged gun-battles. Amazingly there were no casualties on either side until February 21st, when a member of the Coldstream Guards, 20-year-old Michael Doyle, was killed by a single shot while on guard duty in Britton's Parade within sight of Fort Pegasus. Two other members of the same regiment had been killed the night before in an ambush on the Falls, bringing their losses to three in 24 hours. It was a heavy blow to a regiment that had attempted on several occasions to 'buy' its way safely through its tour of duty in the Upper Springfield. An IRA Volunteer recalled how:

> One time, they found an Armalite under a bed in a house. They called all the people in the house together and told them they would leave it there provided no attacks were made on them. On another occasion a four-man patrol ran into a house after a woman who had a rifle up her coat. They told her they knew she had the rifle, gave her the date they were leaving, and asked that no attacks be mounted on them before then. But, even at that point they were in danger, two Volunteers were ready to attack the house when the soldiers appeared with no sign of the woman being under arrest. We refused to make any deals with them, and at the end of their tour of duty, things fell apart badly for them.[16]

On February 22nd 1973, Ballymurphy was again in the headlines with reports of a spectacular escape from Crumlin Road Jail by Jim Bryson, who had been arrested the previous September and charged with possession of a handgun. While being escorted to Crumlin Road Courthouse, linked to the jail by an underground tunnel, Bryson produced a gun and he and another prisoner overpowered their guards and stripped them of their uniforms. They then casually walked through the courthouse towards freedom, but only Bryson made it.

Once outside, he discarded the uniform, headed for the Shankill Road, and hitched a lift to the Falls from two unsuspecting armed off-duty UDR men who thought they were running a mercy mission to the Royal Victoria Hospital! That night an enraged patrol of the Coldstream Guards fired indiscriminately from the darkness of blacked-out Ballymurphy Road at a group of children celebrating the escape around a bonfire in Ballymurphy's Bullring. But they only succeeded in adding to the drama of the escape. From then onwards the man who would soon resume his position as IRA O/C of Ballymurphy was known in his home ground's folklore as 'Houdini'.

In March, as the shooting continued, there were more casualties. On the first day of the month a soldier was grazed in the head while on patrol in Ballymurphy Drive. The next night two young men were shot in the legs in a punishment shooting carried out by the Officials. Four days later another member of the Coldstream Guards, Anton Brown (22), was killed by a single shot in Whitecliff Crescent.

Then, on the night of March 9th, in dense fog, the military went to answer a 'bomb scare' in the vicinity of Corry's timberyard, only to come under fire. Reinforcements were immediately summoned and a tight cordon thrown around Corry's. With a helicopter circling overhead, the IRA unit, it seemed, was trapped. There followed a night of sniping, the British maintaining a ring of steel around the yard, waiting for dawn so they could move in. But when dawn came, there was no IRA unit in Corry's. The soldiers had spent the night replying to one another's shooting.

On April 12th, the first Ballymurphy Volunteer to be killed in 1973 died in the Lower Falls. It had been a day of rockets, grenades and sniping throughout Belfast. Edward 'Mundo' O'Rawe (27) and a companion, Sean Rowntree, both of whom were unarmed, were in Cape Street, when they were stopped and searched by British troops. (An American woman then living in the Falls later produced photographs of both men spreadeagled against a wall and 'covered' by the soldiers.) They were then gunned down in cold blood. Edward O'Rawe was killed and Sean Rowntree was seriously wounded.

On April 18th, 20-year-old Gerald FitzGerald of Ballymurphy was sentenced to 20 years for a claymore mine attack on the Paras in Rock Grove in the early hours of July 13th 1971. 'Fitzy' would become another Ballymurphy escapologist of renown, having already escaped once in one of the IRA's more daring operations. During the attack for which Fitzy was jailed, he had been shot and captured by the paratroopers. Three days later, on July 16th 1971, as he lay under armed guard in the Royal Victoria Hospital, the Ballymurphy IRA sprang him.

At 6am a 'doctor' in white coat and surgical mask walked up to the two RUC guards, pulled a sub-machine-gun from under his coat, clubbed one of the RUC men and held the other up. He was joined by three more 'doctors', also with sub-machine-guns up their coats. Three other Volunteers were holding the night porter prisoner. One of the IRA men then lifted the wounded Fitzy fireman-style and carried him from the hospital to a waiting car, whereupon he and his rescuers disappeared, Fitzy going to a hospital over the border. That morning in Ballymurphy, leaflets that had been prepared in advance were distributed depicting Fitzy's rescue!

Once he had recovered, Fitzy returned to Belfast but was again captured, and jailed for his part in the 1971 ambush. Eighteen months later, on October 13th 1974, after months of tension and several riots at Long Kesh, republican prisoners burned the camp to the ground. During the next few weeks, while the prisoners lived among the rubble of what remained of the compounds, one Cage spent its time digging a tunnel to the outside. On November 6th the first of 33 escaping prisoners reached the nearby M1 motorway in the darkness of the winter's night – and ran straight into military gunfire. Hugh Coney was shot dead. All the others were arrested.

Three months later twelve of those prisoners were at Newry courthouse awaiting trial on charges arising from the burning of Long Kesh and the attempted escape when they noticed some corroded bars in a lavatory window. They prized open the bars, scaled a 24-foot fence and escaped, all but two getting safely across the border despite a massive British dragnet. Among them was Gerald Fitzgerald.*

Meanwhile the attacks went on in Ballymurphy, with the first RPG-7 rocket fired in the area on April 20th 1973. The Taggart was the target and the blast was accompanied by a brief exchange of gunfire. Five days later another single-shot attack seriously wounded a soldier in New Barnsley. On May 2nd a rocket fired at the military post in Blackmountain School struck the roof of a house in Highfield. There followed a week of sniping and gunfights throughout the Upper Springfield, a soldier being hit in the leg on May 8th, during an attack on two military vehicles on Whiterock Road. On May 10th another rocket hit the Taggart, exploding harmlessly on the perimeter wall. On the 16th a soldier was wounded by a ricochet near Corrigan Park.

On May 17th rioting erupted in Springhill Avenue. That evening at about 9pm when everything had quietened down, young Eileen Mackin from Ballymurphy and her friend Lucy Kelly, both 14, went for a walk through Springhill. Without warning loyalist gunmen opened fire from Springmartin, shooting both girls. Eileen Mackin, who was hit in the stomach, died three hours later. She had been a member of Cumann na gCailini.

As May came to an end the tragedy of Ballymurphy was inimitably expressed during an IRA attack on Vere Foster army post. After a rocket had exploded on the protective wire of the post within the primary school grounds and the IRA and British army had engaged in a brief gunbattle, the media turned up to interview George McElwee, the school principal. His statement was simple and matter-of-fact, yet he could hardly have more clearly sketched the extent to which the war had distorted existence in the Upper Springfield.

> The children have a drill for such times: they fall to the ground immediately. They did this and there was no panic and no tears. I went down myself immediately I heard the rocket fired, and in the first three classrooms found children and teachers on the floors and no sound. In the fourth the teacher was reading the children a story in the corner and they were listening.[17]

The children he was describing were aged between five and eleven years old.

May ended with the local government elections which were designed

*In 1983, at Roundwood, County Wicklow, Fitzy was among a group of IRA Volunteers attempting to kidnap a wealthy businessman who would be held for ransom. The Irish Special Branch, however, were waiting in ambush. The surrounded Volunteers alleged that they were ordered to drop their weapons and put their hands in the air, and that when they had done so, the Special Branch shot them. Four, including Fitzy, were wounded; and five, including Fitzy, were captured. The Ballymurphy man was later sentenced by Dublin's political courts to ten years in Portlaoise Prison.

as a lead-up to the Assembly elections. The results, published on June 2nd, showed a collapse of the centre around whom the whole power-sharing concept was balanced, and must have been viewed with dismay in Whitehall circles.

Two weeks later, on June 16th, a loyalist organisation for the first time claimed responsibility for sectarian murders with the release of a statement from the previously unheard of Ulster Freedom Fighters. (On September 6th the UFF issued another statement in which 'Captain Black' claimed responsibility for 13 sectarian murders, 17 attempted murders and 18 bombings since May 13th.)[18] Although in time this organisation would be identified as no more than a cover name for the UDA, the British have consistently refused to proscribe the UDA in the same way as the IRA.

Indeed British attitudes to pro-British loyalist violence have always been quite accommodating and were admirably expressed by the Secretary of State of the Six Counties in 1980. After loyalist gunmen seriously wounded Alfie Copeland (28), at his work in Curran's butcher's shop at the Whiterock/Springfield junction, Humphrey Atkins stated that the 'people' (loyalists) who had carried out the shooting were 'playing into the hands of the terrorists' who of course were the republicans.

On Sunday July 1st Reginald Roberts (25) of the 2nd Light Infantry was shot dead in Ballymurphy's Bullring. The military responded with a full scale invasion of the estate and the systematic wrecking of homes. A week later, as loyalist violence increased in the run up to the Twelfth the whole area erupted. Beginning on the morning of July 9th, and lasting for 48 hours, the area was engulfed in heavy rioting, hijackings and burnings, and lengthy gun-battles. On the 9th a soldier was shot in the shoulder, the only casualty of two days' heavy fire. On the 10th, a rocket hit the Taggart; and two more soldiers were wounded on the 17th.

From then until the festival ceasefire, there were continuous gun-battles and sniping attacks, but without casualties. There were also numerous riots, all triggered off by ongoing events. There was rioting on July 19th, following the capture of Gerry Adams, Belfast Brigade commander since the previous September, along with two senior members of the Belfast Brigade. There was rioting on July 29th, after a protest march in support of Michael Farrell and Anthony Canavan of People's Democracy who were on hunger-strike for political status. There was rioting on August 1st, following the arrest of two Volunteers caught with a rifle. And there was the annual rioting of August 9th, to commemorate the introduction of internment. Then the double tragedy of the Murphy family struck on the 10th, and two days later, as the festival began, 12-year-old Cathy McCartland, a member of Cumann na gCailini, was killed in a fall.

Other trouble too was brewing. Ever since the 1971 feud between the Provisionals and Officials, relations had been strained between the two organisations. On June 19th 1972, the situation was further exacerbated by the death of 37-year-old Desmond Mackin who had been shot in the leg during a Provo raid on the Officials' Cracked Cup Club in Leeson Street. Since the beginning of 1973 the situation had been worsening with people on both sides being beaten up in clubs and in their neighbourhoods and teenage supporters fighting it out in all nationalist areas.

In late August Jim Bryson, who had been in Dundalk for some time, returned to Ballymurphy to warn off the Officials in what was essentially a Provisional stronghold. In the still-flourishing Maggie's Tavern this led to the pistol-whipping of a number of Officials which in turn led to the passing by the Officials of a death-sentence on Bryson. The sentence was to be carried out on August 31st.

From late that afternoon there wasn't a child to be seen in the lower end of Ballymurphy Estate, where both Officials and Provisionals could be seen carrying weapons openly. Then at 7pm the shooting started.

Earlier, Bryson and three other Volunteers had been having a meal in a safe house in New Barnsley when a courier arrived to say that members of the Official IRA were calling at houses in Ballymurphy estate looking for him. At the same time another Provisional, on his way to Bryson's home in Ballymurphy Road to bring a similar warning, was shot at by Officials from an entry on Whiterock Road, the bullet passing through his hair.

On hearing what was happening in Ballymurphy, Bryson immediately sent for a car, with the intention of engaging those who were seeking him out, and drove down to Ballymurphy with the three other Volunteers. In the middle of the estate they encountered Thomas Russell, a member of the Officials, and called him to the car. Bryson told Russell to go to the Officials and advise them to think again. No sooner had they released Russell, however, than the four Provisionals came under fire from the derelict flats above the Bullring.

Believing that they were being shot at by the Officials, they abandoned the car in Whitecliff Crescent at the lower end of the estate and moved through the gardens up to Whitecliff Parade where they engaged the gunmen in the flats for 20 minutes. Unknown to the IRA men, however, the flats were occupied by a patrol of the Royal Greenjackets who were using them as an observation post.

Eventually Bryson decided to flush out the 'Officials'. Simultaneously, neighbours spotted soldiers climbing over the railings from St Bernadette's School and moving into entries on Ballymurphy Road adjacent to the entrance to Whitecliff Parade. They shouted a warning to the Volunteers; but whether or not the warning was understood is unclear.

It would appear that the plan was still to head towards the Bullring when the four men pulled back from Whitecliff Parade. Either way, the car, with Bryson at the wheel, reversed out into Ballymurphy Road – in clear view of the flats – and was riddled from the observation post. Nineteen-year-old Paddy Mulvenna was killed instantly and Jim Bryson was badly wounded.

Bryson, who had been shot in the head, nevertheless managed to take off down Ballymurphy Road. But the car crashed on a bend in the street, two doors away from where Bryson's wife was now living with their child. Despite being seriously wounded, the IRA commander was still conscious enough to order the other two Volunteers to take what they could of the weapons and get clear. When one of them reached for Bryson's handgun, however, he found the gun held in a tightly-clenched fist.

But by the time the British army closed in on the car, Bryson was unconscious and would die from his wounds on September 22nd. A third Volunteer, 18-year-old James 'Bimbo' O'Rawe, was wounded while trying to escape. And as the shocked residents of Ballymurphy Road crowded out of their homes, the ubiquitous ice-cream van came up the street playing 'Three Blind Mice'.

A short time afterwards, two unarmed women who were members of the Provisionals were shot at by Officials firing from Glenalina Crescent into Ballymurphy Road. In a subsequent military raid two Thompson sub-machine-guns were found in a house in Rock Grove. They belonged to the Officials, and were later described in the political courts as weapons that were on hand 'to shoot a man who has since been killed by the security forces', i.e. Jim Bryson.

Bryson's funeral was a massive show of strength by the Provisionals with thousands of republicans marching to Milltown Cemetery in military formation. Giving the graveside oration, Maire Drumm, Sinn Fein Vice President, told the mourners that 'generations yet unborn will live to hear the name of Captain James Bryson'. In Ballymurphy he was already a legend.

Although the Officials and Provisionals met in Dublin on September 10th to try to defuse the situation, the bitterness caused by the Bryson and Mulvenna killings – and the gloating afterwards by Officials in Belfast – led directly to the bitter feud of the autumn of 1975 when the two organisations fought openly on the streets of Belfast while the British looked on contentedly.

The day after Patrick Mulvenna's death, another Ballymurphy Volunteer, 19-year-old Anne Marie Pettigrew, died in hospital from injuries received during an explosion in Elaine Street nine days earlier. A member of Cumann na mBan since 1971, she had been an explosives specialist and part of a unit that planted incendiaries all over the North. The explosion had occurred when she and another Volunteer were experimenting with new methods of assembling incendiaries.

The sniping in the Upper Springfield continued through the remaining months of 1973, but there were no further deaths in the area until November 12th, when 15-year-old Bernard Teggart from New Barnsley was abducted from St Patrick's Training School and shot dead. When he was found dying in the grounds of Bellevue Park at 10pm a placard with the word 'tout' written on it was pinned to his chest. He had been shot by the IRA for allegedly supplying information to the British. The boy's father had been murdered in August 1971 at the Taggart by the paratroopers. The killing of Bernard Teggart had a particularly brutalising effect on the Upper Springfield. Most people felt that, regardless of how he might have transgressed, his youth and the fact that he was not the brightest of youngsters should have spared him such a harsh and final judgement.

The area's next killing occurred in Whiterock on February 4th 1974, when 43-year-old Vincie Clarke died in a hail of bullets outside his mother's home. Neighbours rushed out to find his body slumped over the bonnet of his car, and another car speeding away from the scene. This was the same Vincie Clarke who was fixing his truck the day Arthur McKenna and Alexander McVicker were shot dead by the IRA in 1970.

To this day, there is a strong belief in Ballymurphy that Jimmy McKenna had chosen Vincie Clarke for his long-promised revenge, and had been in the car with the loyalists who shot him. It is said that he was also behind the killing in July 1973 of Clarke's brother, Robert, who was ambushed by loyalists outside a builder's yard in the city. There is no evidence to support these beliefs. Yet, until Jimmy McKenna's death in 1986, the area was haunted by the image of a lone vigilante who was out there somewhere, armed with god knows how many guns, waiting to avenge his brother's death.

In the coming weeks there were several confrontations between loyalists and nationalists at the Springhill/Springmartin interface, shots being exchanged on occasions, but without casualties. Then on April 13th, a 37-year-old Springfield Park man was shot in the leg as he stood on a ladder painting his house, the incident causing yet another exchange of gunfire between Ballymurphy and Springmartin.

A week later, on April 20th, 20-year-old James Corbett, an ex-internee from New Barnsley Drive was shot dead by the IRA. At 3pm a man called to the house, spoke to his wife, and went upstairs to talk to Corbett. A few minutes later both left the house. In less than two hours James Corbett's body was found at the Turf Lodge roundabout. He had been shot twice in the back of the head for allegedly acting as an informer.

On May 25th a cow on Black Mountain was killed when it stood on a landmine meant for soldiers who were raiding a nearby farmhouse. The British then came under fire from an IRA unit further up the mountain. That evening, another type of explosion was heard in New Barnsley. As a massive loyalist political strike gripped the North, the city's gas supply had been run down, and people were now cooking in their fireplaces and back yards. The gas service had warned that they were maintaining only minimum pressure in the pipes to prevent air from getting in and causing explosions. But, they warned, people weren't to attempt to cook, otherwise they could expect such explosions. But there are sceptics everywhere. In the Upper Springfield, their exact locations were being pinpointed by the roar of the warned-against explosions.

* * *

The power-sharing Executive officially took office on January 1st 1974, as Dolours Price (22) her sister Marion (19), Gerry Kelly (19) from Whiterock, and Hugh Feeney (21) entered their second month of force-feeding in British jails. By using wooden clamps and tubes, and daily assaults on the prisoners, the Whitehall administration was attempting to break the prisoners' morale before their hunger strike could reach proportions that would compromise the SDLP position within the newly imposed British 'solution' in the Six Counties.*

At the same time the British army was launching a renewed assault on republican areas in an attempt to destroy resistance from that quarter. Mass arrests of children from ages ten and eleven upwards were followed by torture and interrogation in army bases. Such was the level of brutality that Deputy Executive Gerry Fitt, Minister of Health and Social Services, Paddy Devlin, and SDLP Assemblyman for West Belfast, Des Gillespie, were forced to publicly condemn Francis Pym, the new Secretary of State, on January 6th.

Commenting on the torture of groups of '15 to 20 boys at a time', at Fort Monagh in Turf Lodge, Paddy Devlin said that he found it 'peculiar' that at 'a time when the Secretary of State is assuring us in the SDLP that he intends to phase out internment forthwith, these arrests are being carried out, and, to say the least, interrogation in depth is being used on these young boys'.[19] The Association for Legal Justice was simultaneously describing Springfield Road RUC/British army Barracks as a new torture centre that 'seems destined for a place in history along with Girdwood, Ballykelly and Palace Barracks, Holywood'.[20] Referring to the treatment meted out to groups of young people 'aged 13 to 17' the human rights group spoke of 'an administrative practice of torture and brutality' at the base.

In the 26 Counties Patrick Cooney, Minister for Justice in the Coalition government, was wholeheartedly throwing his weight behind the British anti-republican drive, assuring the world on January 15th, that those who 'harboured' IRA members henceforth ran the risk of losing their homes and having their businesses closed down.

On January 22nd the Stormont Assembly met for the first time since the formation of the Executive. In the rumpus that immediately began, 18 loyalists were ejected by the RUC for causing uproar in the chamber. When Paisley was asked to vacate a seat allocated to the Executive, he turned on the speaker, Nat Minford, bellowing, 'You'll not jackboot us with your British armoured cars and your British army!' Kennedy Lindsay, meanwhile, was busy spitting in Brian Faulkner's face and dancing from foot to foot on the Speaker's table, microphone in hand, screaming 'We've purged the Temple!' As the circus atmosphere proceeded in the coming weeks, the SDLP continued to make perfunctory noises about ending internment, apparently unaware that internment would come to an end – as soon as the British were satisfied that the Diplock courts would fulfil the same purpose.

Meanwhile, overall loyalist opposition to Sunningdale had crystallised around the United Ulster Unionist Council (UUUC), formed in December. The focus of attack was the proposed Council of Ireland, an

---

*On June 7th, 1974 the Price sisters, Gerry Kelly and Hugh Feney ended their 206-day fast. The British, having abandoned force-feeding, conceded their demands.

epitome of ambiguity that was the Agreement's Achilles' heel. While
Faulkner argued that the Council would strengthen the North's constitutional position, the SDLP was assuring nationalists that it was downhill
to reunification. The Dublin Coalition, keen for any settlement within a
Six-County context, was initially happy to go along with Faulkner in
playing down the council's role. The 26-County Prime Minister stated
that there should be no pressure on the issue of partition (Dublin and
London having agreed that the SDLP should participate in a recon-
structed Stormont).

However, by September 1973, three months after the Assembly elections, the SDLP had swung Dublin to its own interpretation of the
Council of Ireland[21] so that both entered Sunningdale with their sights
on a clear interim step towards Irish unity. Otherwise, the SDLP argued,
its electoral support would be seriously undermined. The British, meanwhile, were interpreting the 'matters of substantial mutual interest'[22] to
be co-ordinated by the Council as tourism, regional development and
transport. Consequently, the Executive took office with this key issue
still unresolved.

On January 4th the anti-Sunningdale unionists scored a major victory
when the Ulster Unionist Council rejected the Sunningdale package with
a majority of 80, forcing Faulkner's resignation as party leader. He stayed
on as leader of the Executive, but he was now without a party or party
machine at what proved to be a crucial moment. In Britain a miners'
strike and general industrial chaos had brought down the Tory government of Edward Heath and an election had been called for February
28th.

The Assembly alliance fell apart, with all three parties competing for
seats and Faulkner's Unionists in disarray. By contrast, the anti-
Sunningdale Unionists, led by Harry West, made a pact with Vanguard
and the DUP so that only one candidate stood in each constituency. The
results were a disaster for the Executive, and particularly for Faulkner.
The UUUC won eleven of the twelve Six-County seats.

In the marginal constituencies of Fermanagh–South Tyrone and Mid-
Ulster the SDLP stood against the outgoing MPs, Frank McManus and
Bernadette Devlin. The seats were lost to the loyalists as a result. At
Westminster, Harold Wilson became Prime Minister of a Labour govern-
ment, and Merlyn Rees was despatched to Stormont to keep Sunningdale
afloat.

Over the next two months, while Faulkner's Unionists back-tracked
furiously on the Council of Ireland, and the SDLP pushed for its speedy
implementation, the IRA nudged the UUUC stormtroopers on with a
relentless bombing onslaught that reduced tens of millions of pounds
worth of property – mainly unionist property – to rubble. Lengthy gun-
battles were also taking place between the IRA and the British army,
while military security measures were ridiculed by IRA successes.

Small easy-to-conceal incendiaries, many no bigger than a cigarette
packet, were being slipped through the most stringent checks, while
Belfast's Grand Central Hotel, British army headquarters in the city's

fenced-off security zone, was blitzed on March 7th, and again on the 28th, by 1,000lb 'earthquake bombs' that turned the whole of Royal Avenue into a demoralising shambles. Whole areas of the city were bombed out of existence during this period as were the centres of most provincial towns.

The pressure on Faulkner filtered through to Dublin. Cosgrave dropped all talk about unity, declaring on March 13th, that 'the factual position of Northern Ireland is that it is within the United Kingdom and my government accepts this as a fact'. The SDLP, at the same time, was flexing its Ministerial muscles in Stormont. On April 3rd Ivan Cooper, SDLP Minister of Community Relations, announced the axing of the Community Relations Commission. On the same day Austin Currie, SDLP Minister of Housing, dismissed calls for an amnesty for rent and rate strikers, announced an increase in deductions to be made under the Payment of Debt Act from strikers' welfare benefits, and added his infamous punitive collection fee.

On April 18th Harold Wilson visited the North to reaffirm his government's support for Sunningdale and prop up the morale of his forces whose bases across the Six Counties were being blasted by the IRA. Six days later, in an effort to deaden loyalist opposition, Roy Mason, British Defence Secretary, warned that pressure was mounting in Britain for a withdrawal of troops. But the UUUC campaign went on unscathed, accompanied by increased loyalist attacks on nationalist civilians. On May 2nd five were killed and 18 injured in the bombing of the Rose and Crown Bar in Belfast. During the next seven days, ten more were killed in a spate of attacks that also left many wounded.

Finally the UUUC decided to force the issue. Its Assembly members put forward a motion that the Council of Ireland be rescinded. The loyalist Ulster Workers' Council (UWC), formed in December, threatened strike action if the motion failed. On May 14th it was defeated in Stormont by 44 votes to 28. The UWC called its strike.

The stoppage was immediately effective, though nowhere on the scale hoped for by the UWC. During the following days this was remedied by the Ulster Army Council, a co-ordinating body of the loyalist guerrilla groups, who were providing the muscle to enforce the strike. Open collusion between the state forces and the masked heavies at the loyalist barricades (often hijacking vehicles in full view of troops and the RUC) further discouraged anyone thinking of running the gauntlet to work.

On May 16th, as the violence at the barricades intensified, William Craig warned that Sunningdale had to be ditched. 'If they don't realise this there will be further actions taken against the Irish Republic and those who attempt to implement the agreement.'[23] The following day three car-bombs in Dublin, and a fourth in Monaghan town, left 31 dead and over 100 injured. (Former Military Intelligence officer, Captain Fred Holroyd, later blamed British military intelligence for the bombs.) And still the strike went on.

On May 19th Merlyn Rees declared a state of emergency in the North, giving him the power to use troops to maintain essential services. But the inactivity of his army belied the gravity of any British threat. British officers in the North had already decided that, even if Whitehall ordered them to move against the loyalists, they would refuse to do so – which actually happened on May 24th, shattering the illusion of British democracy. As explained three months later by one of those officers: 'For the first time the army decided that it was right and that it knew best and that the politicians had better toe the line.'[24]

By now cracks were also beginning to appear in the Executive, with several Faulknerites calling for talks with the UWC. On May 21st the UWC declared an embargo on all oil and petrol supplies, and there were twelve-hour power cuts in Belfast and long queues for milk and food. Two days later, Brian Faulkner, Gerry Fitt and Alliance Party leader, Oliver Napier, flew to London to demand that troops be used to break the strike. Fitt threatened an SDLP resignation from the Executive if the military did not take over essential services by May 27th. On May 25th British Prime Minister, Harold Wilson, went on nationwide TV, castigating the strikers as thugs and bullies, 'people who spend their lives sponging on Westminster and British democracy and then systematically assault democratic methods'.[25] Meanwhile, three nationalists had been murdered, two of them near Ballymena by UAC strike-enforcers who were wrecking pubs in County Antrim that had defied the strike.

At 5.15am on May 27th Fitt's demand was conceded. The BP oil refinery at Sydenham outside Belfast was taken over by the British government, occupied by troops, and shut down. Soldiers then moved in on oil storage depots and petrol stations, which were sandbagged and put under heavy armed guard while government officials handed out fuel permits to essential services.

The UWC threatened that if the military went near the power stations, they would close them down completely, along with water and sewage plants, two services already severely threatened by the strike itself. With the Six Counties on the verge of chaos, the flour mills announced that they were closing down, and hospitals warned that only emergency operations were being carried out. Despite Faulkner's pleas, however, Rees was still refusing to talk to the UWC. On May 28th the strikers announced the final turn of the screw; at Ballylumford power-station, where one of three generating sets was already closed down, they were now in the process of running the others down.

At the same time, thousands of farmers and their tractors were converging on Stormont for a mass rally. But the battle was already won. Just before 2pm, the Executive collapsed, Faulkner's unionists having resigned. The loyalist strike had been an absolute victory; and Sunningdale, and all it stood for, was dead. Bonfires blazed throughout loyalist areas; and in Ballymurphy, where there were mixed feelings about the power-sharing adventure, there was also a secret desire to light a bonfire or two to celebrate the final nail in the coffin of the Six-County state. On May 29th, the British prorogued the Assembly for four months. It was never resurrected.

Following the collapse of Sunningdale the political situation was one of deadlock. The impossibility of any internal 'solution' lay fully exposed. Power-sharing, the minimum concession required by the nationalist middle class, was a blasphemous capitulation as far as loyalists were concerned. In a state based on loyalist supremacy, religious bigotry and political discrimination, any move away from the status quo would fracture the existing power-base. Concessions could not therefore be made to the nationalists.

On the other hand, the state as it stood, and the fact that it was set up by force of arms against the wishes of the vast majority of the Irish people, would guarantee a permanently rebellious nationalist community, with the general population of the 26 Counties supportive of the nationalist revolt and hostile to the Six-County state. 'Northern Ireland' was a political failure, a failure guaranteed from the beginning by its intrinsically unstable make-up, which had prompted insurrections on an almost permanent basis since 1921.

In a sober assessment of British prospects for a stable North, Brigadier J.M. Glover of British Defence Intelligence Staff would declare in November 1978 – four years after Sunningdale had bankrupted British political options in Ireland – that the republican war against Britain 'is likely to continue while the British remain in Northern Ireland'. There were therefore only two other options available to the British after Sunningdale; withdrawal and the abolition of the Six-County state; or consolidation of its position by the extermination of the opposition.

Fifteen years after the collapse of Sunningdale the war goes on as ever, both sides locked in stalemate, and the IRA prepared for a war of attrition on an indefinite basis. The political situation, meanwhile, remains as deadlocked as it was at 2pm on May 28th 1974.

References
1. Martin Dillon/Denis Lehane, *Political Murder in Northern Ireland* (Penguin, London, 1973).
2. *Irish News*, Belfast, July 3rd 1973.
3. *Hands Off Ireland*, No. 9 (1979), p. 12.
4. Tony Spencer, *A Tale of Two Surveys* (Queen's University of Belfast, 1973), pp. 59 and 122.
5. *Ballymurphy Benefit Campaign* (Upper Springfield Resource Centre, 1983), p. 6.
6. *Irish News*, Belfast, September 6th 1973.
7. Ibid.
8. *Open the Window; Let in the Light* (St John's and Corpus Christi Parish Council Steering Committee, 1975), p. 4.
9. Ibid., p. 7.
10. Spencer, AECW, *A Tale of Two Surveys*, p. 29.
11. Ibid., p. 30.
12. *The BUS Report on the Belfast Urban Motorway* (Holy Smoke Press, Belfast, October 1973), p. 3.
13. Ciaran O'Kane, 'Co-operative Self-Help in Belfast' in *Co-operative Self-Help and Local Economic Development and Some Contributions,* edited by John Darby and Geoffrey Morris (Northern Ireland Community Relations Commission, 1974).

14. *Spotlight* (Ballymurphy Detached Project ('42), October 1973.
15. Ibid., April 1974.
16. Interview with the author.
17. *Belfast Telegraph*, May 30th 1973.
18. *Irish News*, Belfast, September 7th 1973.
19. Ibid., January 7th 1974.
20. Ibid.
21. Paul Bew and Henry Patterson, *The British State and the Ulster Crisis* (Verso, London, 1985), p. 58.
22. *Northern Ireland Constitutional Proposals,* HMSO, London, March 1973, Cmnd. 5259, White Paper, pp. 29–30.
23. *Newsletter*, Belfast, May 17th 1974.
24. Michael Farrell, *Northern Ireland: The Orange State* (Pluto Press, London, 1976), p. 320.
25. *The Times*, London, May 26th 1974.

Part II

The Wars Go On

13

A Test of Wills

By May 1974 most of the major influences that would shape the Upper Springfield's future were already in place, although the story was by no means over. The work of the BTA and the early influxes of refugees had brought cohesion, stability and organisation to a community that had been little more than a transit camp. The riots of 1970 and 1971 had brought solidarity and pride, and a realisation of the power of a people united.

Internment had been a crushing blow, but it too had been overcome, with the initial shock and terror changing to determination and resilience. And the humiliation and fracturing of Motorman had been turned into a further gritting of the teeth. Each trauma had, in its own way, increased rather than decreased the community's capacity to function and resist. And the longer the conflict went on, the more politicised and radicalised the people became. The programme of political and social action undertaken by the area's action groups had merged into a coherent, militant framework that was already being admired and envied by community and political activists from all over the world.

When Sinn Fein, as a revolutionary movement, was finally to become involved in working-class politics in 1982, it would find in Ballymurphy an area in which the people were already well enough in control. Fifty-three community groups were still beavering away at the area's problems, with new issues being constantly tackled as soon as they arose. And, although Sinn Fein had not been involved as an organisation, many republicans in the area were deeply committed to local political agitation, the whole Ballymurphy development clearly stamped with the extra radicalisation injected by homecoming POWs over more than a decade. True, there were still many battles to be fought; but the score of victories, prior to 1974, and between 1974 and 1982, was, by any count, impressive.

Throughout the 1974–82 period, Ballymurphy's struggle ran parallel with the efforts of Whiterock man, Joe Hughes, a remarkable fund-raiser who pumped his heart out for others until it literally killed him. Born in 1942 with cerebral palsy, Joe was so severely disabled that his sole means of mobility was to push his wheelchair backwards with one foot. Still, by using his very disability – in the form of marathon wheelchair pushes – he single-handedly raised tens of thousands of pounds for a battery of causes.

In May 1974 he offered his services to the '42' project – undertaking a sponsored May push from Swords to Dublin – and for the next nine years was heavily involved in the community politics of the Upper

Springfield. Otherwise, the man who had spent twelve years of childhood in units for the mentally handicapped was off travelling Europe or hitch-hiking across Canada.

Joe's efforts were officially recognised in 1977 when he was awarded the Spastic Society Award and the following year he made history by being the only Ballymurphy person ever to receive an MBE, and what's more, to be fully supported in his acceptance of his imperial title. This was followed in 1981 by the William McKeown Award, and a People of the Year award in Dublin in 1982. When Joe died of a massive heart attack in the Royal Victoria Hospital in February 1983, tributes were paid to him from many quarters. Des Wilson called him 'one of the world's workers', while another of his old friends, writing of the personal struggle that Joe had been fighting since the first day he realised he'd been born on the minus side of fortune, described him as 'Joe Hughes who always did the impossible. Joe Hughes who believed there was no place he couldn't go and nothing he couldn't do. Joe Hughes in the wheelchair – a truly remarkable man who gave us all courage.'[1]

Two months after Joe Hughes' push from Swords to Dublin, as summer festivities were organised throughout the Upper Springfield, the British government published another White Paper. In it they demonstrated that they learn slowly. There would be another conference – a Constitutional Convention where those elected would seek a formula for devolved government. This formula would be subject to a London veto, would not be a return to the old-time Stormont, and would have to include some kind of power-sharing.

In Ballymurphy the plan was greeted with derision, and people got on with the important business of enjoying the summer. There were children's camps, the playscheme, another community festival, and '42's' educational trips for the younger children, which also proved educational for some of the adults. Greg Dormani, a New York student who would eventually spend over a year in Ballymurphy, accompanied one of the first trips – to Bellevue Zoo. He came back to Ballymurphy, gog-eyed. 'Shit man,' declared Greg, 'I ain't never seen anything like it. Those kids were climbing up the bars of the tiger's cage!' Witnesses of Ballymurphy children's assaults on British armoured cars might justifiably have wondered who in this case posed most danger to whom.

Meanwhile, the shootings and ambushes continued in the area, with several people wounded during June, and there were three determined attempts to burn down Corry's timberyard. On June 29th David Smith (26) of the Cheshire Regiment was seriously wounded in an ambush at the Whiterock/Springfield junction. He died six days later. On July 4th, the day the White Paper was published, there was a prolonged gun-battle at the same spot.

On July 22nd the only Ballymurphy Volunteer to lose his life in 1974 died while interned in Long Kesh. Twenty-three-year-old Paddy Teer had suffered head injuries in mid-July when British soldiers entered Cage 3 of the camp in force and beat up the prisoners. On July 19th he collapsed during an exercise period and lay for two days without medical attention before being taken to the Royal Victoria Hospital. He died of meningitis three days later.

On the wider front the IRA had resumed its bombing in the North and in Britain and the whole cycle of shooting, bombing, arms raids, mass military swoops, torture, loyalist assassinations, prison protests, street agitation and general state repression had been renewed since the collapse of the Executive. On August 8th and 9th there were the additional riots associated with the anniversary of internment, leading in Ballymurphy to the ritual petrol-bombing of the Taggart and the sealing of the district with barricades and burning vehicles. On August 12th, ten days after a British evacuation from Vere Foster School, twelve-year-old Catherine McGartland from Moyard climbed up on the roof to rub out an embarrassing 'Catherine loves Tony', and fell to her death through a skylight. A member of Cumann na gCailini, she was given a military funeral through Ballymurphy.

On September 6th, in the build-up to the second Westminster elections of 1974, Garret FitzGerald, Dublin's Foreign Affairs Minister, gave an interesting insight into his government's thinking. There should be no attempt at reunification, he said, as it would only add to loyalist fears and thus endanger the lives of nationalists in the North.

In a continuation of a most remarkable piece of revisionist juggling he went on to say that there had been many pogroms over the years in the North and that in the past five years tens of thousands of Catholics had been forced to flee from their homes – all a result of the IRA campaign of the previous four years![2] FitzGerald had conveniently forgotten that, in Belfast alone, almost 4,000 of these families were burned out in August and September 1969, long before there was any IRA campaign.[3] But Dublin wasn't finished yet. On September 21st Patrick Cooney, Minister for Justice, suggested a referendum in the 26 Counties aimed at abolishing Articles 2 and 3 of the Irish Constitution – those claiming jurisdiction over the Six Counties. What were the good loyalists of the North supposed to think, wailed Cooney, when a gramophone record celebrating an IRA prison escape was so popular in the South that it might soon be a chart-topper?

Four days later Dublin's paranoia of being embroiled in the Northern conflict reached hysterical proportions in a document prepared by Conor Cruise O'Brien, the government's political censor and Minister for Posts and Telegraphs. Dublin must play a low profile, O'Brien urged, so that there would be no 26-County boost to hard-line loyalism, otherwise, there could be a loyalist declaration of UDI, possibly followed by a British disengagement, and then a civil war. In this event there would be raids and bombings in the South, heavy casualties among Northern nationalists, and massive disruption of both economies, with widespread and lasting unemployment. The SDLP, he said, had told him that there would be some 250,000 refugees flooding over the border, among them 'large numbers of teenagers who, by reason of the conditions in which they have grown up, are tough, violent and virtually ungovernable'.[4] Little wonder that Dublin has spent all its energies since in maintaining the partition of Ireland, allowing Britain to take care of all those ungovernable teenagers.

In the Upper Springfield, dominant worries over the same period included the urban motorway, the dangers of vandalism to the new prefabricated library, and the packs of 'savage dogs' which were, according to 'Dog Lover', 'returning to the wild state' and 'attacking anything that moves'.[5] There was also an air of pride regarding the latest communal achievement – the completion of 'The Sloan's' social club.

The inspiration was Larry Sloan's, hence the name of the club, in memory of his 16-year-old son Michael, accidentally killed during an arms training session in 1972. A working men's club, Larry thought, would be good for the area, so, early in 1974, he gathered around him a team of selfless stalwarts and they set to work. Having little time for bureaucracy, Larry and his men dispensed with the usual trivia of leasing land, seeking planning permission, and other such irrelevancies, and chose their spot adjacent to the BTA community centre on land that belonged to Belfast City Council – or so the Council thought.

They then borrowed a JCB, dug a large hole, and laid, as Larry put it, 'more founds than would have held the *Queen Mary*'. In the process they broke the main electricity cable and had to pay for its repair. Using mainly unskilled voluntary labour, they went on to connect up with the local sewage system, and construct what must have been the ugliest, but most gallant, building in Belfast – just concrete blocks in a box shape with a flat roof. Then the booze was ordered, and the most famous of Ballymurphy's drinking institutions got under way. As Larry Sloan would recall:

> We had a dog shot dead in it, the Brits came in and fired 20 or 30 rounds in the club and we had two Brits wounded leaving it. The Brits hated it and they burned it three times, but we never closed one day. It opened at nine o'clock in the morning and closed at two o'clock the next morning. We helped local groups and paid funeral expenses, it was one of the finest clubs around.[6]

In 1979 an exasperated City Council would take the Sloan's to court in an effort to reclaim the land, only to discover that they couldn't prove ownership! A year later the whole shebang would move to more salubrious premises, but the council's headache would remain, simply transforming itself into a repair shop for the Black Taxis. In the autumn of 1974, history was indeed in the making.

Despite Dublin's pandering to the loyalists, the results of the Westminster elections, held on October 10th 1974, were the death knell for Faulkner's Unionists. The UUUC received 407,778 votes, while Faulkner's Unionists got only 20,454, hardly a promising sign for the Convention elections scheduled for May 1st 1975. Five days later the cauldron that had been boiling in the prisons finally exploded. On the night of October 15th 1974, republican prisoners in Long Kesh burned the camp to the ground. Fierce hand-to-hand combat followed between the prisoners and hundreds of soldiers armed with clubs and rubber bullets, and supported by dogs, and helicopters spraying CS gas from the air.

The next day republican women in Armagh Jail seized the governor and three other prison staff and held them hostage for 24 hours. There was also a riot in Crumlin Road Prison in Belfast and Magilligan Prison Camp outside Derry was set on fire. In Long Kesh alone, 23 soldiers, 14 prison officers and 100 prisoners were injured, and as the news of the prison uprisings went on the air, riots broke out in republican areas across the Six Counties. From the evening of October 15th to the morning of the 18th, the Upper Springfield was again virtually a No-Go area, with hundreds of youths armed with stones, bottles and petrol bombs engaging the military whenever they appeared.

A month later, on November 21st 1974, bombs devastated two public houses in the centre of Birmingham. Inadequate warnings resulted in 21 deaths and a further 180 casualties. Although nobody claimed responsibility, it was, as suspected at the time, an IRA operation. As part of the hysterical racist response that framed The Birmingham Six for the bombing, the British Labour Party – returned to power with a decreased majority – introduced the anti-Irish Prevention of Terrorism Act (PTA).

The Act's provisions allowed detention for interrogation of up to seven days (a provision already in force in the North), gave the police sweeping powers to arrest and enabled the British government to 'exclude' Irish nationals from England, Scotland or Wales and deport them to either part of Ireland. In the first six years of its operation, the PTA would bring about the detention of over 5,000 people. Of those, only 69, or 1.4 per cent were charged with any act covered by the PTA.[7]

On November 28th 1974 Paul Hill (20) of New Barnsley became the first victim of the PTA. He and his girlfriend, Gina Clarke, were arrested in Southampton. He was charged, along with three others, with an earlier IRA bombing in Guildford in Surrey. His mother, Lily, later described the methods used to extract 'confessions' from the Guildford Four.

Paul was prevented from seeing the NCCL solicitor that the family in England had got for him ... He was held naked in a cell in his bare feet with nothing but a towel. He was beaten and threatened with a gun. He was handcuffed while he was interrogated. He was prevented from sleeping and given no food. Threats were made that they'd give his girl-friend, who was pregnant, 30 years. They even produced her at one point to make it look like she was getting interrogated too ... In the end he couldn't take any more and he signed, as did the others ... Later on it was found that there were 101 discrepancies in the statements, but it didn't matter to the court. The statements, which were retracted, were the only evidence against them. The one attempt at an ID parade was with Carole Richardson; and then a policewoman got picked! ... When I went over to see him in court, I was refused permission to go in. They wouldn't even let me into the street. Eventually, when I got seeing him in Winchester Prison, he looked terrible. So thin and nervous and he kept rubbing his face. He looked in shock.[8]

In October 1975 the Guildford Four were convicted as charged. Paul Hill was given the longest sentence ever passed in a British court and had his name entered in the *Guinness Book of Records*. Two months later an IRA unit, captured after the Balcolme Street siege, admitted the Guildford bombings. Their statements gave precise details of the operation, some of which were new to the police. Nevertheless, the Guildford Four remained in prison until 1989. Along with the Birmingham Six and the Maguire/Conlon family, they were victims of guilt-by-birth – they were Irish.

As well as paving the way for a full-blooded assault on Irish nationals in Britain, the Birmingham bombs sent the loyalist killer squads into a frenzy. On November 22nd they hit the People's Garage, part of Whiterock Industrial Estates, on the Upper Springfield Road. A car drove into the forecourt and as the 20-year-old attendant, Geraldine Macklin of Westrock Drive, approached it, she was shot dead. The garage manager, Seamus Mac Seain, was shot in the abdomen.

By the end of November, Geraldine Macklin was just one of 35 people killed in the month's sectarian attacks. Belfast, where 18 of November's killings had occurred, was a city stalked by terror where only fools strayed onto the main roads and nobody went near the city centre after six o'clock in the evening. The Provisionals continued their bombing campaign while the Officials, now among their most vitriolic critics, condemned 'the men of violence' from their new-found pedestal of ideological purity. But, despite public utterances, there were grave differences of opinion within the Officials' camp on the question of armed resistance to British rule.

Ever since the unilateral truce declared by the Official leadership in May 1972 there had been simmerings of discontent within the ranks. The most prominent of the dissidents was Seamus Costello, a veteran of the Border Campaign and an elected representative of Wicklow County Council. At the Official Sinn Fein Ard Fheis in December 1974, Costello's faction attempted to swing the Officials back towards a military offensive, having failed in a similar attempt the previous year. When they again lost the vote, the 80 or so delegates who felt that the war in the North should be supported left the conference and established the Irish Republican Socialist Party.

Initially the IRSP did not have an armed wing. However, many of the former OIRA Volunteers who made up the bulk of the new organisation had taken their guns with them when they defected. At the same time the remaining members of the OIRA, furious at the loss of the 'stolen' weapons, were only too ready to have a crack at the 'Irps'. Their first strike was in Ballymurphy. On February 20th 1975, Hugh Ferguson of Whiterock, chairperson of a local branch of the IRSP, was shot dead on a building site close to his home. Five days later OIRA Volunteer Sean Fox of Andersonstown was killed in retaliation. In the ensuing feud which lasted until mid May, the tally of victims included Billy McMillen, long-time commander of the Belfast Officials who was shot dead, and Sean Garland, national organiser of Official Sinn Fein who was badly wounded in Dublin.

By the time the feud was over the IRSP's armed wing, the People's Liberation Army (PLA), was firmly established, although it maintained an official distance between itself and the IRSP. In February 1976 the PLA merged with a group of former OIRA Volunteers to become the Irish National Liberation Army.

Despite the IRSP's continued denials that it had an armed wing, the INLA would in time become closely interlinked with the IRSP. It and the IRSP would together face a future of intensive state repression on both sides of the border, and ongoing internal divisions that would result in split after split, culminating in the bloody feud of 1986–7. By then there were four separate factions calling themselves the INLA – three of which later merged into the Irish People's Liberation Organisation (IPLO) – and a string of dead bodies testifying to the bitterness of the fragmentation.

Shortly after the 1975 feud between the PLA and the Officials, the IRSP suffered its first split when Bernadette Devlin McAliskey and eleven other members resigned, accusing the IRSP of having lost sight of the class war and concentrating on the national question. They were also unhappy with the emergence of the PLA as an armed wing of the party. In October 1977 the new party would suffer one of its severest blows with the assassination in Dublin of Seamus Costello as he sat reading a newspaper in his parked car. At the time the IRSP suspected either British intelligence or Irish Special Branch involvement in the murder. However, on June 4th 1982, a 37-year-old man was shot dead from a passing motorbike as he left a pub in Dublin. The INLA issued a statement saying that the dead man, James Flynn, was a member of the quiescent Official IRA and the gunman who had killed Seamus Costello.

On December 10th 1974, a group of Northern Protestant ministers, led by the Reverend William Arlow, met in Feakle, County Clare, with the entire core of the Provisional Republican Movement. The meeting was disrupted when the IRA's representatives received a tip-off that the Irish Special Branch were on their way to Feakle, but not before significant progress had been made. When Arlow returned to Belfast, he was in a position to offer the Northern Ireland Office IRA terms for a Christmas ceasefire with a possible extension to a bilateral truce.

On December 18th Arlow and his colleagues flew to London to meet with Rees and Sir Frank Cooper, Permanent Secretary and chief policy maker at the NIO. The following day Arlow flew to Dublin to meet the Provos. On Friday, December 20th, the IRA announced a cessation of hostilities from December 22nd to January 2nd 1975. On New Year's Day they issued a further statement saying that they would extend their ceasefire until January 16th. When the British failed to respond to either of these gestures, the IRA offensive was renewed. Five days later another Ballymurphy Volunteer was killed. Twenty-two-year-old John Stone, who had been on the run from the British for two years, was transporting a bomb along with another Belfast Volunteer, John 'Bap' Kelly when the device exploded prematurely, killing both men.

The renewed IRA offensive met with a negative reaction. Many people in the war-torn nationalist areas felt that the British should be given more time to respond, and that perhaps they might end internment. The British, for their own ends, were also anxious for a prolonged truce. Negotiations between the IRA and the Wilson administration were re-established and on February 11th 1975 the IRA announced a second 'indefinite' truce. The IRA agreed to halt its attacks on state forces in return for a calling off of military repression and a number of political concessions. These included the opening of 'incident centres' – one above McEvoy's shop in Ballymurphy – that would be staffed by Provisional Sinn Fein members and would have a direct telephone link with NIO officials based in an office in central Belfast. Their purpose would be to monitor the truce and prevent any repeat of the Lenadoon incident that had brought about the collapse of the 1972 truce.

For the British the 1975 truce was a major coup. At a small price they had managed to secure an end to the fighting. And this at a crucial moment when they were about to open up a new front in their war against republicanism. Ten months earlier, Rees, in a speech to the House of Commons, had spoken of a long-term British strategy of 'normalisation' in the North.

The plan was to push the RUC into the front line against the IRA, with the British army playing a secondary role, so that the war was seen as more of a 'law and order' problem. 'Normalisation' and 'criminalisation' would then neatly complement one another in portraying the war as a 'criminal conspiracy' being dealt with through the 'normal' processes of the police and courts. The fact that the RUC had been retrained into a fully armed military force and that the courts had also been militarised would not be immediately recognisable to the outside observer, giving the British an additional angle in the propaganda war.

There was also the inherent move towards 'Ulsterisation' which meant that the RUC and UDR would take more of the brunt of the war. In turn fewer British soldiers would come home in boxes and the conflict could be explained away as a row between those irrational 'Paddies'. The British also hoped that the truce would provide a more convivial atmosphere in which to proceed with the Constitutional Convention. And it would bring an end to the bombings in Britain.

As far as the IRA was concerned the truce would give their supporters and themselves a welcome break from the war. It would enable their units to recruit and regroup and it would allow the Republican Movement to introduce its political programme to the community at a time when the class dimension of the struggle was being pushed to the fore by the more radical elements of the IRA and Provisional Sinn Fein.

At the same time the incident centres would establish the Provisionals as the recognised guardians of the community's welfare, and a de facto police force of the ghettoes. But the most forceful incentive for the 1975 truce was the promise made by the Wilson administration *that they would withdraw from the North if the Constitutional Convention failed.* Although the British subsequently denied this claim by the IRA, Reverend William Arlow stated in May 1975 that he believed 'that the British government has given a firm commitment to the IRA that they will withdraw the army from Northern Ireland'.[9] As the IRA well knew, the chances of the Convention succeeding were nil.

On February 13th, two days into the 1975 truce, a St Valentine's Day card exploded in a house in Whiterock Gardens. Seven-year-old Deirdre O'Kane had run upstairs to her mother, Monica, with the morning post. A few minutes later, as they both opened the card, it blew up in their faces, injuring mother and daughter. The card-bomb was one of five posted to nationalists in the city. A second in Whiterock failed to explode only because the alarm had been raised before the recipient, Davie Walsh, tried to open it.

That night there was a related bomb scare in Ballymurphy Road. A car, hijacked in loyalist Silverstream, was abandoned outside '42' – with an ominous Valentine card on the front passenger seat. The British army cleared the surrounding houses, but the '42' clan, just home from the pub, dismissed the military panic. They returned to the house, opened the windows 'to let the blast through', and put on the kettle for hot whiskies. Donal Fagan, who was now living part-time in the house, armed himself with a crowbar. Then, as soldiers dived for cover, and Claude, a culture-shocked French photographer staying at '42', proclaimed the presence of lunatics, the well-oiled Donal – on whom fortune persistently either smiled or frowned signally – ripped open the boot of the car. Lucky for all at '42', there was no bomb.

Another of the Ballymurphy Road crew's lucky escapes occurred on the night of Sunday, August 24th 1975. Two carloads of community activists from '42' were returning from the project's holiday home in County Cavan. Shortly after crossing the border, on its way through South Armagh the first car passed two UDR vehicle checkpoints, the second of which was in the process of being set up. The second car, some 15 minutes behind, later reported passing through only one checkpoint. In the interim two nationalists on their way home from a football match in Dublin's Croke Park were machine-gunned by the Protestant Action Force (a cover for the then legal UVF) – the ghost patrol operating the second 'UDR' checkpoint!

Meanwhile, as the spring progressed, the ceasefire between the British and the IRA made little difference to life in Ballymurphy. On March 9th the ongoing feud between the Officials and the PLA returned to the district. Two men burst into a house in Whiterock Parade with guns blazing, but their intended victim managed to escape. Four days later a blast bomb exploded in Britton's Parade in the same area, and a four-year-old girl was injured by flying glass. During the weekend of April 5th to 7th, in an orgy of sectarian shootings and pub bombings that left eleven dead and 82 injured, another local man died.

Kevin Kane (18) of Springfield Park was one of two nationalists killed when a cylinder bomb was tossed into McLaughlin's bar on the Antrim

Road on the Saturday afternoon. On the Sunday night three members of the (Officials') Republican Clubs were shot in the legs at Moyard Social Club by the PLA.

By the middle of April 1975 the situation in the North was such that it was virtually impossible to know who exactly was attacking whom. Along with the IRSP/Officials feud, another feud had been raging between the UDA and UVF since mid-March. There was also the continuing sectarian slaughter, with loyalists and nationalists being gunned down in the streets and blown up in pubs. And there was the British army's role, which combined overt killings with its covert surveillance and destabilising programme, the full extent of which will never be known. What is known, however, is worthy of comment.

During the second week-end of April, Sir Frank King, GOC, launched a caustic attack on the British government's agreement with the IRA, and particularly on the release of republican detainees from Long Kesh. A total of 200 had already been released, King told his Nottingham audience, and 370 more would be out before the end of the year. He lambasted the politicians for negotiating at a time when, he believed, the IRA was on the run. As a result of his speech, King was recalled to Belfast by Merlyn Rees as the British establishment did its utmost to gloss over the general's insubordination. But the general was not alone.

During the early months of the truce there were several incidents in which innocent civilians were gunned down by soldiers in deliberate attempts to force a resumption of IRA hostilities, while the SAS continued its covert war, regardless of the truce. Again it is impossible to say how many 'sectarian' or 'internecine' shootings and bombings were carried out by undercover soldiers, but such operatives certainly accounted for a number of deaths in 1975.

In the truce's initial phase, prior to January 16th, John Francis Green, an IRA Volunteer who had escaped from Long Kesh, was murdered in a farmhouse in County Monaghan by an SAS death-squad under the command of Captain Robert Nairac who was subsequently killed by the IRA in South Armagh in May 1977. The UVF claimed Green's killing in March 1975, and this claim seemed confirmed when one of the guns used, a Star pistol, was found on the roadside outside Newry following the UVF massacre of the Miami showband in July 1975.

However, it later transpired that both operations were the work of the same Kitsonian 'mixed gang', recruited by Nairac to engage in murders and abductions on behalf of British intelligence.* It also transpired that the UVF bomb that exploded and killed two of the Miami killers as they attempted to load it into the showband's van, was meant to kill the whole UVF team. Nairac, having decided that the UVF team knew too much, had double-crossed them by sabotaging the fuse on the bomb.[10] It was also later revealed by two former Military Intelligence Officers, Captain Fred Holroyd and Colin Wallace, that British undercover opera-

*In another twist in the relationship between the state forces and the loyalist killer squads, two of the men later charged with the Miami massacre turned out to be soldiers in the UDR militia.

tions in the mid 1970s were directly responsible for some 30 killings in Ireland, along with the Dublin bombings of 1974.

According to Holroyd, the reason for this splurge of killings can be traced to a feud then in progress between MI5 and MI6, the internal and external arms of the British secret service. The truce with the IRA had been negotiated by a British team which included the permanent secretary of the Northern Ireland Office, Sir Frank Cooper, and the MI6 Head of Station, James Allen. To undermine what they saw as an MI6 sellout to the IRA, MI5 and sections of the British forces used agents in loyalist groups to push the IRA into a sectarian conflict in the North.

Direct evidence of prowling SAS operatives turned up several times during the truce. On April 19th, two months into its 'indefinite' phase, the IRA wounded an undercover soldier in an unmarked car on the Falls Road. The soldier escaped, but a tape containing the names of 30 local Provisionals was found in the van. On July 8th another undercover soldier was involved in a traffic accident at the junction of Leeson Street and the Falls Road. The soldier ran off and his car was set on fire by local people, but a US-made machine-pistol and photographs of 51 Belfast Provisionals were confiscated from the vehicle by the Official IRA. A killing carried out by such an operative could in no way be traced to the doorstep of the British army.

In addition to the general maelstrom of 1975 the IRA continued to operate on a low key, retaliating for British violations of the ceasefire, or at times it seems, simply unable to control some of its members. But anti-British operations by republicans were minimal compared to the level of two-way sectarian attacks and 'knee-cappings' – punishment shootings carried out against suspected collaborators and alleged criminal elements. The policing role of the Provisionals during the ceasefire brought a considerable rise in knee-cappings as the IRA turned its attention to the burgeoning problem of the 'hoods'.

A sizeable section of the generally unemployed youth population whose excitement threshold had been raised sky-high by the Troubles, but whose role in the war had diminished since the earlier days, had now turned to petty crime and joyriding, both to amuse themselves and to supplement their state benefits. The IRA's interest in the hoods was twofold: first, their activities – house-breaking, robbing the milkman and the baker, stealing cars and driving recklessly through the streets – were bringing added pressures on the already beleaguered communities; and secondly, these activities were placing them in a position in which they could be blackmailed by the RUC (and often were) into becoming low-grade intelligence-gatherers for the British.

There was also the added concern for the youngsters themselves, who were in danger of being shot dead at any moment as they cruised about areas like West Belfast in their stolen cars. (In June 1972 the first joyrider to be summarily executed by British forces was killed on the Whiterock Road. Three young men, James Bonner, Patrick McGaughan and Patrick Canavan, were fired at when they drove through a military checkpoint, and James Bonner was killed.)

During 1975 knee-cappings were occurring on an almost weekly basis in the Upper Springfield, as they were throughout the North. By the end of October a total of 374 punishment shootings had been recorded since the beginning of 1973. But the problem of the 'hoods' refused to go away.

On January 30th 1987 the confrontation between the republicans and Ballymurphy's more wayward youth reached an unprecedented stage when the 'Whiterock and Westrock joyriders' threatened the 'so-called Provies' that if they didn't lay off, the joyriders would take action against the IRA and those in the community who reported them to the IRA! Along with raising howls of laughter locally, the joyriders' ultimatum brought a reminder from Ballymurphy's Sinn Fein councillor, Sean Keenan, that 'the British army with all their resources have been trying to do that for 17 years'.[11] That particular crisis was defused the same night. A small contingent of IRA men moved into Westrock and Whiterock, rounded up all the likely hoodish hit-squad types, fired five shots over their heads, and sent them scurrying back to the safety of their cider. The whole episode being viewed with considerable humour by the community.

By mid-June 1975 the truce was becoming extremely shaky, but both sides were still adamant that all was well, and Rees was still releasing the internees. Meanwhile, everybody who could use a gun or prime a bomb seemed to be working overtime. At the same time the Upper Springfield was entering another phase of its wars with the Catholic hierarchy. On June 16th Des Wilson announced his resignation as curate of St John's parish, sparking off an angry reaction in a community that had had enough of the hierarchy's tramplings.

The latest episode had taken place on April 24th at St Thomas' School. It was prize-giving night at the school and the headmaster, 62-year-old Sean McKeown, had taken the step of inviting his journalist son, Ciaran McKeown – who would later become one of the three central figures of the 'Peace People' – to cover the event, particularly the speech to be made by Canon Padraig Murphy, chairperson of the school's management committee. When Ciaran McKeown arrived at St Thomas', however, he was immediately confronted by the Canon, who produced an article that he (McKeown) had written for the *Sunday Press* the previous May. The theme of the article was 'Shared Schools' and it covered Bishop William Philbin's controversial decision to withhold the sacraments from children attending state schools – the issue that had caused all the trouble at Vere Foster. To the astonishment of both McKeowns, Murphy proceeded to direct the younger man from the building, pronouncing him to be 'persona non grata' in 'any Catholic institution'.

After 18 years in St Thomas', eleven of them as principal, Sean McKeown resigned. To the community, and to Des Wilson, it was yet another insult heaped on top of all the other insults. But Des Wilson had already tendered his resignation on March 2nd, and had it accepted by Philbin in a letter dated April 25th. He had merely kept his silence until June 16th.

The anger felt in Ballymurphy took two days to gather itself into a coherent form. On the night of June 18th, in a spontaneous act, 1,500 people stormed into the hall of St Thomas' School, breaking the locks of the front door as they went, and held a public meeting. Frank Cahill was elected to chair the gathering and after two hours of heated debate a Parish Council Steering Committee was elected with a mandate to fight back on behalf of the people. The ensuing struggle became known in Ireland as the 'Holy Watergate'. Had some of the angrier women at the initial meeting had their way, it would have begun with the 'symbolic' burning out of the parish priest, Canon Padraig Murphy.

The furore caused by Des Wilson's resignation, and Ballymurphy's response, shook the Catholic Church in Ireland to its foundations. The public debate ran for a full month, with priests, academics, newspaper editors, religious correspondents and laity generally sympathetic to Des Wilson's and the Ballymurphy position. One commentator stated that whereas the millionaire recluse Howard Hughes had been given one week to prove that he was still alive, the Irish Catholic Church had been given slightly longer.

Although the hierarchy, from the parish priest to the Papal nuncio, refused to meet Ballymurphy's elected representatives, or to engage in any debate or clarification, their silence served only to further condemn them. On Tuesday June 23rd, 200 pupils from St Thomas' School, against the wishes of their teachers, mass-picketed the canon's house on the Falls Road, Ballymurphy residents picketed churches, and there was a leafleting campaign at the gates of the City Cemetery during a 'Reconciliation Sunday' when Murphy was displaying his 'liberalism' to visiting Protestants. But still no response.

Then the smear campaign – the whispering – began: that Des Wilson had had a nervous breakdown; that he had run off with a woman; that the protestors were all 'lapsed Catholics and communists'. That was the point at which the psychological break happened between the Upper Springfield and the Catholic hierarchy. In the wider Church and the wider community, the 'Holy Watergate' might have run its course in a year or two, but in Ballymurphy, the trenches were dug between the people and *their* priest and the establishment Church.

Over the coming years the practising Catholic population of the Upper Springfield would drop so much that the new Corpus Christi Church would be divided in two, one half becoming a parish centre. This pattern would also show in other urban nationalist areas of the Six Counties, as the republican population, radicalised by years of conflict, came to a more exact realisation of which side the hierarchy was actually on in relation to the people, the state, and its own vested interests. But in Ballymurphy there was also that Des Wilson episode and all it represented.

On his resignation, the Ballymurphy curate issued a statement saying that he had asked to leave the Diocese of Down and Connor because he felt 'the Catholic Church in Belfast had been unable to produce better procedures than those used by the Unionist Party in the days before the present violence.'[12]

In reality, he never left his work. Even though the 'faculties of the Diocese' were withdrawn from him – he could no longer function publicly in the Diocese, and his Church pay was stopped – he continued as before at Springhill Avenue. He is still there today, having become one of the most vocal and respected human rights figures in Ireland, a position that automatically keeps him well outside the confines of established Irish Catholicism.

In 1982 75-year-old William Philbin was replaced by 65-year-old Cahal Daly as Bishop of Down and Connor. One of the new bishop's first moves was to 'reinstate' Des Wilson, returning to him the faculties of the Diocese. However, despite this cosmetic move, none of the conditions prevailing in 1975 had changed in any way that would make the Ballymurphy priest alter his stance. While accepting the bishop's gesture by turning up in Corpus Christi at a Mass at which he was officiating, to a spontaneous round of applause from the congregation, Des Wilson would remain outside the fold. Indeed, within a short time, Cahal Daly had occupied William Philbin's position symbolically as well as physically, breathing SDLP politics from the pulpit and rounding on republicans and their working-class supporters at every opportunity.

In August 1986 the uneasy peace between Des Wilson and Down and Connor came to an end when the Ballymurphy priest walked out of a funeral Mass in protest at the Bishop's comments. Paddy McAllister, a Black Taxi driver, had been murdered in his Rodney home by the UFF. Yet the Bishop somehow managed to use the occasion to launch another attack on republicanism and suggest that nationalists' problems could all be attributed to this one source. 'I was under no obligation', Des Wilson recalled, 'to listen to that kind of stuff.'

Throughout June and July 1975 the sectarian attacks and the UDA/UVF feud continued, but the IRA remained generally inactive against crown forces. In the Upper Springfield the only serious attack of the two months came on June 20th when a 48-year-old man was wounded from a passing car in an attempted sectarian assassination in Springhill Avenue. In August, however, the general atmosphere began to change. In line with escalating republican attacks across the North, activity in Ballymurphy began to increase.

Early in the month there were a number of shooting and blast bomb attacks. On the night of August 8th, as the annual internment anniversary got under way, serious rioting broke out in many areas of the North, giving way in West Belfast to heavy gun-battles between the IRA and British forces. In Ballymurphy the Taggart and Fort Pegasus came under siege and an RUC man was wounded by gunfire. The rioting continued throughout August 9th and gave way again on the afternoon of the 10th to further gun-battles, beginning in Divis Flats, and spreading up the Falls to Ballymurphy and Turf Lodge. On August 11th the shooting in republican areas of West Belfast spread to the Shankill after an attempted bank robbery was foiled. Then on August 12th the shooting died down. And the rather odd truce was found to be still holding!

By the end of August, however, the deal between the British and the IRA began to become undone in earnest. The Convention was hopelessly deadlocked, as the IRA had expected, but noises from London gave no indication of any imminent troop withdrawal. On August 27th the IRA resumed its bombing campaign in Britain in an attempt to prod the British government into its pull-out declaration. Nothing happened. At the end of September the bombing was resumed in the North, as were full-scale attacks on British forces. Still nothing happened – and still the 'truce' officially remained! There was clearly going to be no British withdrawal.

In the Uppet Springfield the sound of blast bombs and gunfire became more frequent, and the killing began again. On September 9th 41-year-old George Quinn of Glenalina Road, a socially withdrawn man who enjoyed going for solitary walks, was found shot in the head at Turf Lodge roundabout. He had been killed by loyalist gunmen. On September 26th a warning was phoned to St Thomas' School that an unexploded mine lay in Corrigan Park at the rear of the school. The British army, for whom the mine had been intended, arrived to investigate and triggered it off, injuring two soldiers. Afterwards, the *Belfast Telegraph* reported, 'an army expert fired a single shot at a suspicious saucepan near the scene of the explosion'. On October 10th, 24-year-old Sean McNamee was shot dead at the Whiterock Industrial Estate when he grappled with three raiders during an armed robbery at the Macweld Engineering Plant which he and his brother owned. The raiders were members of the Official IRA. Then on October 29th the area became engulfed in a new wave of violence as feuding broke out in Belfast between the Officials and Provisionals.

Not since internment week in 1971 had anything in nationalist areas of Belfast been as bad as the two weeks that followed October 29th 1975. The feud began at about 6pm that evening when the Provisionals launched 31 separate attacks in the space of half an hour against known Officials, several of them in Ballymurphy. One man was killed and 20 were wounded. Immediately Belfast's Officials armed themselves and struck back, and the cycle began, with British forces staying well in the background. During the next two weeks of inter-street war, people stayed indoors after dark in nationalist areas, something that the years of loyalist terror had failed to achieve.

In the Upper Springfield, streets were patrolled by armed men, and in some cases both factions could be found dug in in gardens or in bushes at opposite ends of the one street. Shots were fired from back gardens into people's homes at night, doors were kicked in and houses sprayed with sub-machine-gun fire, and cars passed one another in blazing shoot-outs on the main roads. But the worst aspect was that the shooting was not confined to actual members of both organisations, 'supporters' also became targets and that meant almost everyone in the community. In an atmosphere of unparalleled fear, nationalist Belfast watched appalled as the casualty toll mounted until eleven people were dead and

50 wounded in hundreds of incidents. Among the dead was a six-year-old girl who was struck by a bullet during a Provo attempt on her father's life.

The initial spate of shootings was followed in the Upper Springfield by sporadic sniping by both groups, then further casualties on October 31st. That afternoon a 15-year-old boy was wounded near Kelly's bar and shortly afterwards a burst of shots fired at a group of youths standing in New Barnsley Crescent injured a 16-year-old girl. On November 3rd 22-year-old ex-internee James Fogarty, a former member of the Officials, was shot dead at his home in Rock Grove in front of his wife and child. Three nights earlier shots had been fired into his home, narrowly missing his wife.*

On November 7th a bomb was thrown by the Officials at Kelly's Bar in response to the bombing of a number of Falls Road (Officials') pubs by the Provos. On November 8th a pensioner was shot at while getting out of a car in Ballymurphy Road. On November 11th 19-year-old John McAllister of Ballymurphy Drive was shot dead as he waited for a bus on the Springfield Road at the top of Springhill Avenue. He was killed apparently because his mother, Ethel, was a prominent member of the Republican Clubs (Officials).

The feud finally came to an end on November 13th, the day after the killing by the Officials of 28-year-old John Duggan, chairperson of the Falls Taxi Association. The Black Taxis, supported by most residents of the Falls, formed a huge cavalcade of protest, demanding an immediate end to the shooting and bombing. It was later conceded by the Provisionals that this period of self-destruction played directly into the hands of the British, whose 'criminalisation' propaganda was greatly boosted by what was widely portrayed as a gangland vendetta. It also drove the dwindling Officials and their supporters further into their ideological ghetto so that they became vicious opponents of the republican struggle, eventually adopting a pro-partition stance, and effectively becoming another shade of unionism.

Meanwhile, on November 12th the truce had eventually come to its official end when Merlyn Rees severed his government's telephone links with the Sinn Fein incident centres. The British were simply acknowledging the obvious – the war was back in full swing – no concessions were going to be made in the face of the collapsing Convention and Whitehall had reaped all possible advantages from the exercise.

The British were now ready to move forward with their dual policy of 'criminalisation' and 'normalisation'. The new legal and judicial framework proposed by Diplock was firmly in place so that internment without trial, and its attendant concentration camps, could be ended without any British loss of tactical advantage. In fact, the sooner it was ended, the sooner the new policy could get under way. On December

---

*A year later, James Fogarty's wife, Maureen, unable to take the strain any longer, committed suicide.

5th the last 46 men were released from the internment cages of Long Kesh. Among them were several men from Ballymurphy.

* * *

Maura McCrory of Dermott Hill recalls the period of 1976 to 1979 as 'one of the most horrific of all, the time when Castlereagh was turned into a torture chamber with just one aim, get as many of our people as possible into the H-Blocks, whether they're "guilty" or not'.[13] Maura McCrory was a member of the Relatives Action Committee during the three years of what became known in Ireland as the 'H-Block conveyor belt'.

The powers given to the RUC under the Emergency Provisions Act (EPA), coupled with the 'legal' changes wrought by the Diplock system, were specifically designed to achieve the same results as might be achieved through internment, while avoiding the international flak caused by the latter.

Under the new arrangements suspects could be interrogated for up to seven days, they could then be held in remand for up to two years with no hope of bail, and, if no 'evidence' was available, they could be released immediately prior to their scheduled court appearance – internment by remand. The onus of proof was shifted from the state to the accused and – the kernel of the Diplock system – confessions induced under torture were admissible in court unless the accused could prove that his or her injuries had not been 'self-inflicted'. These 'confessions', either verbal or written, were sufficient to secure convictions in the political courts. No corroborating evidence was required. Now, that internment had ended, it was a means of jailing *suspects* as well as those apprehended during anti-state activities. The onus was therefore on the RUC 'to build up an atmosphere in which the initial desire to remain silent is replaced by an urge to confide in the questioner'.[14]

The assault and torture of suspects, always a casual part of the state's apparatus, now became the full-time occupation of those employed in the various interrogation centres. The 'conveyor belt' of interrogation–Diplock Court–H-Block was under way. The personal account of Brian Pettigrew (21 at the time), who had been wounded during the 1972 Westrock massacre, was fairly typical. He was arrested in February 1977 and taken by Saracen to Springfield Road Barracks at 4am :

There was no bedding in the cell and the light was kept on all the time ... At about 8 o'clock the first interrogation began ... I was put up against a wall and punched and slapped about. When I didn't answer the way they wanted, one of them says 'Let's get the machine'. They brought out this sort of blackboard easel that came apart in two halves. Then they put a plastic binliner over my head, it came down to my waist. I felt this thing, the easel, go around me so I was locked inside. They tilted the top against the wall so I was leaning at a 30 degree angle with my hands pinned down to my sides and the back of my head against the wall. My trousers were pulled down to my ankles and they started beating me between the legs with some kind of plastic stick. That went on for maybe half an hour ...

Then they'd put me in this big tin cabinet and bang on it, with them screaming on the outside. It was terrifying. Then it was back to the wall for another beating, and then the cabinet again, and so on ... They made you do press-ups. They took my shoes off and if I refused to do the press-ups, they'd beat the soles of my feet with the plastic thing. There was always three of them, plainclothes, in the room at the same time. They'd stand around you, pushing you from one to the other, slapping you around the head, punching you in the stomach. They also had a telephone with three wires and loops, and they put these on my fingers, saying I was going to get electric shock treatment; but nothing happened.

It was just a scare tactic. Then they brought me to a window, opened it, and lifted me up with my head pushed out, threatening to throw me out ... There was also general abuse of my family. I had a sister killed in an explosion and they got at me with that. There was one detective would've come in after all the rough treatment and try and act friendly, then the others would come back in and the brutality would start again ... In three days, there were 12 or 13 interrogations, all involving that kind of brutality. Afterwards, I complained but nothing ever came of it.[15]

Brian Pettigrew, battered and disoriented, finally 'confessed'. Without a shred of supportive evidence, he was given a ten-year sentence by the Diplock Courts. Scores of other Ballymurphy men suffered varying degrees of the same treatment, among them Eddie Rooney, who was seriously injured when he was thrown from an upper-storey window of Springfield Road Barracks to bounce off a parked car 25 feet below.

In November 1977 Amnesty International arrived in Belfast to conduct an investigation into torture in the Six Counties. They published a damning report in June 1978. Nevertheless, the practices condemned by Amnesty were to continue. Eventually an RUC doctor, Robert Irwin, appalled at the injuries he was still treating, spoke out. His televised interview of March 11th 1979 caused a political storm and prompted a British smear campaign against Irwin. It also forced the British government to publish its own *Bennett Report* on the allegations five days later. Although seen by many as an attempted whitewash, its findings were sufficient to bring a US embargo on arms sales to the RUC and oblige the British to look for other means of facilitating the machinations of the Diplock courts.

But the exposure and neutralisation of the torture centres were not the only problems facing 'criminalisation' by 1979. The second arm of the new strategy was the phasing out of political status, as proposed by the *Gardiner Report* of January 1975. The Second World War type compounds of Long Kesh were to be replaced by cellular high-security H-shaped blocks, changing the POW image to a penal image and everybody convicted in the Diplock Courts of acts committed after March 1st 1976 was to be treated as a common criminal. On March 27th, as Sinn Fein negotiated in vain behind the scenes with the NIO, the IRA warned: 'We are prepared to die for the right to retain political status. Those who try to take it away must be fully prepared to pay the same price.'[16] On April 8th they shot dead Pacelli Dillon, the first of 18 prison officers (and one civilian prison worker) who would be killed by republicans before the H-Block issue was resolved.

The Relatives Action Committee, to which Maura McCrory and many other Ballymurphy women belonged, was formed in April 1976 in response to the growing concern over the impending confrontation in the prisons.

To my knowledge Ballymurphy RAC was the first to be set up. There were very high feelings among the people. Up till then the prisoners had been recognised as political prisoners. Now, the Brits were going to try and take that away from them. It was clear to us that a lot of work, a lot of organisation, would have to be done on the outside. In the end it would be up to us, the relatives and the community, to do whatever could be done.[17]

Over the next five months, as nationalist areas steeled themselves for the inevitable, the British poured out an endless stream of criminalisation propaganda. Those who had publicly been policing large areas of the North suddenly became 'Godfathers' and 'small groups of criminals' with 'no support in the community'. At the same time the enforcers of the new policy and the 'conveyor belt' were moved into position.

Former chief superintendent of the London Metropolitan Police, Kenneth Newman, took over from James Flanagan as chief constable of the RUC on May 1st 1976. Newman had spent the previous three years reorganising the RUC, building up its intelligence-gathering capacities until they were among the most sophisticated in Europe, and establishing Castlereagh as a central specialist interrogation centre. The new chief constable and his reshuffled retrained forces – supported by a network of informers and interrogation centres – were to be the new instrument of British military success against the IRA.

On the political front, Merlyn Rees was replaced in August 1976 by Roy Mason as Secretary of State. The Convention had collapsed on March 4th, and the politically-minded Rees was no longer needed. Mason, former Defence Minister, was the ideal man, as far as the Labour government was concerned, to implement the new militarist approach to the North, a role he clearly relished. In November 1977 the Mason/Newman team was further bolstered by the appointment of Major General Timothy 'Bull' Creasey as GOC.

Creasey's career had included specialist counter-insurgency operations in support of the feudal Sultan of Oman between 1972 and 1975. Prior to his appointment to the Six Counties, he had been stationed in Bradbury Lines, Hereford, the headquarters of the 22nd SAS. It was Creasey's responsibility to speed up 'Ulsterisation', passing the war over from the British army to the locally recruited RUC and UDR, and where this was not possible (in staunch republican areas) to bring the war to the enemy.

By the time of Creasey's appointment, the H-Block issue had taken off.

On September 14th 1976 17-year-old Kieran Nugent became the first person to be convicted in the political courts for an act committed after March 1st. On arrival at Long Kesh, he refused to wear prison uniform and became the first of the 'Blanket Men'. Over the coming months, as the conveyor belt funnelled its victims into the cells of the H-Blocks, the battle of wills between the British government and Irish republicans began to centre around one issue – political status.

Twenty-seven year-old Jimmy Duffy of New Barnsley was the first of Ballymurphy's Blanket Men. He had been wrongfully convicted of assaulting a soldier during a British army shoot-up of the Sloan's Club and sentenced to three years. He described conditions during his own mini blanket protest in Crumlin Road Jail:

> There were only four of us there, me, Fra McCann, Joe Maguire and Gerard Murray. They classed us 'short-termers', under three years, so they wouldn't send us to the Blocks. After I was sentenced early in 1977 I went straight on the blanket. We were locked up 24 hours a day. We weren't allowed any covering, no blanket, to go out to the toilets. Going to the toilet or going for a shower we had to go naked ... The food was bad and they only gave us small amounts ...
>
> All you had was the bed, three blankets and the mattress. Then every 14 days you were trailed naked in front of the governor and charged with not conforming. You lost 14 days remission and all your privileges and got three days on the boards [solitary confinement]. That entailed everything being taken out of your cell. So, during the day you were naked in a bare cell, no blanket or nothing, and that was mid winter. At 8 o'clock at night they gave you your mattress and blankets back, and they were took out again at 8 o'clock the next morning. And that happened to you every fortnight ...
>
> I had done about 18 months when the no-wash started. We got a 'comm' from the O/C of the Blocks telling us about it, and that it was up to us if we wanted to take part. So we decided among ourselves that we would join the stepping up of the protest. The 'remands' had been shouting over, telling us they'd back us up. The screws on that night must've heard, and the next morning we were brought before the governor individually. He says we weren't going to foul his prison up and he was sending us to the H-Blocks with the rest of them. I lost about four and a half stone in the Crum. I also ended up with sciatica – from the cold of the concrete floor. There was also some violent treatment, but nothing like what went on in the Blocks.[18]

In Long Kesh the blanket protest had brought a brutal response from the prison regime. Protestors were kept locked in their cells 24 hours a day, naked except for a blanket. Between 7.30am and 8.30pm they remained on a bare concrete floor without bed, mattress or reading material. The only furniture was a single chair, normally shared by two men, and a chamber-pot. They were denied exercise, fresh air and proper food, and were regularly subjected to beatings and degrading treatment. Prisoners were dragged by the heels along corridors and beaten off the grillwork on their way to the humiliating anal searches, while warders kicked and batoned them.

Seamus Martin of New Barnsley was 21 years old when he arrived in the H-Blocks in September 1977. He and five others had been apprehended after a bombing in Belfast. The IRA unit to which he was attached had planted four bombs at Balmoral Showrooms and were attempting to make their getaway when the military and RUC arrived with guns blazing. Seamus Martin and Gabriel Corbett were shot and all six were arrested. Among them were Bobby Sands and Joe McDonnell, who would soon be part of the most shattering experience faced by Irish nationalists since the spaced-out executions of the 1916 Rising in Dublin. Seamus Martin described the depravity that was already part of the Long Kesh regime by September 1977:

I was lucky: I was shot and they took me straight to Musgrave Park's military wing; the others were taken to Castlereagh. Bobby got a really bad time. His mother didn't even recognise him when he came out of Castlereagh ...

When we got to the Blocks there was already a kind of routine of brutality and vindictiveness. Petie Clarke got glass in his food; I got maggots in mine. You'd put your water-gallon out and the 'shite orderlies', as we used to call them, would come along and fill it. They'd put maggots and shite into it all the time, and they'd piss in the gallons too. But if you had kept thinking about it you wouldn't drink, you wouldn't eat.

If you were going out on a visit you left your cell with your wee towel in your hand and they brought you to Room 26 where the prison uniforms were. Then they threw you right up against the wall. You got your legs spread apart and they used a torch and mirror to look up your arse. If they thought you had something, they got the doctor to give you a search. Sometimes the screws done it themselves. Then they might use the same fingers in your mouth. When you kicked up, they stuck their fingers in disinfectant and then shoved them in your mouth. So you couldn't win either way. If you refused to squat the screws would hold you down and force you into position. If you resisted in any form, they'd beat the crap out of you.

There were also routine beatings going on on a regular basis.[19]

The warders also took to entering the cells in force, battering the men, and kicking over their chamber-pots. Finally, because the use of toilet and washing facilities was being used as a lever against them, the prisoners decided in February 1978 to escalate their protest. They would no longer wash, clean their cells or slop out. From then on they daubed faeces on the walls to keep it off the floor and slept on urine-soaked mattresses, surrounded by maggots and the stench of human excretions and rotting food. In response, the prison regime went berserk.

Once the dirt protest started, it became a complete battle of wills between us and the screws. They were out to break us, that was all they lived for. The beatings had been very heavy in the early days, but they had slowed down a little by the beginning of 1978. But, with the dirt protest, they really started again, especially in H3 and H4. They also started the forced baths and used that as a terror tactic. They started in H4 and there was nothing but slaughter matches, one whole wing beaten in one day, until they got to H5. Then they stopped. They used to do that: use different levels of violence in each Block to try to sow dissent.

Then they started using the doctor, Mengles we used to call him, and he'd come in and pick out individuals. He used to wear a dickie-bow ...

Most of the beatings happened in wing shifts, when they came to clean the cells. Or sometimes they'd come into the cells. The wing shifts happened about every nine days. The screws were paid according to the cell, so the more they could do, the more money they got.[20]

With the onset of the 'dirty protest', life in the H-Blocks reached new depths.

You had to pour your piss out under the door. To make sure it didn't come back in again, you beat your bread into a pulp and sealed the bottom of the door like a wee dam. Then at one end of the door you built a wee round wall so you could pour out without it coming back in again. Screws with squeegies would then come down and mop up. Or, if you were unlucky, you might get a screw who liked to use the hose. Then your cell and you and everything else got soaked in ice-cold water. In some cases they blasted the men with steam machines that were used to clean down the cell walls. They'd also use ammonia, throw it under the cell doors or in the window at you.[21]

Dysentery and diarrhoea became rampant until the bearded, filthy H-Block men began to resemble the inmates of Dachau. Yet, the protest ground on without a chink in the British position, while the RAC, led by blanket-clad men and women, marched up and down the Falls Road in a futile attempt to draw world attention on what was happening in the H-Blocks, efforts that were severely hampered by the media's prostration before the 'Peace People'.

On August 10th 1976, a British mobile patrol was chasing an IRA unit along Finaghy Road North. They riddled the IRA car and killed the driver. The car then ploughed into Andersonstown woman, Ann Maguire and her four children. Three of the children were killed – either by the car or by British bullets. The fact that the subsequent results of autopsies and an inquest were never published brought many to believe that the soldiers were the actual killers. Nevertheless, the British turned the tragedy into a major propaganda coup.

That night, Ann Maguire's sister, Mairead Corrigan, broke down on TV. Watching the programme was Betty Williams, who got in touch with Mairead Corrigan after deciding that something had to be done to stop the war. They were later joined by journalist, Ciaran McKeown, and on a deeply emotive tide, spurred on by a multi-million-pound British propaganda effort, the Peace People took to the streets. Although their one-sided condemnation of violence soon lost them whatever support they had in republican areas, the media continued to buoy them up until their final collapse in October 1977, following the two women's acceptance of the Nobel Peace Prize, and their decision to keep the prize money for themselves.

Meanwhile the war went on relentlessly, but with a major shift in IRA structures, forced on the Volunteers by British intelligence successes and the effectiveness of the RUC torture centres.

In 1977 the old structures of Brigades, Battalions and Companies was replaced by a virtually impenetrable cell structure, with small groups of Volunteers specialising in particular jobs. We took to wearing masks and often operating outside the area. This threw Brit intelligence into total disarray and limited the damage that could be done in Castlereagh. As part of the same strategy, Volunteers from other areas operated in Ballymurphy. Some of these units were in place as early as 1976. For example, Paul Marlowe who was killed in the big gasworks explosion in October 1976. He was an ex-SAS man who was on the Brigade Staff, and he operated as a sniper in the Murph.[22]

The cell structures, though deadly efficient, had their own inherent disadvantages. Operations became less spontaneous so that the nature of IRA activity began to change. Targets became more selective and streamlined, chosen more for political impact than spectacular results, although bombing attacks continued on a regular basis to show that nothing in capacity had been lost. The low profile of the IRA during its period of reorganisation fooled Mason into believing the Movement was being destroyed. At the end of 1977 he declared bumptiously that British tactics were 'squeezing' the IRA, 'like rolling up a toothpaste tube'. Twelve years later, and Roy Mason, by his own admission, is a frightened man who walks about in constant fear of the same IRA.

Throughout, Ballymurphy's war continued. On February 14th 1976, as the British wheeled the 'conveyor belt' into place, and sectarian attacks against nationalists increased, four Ballymurphy Volunteers drove over to Highfield, where they shot and wounded two loyalist youths. As they sped off into the darkness, a military patrol gave chase and opened fire. Twenty-five-year-old Jimmy McGrillen was killed, one Volunteer escaped, and two were arrested, one having been shot in the neck.

In March Harold Wilson resigned as British Prime Minister and leader of the Labour Party, and James Callaghan took over. It mattered nought in Ballymurphy. People were far more interested in the presentation of the Xirinacs Peace Prize to Des Wilson by the Spanish section of Pax Christi. Then tragedy struck the area again. On March 23rd the military lifted Tommy Fegan of Ballymurphy Road. A neighbour saw the arrest and ran to his home with the news. Mary Fegan (56), a popular local woman who was also the mother of Ballymurphy's largest family (26 children of whom 11 had died), ran into the street to protest at her son's arrest. As she reached the Saracen taking Tommy away, she collapsed of a heart attack and died in the street. Tommy Fegan was thrown out of the vehicle which then drove off.

In May there were a number of loyalist shooting incidents between the Upper Springfield and Springmartin. These culminated on the 30th of the month in the murder of 31-year-old John Ritchie, a milkman from Moyard Park. He was found shot dead in his milk float at the top of Springhill Avenue. He had been on his usual Sunday morning round when he was murdered by loyalists from Springmartin.

Eleven days later, on June 10th, the Taggart came under sustained attack for the first time in months. A Volunteer ran up to the back wall, lobbed a bomb over the top, and withdrew under cover fire. A concentrated hail of bullets was then directed at the base from vacant flats and houses in Moyard, while the children and staff at Vere Foster again threw themselves on the floor. On June 27th a loyalist gunman on the back of a motorbike fired from the Springfield Road at a group of people in Springhill Avenue, but missed.

At the same time, community ventures continued: festivals and play-schemes were organised; co-operatives flourished; and '42' purchased a holiday home that had previously been on loan from the eccentric Lord Kilbracken of Killegar. There was also still talk of a British withdrawal, though the signs were very much to the contrary: the forts were being further fortified; railway-crossing gates were being erected at strategic points so that the area could be cut off at a moment's notice; and the information-gathering went on through dawn raids and head-checks and the continued questions about the colour of the living-room wallpaper, the dog's name, and the shape of your granny's nose.

By mid-summer the sectarian shootings and bombings had again become a nightly onslaught. Despite the long bright evenings, few people ventured out of the Upper Springfield at night to socialise. Movement was generally confined to IRA Volunteers carrying bombs and incendiaries into the city centre or launching attacks on the British army. At this point the IRA was beginning to scale down its level of localised activity in the ghettoes in line with its efforts to thwart British intelligence and deaden the impact of the interrogation centres which were getting into full stride in July 1976. As many republicans had become known to the British through their intelligence work during the 1975 truce, local attacks were becoming a liability to the IRA. After an attack, all the British had to do was pick up as many suspects as possible, whisk them off to Castlereagh, and get one or two to break under torture.

None the less, although Ballymurphy Volunteers were increasingly involved in attacks in other parts of the city, ambushes and sniping continued to be a regular feature of life in the area. During July and August, three soldiers were wounded, and a nationalist and loyalist injured in sectarian exchanges. Then, in the early hours of August 27th, the military set fire to the Sloan's Club, and only prompt local action prevented the building from being gutted. On September 19th the troops came back and there was a massive brawl in the club, during which soldiers shot up the place and killed an Alsatian dog in the process.

Three weeks later, on October 10th, an IRA unit, in oilskins and fishing waders, entered the culvert enclosing the Clowney stream and made its way up under the Lazy Acre to the Taggart, a quarter of a mile away. Using flashlamps, and securing a quarter-mile of cortex to the concrete tunnel with a Hilti gun, the ASU carried 200lbs of explosives and 200lbs of sand (to support the bomb) in rucksacks, and laid a mine under the Springfield Road at the Taggart entrance. The road erupted in a massive blast the following day as a foot patrol left the base. The soldiers were lucky to escape with minor injuries.

On October 23rd young people from the area joined other republicans on the Falls Road to oppose a march of the Peace People, against whom there was already strong resentment in republican areas, particularly since the plastic-bullet killing of 13-year-old Brian Stewart of Turf Lodge two weeks earlier. Feelings were running high and the march was stoned and, deliberately or by accident, Canon Padraig Murphy was struck on the head with a half brick. The following morning a small mine, detonated in New Barnsley, injured one member of a passing military foot patrol, one of seven soldiers wounded in the North that day. Over the next two months sporadic sniping continued in the area, as did knee-cappings.

The cat-and-mouse nature of Ballymurphy's war was again highlighted in December. The IRA laid the bait by detonating a small charge outside the enclosed reservoir on the Whiterock Road. They also spilt some animal blood at the scene to give the impression that a Volunteer had been injured in a premature blast. Meanwhile, two mines had been planted inside the railings of the reservoir to catch the investigating troops. To avoid detection of the command wire, it was run up a telegraph pole and along the wires to the detonation point. At the same time, three Volunteers with rifles were positioned in a block of disused flats in Turf Lodge, some 300 yards away. The military, however, didn't fall for it. Guessing that the reservoir had been booby-trapped, they moved in cautiously.

'It took them days,' one of the Volunteers recalled, 'they knew the mines were there, but they were in no hurry to defuse them. They were afraid that we had something else up our sleeves. At the same time, we kept moving about trying to get a "dig" at them. They put up camouflage screens on the Whiterock, and put Brits outside to protect the ones inside. So we hit the guards.' On December 14th one soldier was shot in the chest in the brief exchange of gunfire. The IRA then withdrew, leaving the military to deal with the two devices.

Four days later, soldiers shot dead 17-year-old John Savage from Ardoyne just below the Taggart. The youth was one of three who had evaded a roadblock in a stolen car.

The early months of 1977 were relatively quiet in Ballymurphy. Physically, the area seemed to be reviving itself. The wrecked houses had either been pulled down or rehabilitated; in Moyard the derelict blocks of maisonettes were being restored by squads of locally-recruited labour. On March 1st, amid unionist allegations that cash was being siphoned off the Moyard contract by the IRA, the Housing Executive announced that, following talks with the contractors, the average restoration bill per unit had dropped from £11,000 to £7,000.

At the same time a number of community activists were involved in ongoing dialogue with Lord Melchett, the Minister of State for Health and Social Services, about wider plans for the area. A leisure centre, library, shopping complex and health centre were being planned for the waste ground above the City Cemetery, and a landscaping of the area was being discussed. But all had the backdrop of the rising tide of torture and the H-Block protest. On March 3rd former Stormont Prime Minister and the architect of internment, Brian Faulkner, was killed in a horse-riding accident. His horse, they said in Ballymurphy, was a Provo.

The Upper Springfield remained fairly quiet until July as the IRA reorganised. There were few attacks on British forces, and only three British casualties, two injured by explosions and one by gunfire. Corry's also had two further fires at the beginning of April, and there was rioting in the area on May 18th. A strike instigated by Paisley in early May had petered out after a few days' unsuccessful bullying by loyalist heavies, and had had little or no effect in Ballymurphy where unemployment in most of the estates was running at some 65 per cent and rising.

But one aspect of the strike was viewed with approval, it split the UUUC wide open. The Official Unionist Party and the UDA were furious at Paisley for damaging loyalist credibility with a failed strike, while Paisley was dismissive of their protests, arguing that the strike had worked because it forced the British government's hand. It was an argument that was strengthened two weeks after the strike's collapse. Paisley had demanded tougher measures against republicans, more power for the RUC and a return to the old-style Stormont. Mason responded by increasing RUC members from 5,500 to 6,500, arming them with M-1 carbines to supplement their revolvers and Sterling sub-machine-guns, increasing the RUC Reserve Corps and the UDR, and promising more SAS involvement against the IRA.

Meanwhile, tension between the Provisionals and Officials had exploded to the surface on Easter Sunday, April 10th, in a series of incidents that had all the hallmarks of a British secret service conspiracy and brought two more deaths to the Upper Springfield. On Easter Sunday morning, as the Officials mustered at Beechmount for their annual parade to the Republican Plot at Milltown Cemetery, a parcel bomb exploded on a window sill of an old bakery. Ten-year-old Kevin McMenamin from New Barnsley Drive was killed in the blast and three others were wounded, one man losing a leg. Immediately, the Officials blamed the Provisionals for planting the bomb. This would appear to have been the intention of the bombers, loyalists, for whom the Provisionals, whose parade was then arriving at the Republican Plot, would have been a far more prestigious target.

So convinced of the Provisionals' guilt was the Beechmount crowd that stewards had a difficult time restraining the marchers from racing off to Milltown for revenge. An hour later the angry Officials arrived at Milltown – just as the Provisionals were leaving the cemetery. Jeering and booing broke out. Then, as the Officials entered the cemetery, directly under the gaze of the British army and RUC at Andersonstown barracks, bottles and stones began to fly in both directions and fierce hand to hand fighting broke out. During a half hour's running battles in the cemetery, as British army helicopters hovered overhead, a number of shots were fired by the Officials, and two people were wounded.

By early afternoon the situation had escalated across Belfast, with both sides arming themselves. Three hours after the death of Kevin McMenamin, shooting broke out again, this time close to the junction of Whiterock and Springfield Roads. John Short (49), the dead boy's uncle, and Daniel Mateer (33), both from New Barnsley, got out of a car containing three other members of the McMenamin family. They were about to bring news of the death to other relatives when a second car pulled up alongside. Three Provisionals jumped out and opened fire. John Short was shot dead and Daniel Mateer was hit in the legs.

Only the realisation by both sides that loyalists, possibly being manipulated by the British, had planted the Beechmount bomb (and a second device that was defused) prevented the Easter Sunday incidents from flaring up into another bloody feud. But tension remained high over the coming months.

At about the same time Donal Fagan, still doing youth and community work at '42', had a curious encounter of the kind that illustrates the IRA's relationship with the nationalist community. Chrit Verstappen and Annemieke Ryckenberg, two long-standing Dutch friends of the '42' project, had sent on four postal orders for £150 each from their fundraising efforts in the Netherlands. Donal Fagan went to St James' post office on the Falls Road to cash them.

I had passed the postal orders across and your man was counting the money out. Next thing, the door slammed behind us. A bloke rushed past me with a balaclava and sack, and another guy closed the blinds. I realised immediately what was happening so I pushed the money back. But I couldn't get my hand under the glass to grab the postal orders. We were ordered up against the wall with our hands in the air – six others or so and myself. One bloke covered the door and the other ran in behind the counter, throwing everything he could find into the sack, stamps and all.

So when he came out I waited my opportunity and sort of slowly turned around, my hands still in the air, and says, 'Do you mind if I speak to you?' And he just levelled the gun on me. My heart was bouncing. He says 'What the fuck do you want?' I sort of knew then it was OK. I said, 'I want those postal orders.' He says, 'Who owns them?' I said, 'They belong to a community group in Ballymurphy that runs holidays for kids.' He looks at me for a while, then hands me the bag and says, 'Take them.' So I rummaged through the bag, lifted them out, and turned back to the wall with my hands up in the air again.[23]

And thus it was.

In June 1977 Fianna Fail returned to power in the 26 Counties in a massive landslide victory. The change was viewed in the North with hope; in Ballymurphy, feelings were that at least things couldn't get any worse. These feelings were borne out shortly afterwards when protesting IRA prisoners in Portlaoise Prison were granted political status in all but name, thus defusing the cauldron built up in the prison during the Coalition reign. In July the IRA increased its attacks in the Upper Springfield, and a soldier on foot patrol was wounded in Ballymurphy Drive on the 21st.

A week later, on July 27th, republican areas again erupted in feuding between the Officials and Provisionals. The first attack occurred at 3pm and the gunfire went on without stop until early the following morning, by which time four people had been killed and five wounded. In Ballymurphy, Kelly's Bar was sprayed with gunfire as were several houses, two men were wounded in Springfield Park, and the legendary Tommy Tolan, Jim Bryson's life-long friend and one of the *Maidstone* escapees, was shot dead. He had just returned from his honeymoon with his wife of two weeks, Maureen McGuinness, when the Official IRA ambushed him outside his Divismore Crescent home. Then the feud was over as suddenly as it had begun.

The IRA began August with a bombing campaign across the North, the largest concentration of attacks taking place on the night of August 4th when 20 explosions went off in Belfast and Lisburn. These were followed on August 5th with 58 bomb hoaxes that brought chaos to the Six Counties. On Sunday, August 7th, the annual internment parade again featured a protest in support of the H-Block men, and again exploded into a riot which spread to all republican areas and was followed by gun-battles. On the night of August 8th further gun-battles broke out in Belfast, and the Taggart came under heavy fire several times.

The next day, during rioting in Springhill and Westrock, Volunteer Paul McWilliams (17) was killed in Westrock Drive when he was shot in the back by soldiers stationed in Corry's timberyard. He had been on active service, petrol bombing the military posts when the soldiers started shooting. In immediate retaliation the IRA raked the Taggart with gunfire and killed Louis Harrison (20) of the 3rd Light Infantry. On the same day an undercover RUC squad shot a young man attempting to hijack their car at the top of Whiterock Road. The wounded man was dragged to safety by two friends.

Although much of this violence was associated with the internment anniversary, August 1977 was fuelled with an additional provocation to republicans. In an effort to demonstrate to the world at large that all was now 'normal' in the Six Counties, Mason had managed to convince Buckingham Palace and Whitehall that a visit by the British Queen to mark her jubilee year would be a major psychological boost in the war against the IRA. The visit was arranged for August 10th and 11th and the escalation of IRA activity was a prelude to what they promised would be a memorable tour.

On August 10th, Queen Elizabeth II arrived aboard the royal yacht *Britannia*, sparking off three days of riots, gun-attacks and hijackings in nationalist areas across the North. During her two-day visit she was ferried by helicopter to the safe loyalist towns of Hillsborough and Coleraine in a massive security operation involving 32,336 soldiers, RUC and UDR militia – Operation Monarch – while 800 nationalists were imprisoned in a mini-internment for the duration of the visit. Even then, the IRA managed to breach the royal security net with a small bomb that exploded in a flower-bed at Coleraine University shortly after the Queen had left. While Mason congratulated himself on such a rum example of 'normality', the other normality was being remembered on the Falls Road where a 40-foot length of graffiti asked: 'Will Lizzie Visit H-Block?'

Tension was high in the Upper Springfield for the remainder of August, as it was in other nationalist areas of the city. On August 19th inter-communal rioting broke out between Moyard and Springmartin youths, the first such rioting for a long time. A week later, the RUC and British army, in a display of 'normal policing', raided the unlicensed Sloan's Club and confiscated its entire stock of drink which was carted off in three 4-ton army trucks.

On August 28th attacks against the military continued with an ambush on a foot patrol near Corrigan Park in which a soldier was grazed by a bullet. Three days later a rocket was fired at an army vehicle at the Whiterock/Springfield junction. It struck the vehicle but deflected off to one side, exploding in mid-air and injuring two children of 12 and 13 with shrapnel. This was followed on September 6th by a further ambush on the Springfield Road. The weekly post office delivery of benefits cash to Whiterock Post Office was being escorted as usual by two Saracen armoured cars when the IRA fired into the back of one of the Saracens, injuring four soldiers. At the same time, kneecappings took place regularly, earning one entry at the top of Whiterock Road the nickname of 'Kneecap Alley'.

By the autumn of 1977, however, the sectarian siege had begun to lift from Ballymurphy. As a result of discussions through mediators between loyalist leaders and the Republican Movement in the early months of 1977, and the realisation by loyalist groups that their people were just as vulnerable as nationalists, the wholesale slaughter of non-combatants had been brought to an end. Although loyalist groups have continued to use sectarian murder as a political weapon from time to time, the level of attacks has not at any time in the past twelve years, reached anywhere near that of the early and mid 1970s. Republican involvement in sectarian attacks has not been resumed. Tighter control by the IRA's leadership in the wake of reorganisation has enabled the Army Council to enforce its anti-sectarian policies and prevent freelance operations.

However, the decline in sectarian violence in 1977 did not reduce loyalist violence against nationalists. In the interrogation centres and prisons, other arms of loyalism were savagely assaulting prisoners, while the revamped RUC, under heavy British army protection, was blasting its way back into republican neighbourhoods under the cover of armoured Land Rovers, rifles, sub-machine-guns and a rain of plastic bullets.

Along with the random assault of civilians, the beatings administered to those arbitrarily arrested, and the pre-emptive use of plastic bullets by the thousand, the state forces were also engaging in regular confrontations with H-Block marchers as the situation in Long Kesh continued to deteriorate. Peggy Burns, a prominent member of the Ballymurphy RAC, described how:

> Every time we went on marches they'd line the route, calling us whores and sluts, and what they wouldn't do whenever they got us. When we blocked roads, they ran Saracens through the middle of us. Then they sprayed us with cans, threw bricks at us. The things I've had thrown at me from Saracens: piss, shit and everything. As well as that they used to cut the legs off people with barbed wire hanging from the backs of the Saracens. Sometimes they'd charge you as soon as you got to a particular point, especially if you were going anywhere towards the town. Then they'd really get welted in, and the wee lads would retaliate.[24]

By the beginning of September 1977, 180 republicans were on the blanket protest and the 'conveyor belt' was chugging away in the background. By October condemnation of RUC violence in the interrogation centres was cutting across the nationalist political divide, with the SDLP accusing the force of 'illegal, inhuman and obscene behaviour'. In January 1978 the RAC decided to step up its campaign. On the 22nd of the month the Coalisland branch, led by Bernadette Devlin McAliskey, along with members of Peoples Democracy, sponsored an anti-repression conference in the town. Some 500 people turned up to discuss the Diplock courts, the H-Blocks, repressive legislation and resistance to British policies.

> This was the first attempt to build a broad-based opposition to criminalisation and draw in everyone who supported the prisoners' demands but mightn't necessarily support the armed struggle or Sinn Fein. It was followed (in February) by a second conference in Andersonstown where the same issues, and the possibility of a united front, were again discussed. Although nothing concrete came of either meeting, they were generally welcomed as a step in the right direction – towards a broad based anti-imperialist movement, and in support of the Blanket Men. But then La Mon happened and threw everything up in the air.[25]

Towards the end of 1977 the IRA had gone on a massive fire-bombing offensive across the Six Counties. The smaller devices, containing up to 3lbs of a deadly home-made explosive tied to a can of petrol, were easy to conceal and carry, and their napalm-like effect caused as much damage to a building as a 500lb car bomb. During a two-week period in December a fire-bomb blitz on 20 towns caused more than £3 million of property damage without a single casualty, demonstrating somewhat the folly of Mason's 'toothpaste' optimism. But the new tactic backfired badly on February 17th 1978, seriously damaging the united front against repression and the Blanket Men's cause.

An IRA Active Service Unit (ASU) left a fire-bomb on a window at the La Mon Hotel in Comber, County Down. The warning given was inadequate and the crowded hotel was engulfed in an inferno that incinerated twelve people and injured many others. Along with being a severe setback for the H-Block campaign, the La Mon bombing gave Mason an excuse to move against Sinn Fein. Over the next few days many prominent members of the party, including vice-president Gerry Adams, were arrested and charged with IRA membership. In later court cases those arrested were released, but the swoop succeeded in temporarily disrupting Sinn Fein and associating it in the public eye with the La Mon killings.

Throughout 1978, as the prison protest continued, the huge resources being deployed by the British in their war against the IRA finally appeared to be showing dividends. Intensive surveillance and the swamping of republican areas by state forces were limiting the operational capacity of the ASUs, and the interrogation centres were also taking their toll. With hindsight, however, it has become clear that caution, regrouping, retraining and acquiring new weapons were partly responsible for the drop in IRA activity, and that the situation was in fact beginning to even out into a military stalemate. This fact was acknowledged by Brigadier J.M. Glover in his report of November 1978 in which he accepted that the IRA would continue to be an active force for as long as the British remained in Ireland.

Ten years after the first Derry riots all the British had managed to achieve was to put a lid on the pressure cooker. By entrenching themselves in bunkers, and improving the armour-plating of vehicles and the quality of flak-jackets, the casualty-rate of state forces had dropped, but so had those of the IRA. The Provos had also concluded that there would be no quick military victory and had settled in for a long war of attrition. Instead of concentrating all their efforts at once, they had become selective in targets and timing, pinning down the same number of British forces with less expenditure, while increasing their sophistication and strike-potential.

The 1978 lull and the changing nature of the war were reflected in Ballymurphy by the drop in IRA operations and a year in which only one war-related death occurred. In the first six months of the year there were no more than a dozen sniping attacks on the military in addition to one proxy van-bomb attack on the Taggart. On April 12th, in a diversion from its usual activities, the IRA planted three bombs in Kelly's Bar and demolished it, claiming that too much loose talk went on in the bar, making it a threat to the area's security.

The 'hoods' at this period were also demonstrating a change of targets as they set monthly records for the number of bus drivers robbed on the Springfield Road between the Taggart and the Turf Lodge roundabout. Then, on June 16th, Kevin Dyer (25) of Glenalina Road, who had lived in Forthriver Gardens since his marriage, was murdered by loyalists in Glencairn. He had been drinking with a friend, and afterwards both of them went to a club in the Shankill area. When they left the club the Ballymurphy man was picked up by his killers, taken to Glencairn and killed with an engine casing which was dropped twice on his head.

In July 1978, four months into the dirty protest, Archbishop Tomas O Fiaich of Armagh, Roman Catholic Primate of All Ireland, visited the H-Blocks as whispers grew of a hunger strike on the horizon. On August 1st he released a statement, deploring the conditions in the prison, which reminded him, he said, of 'the spectacle of hundreds of homeless people living in sewer-pipes in the slums of Calcutta'.

A week later, the annual internment commemoration was again turned into a display of support for the H-Block prisoners and was followed by rioting and gun-battles in many republican areas. A banner strung across the Falls Road defiantly declared that 'Stone Mason won't break them', while young people in working-class areas, and IRA Volunteers, underlined the message with action.

Rioting throughout Belfast was widespread. In the Upper Springfield it continued from the morning of August 8th to the morning of the 11th, and was accompanied by several gun-attacks on the Taggart and Fort Pegasus, and on British mobile patrols. On August 11th a bus, hijacked on the Glen Road, was directed to the Whiterock Road where two IRA Volunteers put a small bomb on board and primed it. The driver was then ordered to drive the bus to the gates of the Taggart and leave it outside, which he did. The bomb exploded at 8.30pm, causing slight damage to the base. The area was then relatively quiet until August 27th when a 19-year-old man was shot in the chest, legs and jaw on Dermott Hill Road by the INLA, who accused him of informing and being responsible for the capture of INLA weapons.

In November 1978 Brigadier Glover's report noted that the reorganised IRA was concentrating more on 'attacks against the security forces and away from action which, by alienating public opinion, both within the Catholic community and outside the province, is politically damaging'.[26]

In December, as if to emphasise Glover's other assertion that the IRA could not be beaten, the ASUs were back in action, literally, with a bang. On December 14th 19 bombs went off across the Six Counties. Three days later seven bombs exploded in five British cities. The following day there were three car bombs in London. On December 20th nine hotels were bombed in the North. The next day three soldiers were shot dead in Crossmaglen. In frustration of the British hopes of mid 1978, the year was ending as it had begun. The IRA, finally fully recovered from the effects of the 1975 truce, was climbing back from its lowest ebb towards the year in which it would kill off 'normalisation' and draw the reins on 'Ulsterisation'.

* * *

Ballymurphy's first major IRA attack of 1979 took place on January 26th. A lorry was hijacked, packed with sandbags, and driven close to Fort Pegasus. When two army Land Rovers appeared, Volunteers raked them with gunfire. The occupants escaped, but two teenagers were grazed by stray bullets.

Then in March, Ballymurphy Volunteers were involved in one of the biggest operations ever planned by the IRA in the North. Forty-two bombs were prepared and stored in a warehouse in Short Strand for what a senior IRA Volunteer would later describe as 'the one that if it had come off, would have ended the war'. However, the British were tipped off about the location of the bombs, and a large contingent of SAS was moved into Short Strand in a joint RUC/army manoeuvre. Upwards to 30 Volunteers were to have taken part in the operation, and the heavy deployment of the SAS – many, according to the IRA, arriving disguised as workers in Department of the Environment lorries and vans – would suggest a British intention of devastating the Belfast Brigade with a major killing of Volunteers. However, according to one of the Ballymurphy Volunteers:

> The stake-out was badly co-ordinated by the RUC and the Brits. There were just too many DoE blokes running about all of a sudden. And word had also come in of strange activities around the perimeters of Short Strand. So we decided to abandon the operation and the gear and get the hell out. Volunteers started sending out radio-waves for the Brits to pick up, hoping that they'd think the whole area was booby-trapped. And it worked. The SAS pulled back long enough for all the units to get away. Afterwards, the Brits and the RUC spent ages blaming one another for the screw-up. Then, in July, a Volunteer named Michael Kearney was shot dead near the border for tipping the Brits off about the bombs.[27]

On March 16th, as the war ground on, the *Bennett Report* was published. On March 28th it toppled Callaghan's Labour government. In a crucial vote of confidence, the two non-unionist Six-County MPs, Gerry Fitt and Frank Maguire, abstained. Labour, already on a knife edge, lost the vote by 311 to 310. In the General Election of May 1979 the Tories, under Margaret Thatcher, swept into power, while the Labour Party, riven by internal divisions, was despatched to the political antipodes.

The collapse of Callaghan's government coincided with the launching of a new and devastating offensive by Ballymurphy units of the IRA. 'As a matter of policy', one of the Volunteers would later explain, 'we decided to go for actual Brit soldiers, and the best place to find them was at their bases.'[28] On April 5th a unit of Ballymurphy men moved into a barber's shop directly across the street from Andersonstown Barracks and shot dead two soldiers outside the gates.

This daring attack began the offensive that would last until May 1980 and be instrumental in causing the British to embark on a new 'legal' onslaught against republicans. It also caused the IRA leadership to augment Ballymurphy's weaponry with an M60 machine-gun. On April 11th the unit struck again, this time in Ballymurphy estate. Several bullets, fired at a Saracen from a house in Glenalina Crescent, ricocheted around inside the back of the vehicle and shot two members of the King's Regiment through the head. Christopher Shanley (21) died almost immediately, and Stephen Rumble (19) died eight days later.

Two weeks after the Glenalina Crescent attack another IRA Volunteer with Ballymurphy connections was shot dead. Billy Carson (32) and his wife, Annie, had gone out for the night when two loyalist assassins arrived at their Rosevale Street home off the Clintonville Road. When the two Carson children explained that their parents were not at home, the gunmen left. However, they returned an hour later and sat with the children until their parents came back at 11.30pm. The assassins met Billy Carson at the door and shot him several times. He died in the early hours of April 25th.

On May 4th 1979 Margaret Thatcher came to power to face the full IRA resurgence. The new British Prime Minister, a far-right autocrat and devout monetarist, was already a bitter enemy of republicanism. She had been badly shaken by the INLA assassination in March of her close friend, Airey Neave, Tory spokesperson on the North, whose car had exploded as he left the House of Commons' underground car park, and she was determined to exact vengeance on Irish republicanism.

Knowing little of Irish politics, she despatched Humphrey Atkins to the political graveyard of the NIO to step up the military repression of his predecessor against the IRA, now a highly-politicised guerrilla army bristling with self-confidence. He had hardly settled into his office at Stormont when, on May 9th, the Ballymurphy IRA detonated a booby-trap bomb in Turf Lodge, killing one soldier and wounding another.

The most telling example of what Atkins was up against came on June 6th when the Ballymurphy Volunteers launched an attack on the UDR's 10th Battalion based in South Belfast. A red 10-ton builder's truck, for the second time in two days, drove up the residential Malone Road with six IRA Volunteers hidden under tarpaulin in the back. At a certain point it turned, and came back towards the city, stopping outside the UDR base. On the previous day only one soldier had been in sight so the operation had been aborted, but on June 6th the look-out gave word to strike.

The six Volunteers jumped up, fired over 50 shots into the base and lobbed in two 15lb bombs, one of which exploded. One UDR soldier was killed and two wounded before the truck took off down Windsor Avenue. At one point an off-duty RUC man fired at the Volunteers, but the return fire was so heavy that he decided against pursuit.

However, on the Lisburn Road, two plainclothes RUC men in an unmarked car began to give chase. On Tate's Avenue they were within 20 feet of the truck, firing from the car, when all six IRA men popped up and returned fire. According to the IRA the RUC car immediately screeched to a halt and its two occupants dived for cover behind two women, one of whom had a pram, while the truck drove on unmolested to the Falls. The media said the RUC men 'took up firing positions'.

A month later, as the bombs and bullets continued across the North, the Ballymurphy IRA pulled off another audacious truck attack, this time on the Whiterock Road. On July 18th Volunteers watching through binoculars from a house in Turf Lodge spotted an RUC Land Rover at the bottom of the Whiterock Road. At that point, the RUC had just begun to venture back into the vicinity of Ballymurphy in their Land Rovers, and as yet had not entered the estates. Therefore, the vehicle would not be turning off until it reached the Springfield junction. At a given signal from Turf Lodge, a truck moved off from the top of the Whiterock Road while, further down, several Volunteers took up ambush positions at the spot where it had been estimated the two vehicles would meet. There the Land Rover was rammed up against the cemetery wall and while the truck driver escaped, the concealed Volunteers sprayed it with semi-automatic fire. But the RUC managed to reverse and withdraw, protected by the armour-plating of the Land Rover. The IRA, who had expected the police vehicle to disintegrate, melted off in disappointment.

Three weeks later, on the eighth anniversary of internment, the Upper Springfield, along with republican areas throughout Belfast and Derry, was again the scene of bonfires, binlid-bashing and fierce rioting. Stones, bottles and petrol bombs were hurled at army and RUC armour while the crown forces replied with volleys of plastic bullets fired from the cover of their vehicles. A new British tactic was also deployed – the whole of West Belfast was fenced in by closing the strategically-placed railway-crossing gates on its perimeters so that no barricade material (passing vehicles) was available in the republican stronghold on the nights of August 8th and 9th.

However, the rioting flared again on August 11th and went on for a further four days despite the new tactic. On August 15th two Pakistani men were wounded by the IRA as they drove past the junction of Springfield Road and Divismore Crescent 'for providing essential services to the British war machine in Ireland'.

Regardless of British innovation, the IRA was determined to undo Rees' and Mason's work, particularly in relation to 'Ulsterisation' and 'normali-sation'. By pumping in massive amounts of military and technological hardware and swamping districts with troops and RUC, the British might be able to contain given areas at a given time, but on no account would they be allowed to portray the Six Counties as a stable entity. Nor was there any question of allowing Britain to pull itself out of direct involve-ment in the war by replacing regular troops with the RUC and UDR. On August 27th the double blow that would wreck any such British plans was decisively struck.

Lord Louis Mountbatten, cousin of Queen Elizabeth II, colonial warlord, and last Viceroy of India, had been a long-time summer visitor to a Gothic castle overlooking Mullaghmore, a small village in County Sligo in the South of Ireland. On August 27th 1979 he set off in a boat for a day's sailing with a number of other British aristocrats and a 15-year-old local boy who was acting as pilot. As the boat left port under the watchful eye of a Garda patrol, a massive explosion blew it to smithereens. Mountbatten (79) and his 14-year-old grandson were killed instantly, as was the local boy, Paul Maxwell. The Dowager Baroness of Brabourne died later in hospital. The reaction in Britain to Mountbatten's assassination was one of shocked disbelief and outrage. So much so that the second blow of the day – militarily far more crushing – was almost lost in the media uproar and the howling of the British establishment.

A few hours after the bombing of Mountbatten's boat, the IRA detonated a 1,100lb charge by remote control at Narrow Water outside Newry. The bomb, hidden in a trailer of hay, blew a passing military vehicle 50 feet into the air and killed several soldiers. Shortly afterwards reinforcements arrived and an officer ordered his men into the cover of a nearby derelict house – just as the IRA had anticipated. The ASU, still lying in wait, detonated a second 800lb bomb concealed in the old house and blasted several more soldiers to death. The IRA then withdrew as the panicking survivors careered about in shock and confusion, shooting dead an unfortunate English tourist out for a stroll on the 26-County side of the narrow channel.

Military deaths for August 27th 1979 finally tallied at 18, the heaviest toll taken by the IRA since the 1921 Crossbarry ambush in County Cork when 35 British soldiers were killed. The reins were effectively drawn on 'Ulsterisation'. In Ballymurphy, as in all republican neighbourhoods, Narrow Water was greeted with a hushed awe giving way to a feeling that justice had been done – most of the dead soldiers were members of the Parachute Regiment, responsible for Derry's Bloody Sunday. On the Falls Road, within hours of Narrow Water, a scribe had written, '13 dead but not forgotten, we got 18 and Lord Mountbatten'.

The British army was stunned and demoralised, its officers furious at the politicians. In an effort to reassure her shocked troops, Thatcher flew to the North, had her picture taken in a flak-jacket in South Armagh, and went walkabout in Belfast. Her posturing, however, was somewhat dented when she ran into 63-year-old Harriet Kelly from the Springfield Road.

Harriet, a deeply religious, affable grandmother and a well-known old republican, was already a figure of some respect in the Upper Springfield. She had served six months in Armagh in 1971 'for batin' binlids, and I'm still batin' binlids today'. Since then she had spent a total of ten years on probation for various anti-state activities. On the day in question, Harriet had taken her grandson, Thomas, in town to buy him a tracksuit. She heard someone shout, 'There's Margaret Thatcher!'

The H-Blocks was so much on my mind, and them men and their suffering, that I run up with the intention of getting at her over the Blanket Men. I got through the bodyguards and they all got the shock of their lives. I shouted at her about the prisoners and the conditions they were living in, then I got arrested. An RUC woman went flying and they called up reinforcements. They took me to Townhall Street barracks and kept me in a cell overnight. I just sang republican songs the whole way there and all through the night. That woman [Thatcher] wasn't the way they put her across on TV. She looked to me like a frail weak woman. She put her head down – and so she should – and she blew. Like a cowardly dog she was. I shouldn't compare any woman to a dog, but that's how she was.[29]

The sight of Harriet jostling with Thatcher and her entourage was broadcast worldwide, earning the Ballymurphy woman much local admiration and a further three years' probation. She received many letters of support, one from an English woman who offered to pay any fine imposed by the courts. 'It would be a kindness on your part', the woman wrote, 'not mine.' Some weeks after the Thatcher incident, Harriet again offered to take her grandson to buy his tracksuit, but the little boy, still harbouring vivid memories of holding a shopping trolley as his grandma was hauled off to international stardom, wanted nothing of it. 'No way', he said, 'do I want any tracksuit or trips down town with granny.'

Thatcher's visit failed to detract from the realities faced by the generals. Despite ten years of military oppression, despite internment, Diplock Courts, torture and Mason's boasts, the IRA was still there, as effective as ever. The events of the past few months – especially the Short Strand bombs and Narrow Water – had demonstrated the bankruptcy of British government policies and angered the army brass who had never been keen on the idea of playing second fiddle to the RUC. As far as they were concerned all this 'cops and robbers' charade in the middle of a very real war was just a lot of nonsense.

The only way Thatcher could contain military dissent was by promising more force, more personnel, more covert operations, and more political moves against republicanism, particularly in relation to the 26 Counties. As a first step, she summoned the Taoiseach, Jack Lynch, to London for a ticking off, and demanded greater co-operation in intelligence and security matters. Lynch promised to comply, and also agreed to British army helicopter overflights along the border.

The next step was taken on August 31st with the announcement that the RUC was to be boosted by 1,000 extra recruits from 6,500 to 7,500, and the RUC Reserves were also to be strengthened. This would bring total British forces in the North to 31,500, 500 more than the 1973 figure – when the war was at its height. In a further commitment to covert action, Maurice Oldfield, former chief of MI6, was drafted in as 'spy supremo' with the dual task of streamlining RUC, UDR and military intelligence and stepping up the activities of the SAS and British secret service in the North. Clearly the British were not yet winning the war, nor were they containing it, militarily or politically. August 27th had shown that British military strategy was going nowhere.

In October 1979, as the IRA offensive went on, the political struggle was renewed, both by the British and the supporters of the H-Block men and the republican women in Armagh who were also demanding a return to full political status. (As clothing was not an issue in Armagh, there was no blanket protest, but the women were no longer co-operating with the regime.)

The British initiative, aimed at counteracting negative publicity in the USA after the Bennett Report, was launched by the Secretary of State, Humphrey Atkins. He announced plans for an all-party conference at Stormont to look at possible paths to devolved government in the Six Counties. The affair proved one more British flop. The Official Unionists boycotted it because it did not guarantee a return to the old Stormont, while the SDLP initially refused to attend because there was no guaranteed 'Irish dimension'. As a result of the SDLP refusal, party leader, Gerry

Fitt, resigned. He was replaced by John Hume MEP, whose nationalism was a little 'greener' than Fitt's. However, once Fitt was gone, the SDLP did a volte-face and agreed to attend when the rules were slightly changed to allow all parties to submit papers of their choosing. None the less, the conference collapsed in early 1980, having never really been off the ground.

The other October initiative was organised by the RAC at the Green Briar hotel in Andersonstown. There, Sinn Fein, People's Democracy, the IRSP, Women Against Imperialism, the Trade Union Campaign Against Repression, the Belfast Anarchist Collective, the Peace People and a collection of community and political activists from many different areas again discussed the formation of a united front against imperialism – this time without a La Mon. By now, Sinn Fein, under the increasing influence of its radicalised Northern *cumainn*, was steadily moving away from its earlier position of 'Brits out!' only and formulating long-term strategies towards its stated aim of a socialist republic in all of Ireland. Part of this plan was the acceptance that republicans could work profitably with other groups without those groups necessarily supporting the armed struggle of the IRA.

Although some republicans were deeply suspicious of the new policy, especially if it involved working with people who might, on other platforms, condemn the IRA, the four-year crisis in the H-Blocks, and the reported conditions of many of the prisoners who had now been two years on the dirty protest, temporarily discouraged opposition. It was therefore unanimously agreed at the Green Briar that a National H-Block/Armagh Committee be established with the aim of building up a single-issue campaign around the demand for political status.

It was agreed that, given the 'decline in public interest' and the desperation of the prisoners, time was running out. The last card available to the prisoners was already being mooted. As journalist Ed Moloney reported in *Hibernia*, 'the never quite articulated threat of a hunger strike was in the smoky air last Sunday in speeches from Sinn Fein leaders Gerry Adams and Gerry Brannigan as well as in a letter from the prisoners themselves'. And the last thing Sinn Fein or the Republican Movement wanted was a hunger strike.

Meanwhile, during the last four months of 1979, the Ballymurphy ASUs continued to make their mark, and the Ballymurphy death toll continued to rise. Earlier, on June 9th, 34-year-old Joseph McKee of Dermott Hill – whose brother died in the loyalist car-bombing of Conlon's Bar in 1972 – had been shot dead in a random sectarian attack in Castle Street. The gunmen escaped on the back of a motorbike, later found abandoned in North Belfast. The next fatality came on September 10th when 28-year-old Hugh O'Halloran died, having been battered with hurleys two days earlier by an Official IRA punishment squad not far from his Moyard home. Afterwards, before checking his facts, Seamus Harrison, Chairperson of the Belfast branch of the (Officials') Workers' Party, made the embarrassing statement that: 'Our party wishes to place on record its absolute condemnation and disgust at these murders.'[30]

Two days later, Gabriel Wiggins, a father of 14 children, was murdered by loyalist gunmen in his home on the Springfield Road.

Earlier in the month, in another display of British democracy, Pierre Salinger, former White House press secretary to Presidents Kennedy and Johnson, was arrested along with a group of journalists and Sinn Fein members at Ballymurphy community centre where they had stopped as part of a fact-finding tour. Salinger and his entourage were only released twelve hours later after the US Consul had intervened. The Sinn Fein members were held for several days.

September 1979 was also the month when Pope John Paul II visited Ireland. The visit was a masterful piece of stage-management by the Irish hierarchy, aimed at drawing back to the fold the increasingly secularised Irish urban communities, and putting the seal of papal authority on the Irish Catholic Church's traditional anti-republican stance. To the tune of a multi-million-pound religious trinket industry, 1.3 million people – over a quarter of the island's population – turned out for a papal Mass in Dublin's Phoenix Park, while another half a million attended a service in a field at Drogheda. The Drogheda occasion, close to the border, was chosen by the Pope for the delivery of his expected pronouncement on the war in the North. In a message clearly aimed at the IRA, he said:

> Now I wish to speak to all men and women engaged in violence. I appeal to you, in language of passionate pleading. On my knees I beg you to turn away from the paths of violence and to return to the ways of peace. You may claim to seek justice. I, too, believe in justice and seek justice. But violence only delays the day of justice. Further violence in Ireland will only drag down to ruin the land you claim to love and the values you claim to cherish.[31]

It was the old Catholic relationship with British imperialism, albeit tempered to suit changing times. There was no reference to Britain's presence in Ireland, nothing about the torture at Castlereagh, the H-Blocks, the plastic bullet murders of children or British army death squads. The British used John Paul's homily as 'proof' that the IRA campaign had no moral basis.

Within a week new security measures were announced by Atkins. 'It's Provos watch out, I reckon,' Atkins threatened. Three days later Maurice Oldfield arrived in the North. At 4pm that afternoon the IRA responded. An ASU from Ballymurphy had been waiting for six hours for a Derry-registered Mini to come down the Whiterock Road and turn up towards Fort Monagh. When it did, four men stepped from the doorway of a DIY shop and riddled it with bullets. The car crashed and the IRA unit fired more shots into it, leaving one of its occupants, 21-year-old Paul Wright, dead and the other seriously wounded. Both were members of the SAS, shot 'to coincide with Oldfield's arrival'. Shortly after the Volunteers had withdrawn, locals removed an SLR from the car and later handed it over to the IRA.

On October 12th the Ballymurphy Volunteers struck again. Two soldiers were wounded in a 4-ton truck as they left Springfield Road Barracks. The ASU, using its new M60 machine-gun, and four rifles, had been lying in wait in a house in nearby Cavendish Street. Two weeks later, on October 28th, they hit the same barracks again, killing an army sergeant and seriously injuring two RUC men, one of whom later died. This time the ASU had taken over a house in Crocus Street, again opening fire with the M60 and four rifles as the soldiers and RUC left the base. They then escaped through a top floor window and over rooftops.

Although the IRA was operating on many fronts, the M60 attacks were having a debilitating effect on British morale, as neither their flak-jackets nor vehicles could stop the concentrated fire of the heavier machine-gun. On October 29th, in an attempt to find the M60 – which was hidden in a wall-excavation in a house in the Upper Springfield – the British army swamped Beechmount, the Falls and St James in a house-to house search. They also deployed a large force in Ballymurphy, arresting Des Wilson in the process. But nothing was found.

Security bosses were also so worried about the effectiveness of IRA intelligence that they were beginning to believe that the RUC, UDR and prison service were riddled with moles, further adding to state demoralisation. Meanwhile, another Ballymurphy death was recorded on October 21st when 31-year-old John McGuinness died from wounds received in February 1971 during feuding between the Provisionals and Officials. At the time he had been a member of the Officials and had been shot and paralysed, being since confined to a wheelchair under constant medical care.

On December 3rd 1979, eight days after the IRA blitzed 16 targets across the North with 23 incendiary bombs, the Ballymurphy Volunteers, in conjunction with another Belfast unit, shot dead William Wright, the sixteenth prison officer to die as a result of the H-Block impasse. They then lay relatively low for a while as the IRA continued to strike elsewhere.

The confidence with which the Ballymurphy IRA was now operating was evident in all its operations, but most perhaps in one particular attack at the new Sloan's.

The Brits were weighing in constantly at the Sloan's. They were targeting the clubs at the time. A 'remote' was put down near the entrance to the building. But when it was checked, the aerial wasn't picking up the signal. One of the lads then discovered that when it was pressed against some chickenwire that formed part of the fencing behind, it worked, so we attached it to the chickenwire. The Brits weighed in as expected and the lads hit the mine, but only the 'det' blew. (The soldiers already inside the Sloan's, believing the exploding detonator to be a plastic bullet, opened up with their own plastic bullet guns.)

We had used a commercial 'det' with military explosives and it didn't work. We took the mine away and got a military 'det' from Micky Kearney who was in the INLA. Then we came back every night – it was during the long summer evenings of 1979 – and planted the 'remote' and waited. When they didn't weigh in, we took it home with us again and came back the next evening. Eventually the chance came again and it blew, but there were no serious casualties among the Brits.[32]

1979 had also been a critical year in the social and economic development of the Upper Springfield. Ballymurphy Enterprises, which had employed 16 workers in its new purpose-built factory at the top of Whiterock Road, had been driven into bankruptcy towards the end of 1978. Unable to compete with cheap foreign imports, the co-op had been forced to close its doors and sell its premises. The new tenant was the Sloan's Club, now being hounded from its original site by Belfast City Council who wanted their land back.

Garáiste an Phobail (The People's Garage) was also running into financial difficulties and the co-operative building company had long ceased operation. However, Whiterock Pictures was still going strong, having moved premises to a shop cum small factory unit next door to The People's Garage. And Whiterock Industrial Estate maintained its former potential, although attracting industrialists into the area in a time of growing recession was proving a formidable task.

Then on Monday November 5th the British army dealt the death-blow to economic development in the Upper Springfield. During the previous months there had been a number of strange developments at the Industrial Estate. First, the government funding that paid for security was withdrawn; next, the street lighting at the Estate was removed without any reference to the management; then, in a series of mysterious early-morning fires, the Government Training Centre was burned to the ground; and finally, on the morning of November 5th, the British army moved in.

The workers arriving at the estate were lined up against a wall at gunpoint, photographed by the military and told to get lost, that the site was now a military base under the terms of the Emergency Provisions Act. Corrugated iron screens were erected and over the next few days as local residents protested in vain, the economic hopes of the most economically deprived district in Ireland were crushed under the heels of the British army. Although the units which had been operational at the Industrial Estate were later offered alternative accommodation by the NIO, the loss of their Christmas trade that resulted from their eviction from Whiterock destroyed them financially, and all were bankrupt within a short time.

At the same time housing issues were again coming to prominence in the Upper Springfield. In 1979 street lighting had come back to the district for the first time in a decade. Previous attempts by the Department of the Environment to replace the lighting had ended when the British army shot out the newly-installed fittings. However, in the framework of 'normalisation' blacked-out streets were distasteful and had to go. Perhaps it was this new illumination that made people realise just how bad housing conditions were in the maisonette-blocks of Moyard, the box-houses of Springhill and the aluminium huts of Westrock. Whether it was or not, the return of the street lighting certainly coincided with the birth of renewed housing agitation in Greater Ballymurphy.

With regard to Westrock, plans were already underway to replace the aluminium huts, and this was done in 1984/5 by the Northern Ireland Housing Executive along classic Kitsonian lines. Out went the maze of old streets and in came neat cul-de-sacs with one access route and no through road to neighbouring Springhill.

In the years 1982–4 Ballymurphy's decades of agitation also bore fruit when Ballymurphy estate was fully refurbished. Walls were erected around gardens, each house was centrally-heated, and doors and windows were replaced. The 'Orlit' houses were even given a waterproof coat of plaster to cover the cracks and gaps in the brickwork. The same was done for the houses in New Barnsley and Moyard during 1984–6. And at the time of writing, Springhill is being demolished. However, the worst of the Upper Springfield's housing problems – the 17 blocks of maisonettes in Moyard – were to be the focus of the area's most concentrated efforts and one of its finest agitational achievements.

Many of the problems that had plagued Moyard since the rehabilitation of the maisonettes were designer-made, others stemmed from the bureaucratic attitude that anything is good enough for Ballymurphy. In the first instance, the grey blocks themselves, perched on the side of the unlandscaped mountain, were unsightly and uninviting. At night the atmosphere was intimidating and prison-like. The stairwells and verandas were unlit and small fires in the gable-end 'drying rooms' marked the haunts of groups of teenagers whose only recreational outlet was to drink cider or sniff glue.

Conditions inside the flats were no more enticing. The combination of flat roofs and Irish weather brought constant seepage and dampness so that the most prolific growth in Moyard was black mould, the spores of which cause various bronchial problems. In addition, the downspouts ran inside the flats, bringing flooding each time there was a blockage. Another source of flooding was the run-off from the mountain, for which Moyard's drainage system didn't allow. Every time it rained, half the homes in the estate were under several inches of water, while clogging underground pipes pushed sewage up into the streets. This in turn caused epidemics of dysentery, gastro-enteritis and what local mothers simply called 'vomiting and diarrhoea', which affected 60 per cent of Moyard's families in one twelve-month period. The flats were also freezing cold in the winter, and the existence of rubbish chutes in each block led to the estate being overrun by rats and mice.

By 1979 Moyard Housing Action Committee was embarking on a campaign to draw attention to conditions in the flats. In early 1980 they were joined by Rowan Davison, a community worker with the Eastern Health and Social Services Board, Paddy Mooney from the Upper Springfield Resource Centre and Geoff Sirockin, a Queen's University microbiologist who confirmed that the water now constantly running through Moyard's streets was raw sewage. Over the next twelve months, as the enormity of the Moyard problem became clearer, the tenants' demands were narrowed down to one – 'Full demolition of the flats and maisonettes!' – a demand supported by the whole of the Upper Springfield. Within another twelve months the Housing Action Committee had managed to make a political issue out of Moyard and attract the attention of the Irish, British and overseas media.

At the beginning of 1982 they stepped up the militancy of their campaign. In April the Housing Executive offered to spend £15,000 per unit on refurbishing the blocks. The Housing Action Committee, supported by all the tenants of Moyard and the 50 community groups of the district, refused the offer and told the Executive that the people had decided that no workers would be allowed into their homes to carry out any refurbishing work. They also threatened to begin demolition themselves if the Executive maintained its position.

During the next few months there were two fires in the blocks and eight people received injuries and burns jumping to safety after the flames cut them off from the only exits from their homes. Then a young boy from Springfield Park came down with polio, which brought the media homing in on Moyard. It was the first case in the North in 20 years.

Shortly afterwards the Housing Action Committee padlocked the local office of the Housing Executive (a downstairs flat) with all staff inside to demonstrate the vulnerability of anybody cut off from their front door. The Housing Executive and Department of the Environment reacted furiously, blaming Moyard's problems on 'vandals'.

Geoff Sirockin replied that strange vandals were being bred in Moyard: instead of attacking the street lights as one might expect, they were attacking the sewers! The DoE responded by claiming that it had found an old bicycle down one of the troublesome sewers – a miracle given the dimensions of the pipes. The Moyard people responded by blocking main roads in protest.

The war of words between the Moyard Housing Action Committee and the DoE continued until the end of October 1982. By this time Sinn Fein had moved into the sphere of grassroots working class politics, and one of the first issues they took up was Moyard, which greatly widened the dynamics of the debate. Gerry Adams, who had recently been elected on an abstentionist ticket to the Stormont Assembly, and Sean Keenan who would later be Sinn Fein councillor for the area, began to attend meetings of the Moyard demolition campaign and lobby the DoE along lines suggested by the Housing Action Committee. This threw the NIO into consternation, making Moyard an even hotter potato, as the British tried to work out how to cope with the new Sinn Fein politicians.

The turning point came at the end of October when 17-month-old Gerard Smith died in the estate's 'T-Block'. At first it was thought that he had died of gastro-enteritis, linked to the sewage problem. To counter the immediate flood of bad publicity, David Mitchell, Under-Secretary of State at the Department of the Environment repeated his claim that Moyard's sewage system was without fault. At the same time the Upper Springfield Resource Centre was out in the estate photographing DoE trucks and bulldozers carving up the streets to replace cracked and broken pipes. It later transpired that Gerard Smith had died of pneumonia.

None the less Mitchell was forced into a meeting at Stormont with the Housing Action people and their supporters, who now included the West Belfast elected representatives of Sinn Fein, the SDLP and the Alliance Party. After a two and a half hour meeting, during which every argument of Mitchell's in favour of the maisonettes was countered by professional reports, Margaret Keenan, secretary of the Housing Action Committee got up to go. 'There's just one thing I'd like to say before I go,' she politely told the British Minister, 'Moyard is going to have demolition – one way or the other.' On February 21st 1983, at a high-powered meeting between the Housing Executive and Moyard Housing Action Committee, the Executive announced plans to demolish five blocks of the maisonettes.

Afterwards, Sean Gallagher of the Executive accused the Moyard people of 'acting under political influence' and under 'the influence of outsiders', to which the Upper Springfield Resource Centre's magazine replied: 'What a laugh! The Northern Ireland Housing Executive Board, which directs the policy of the organisation, is appointed by the British government. Now Mr Gallagher, it would be hard to beat that for political influence.'[33]

By the end of 1984 the Housing Executive was still insisting on refurbishing the remaining twelve blocks of maisonettes despite the continuing campaign for demolition. By now 'moles' within every government department with which they were dealing were feeding information to the Housing Action Committee so that 'confidential' information was being published in the newspapers by the committee in advance of meetings, to the growing embarrassment of the Housing Executive and DoE. Simultaneously, another group of community activists was drawing up alternative plans to solve the Moyard problem for once and for all.

Two new lots of houses were nearing completion in the area, one between Moyard and Springfield Park and the other at Springhill. It was estimated that these houses would accommodate most of the families in the maisonettes. It was therefore decided that, as soon as the houses were ready, the IRA would be asked to approach the security personnel at both sites, asking that the dogs be kept at bay. This would be done on a Friday evening when the Housing Executive had closed for the weekend. A member of each family in the maisonettes would then be allocated a house, at which point a fleet of vehicles would move in to transfer furniture and other belongings from the maisonettes to the houses. By the Sunday night it was envisaged that all the maisonettes would have been cleared, at which point they would be set on fire.

Perhaps the DoE and Housing Executive guessed what was afoot. At the end of November 1984 the British government announced the demolition of Moyard's remaining maisonettes, marking an astonishing achievement by a small group of determined people.

* * *

The New Year of 1980 began in Ballymurphy with the summary execution by the British army of 16-year-old Doreen McGuinness from Distillery Street for joy-riding. She was killed at a vehicle checkpoint on the Whiterock Road shortly after 10pm on January 1st. A teenage boy in the car was also wounded while the driver escaped after taking his shot companions to hospital. As usual in such circumstances, the military had made no attempt to stop the car with spiked chains or by shooting out the tyres. On the same day the British shoot-to-kill policy backfired in South Armagh when a patrol of paratroopers shot dead their own commander and another soldier in the early-morning darkness. Otherwise, the war continued in its familiar pattern until January 17th when another firebomb disaster occurred.

The bomb, on its way to Belfast, exploded prematurely on a commuter train at Dunmurry. Ballymurphy Volunteer Kevin 'Dee' Delaney (26) and two civilians were killed, and five other people injured as their carriage was engulfed in a huge fireball. Although nowhere on the scale of La Mon, the Dunmurry train bomb again rebounded badly on the IRA. The Catholic clergy used the occasion to play God, and further add to the anguish of the Delaney family, by refusing to allow Kevin Delaney's body into any of the churches in West Belfast. Eventually Mass was said in the Delaney family home in Springhill by Des Wilson and Fr James McAuley – who was visiting, appropriately enough, from South Africa. On January 26th the Ballymurphy IRA showed its contempt for Church politicking when Volunteers shot dead Errol Price (21) of the Duke of Wellington Regiment. A foot patrol was passing Fort Pegasus when three Volunteers opened up with the M60. Immediately the soldiers panicked and opened fire recklessly, wounding two civilians, and afterwards troops went on the rampage in the area, wrecking homes and assaulting civilians, one of whom was spreadeagled against a wall and had a shot fired between his legs. But the Delaney funeral issue wasn't over yet.

Three of Kevin Delaney's sisters had served sentences in Armagh prison. As a mark of respect the republican women in the jail therefore decided to hold a commemorative ceremony for him, wearing black skirts similar to those worn at funerals by Cumann na mBan. A week later, on February 7th, the republican women were told that a special lunch of chicken and apple pie was to be served that day. All the women immediately gathered at the hot plate on the ground floor, where they were instantly surrounded by 60 male and female warders, many drafted in from Long Kesh for the occasion. They were then beaten, punched and kicked by the combined force of warders, and afterwards locked in 'B' Wing's two association cells while their own cells were searched and wrecked.

The women were then returned to their cells, but were informed that they would later be brought to the guardroom to be punished for their involvement in the earlier trouble. Male warders in riot gear, armed with batons, came back into the cells and the women were beaten up again. Afterwards they were confined to their cells for 24 hours and refused access to the toilets.

By February 12th the women in Armagh had joined the 'dirty protest'. Anne Marie Quinn from Whiterock Road later gave an account of the events of February 7th which was handed over by her parents to the prison chaplain, Fr Raymond Murray. Here, she describes the second assault.

> Before we knew what was happening three men in riot gear and more behind them charged into the cell. I was banged against the wall with a riot shield and two men jumped on me – one jumped and dug his knees into my chest. I yelled with pain. The other one twisted my arms ... I didn't even notice Eilis being dragged from the cell but I heard her screams from downstairs ... they kept twisting my wrists till I thought they were broken or would break ... A few hours later a nurse came in to me and took note of the bruises and scratches on my wrists, arms and below my left eye. My shoulders, back and ankle were also hurt but show no marks. I am five foot one inch and weigh eight stone ten pounds. The three officers who attacked me were at least five foot ten inches and looked heavy men.[34]

The Republican Movement, which had been restraining the women from joining the dirty protest, and the H-Block/Armagh Committee, were dismayed by the new turn of events. As the street protests continued into March, small-scale rioting in support of the prisoners had become almost continuous in republican areas where children could also be seen emulating their elders with assaults against British armour. In one such Ballymurphy assault on February 10th, nine-year-old Hugh Maguire and a group of his peers attacked two speeding Saracens with stones and other street debris on the Springfield Road. An iron bar rebounded from one of the Saracens, killing Hugh and sparking off a large-scale riot.

On February 15th the Ballymurphy IRA struck again. A soldier was wounded by gunfire as he worked at the top of a 70-foot mast in the new base at the former Industrial Estate. Four shots had been fired from a house in Divismore Crescent 400 yards away. The military responded with a new tactic: immediately, a helicopter from the fort dropped troops at the Whiterock/Springfield junction, within a few more minutes dozens of vehicles had arrived and the whole of Ballymurphy was sealed and systematically searched.

The suddenness of the operation left two of the three Volunteers involved trapped in a safe house. One managed to escape, but the other was upstairs with the unit's two rifles when the soldiers raided. Preparing for the worst, he stood behind a bedroom door, put the rifles beside him, and pulled out a hand gun. A soldier entered the bedroom. The Volunteer raised the hand gun, ready to shoot as soon as the door was pulled back. Then he heard the soldier shout 'Nobody here!' and leave the room again.

From that point on, IRA timing had to speed up dramatically. Instead of the previous half hour's grace between operations and military responses, the Volunteers henceforth had to disappear totally within minutes. The fact that military and RUC follow-up searches seldom produce results demonstrates how effectively this has been accomplished. It took exactly a week for the Ballymurphy units to perfect their vanishing ability. Then they were back at Springfield Road Barracks where they narrowly missed a soldier in another M60 attack.

On occasions, however, luck, more than skill, prevented Ballymurphy losses.

This particular house was very strategically placed. To get in, we broke a wee window at the top of the door. There were three Volunteers involved and we were waiting for the Brits to mount a checkpoint. Next thing was, a huge foot patrol, about 18 Brits, came on the scene. And they started doing a P-check outside the house. We couldn't hit them because there were more Brits at the top of the Rock. One of the Brits was taking cover near the door when he says, 'Hey Sarge, this house has been broken into!' And he's looking in at the glass lying on the floor. The three of us aimed at the door – two rifles and a short. They rapped the door and we just stayed still. We were ready for them kicking the door in. But for some reason they let it drop and went on.

Shortly afterwards we were back up the stairs again when we heard a key being put into the lock of the front door. So I went down the stairs. I had a Skooby-Do mask on and a Belgian FN pointed at the door. But it was only the owner coming back. He never seen me. He just come on in – even though I was right at the bottom of the stairs in front of him – and closed the door again. At that point I put the rifle to his back and said 'Don't move!' And what does he do? He turns around, jumps back and says, 'Jaysus Christ! I thought you were my wife!' Me in my Skooby-do mask and FN rifle!

Each time we took over that house, it cost us £4 for the glass we broke, and it cost the owner the time to put it back in again. So, in the end, he got us a key cut so we wouldn't have to break in.[35]

On 9th April 1980 the M60 squad moved its operations to the Stewartstown Road. An RUC patrol was lured to the local library by a bogus break-in. As they stepped from their vehicles the IRA opened up with the M60. One member of the patrol was killed and two wounded. By this stage two of the Ballymurphy ASUs had merged into a larger unit containing Volunteers from other parts of the city.

Among the operational network organised by this group (safe houses, arms dumps, transport, etc.) was a taxi-driver named James Kennedy, a boyfriend of the sister of two of the Volunteers. After the Stewartstown attack, Kennedy was summoned to drive Volunteers and weapons, including the M60, from the scene. His taxi had also been used during the killing of Chief Prison Officer William Wright and the unsuccessful M60 attack on Springfield Road Barracks. Kennedy was destined to become the first major cog in the next British war-tactic: the 'supergrass' system.

By April 1980 the H-Block/Armagh campaign was steadily gathering momentum. On March 5th Cardinal Tomás O Fiaich and Bishop Edward Daly of Derry had met with British Secretary of State, Humphrey Atkins, in an attempt to break the deadlock. In response the IRA had suspended attacks on prison officers, 18 of whom had already been killed. However, the talks collapsed after a few weeks and the IRA resumed its war on prison personnel.

Atkins' announcement in late March that political status would henceforth be denied all prisoners, including those convicted of war-related acts committed before March 1st 1976, further incensed nationalists, who now suspected the British of attempting to force a showdown in the prisons. Anger turned to protest as the war went on unabated, and Maurice Oldfield, 'spy supremo', appeared to be making little impact in his crusade against republicanism.

In fact, shortly afterwards, in May 1980, the Ulster Security Co-ordinator, suffering from terminal cancer, was to announce his resignation to his old friend and admirer, Margaret Thatcher. He left the North a sick man, having apparently achieved nothing in his seven-month stay. However, those who felt that the former MI6 chief had been wasting his time had underestimated Oldfield and the lengths to which the British secret service were willing to go in the war against Irish republicanism.

After the killings of Airey Neave, Lord Mountbatten and the 18 soldiers at Narrow Water, the British cabinet had decided to exact vengeance on both the IRA and INLA while simultaneously launching a new assault aimed at crippling both organisations. Maurice Oldfield was chosen to head this operation, drawing on a decade of familiarity with the Irish situation and his years of directing the international British spy network. He chose three key areas to launch the British counter-attack.

First, he centralised all intelligence under the Ulster Security Liaison Committee (USLC) at Stormont, thus ending the rivalry and information-hoarding that caused botch-ups like the SAS/RUC operation against the IRA bombers in Short Strand. Later, after Oldfield left, the USLC, under its new Director, Sir Frank Brooks Richards, was moved to RUC Headquarters at Brooklyn where MI5 was based.

Oldfield also introduced closed-circuit TV systems on all vantage points across the Six Counties – from tall buildings and barrack radio masts to mountaintops – along with new computer systems linking all RUC vehicles, posts and personnel to a central computer. Some £300 million was spent on this elaborate network of intelligence-gathering equipment.

Secondly, based on his earlier experiences in the Middle East, the spy chief began to organise units that would eliminate enemies of the state. The SAS, MI5 and specialist RUC units were to form officially-sanctioned death-squads who would methodically hunt down and murder suspected guerrillas. The new RUC Special Support Units (SSUs) would be trained in Britain by the SAS to become the operational arm of MI5 in the Six Counties. And thirdly, using the age-old methods of 'turning' enemy agents, key persons within the IRA and INLA would be brought over to the British side to be used against their former comrades. In the Six Counties context a combination of 'turned' guerrillas, political courts and the policy of 'criminalisation' coalesced perfectly to become the 'supergrass' system; and James Kennedy was its spearhead.

Kennedy, however, was not the first disaster to strike the Belfast Brigade's 'M60 squad'. On May 2nd 1980 Robert Campbell (27) and Paul 'Dingus' Magee (33) of Ballymurphy, along with Angelo Fusco (24) and Joe Doherty (28), had taken over a house on the Antrim Road for another M60 attack when the RUC was alerted to their presence. Within minutes an eight-man patrol of plain clothes SAS soldiers drew up in two cars. As they jumped from the vehicles to surround the house, the Volunteers opened up with the M60, killing SAS Captain Herbert Richard Westmacott and forcing the soldiers to retreat. In the ensuing siege the IRA position became hopeless, and the ASU surrendered.

A few weeks later the lost M60 was replaced, but the M60 squad was beginning to come under severe pressure from the British and the RUC whose intelligence was linking individual Volunteers to various IRA operations. They were also becoming increasingly worried about James Kennedy. He had already been picked up and questioned by the IRA in October and November about loose talk in the clubs. Kennedy was also becoming worried, so he went to Dublin to be out of circulation for a while. This further strengthened IRA suspicions, and he was again arrested and questioned by Ballymurphy Volunteers on his return.

In the end he panicked and went to the RUC. He first approached an RUC man whom he knew when they met at a vehicle checkpoint. After three meetings with this man he was handed over to the Special Branch. Shortly afterwards most M60 squad Volunteers known to Kennedy were arrested. They were charged on Kennedy's word in the political courts at the beginning of September 1980. Kennedy, meanwhile, had been given immunity from prosecution and the guarantee of a safe passage out of the country.

In the meantime British intelligence had begun to strike back for the killing of Airey Neave by the INLA. At the beginning of June John Turnley, a Protestant who was a leading member of the Irish Independence Party, was assassinated by three loyalists who had been recruited by the SAS. On June 26th Miriam Daly, a leading member of the IRSP, was tied to a chair and shot dead in her Andersonstown home in the middle of the day.

These killings were followed in October by the double murder by pro-British gunmen of Ronnie Bunting and Noel Lyttle, also leading members of the IRSP. Three months later Bernadette Devlin McAliskey, prominent in the H-block/Armagh campaign, and her husband, Michael, were seriously wounded at their home near Cookstown. All operations were carried out in nationalist areas in a cool calculated manner. Two involved the smashing of front doors with sledge hammers, a method of entry used by the SAS in Twinbrook during a raid on an H-Block meeting at about the same time.

In the McAliskey attack the gunmen got into the house, carried out the shooting, and were immediately apprehended by uniformed soldiers who appeared from nowhere. They later claimed that they had been staking out the house in search of wanted republicans. However, in March 1984, an attempted assassination of Gerry Adams in Belfast also culminated in the immediate arrest of the would-be assassins by a plain clothes soldier who just happened to be passing at the time. In both cases prestigious targets were to have been assassinated, eliminating enemies of the state. In both cases the military happened along in time to nab the culprits and pick up the honours, but not in time to prevent the attacks. The coincidence begs the obvious question.

On June 25th 1980 Brian Keenan of New Barnsley Park was jailed for 18 years at the Old Bailey for organising IRA operations in Britain. He had been National Director of Military Operations, known by the code name of 'Dog' which had been affectionately changed to 'God' by many of the ASUs. On July 1st, after an IRA knee-capping at the BTA community centre, Volunteer Terence O'Neill (23) was shot dead by the RUC in Glenalina Road. Later, rioting broke out when the RUC and British army sealed the area in a search for a second Volunteer who had escaped the RUC fusillade.

On July 20th the whole district was again engulfed in rioting – which was widespread throughout the North – in support of Martin Meehan of Ardoyne who was on hunger-strike. Meehan and two others had been jailed on the uncorroborated word of an informer named McWilliams who alleged that he had been kidnapped and held by them. Meehan went on hunger-strike to protest his innocence. (This case was later seen by many as a dry run through the political courts to see how uncorroborated 'evidence' would fare, as this was to be the prime weapon of the 'supergrass' system.) The rioting continued until July 24th, the day after Meehan was persuaded to end his hunger-strike after 66 days without food.

Rioting again flared over the week-end of August 9th and 10th. The internment commemorations and H-Block/Armagh protests led to violent confrontation, hijackings, bombings and gun-battles. Two soldiers and two civilians died and scores were injured. One of the dead was 21-year-old Micky Donnelly of Cavendish Street, a social worker who had been visiting a group of disabled children in Ballymurphy. According to eyewitnesses, he was arrested by troops on the Falls Road, taken to the back of a Saracen and murdered by a plastic bullet fired at point-blank range.

On Friday, August 15th, West Belfast experienced its worst flooding in 50 years. At one point over a mile of the Falls Road was submerged, with the water two to three feet deep in places. The Upper Springfield was badly hit, with floods rushing through the houses on the slope of Black Mountain and settling in the hollows of Ballymurphy, where many residents had to move upstairs for a day. Children were photographed by the *Irish News* swimming on the Whiterock Road – Ballymurphy style, with their clothes still on!

A week later the new Sloan's Club was bombed. Fifty-four-year-old Evelyn Clarke and her daughter were cleaning the premises when two men called looking for a drink. They were told it was too early. They left, and a few minutes later a bomb exploded at the front door, causing slight damage. On October 16th a booby-trap bomb meant for the army exploded near St Peter's School when a dog tripped the switch.

Meanwhile, on the broader front, the situation in the H-Blocks and Armagh was becoming desperate. Charles Haughey, the new Taoiseach who had ousted Jack Lynch in December 1979, had been to see Thatcher in May, but the British were refusing to give way on criminalisation. The climate outside the prisons was as explosive as that in the H-Blocks and Armagh, with rioting following almost all protests. The RUC, under its new chief constable, John Hermon, was still attempting to blast its way back into republican areas under the cover of armoured cars and plastic bullets, but could still only come in with massive military support.

Finally, the dreaded letter was smuggled from the H-Blocks, announcing that seven prisoners were to begin a hunger-strike for political status on October 27th. On Sunday, October 26th, 20,000 people marched in their support through West Belfast. The following day, the hunger-strike began. The prisoners' last card was being played after more than four years of protest and brutalisation.

Over the next month the National H-Block/Armagh Committee organised marches, pickets, vigils and demonstrations throughout Ireland in support of the hunger-strikers, but Thatcher and her government remained as uncompromising as ever. In the 26 Counties, efforts were concentrated on the Fianna Fail government – still riding on its republican rhetoric – and the Irish Catholic hierarchy. The only hope of shifting the British lay in coaxing the Irish establishment into supporting the hunger-strike on humanitarian grounds.

By late November, when there was still no sign of movement by the British, three women in Armagh Jail joined the hunger-strike. This greatly accelerated the growing support for the prisoners: three 'Irish girls' could not be allowed to die of hunger in a British prison. At the same time the IRA, which had scaled down its activities so as not to alienate any potential 'humanitarian' support for the protesters, struck in London on December 2nd, detonating two bombs at the Territorial Army base in Hammersmith.

Four days later 25,000 people marched through the centre of Dublin urging the Dáil to act. On December 8th Haughey met Thatcher and pushed for a compromise as serious rioting spread across the North. On December 10th a senior member of the NIO visited the seven H-Block hunger strikers to discuss the crisis. On the 15th, Charles Haughey described the Six-County statelet as a failed political entity and spoke of the prison crisis as the most serious problem facing the Dáil. By then 30 other H-Block men had joined the fast and Sean McKenna (27), one of the original seven, was nearing death.

Then, on December 17th, the deadlock was broken. The British government produced a 34-page document outlining their proposals in relation to the prisoners' demands and despatched it to Belfast by courier. The plane touched down at Aldergrove in the late afternoon as Sean McKenna's condition became critical – he was at that stage wrapped in foil – and the document was read by Fr Brendan Meaghar who had been involved in the H-Block negotiations. He informed Cardinal Tomás O Fiaich that the document, which, in his opinion, contained the basis of a settlement, was in transit. The Cardinal in turn informed the prison chaplain who passed word on to the hunger-strikers.

At 6.30pm that evening, the prisoners, acting in good faith, called off their protest. They had decided not to wait for the arrival of the document in case the delay would cost Sean McKenna his life. Later, when the priest mediator arrived, the six lucid hunger-strikers and Bobby Sands, IRA O/C of the prison, read over the document and agreed that it provided a basis on which they could negotiate an agreement.

However, the British took immediate advantage of the calling off of the hunger-strike and issued a statement saying that no concessions had been made. They then published a two-page version of their document which gave a very different impression to that of the original. Sinn Fein attempted to counter the British propaganda move by claiming a victory for the prisoners, but the media had already bought the British version. None the less the H-Block and Armagh prisoners still believed that the NIO would go on to implement the deal when the dust had settled. They therefore maintained their side of the bargain and adopted a wait-and-see attitude, hoping that the British back-tracking was nothing more than face-saving bluster. The end result was a propaganda victory for the British, who had managed to give the impression that the hunger-strikers had surrendered in the face of an unbending British determination not to concede their demands.

*　*　*

The December 8th Dublin meeting between Haughey and Thatcher had been followed by a joint communiqué in which the status of the Six Counties was again reaffirmed. Although Haughey was to denounce the statelet as a 'failed political entity' on December 15th, an acceptance of the colonial arrangement would still provide the basis for a summit between the leaders to be held in Dublin on December 20th.

Ever since the attack at Narrow Water the British government had been taking seriously the military advice that the North could not be stabilised without the active participation of the Irish establishment. One of Thatcher's aims therefore was the creation of some kind of all-Ireland co-ordinated anti-republican drive with the British in control and the Dublin administration serving as a junior partner. Both leaders were also keen to see a devolved administration back at Stormont, but realised that the IRA was not about to accept any such 'solution' to the conflict, again emphasising the importance of an all-out drive against republicanism.

However, the new links would have to be very carefully forged to avoid outraging Haughey's 'republican' support and stirring the loyalists into violent opposition. After the summit, they would begin the process by establishing study groups to look at areas of joint interest such as tourism, energy and 'anti-terrorist' action, all to be viewed in the wider framework of 'the totality of relationships within these islands'.

Despite the care with which the new measures were announced, the loyalists reacted furiously to this 'sell-out' of their 'British heritage'. In February 1981 Paisley launched a 1912-style Covenant against the latest 'British treachery' and set off on a series of rallies which he called the 'Carson Trail'. In one of the more outlandish of his Carson Trail pranks, he invited a small group of journalists to an Antrim hillside on the night of February 5th 1981 to view 500 men waving bits of paper above their heads. These, he assured the reporters, were gun-licences, and the men were part of a Third Force which would save the Six Counties from the British sell-out.

In November 1981 Paisley would march 8,000 members of the Third Force through the village of Newtownards, earning him the nickname of 'The grand old Duke of York'. Then his latest army would evaporate away. Had a Catholic religious leader in the Six Counties marched through a nationalist town at the head of 8,000 masked men in paramilitary garb, the British government would most likely have declared martial law.

Meanwhile, as Paisley did his best to shift media attention away from the H-Blocks, it was clear by the end of January 1981 that the British had reneged on their part of the deal with the republican prisoners. On January 23rd the relatives of 20 men who had gone off the dirty protest handed in clothes for them to wear. The administration refused to distribute them. Two days later a special meeting of the H-Block/Armagh Committee was held in Dublin to discuss the renewed deadlock. The following day the IRA blitzed 100 businesses across the North.

Then, ominously, on January 27th the prisoners in Long Kesh smashed up the furniture in their cells. On the 29th, 96 men went back on the dirty protest, bringing the total to 417. During February, as a second hunger-strike loomed, rioting returned to the streets of Belfast and Derry. And on March 1st 1981 28-year-old Bobby Sands, IRA O/C in the H-Blocks, began the new hunger-strike. He was joined two weeks later by Francis Hughes, a legendary IRA figure from south Derry. A week later, on March 22nd, they in turn were joined by IRA Volunteer Raymond McCreesh (24) and INLA Volunteer Patsy O'Hara (24).

The 1981 hunger-strike was given a major profile boost in early April. Frank Maguire, the independent Westminster MP for Fermanagh–South Tyrone had died suddenly, and a by-election was to be held for the seat on April 9th. Bobby Sands was put forward for election by the H-Block/Armagh Committee. All nationalist opposition stood down, the SDLP reasoning that opposing the hunger-striker would ultimately damage the party.

The international media flocked to the Six Counties to witness the contest between the IRA prisoner and Official Unionist Harry West, campaigning on a purely 'anti-terrorist' ticket. As the election approached, the SDLP began to shift uneasily. They could not support West, nor could they oppose Sands. Instead, they began to suggest that nationalists who did not support the IRA should boycott the polls, knowing well that a small abstention in the marginal constituency would be sufficient to prevent a republican victory. They were ignored. On April 9th, Bobby Sands, now six weeks on hunger-strike, became Westminster MP for Fermanagh–South Tyrone with 30,492 votes.

Rioting was now non-stop in republican areas. Ballymurphy was again almost a No-Go area, with British forces under constant attack and vigilantes patrolling the streets. Protest, pickets and vigils continued, as did sporadic IRA attacks on military patrols. But there was also a growing feeling of powerlessness in the ranks of the Ballymurphy H-Block/Armagh Committee.

> There were protests in the city, torchlight processions, public meetings, posters in all the windows, white-line pickets, and there was the H-Block 'cell' in the Bullring flats. People kept vigils there at night and it was a kind of focus during the day. But there was a terrible lot of waiting. People were doing all they could, but in the end, the final conclusion was beyond their control.[36]

Towards the end of April various delegations and individuals arrived at Long Kesh in attempts to persuade Bobby Sands to end his hunger-strike, but the IRA man was adamant that there would be no repeat of the previous December. The British would have to yield to the prisoners' five demands – the right to wear their own clothes, the right to free association, full remission on their sentences, no penal labour, and the right to organise their own educational and recreational programmes – before he would end his fast.

Shortly after 1.30am on Tuesday, May 5th 1981, nationalist areas across the North erupted as sirens, whistles and bin lids announced the death of Bobby Sands. Petrol bombs, stones and grenades were thrown at British forces. Factories and other business premises were set on fire. British army and RUC bases came under gun-attack. In the Upper Springfield the barricades were strengthened, 50 women gathered at the 'H-Block cell' and knelt to say the Rosary, and hundreds of young people flooded from their homes to attack the military/RUC bases. By dawn the Taggart was ablaze as a continuous shower of petrol bombs rained from the flats behind. Ballymurphy, Springhill, Moyard and New Barnsley were thronged with masked rioters and thousands of plastic bullets had been fired. In the 26 Counties the cabinet met to discuss the crisis while Britain went on full nationwide security alert.

Within a week of Bobby Sands' death the IRA had wreaked economic devastation with a spate of bombs and incendiaries. The lull was over. The Upper Springfield remained sealed throughout as local IRA units launched gun-attacks on the Taggart and Pegasus and on mobile patrols on the main roads. On May 11th two soldiers were wounded at the Whiterock/Springfield junction as they accompanied the weekly cash delivery to the post office. As a result the military forced their way into Ballymurphy estate and descended on the H-Block office in the Bullring. There, they confiscated a quantity of petrol and arrested Liam Wiggins, emptying a container of petrol over him as they dragged him off. To give an air of added importance to the operation the raiding party had sealed off the Bullring with white tape to prevent access.

But the whole exercise lost much of its intended gravity when a local man with a penchant for alcohol came staggering down the street, scissors in hand, and snipped the tape. 'I now declare this street open', the scissors-man slurred. He then went back home as the assembled crowd jeered at the soldiers and RUC, making a mockery of the guns trained on them. The next day 27-year-old Francis Hughes died and the rioting and violence in Ballymurphy became more frenzied as nationalist anger intensified.

On May 13th the Ballymurphy IRA set up a rocket attack on an RUC mobile patrol, but the striker of the launcher was missing and the rocket failed to fire. The following day they returned with a home made striker in place and cut an RUC Land Rover in two, killing RUC man Samuel Vallelly (23) and wounding two others. A Volunteer later recalled how:

> During the whole period of the hunger-strike we operated quite openly in the area because the support from the people was so intense. With the area practically a No-Go area and everybody working with us, it was almost like the early 1970s. The Brits were getting hit from every side.[37]

On May 15th, as the attacks on the military and RUC went on, there was rioting at the Springmartin/Springhill interface. There had also been shooting from Springmartin, and fire had been returned on several occasions. On May 21st the violence was further fuelled by the death of Raymond McCreesh and Patsy O'Hara. Gunfights, rioting and grenade attack were widespread. In Ballymurphy the Taggart came under sustained attack and twelve Bass Ireland lorries were hijacked to strengthen the barricades, while 23-year-old Seamus Rooney was shot in the stomach by an undercover army unit.

By now the IRA had announced its full commitment to the renewal of the war – on May 19th a 1,000lb bomb in South Armagh had blown an army Saracen to pieces, killing all five occupants. Meanwhile, the republican funerals were drawing massive crowds: 100,000 people had followed Bobby Sands' cortege as it wound its way from Twinbrook to Milltown Cemetery – the equivalent of 1,200,000 people following the coffin of a national figure in Britain.

For the British, the hunger-strike was a political disaster. Over a decade of carefully-nurtured international propaganda was in tatters as the IRA engaged in massive shows of strength, uniformed Volunteers accompanying the coffins and firing the traditional IRA volleys with rifles instead of the standard hand guns. Far from being 'criminals' without support, the Provisionals were being clearly seen as a people's army who had the full support of a considerable mass of the Irish population.

By the time the hunger-strike had ended – eventually being undermined by the Catholic hierarchy through Fr Denis Faul who managed to convince relatives to begin requesting medical intervention at the last critical moments – ten H-Block men had died, and the British had been forced to concede most of the prisoners' demands. At the same time the IRA had demonstrated its electoral support through the election of Bobby Sands, and his replacement by his election agent, Sinn Fein member Owen Carron, who actually won more votes than Sands. There had also been considerable electoral support for hunger-strike candidates in the Dáil elections on June 11th 1981.

Although the British House of Commons introduced a bill in late June to exclude convicted prisoners from standing for election, they were now faced with a new problem in their propaganda war. Sinn Fein had been catapulted onto the political stage with spectacular results, and the party was already making plans for an electoral intervention into Northern politics on a grand scale. Meanwhile, the Irish people as a whole had been deeply shaken by the hunger-strikes and the British response. Black flags lined the roads from Bantry Bay to Malin Head and the country was completely polarised between the mass of the Irish people who supported the republicans and the British and Irish establishments, desperate to win back the ground that had been lost.

Although the hunger-strike eventually ended on October 3rd, after 217 days, it was to prove as significant an event in Irish history as the execution of the leaders of 1916. For republican communities such as Ballymurphy, it was the springboard for a renewed offensive against British imperialism in Ireland. The sacrifice of the H-Block men had brought to mind again the immortal words of Terence MacSwiney, IRA Lord Mayor of Cork, who died during another hunger-strike in 1920 at the height of the War of Independence. 'It is not', MacSwiney had said, 'those who can inflict the most but those who endure the most who will conquer in the end.'

References

1. *Andersonstown News*, Belfast, February 26th 1983.
2. *Belfast Telegraph*, September 7th 1974.
3. The Community Relations Commission reported an official figure of 3,570 families displaced in the County Borough of Belfast during August and September 1969. The true figure is probably well in excess of 4,000, 90 per cent of whom were nationalists.
4. *Belfast Telegraph*, September 26th 1974.
5. *Spotlight*, April 1974. Ballymurphy Detached Project.
6. Larry Sloan of Ballymurphy (1986 Interview).
7. Kevin Kelley, *The Longest War* (Brandon Publishers, Dingle, 1982), p. 228.
8. Lily Hill of New Barnsley (1988 Interview).
9. *Belfast Telegraph*, May 26th 1975.
10. *Sunday World*, Dublin, March 1st 1987.
11. *Irish News*, Belfast, January 30th 1987.
12. *Andersonstown News*, Belfast, June 21st 1975.
13. Maura McCrory of Dermott Hill (1985 Interview).
14. *Diplock Report*, para. 84.

15. Brian Pettigrew of Ballymurphy (1988 Interview).
16. Tim Pat Coogan, *On the Blanket* (Ward River Press, Dublin, 1980), p. 66.
17. Maura McCrory of Dermott Hill (1988 Interview).
18. Jimmy Duffy of New Barnsley (1988 Interview).
19. Seamus Martin of New Barnsley (1988 Interview).
20. Ibid.
21. Ibid.
22. Interview with author, 1987.
23. Donal Fagan, former youth and community worker in Ballymurphy (1987 Interview).
24. Peggy Burns of Dermott Hill (1988 Interview).
25. Maura McCrory of Dermott Hill (1985 Interview).
26. Brigadier J.M. Glover of British Defence Intelligence Staff, *Northern Ireland, Future Terrorist Trends,* internal report (November 1978).
27. Interview with author, 1987.
28. Interview with author, 1987.
29. Harriet Kelly of Springfield Road (1987 Interview).
30. *Irish News*, Belfast, September 12th 1979.
31. *Irish Times*, Dublin, October 1st 1979.
32. Interview with author, 1987.
33. *Resource* (Upper Springfield Resource Centre, Belfast, February 1983).
34. *Black February, Armagh Prison – Beating Women in Prison,* compiled by Fr Denis Faul, February 1980.
35. Gerry Sloan, formerly of Ballymurphy (1987 Interview).
36. Jim Moody of Ballymurphy (1988 Interview).
37. Interview with author, 1987.

14

Counter-Attack

On June 10th 1981, three and a half months into the second hunger-strike, when nationalist morale sorely needed a boost, the bulk of the M60 squad shot their way out of Crumlin Road Jail. The escape was a major embarrassment to the British government whose own sources admitted that it could not have come at a worse time. With four hunger-strike deaths and a reeling British propaganda machine, it again reminded nationalists, and the assembled world media, of the omni-present resilience of the IRA.

The M60 trial had begun in early May. During the following weeks James Kennedy had given his evidence and the accused had been duly convicted. On June 12th eight of the squad received sentences ranging from ten years to life with a minimum recommendation of 30 years. But by then, seven of those eight, and another republican, accused of killing a UDR soldier, were drinking toasts in safe houses across Belfast.

The escape had taken place during a specially-arranged legal visit. Ballymurphy man, Gerry Sloan, later recalled:

> We had two .25 pistols – one not working – and we got a few plastic knives and cut teeth in them to give us extra weapons. A few of us had £1 notes in our mouths as well. You needed your bus fare, you see. But because of the long wait in the holding cells I ended up chewing mine to pieces ... As the legal visit ended we all got up to go out, with screws in front and screws behind. Then we turned on the screws and held them up.[1]

After releasing the others who were to go on the escape, the IRA men arrested all warders in the immediate vicinity, locking them in the cells along with lawyers and civilian prisoners. One of the IRA men then dressed as a solicitor and two put on warders' uniforms. After securing 'D' Wing and arresting a further large body of warders, they broke out into the yard of the jail and made for the main gate, which actually consisted of three gates. A warder was forced to open the first.

> There should've been a Brit there and we'd expected to collect his SLR. So one of the Volunteers walked down a corridor looking for the Brit. He had a 'short' with him. Next thing was, he found himself in a room with six Brits watching TV. So he hid the short. The Brits asked him what he wanted, and he just said 'Nothing' and walked out again. At this stage the rest of us had collected a few more screws, and a PO who was a bad one. Beaky tried to attack him but he got away and ran into an office. Beaky then started smashing down the windows! 'Come on,' I shouted at him,

'let's get to hell out of here!' So Beaky left the screw and we went out through the second main gate.

Here, right below a Brit sentry box, there was a small wicker gate where visitors came in and out, which led on to the Crumlin Road. We headed for that, but the screw there realised something was wrong. He put his arm down behind the bar so we couldn't open the gate. About five of us tried to batter him to get it opened. Meanwhile, the Brit up in the sentry box sees all these screws fighting at the gate, so he pulls back the shutter and asks what's going on. At that point we got the gate open and got out onto the Crumlin Road.[2]

The eight escapees ran up alongside the jail towards the car park where two cars were waiting, ignition keys under the floor-mats. As they did, an unmarked RUC car pulled up at Crumlin Road Court house, directly across the street. Two RUC men jumped out to give chase, running along the other side of the street, while the car followed. In order to create pandemonium on the Crumlin Road and make it more difficult for the RUC to shoot, the Volunteers began smashing windscreens of passing cars. They then ran across the Crumlin Road towards the car park.

At that point the RUC started shooting, and one of the Volunteers fired four shots in reply. The eight men then jumped into the waiting cars, both 'pointing in the right direction'.

Dingus was driving the car I jumped into. As I got in I saw his head go below the steering wheel as he let out a scream. At that point the back windscreen came in on top of me. I thought 'Driver dead' and just went straight on out the other door. There was now a point blank gunfight with a cop with a revolver blazing away at us. (It turned out later that Dingus had only been clipped in the ear and was down under the wheel because he couldn't find the ignition!) Four off-duty RUC men, who were coming down the Crumlin Road, then jumped out of their cars and started shooting too. So did a military policeman who was on the roof of the courthouse, and some of the sentry boxes opened up as well. It was a pure fluke that we got out of there alive.

I ran, and seen some of the others ahead of me, all of us heading for the Shankill. Joe was stripping off his screw's jacket and I was getting rid of the batons I had collected. Next thing I knew there was this kid running ahead of me shouting 'This way! This way!' He must've thought I was UVF. The lads took a left and I went on straight with the kid still running in front. The sirens were going off everywhere as I got onto the Shankill Road.

At that point I stopped to take stock. I decided to wait for a black taxi. Then I jumped into the front seat, said I was UVF, and hijacked the taxi, telling the driver to head for the Falls. We went towards the Falls, along Northumberland Street, but two Brit jeeps came and threw up a road-block. I told the taxi to stop, and cut down a side-street – straight into a foot patrol running up towards me. There was an old woman at her front door, so I walked up past her in through the door and through the back of the house, back to the Shankill Road. There was a good-looking girl there, about 23 years old, standing at a bus stop.

So I went up to her and said 'Listen love, I'm sure you've heard this a

thousand times, but I've lost my bus money. You wouldn't have any odds
on you?' I'll always remember it: she gave me nine bob, four tens and a
five pence piece, and I took a taxi to Springmartin. From there I went up
onto the mountain and crossed over to Moyard. I went into the first house
I saw with a hunger-strike poster in the window, and said to the woman,
'Provisional IRA. I need your help.'

Meanwhile, our Tony had made it into Castle Street, where he ran into
one of the bars to see if he could find anyone he knew. As luck would have
it the first person he saw was another Volunteer from the same unit. After
telling him he had just escaped, he said 'Give us the price of a drink', so
the Volunteer handed him a fiver. Tony shouted for a glass of orange juice,
at which point the other fella reached out and grabbed back the fiver.
'You're not getting no fiver of mine', he says, 'for a bloody glass of orange
juice'.[3]

Six of the M60 escapees had Ballymurphy connections. Four of them –
Michael 'Beaky' McKee, Gerry Sloan, Paul 'Dingus' Magee and Robert
'Fat' Campbell, who planned the escape lived in Greater Ballymurphy
while Angelo Fusco and Tony Sloan had lived there. The escape was
therefore heralded in the Upper Springfield with bonfires, wild celebrations and a week of house parties, some of which featured Gerry Sloan as
guest of honour while the British scoured the city looking for him and
his comrades. Since two of Larry Sloan's sons were among the escapees,
June 10th was a special night at the Sloan's Club with the drink flowing
like water.

Ten days after the escape, as if to underscore their recent prison
triumph, the Ballymurphy IRA mortar-bombed Fort Pegasus from a
hijacked truck parked in Whiterock Drive. The area had first been partially cleared of civilians, but nevertheless a young boy received shrapnel
wounds as the base was blitzed and five soldiers wounded.

The next day 'Dingus' Magee turned up at the annual Wolfe Tone
commemoration at Bodenstown, having walked openly in the
Provisionals' parade from the nearby town of Sallins. A later attempt by
armed Special Branch men and Irish troops to arrest him was foiled
when sections of the crowd threw missiles at the checkpoints and lay
down on the road, causing a huge traffic hold-up. However, six of the
escapees were later arrested in the 26 Counties and jailed for the Crumlin
Road escape. At the time of writing another, Joe Doherty, awaits extradition from the United States under terms agreed between Ronald Reagan
and Thatcher in 1986 which ended sanctuary in the US for Irish political
refugees.

On June 11th republicanism received another boost to its morale
when two H-Block prisoners, Paddy Agnew and hunger-striker Kieran
Doherty, were elected to Dail Eireann in the 26-County general election.
As a result Fianna Fail were pushed out of government by a coalition of
Fine Gael and the centrist Irish Labour Party. But the long-term effect
was increased repression in the 26 Counties (as with the jailing of the
M60 squad) and increased collaboration with the British. At the begin-
ning of July, Gardai, under the direction of the new regime, arrested a

three-man SAS death squad in County Monaghan – then escorted them
safely back across the border. On August 25th the new Taoiseach, Garret
FitzGerald, laid the foundations for an era of Irish and British
'McCarthyism' by refusing to meet with Owen Carron, the MP for
Fermanagh–South Tyrone. Already, at the end of June the British had
responded to Bobby Sands' election with the 'Sands Bill' excluding convicted felons from standing for election. It was a case of tailoring the
rules to the desired result.

Now FitzGerald was adding his own touch – which was adopted the
following day by Thatcher who also refused to meet Carron to discuss
the H-Block impasse. Then on September 18th Jim Mitchell, the
Coalition's Minister for Justice, ordered the release from prison of Keith
and Kenneth Littlejohn, two British agents jailed for 20 years in 1973 for
their part in a bank robbery while trying to infiltrate republican groups
in the 26 Counties.

Meanwhile, the H-Block deaths, the rioting, the gun-battles and the
bombing went on. On July 8th Joe McDonnell died after a 61-day fast
and a new burst of anti-state disorders flared up. A day later, during
widespread hijacking and rioting, an RUC man was wounded by gunfire
in Springhill Avenue and the Taggart came under prolonged petrol-bomb
attack. On July 10th Hugh O'Neill (21) was accidentally shot dead in a
house in Ballymurphy Road. On the same day two Ballymurphy men,
Micky Brady and Paddy Adams, were among five people arrested after
British Marine Commandos and the RUC shot up Joe McDonnell's
funeral and attempted to capture the firing party.

The lads had come out that wee bit early and the helicopter had picked
them up. After firing the salute they went back into the house. Then
myself and Micky, realising the danger of them getting caught, went in
behind them. As the lads were attempting to get out of the combat gear
and break down the weapons, two jeeploads of Brits – they must've been
packed like sardines – came flying down St Agnes' Drive. They came
running towards the house. Micky looked out the back window and said
the back was still clear. Micky went out first. As I got out through the
window I saw him crouched down with his hands above his head, and
Brits at the bottom of the garden with rifles levelled at both of us. I had
one of the rifles and was heading down the back with it before I saw the
Brits. I began to back slowly backwards to the house. Then I heard more
English voices from the entry on my right.[4]

Paddy Adams swung around with the rifle in his hands and was shot in
the back from the bottom of the garden. The force hurled him back
through the window into the house. The soldiers rushed in after him,
battered him with butts and muzzles, and began firing wildly through
the ceilings at the people upstairs. They then opened up on the crowds of
mourners outside, wounding several people. Of the five arrested and sentenced as a result, only two were actual members of the IRA firing party.

The IRA retaliated that day with several attacks on crown forces, including a blast-bomb attack on Fort Pegasus. Three months later an ASU planted a booby trap bomb under the car of Lieutenant-General Sir Stuart Pringle, Commandant-General of the Marines, outside his London home. Pringle lost a leg in the explosion.

On July 13th hunger-striker Martin Hurson died and the rioting and protests went on as the IRA continued to operate throughout the North. Fort Pegasus and the Taggart again came under heavy attack and a soldier was shot in the arm in Springhill during one of several sniping attacks. Throughout, the RUC and British army maintained a constant assault with plastic bullets on nationalists: both in riot and non-riot situations. On July 19th the Dublin establishment joined the assault when thousands of riot police, backed up by armed troops, attacked an H-Block demonstration on its way to the heavily guarded British Embassy.

In August four more hunger-strikers died, and the killing, burning and rioting went on. By now the SDLP, the Catholic hierarchy and the Dublin government had all begun to worry about the spiralling violence in the North and the obvious open support for the IRA, and were calling on Britain to make concessions. Carron's election victory on the 21st further added to the worries of the Irish establishment groups. It was becoming clear that British intransigence and lack of political acumen were destabilising the whole island and internationally demolishing Dublin's and London's propaganda efforts of a decade.

By the end of August a serious rift had developed between the two governments, with the Coalition threatening to engage in a worldwide campaign in favour of concessions. On September 15th 1981 James Prior replaced Humphrey Atkins as colonial overlord of the Six Counties. Three weeks later, at the beginning of October, the hunger-strike finally came to an end. In the Upper Springfield the turmoil petered out as the community sat back to absorb the blow.

Ballymurphy recovered as it always had. In a community emotionally and physically scarred by seven months of virtual civil war, the IRA moved back into the shadows for a while and the community activists stepped forward with their eternal optimism undented. A new report had been published on Ballymurphy estate by the Belfast Areas of Need (BAN) Sub-group for the area, and with it had come a new dynamism from the old community stalwarts. Although painting a glowing picture of a caring human environment, the report commented: 'It is perhaps intimidating, if not depressing, to note that many of the environmental problems raised in this paper have been voiced many times before.'[5]

Yet again the old catalogue of deprivation was recounted, and it was stressed that military occupation of the area had 'increased the problems, made solutions more difficult and have provided a handy excuse for the authorities'. It was also pointed out that over 90 per cent of the people residing in Whiterock ward – covering Greater Ballymurphy – left school without having ever passed an exam. Over 50 per cent of the eleven-year-olds had a reading age of nine or less compared to a 24 per cent Belfast average which in itself was nothing to boast about.

As expected, unemployment was another major concern. A Housing

Executive survey in 1978 had shown that 48.7 per cent of the 'heads of household' were unemployed. However, the true figure was by then far higher as was demonstrated by a 1982 tally which showed that only 13 per cent of the 'heads of household' were employed by that date.[6] The report noted that Ballymurphy's chronic unemployment created 'a culture and ongoing cycle of deprivation'.

As 1981 closed in Ballymurphy with a half dozen non-fatal shootings, the British moved forward with the 'supergrass' system. Thirty-eight people from North Belfast were charged with war-related acts on the uncorroborated word of one Christopher Black, who had been promised immunity on IRA-related charges, a large sum of money and a new identity if he agreed to work for the British in the political courts.

* * *

The support shown to the IRA and Sinn Fein during the hunger-strikes had stunned the British establishment, as had the other effects of the prison protest. Criminalisation was in tatters; a decade of propaganda had been given the lie internationally; the Republican Movement had taken up the long-standing British challenge to go to the ballot-box and demonstrate its mandate, and had twice been given the support of Fermanagh–South Tyrone; and Dublin had temporarily pulled away from the British line.

Furthermore, not only had the IRA achieved a tremendous moral victory through the hunger-strikes, but it was also faring well militarily. The reorganised ASUs had demonstrated a ruthless efficiency over the past three years and had been very difficult to penetrate. Also, with the interrogation centres emasculated, the political courts were lying semi-fallow. It was imperative for British morale that the new offensive be set in motion as soon as possible. However, after the adverse publicity of the hunger-strikes, new repressive measures would have to be coupled with some kind of political gesture that would soften Dublin and the SDLP.

South of the border, the Irish establishment was also in disarray. The whole country had been destabilised by British intransigence. The IRA and Sinn Fein had taken leaps forward in the Six-County political arena. The SDLP had been shown to be an impotent force to whom the British did not listen. And a new legitimacy had been given to the IRA's armed struggle. Anti-British sentiment in the South was at its highest since Bloody Sunday. Dublin would therefore be relieved at any political concessions that could be sold as a step forward for the SDLP or the Irish establishment, or both. It was ripe bargaining time for Whitehall.

Nevertheless the British wanted desperately to get it right. Any overtures to Dublin would be strictly in the post Narrow Water mould: the 26 Counties would have to be somehow incorporated as a junior semi-autonomous partner into the British military machine in Ireland. Dublin would of course demand some reforms to bolster the flagging SDLP's popularity. But as this also suited British interests, they would be happy to concede any minor arrangements that did not detract from Britain's overall military strategy in the North – which included increasing military co-operation to its maximum and somehow forcing Dublin to abandon its constitutional position on extradition.

Under the Articles of the Irish Constitution a fugitive could not be extradited for a political offence, which meant that, short of being murdered or kidnapped by roving squads of the SAS, republicans were relatively safe once they crossed the border. By allowing IRA personnel to claim sanctuary as political refugees, the British reasoned, the Irish government was not playing cricket on 'criminalisation' and this was simply not good enough. Therefore, as the 'supergrasses' and state death-squads were lined up for a frontal attack on republicans, the British began to negotiate with Dublin. And Dublin began to negotiate with the SDLP.

On October 7th Garret FitzGerald met with a high-level SDLP delegation for secret talks on the 'possibilities for political changes in Ireland'. On October 27th James Prior, the new Six-County Secretary, met with FitzGerald in Dublin and the ground was laid for an Anglo-Irish summit to take place in London on November 6th. Meanwhile, on November 1st Sinn Fein, at its annual Ard Fheis in Dublin, endorsed a new policy of electoral intervention in order to 'push out the SDLP and become the new leadership of the nationalist people in the Six Counties'.

Sinn Fein President Ruairi O Bradaigh told the conference that the party should now 'develop fully the gains made at such cost during the past year and consolidate them'. In support of the new strategy, Danny Morrison, publicity officer, went on to ask: 'Who here really believes we can win the war through the ballot box? But will anyone here object if, with a ballot paper in this hand and an Armalite in this hand, we take power in Ireland?'[7] With this clear threat hanging over the SDLP and the designs of both the British and Irish establishments, the London summit took place five days later.

The outcome of the Anglo-Irish summit was a masterpiece of ambiguity, combining a British package of false promises of economic and energy co-operation with an Irish package of exactly what the British desired. The principal decision outlined in the communiqué issued afterwards was that an Anglo-Irish Inter-Governmental Council was to be created. This new body would not have a Parliamentary element to it, but would give institutional expression to an unspecified 'unique' relationship between Britain and the 26 Counties. it would 'involve regular meetings between the two governments at ministerial and official levels to discuss matters of common concern'.[8]

For FitzGerald, however, the trump card was his claim that Britain had moved significantly on partition. First, he repeated the wish of the Irish majority for reunification, then went on to argue that reunification was now a distinct future possibility because the British had agreed that they would not stand in the way of such a change if the majority in the North wished it. FitzGerald's agreement with this stance – that no change in the North's constitutional position would be sought without the consent of the loyalists in the artificial Six-County state – flew in the face of the Irish Constitution, copper-fastening partition and strengthening the loyalist veto. It also ignored the 60-year history of the North, which made Thatcher's promise a pretty safe bet.

The British, on the other hand, had successfully laid the foundations of their long-term strategy in relation to Dublin. Both Thatcher and FitzGerald, the communiqué informed, commended the level of co-operation between British and Irish state forces, and both acknowledged the difficulties which remained to be resolved over the problem of *extra-dition*. They also agreed that their respective law officers should now consider how the existing barriers could be overcome. Shortly afterwards, the six captured Crumlin Road escapees were jailed in the 26 Counties, as was Gerard Tuite, another IRA man who had escaped from an English prison. The Irish Constitution was now simply being ignored as the Dublin regime slithered willingly into the British web of indirect colonial rule.

However, on January 28th 1982, the day before the first meeting of the Inter-Governmental Council was to take place, FitzGerald's government was toppled when it lost a vote on its budget proposals. For the British, it could hardly have been more untimely – coming just as James Prior leaked news of plans for a new Assembly at Stormont. Prior's plan was for 'rolling devolution', the voluntary sharing of executive powers, and a system of decision-making that incorporated a 'weighted majority' of 70 per cent. Initially, the 78-seat Assembly would function as a consultative body with executive powers being gradually transferred if the natives behaved. Prior had been counting on FitzGerald's support in convincing the SDLP to go along with the re-establishment of Stormont, but the 26-County elections of February 18th returned Fianna Fail with a minority government, and Haughey was back as Taoiseach.

Charles Haughey had ousted Lynch as leader of Fianna Fail on the basis of his harder anti-British line and his stated commitment to obtaining a British withdrawal from the North. The Anglo-Irish Inter-Governmental Council could, with a good stretch of the imagination, be sold as a small step in the Fianna Fail direction; a return to Stormont could not. On March 22nd Haughey and John Hume issued a joint state-ment, rejecting rolling devolution as 'unworkable'.

At the end of April, Prior's White Paper was published. However, by then, the Irish question had been dwarfed by the Argentinian invasion of the Falklands/Malvinas Islands and the likelihood of a war in the South Atlantic. Consideration of Irish objections to rolling devolution were further nullified by Haughey's subsequent stance when he refused to give unconditional support to the British position during the conflict that followed. Thatcher turned her back on Dublin, the Anglo-Irish Inter-Governmental Council died at birth, and rolling devolution went ahead, with elections for the Assembly announced for October 20th.

In further emphasis of the new cold war between London and Dublin, the British army deliberately detonated 1,000lbs of unprimed IRA explo-sives in West Belfast's Springfield Avenue on June 28th, causing widespread and extensive damage to nationalist homes and property in a crude and transparent attempt to discredit the IRA. Less than two weeks later Haughey and Thatcher clashed again over extradition. On July 9th, as intimidation of nationalists peaked in the build-up to the Twelfth, the European Parliament voted 81 to 54 with ten abstentions, in favour of a British-sponsored motion calling on all EEC governments to sign and ratify, 'without reservation', the European Convention on the Suppression of Terrorism. Afterwards, the Irish Foreign Affairs Department issued a statement explaining its opposition to the motion. In it Haughey's Fianna Fail government said: 'The Irish position on extradition remains as stated in accordance with the generally accepted principles of international law which accepts the principle of non-extradition for political offences.'[9]

Relationships between London and Dublin remained hostile until Haughey's Fianna Fail government was defeated in a vote of confidence on November 4th 1982. Twenty days later, FitzGerald was back as Taoiseach, leading yet another coalition of Fine Gael and Labour with a slim majority in the Dail. It was talking time again – with renewed urgency – between London and Dublin.

Two weeks before the collapse of Haughey's government, the Stormont elections had taken place with both the SDLP and Sinn Fein standing on abstentionist tickets. The results shook the British and Irish establishments. Sinn Fein, after 20 years of non-involvement in Northern elections, and with the combined voice of Dublin, the SDLP and the Catholic hierarchy railing against them, had managed to capture five of the seats contested in their limited 'electoral intervention', with Ballymurphy man, Gerry Adams, topping the poll in West Belfast.

At the Sinn Fein Ard-Fheis in Dublin at the end of October, Adams and the Northern leadership, flushed with the election results, won another victory when federalism was dropped from the party's *Eire Nua* policy. Sinn Fein was now committed to its original aim of a united Ireland with no sops to loyalism. With Sinn Fein on the ascent, and the gun, bomb, mortar and rocket attacks continuing as ever in the North, the common interests of London and Dublin demanded a new political offensive against republicanism.

In the Six-Counties, Britain was already stepping up repression. With the 'supergrass' system well in place, mass swoops, arrests and the wrecking of homes in nationalist areas had become daily events. These were not simply arrest operations, they were designed to intimidate whole communities, spread fear and suspicion, and break down community cohesion and people's confidence in the Republican Movement.

On August 25th the 'supergrass' system had been complemented by the introduction of a policy of premeditated state murder. Former Blanket Man, Eamon Bradley, come out of a Derry pub with a friend, and was immediately shot dead by a waiting patrol of British soldiers. Oldfield's death squads went into action almost three months later when the SAS-trained Special Support Unit (SSU) of the RUC ambushed and killed three unarmed IRA Volunteers in County Armagh on the night of November 11th 1982. Less than a fortnight later, the SSU, in conjunction with MI5 and the SAS, killed a 17-year-old youth, who had no connection with the Republican Movement, in a stake-out of a barn in the same county. On December 12th, in a third SSU ambush, two unarmed INLA Volunteers were shot dead in Armagh city. This ambush, seen by many as a vengeance killing for the INLA bombing of the Droppin Well pub in Ballykelly in which eleven soldiers and five civilians were killed, sparked off widespread condemnation and ultimately led to the ill-fated and notorious Stalker Inquiry.

As 1982 drew to a close, the British counter-attack had become a murderous reality.

* * *

The year of 1982 had begun rather ominously in the Upper Springfield when a large pig, that had been looting bins for weeks as it ran wild through the estates, was drowned. It had fallen through ice at the 'Rock Dam', a water-hole at the base of the mountain, adjacent to New Barnsley. In March, shortly after the discovery of the hapless pig, the area had its first 'supergrass' – Jackie Goodman, a member of the IRSP, agreed to implicate 36 people connected with the party in INLA war-related acts. (Goodman later retracted in one of the first blows to the new British tactic, whereupon the RUC produced yet another 'supergrass' and re-arrested most of those released on his retraction.) On March 30th RUC sergeant David Brown was shot by the IRA as he collected one of the Taggart's cleaners from her home at Springfield Crescent. He died almost three weeks later to become the Upper Springfield's first fatality of the new year.

Meanwhile, the area's community activists maintained the new impetus that had followed the hunger-strikes. The CAB and Resource Centre had liaised with the Law Society to establish a legal advice centre, Belfast Women's Aid had re-established an advice centre at the Resource Centre, several community groups were involved in a city-wide campaign against a proposed 22 per cent rent increase and plans were under way for a massive benefit take-up campaign.

The idea of a take-up campaign had followed a similar campaign in Scotland's Strathclyde, but the model chosen by the Upper Springfield Resource Centre was of its own making. A systematic door-to-door survey was to be conducted to establish every family's entitlements. In the first twelve months, the campaign netted £100,000 in unclaimed benefits in Ballymurphy estate alone (660 houses), where, it was discovered, 87 per cent of households survived on state benefits. It eventually took one and a half years to survey the whole area, resulting in an initial uptake of over £1 million and a continuing full uptake of all available benefits.

The publicity surrounding the campaign was such that, within a short time, those involved were travelling all over the North helping to set up other schemes. In financial terms, the campaign was a tremendous boost to the community and an infectious morale-boost as it spread from area to area. Figures given by the Falls Road office of the then Department of Health and Social Services – which covers the Upper Springfield – show that between April 1982 and March 31st 1987, £8,378,900 was paid out in Single Payments alone (furniture, fuel, clothing, etc.) compared to £419,223 for the previous five years. The success of the campaign inspired the growth of a welfare rights 'industry' in the North, and gave Sinn Fein the vehicle on which to launch its community politics programme at the end of 1982.

Meanwhile, the war continued. On May 2nd Francis Toner (26) of Ballymurphy Drive, a voluntary driver on the Long Kesh buses, was shot dead by loyalists as he worked behind the counter of a fruit shop on the Antrim Road. On July 24th, 18-year-old Paul McCullough was wounded by the military on Whiterock Road. His mother, Maureen, had given him £1 to go for chips at a chip-van near the community centre. 'He was only out through the door', she recalled, 'when he was shot in the back. People told me that the Brits came over the graveyard wall and just opened up on him and the other wee lads'.[10]

On September 27th Corporal Leon Bush (22) of the Worcestershire and Sherwood Foresters was killed at the security gates on the Springfield Road end of West Circular Road, which leads into the loyalist Highfield estate a short distance from Springhill. He had been part of a patrol that arrived to open the gates at 7.10am, and had detonated an INLA booby-trap bomb. On October 14th, two days after a group of Ballymurphy children were discovered playing football with a live grenade, the IRA triggered another booby-trap but failed to inflict British army casualties. Six days later Sinn Fein rocked the Irish political scene with its Assembly election successes, effectively placing a veto on any desire the SDLP might have of participating in Prior's 'rolling devolution'.

Faced with an unprecedented political threat from a party as uncompromising as Sinn Fein, the SDLP could not afford to risk backtracking on its abstentionist promise to the nationalist electorate. Republicans were jubilant. In Ballymurphy there were wild celebrations at the victory of Gerry Adams – 'our Gerry' – who had been elected as one of West Belfast's three Assembly members. Within days of the election results, however, Ballymurphy's euphoria had been turned to horror by a return of the Shankill Butchers.

Two days after the Assembly elections, an IRA unit in South Armagh abducted a UDR sergeant, Thomas Cochrane, close to the village of Markethill as he made his way to work. That night, Joseph Donegan, a 48-year-old father of seven from Britton's Parade in Whiterock Estate, was among the many people who attended the usual Friday night social evening in the Pound Loney Club behind Divis Flats. As it happened, Gerry Adams was also present at the club and a heavily armed IRA unit was in the area. In the early hours of Saturday, October 23rd, Joseph Donegan left the club alone to make his way home. Shortly afterwards the UVF announced that they had kidnapped the Whiterock man and were holding him hostage against the safe return of Sergeant Cochrane.

In those circumstances the IRA's GHQ staff sent a courier to South Armagh to order the soldier's release, but the courier failed to get through the heavy security cordon. Unaware of the Belfast kidnapping, the South Armagh Brigade executed Cochrane on October 23rd, but then, hearing of events in Belfast, withheld the news in the hope of buying time for Joseph Donegan. On the evening of October 24th, as the families of the kidnap victims publicly appealed for the release of both men, Fr Des Wilson was called to the telephone at Springhill Community House. The caller was from the UVF. Joseph Donegan, he said, had five minutes left if Cochrane was not released.

By then it was all over Belfast that the Ballymurphy man was in the hands of Lenny Murphy, the former leader of the Shankill Butchers, who had been released from prison two months earlier after serving six years for possession of weapons. Although Murphy had led the gang found guilty of 20 murders, had himself been involved in sectarian killings since 1972, had poured cyanide down the throat of his co-accused in Crumlin Road Jail in 1973 to prevent evidence being given against him in a murder trial, and had publicly shot to death a loyalist named Noel Shaw in the Lawnbrook Social Club on the Shankill Road in 1975, he had consistently managed to evade murder convictions. The rumour that he was behind the latest kidnapping was given some substance on the morning of October 25th when the horribly mutilated body of Joseph Donegan was found in an entry at the rear of Lenny Murphy's former home. The RUC arrested Murphy and questioned him over several days, but he was released without charge.

Three weeks later, however, on November 16th 1982, the IRA brought an abrupt end to Lenny Murphy's bloody career. Shortly before 7pm the 'Master Butcher' arrived at his girlfriend's house in the loyalist Forthriver Park area. As he climbed from his Rover saloon a blue Marina van drew up alongside. Two IRA Volunteers, armed with a sub-machine-gun and a .38 Special, jumped from the van and opened fire. Lenny Murphy was hit at least 20 times and died instantly. Joseph Donegan of Ballymurphy was thus the last victim of the Shankill Butchers.

By then the Upper Springfield awaited the inquest verdict on 17-month-old Gerard Smith, victim of living conditions in Moyard's maisonettes, who had died on October 14th in the isolation unit of Belvoir Park Hospital.

* * *

On January 3rd 1983, as the war in the North entered its 15th year, the IRA officially confronted the Irish Catholic hierarchy on its policy of subtly supporting British rule in Ireland. From its Dublin headquarters the Army Council challenged the bishops and particularly Bishop Cahal Daly of Down and Connor, to morally pronounce on the question of partition and the British presence in Ireland. In its long-standing tradition, the hierarchy refused to comment.

On the day of the IRA's challenge, the Belfast-based Association for Legal Justice also slated Cahal Daly for his 'consistent silence' on state violence. While roundly attacking republican acts of war, the Church had remained generally inactive on issues such as the torture of nationalists, the H-Block nightmare, plastic bullet murders, death squads, summary executions, and the most recent British tactic, the strip-searching of women POWs in order to humiliate and demoralise them.

When the hierarchy did meet with the NIO in January 1983 as the strip-searching tactic gathered momentum, it was to discuss unemployment in West Belfast and ways of alleviating it. Thus, they hoped, anti-British sentiment might be lessened. By then employment in Ballymurphy was down to 13 per cent and many other nationalist areas of the city were at similar levels. People in the Upper Springfield were incensed by the hypocrisy of the same religious leaders who had watched in silence while Whiterock Industrial Estate, with its potential of 1,000 jobs, was turned into a military fort.

'They were never supportive of the people's efforts', Frank Cahill recalled. 'In fact, when the early community development was going on in this area, when we were trying to raise funds for the community centre, they would only loan us St Bernadette's School for our bingo on condition that 50 per cent of our takings was handed over to the Church.'

At the end of January 1983, as the Catholic Church maintained its public and private wars against the republicans, the Dublin government threw a life-line to the SDLP, still reeling from Sinn Fein's electoral successes. During the party's annual conference, a letter from Garret FitzGerald was read to the delegates. In it the Coalition Taoiseach promised to give full and careful consideration to an SDLP proposal for a 'Council for a New Ireland' to discuss the North's future in the whole context of Anglo-Irish relations. Already there had been much media speculation of a renewal of the Anglo-Irish process.

Shortly before Christmas Prior had annoyed Dublin with a pre-emptive demand that extradition should top the agenda of any new round of talks, clearly suggesting that the British were again ready to negotiate. Then on January 18th Peter Barry, Minister for Foreign Affairs in the new Coalition, arrived in Belfast for a two-day 'fact-finding' visit amid further rumours of renewed London–Dublin talks. During a meeting with John Hume in Derry on January 19th, Barry was pressed for his government's support for the 'Council' idea, and FitzGerald's letter was a result of that meeting. Less than three weeks after the SDLP Conference, Hume was in Dublin meeting with FitzGerald, Labour Party leader Dick Spring, and Charles Haughey of Fianna Fail. After two days of talks it was announced that moves to set up the 'Council for a New Ireland' would begin in March. Hume returned to the North claiming a major historical triumph.

Meanwhile, on February 16th, the first loyalist 'supergrass' trial was rushed into the Diplock Courts with 16 alleged members of the UVF charged on the testimony of Joseph Bennett. Bennett had been arrested in May 1982 and granted immunity on a murder charge. There is much evidence to suggest that the timing of the subsequent 'supergrass' trial was an attempt to show the world how 'impartial' the system really was. The Bennett trial ended in April 1983, four months before the end of the

Black trial, with 14 of the 16 accused being convicted in a judgement that was widely criticised. Bennett had been tripped up in his own lies over and over again. His performance was so bad that relatives of the accused had actually made preparations for an acquittal celebration when the convictions were announced.

Many observers felt that the verdict was needed by the 'supergrass' system at that time, regardless of the quality of Bennett's performance, and that the sentences would be overturned on appeal. Which they were. Those who argued from the beginning that the loyalist 'supergrasses' (seven out of a final tally of 30) were nothing more than window-dressing were to find that by September 1985 not one loyalist remained on remand or sentenced on the uncorroborated word of a 'supergrass'. Another feature of the Bennett trial was the midstream intervention of Sir John Hermon, Chief Constable of the RUC. Confirming the stakes invested in the system, Hermon said: 'On this matter there is much at stake for the terrorists and the community. The outcome is crucial to the well being of Northern Ireland and it is essential that there should be a general public understanding of the facts.'[11] Trial Judge Murray accepted that, had there been a jury in the Bennett trial, Hermon's remarks would have constituted contempt of court.

On March 11th, as the fiasco in the Diplock Courts continued, the Irish government formally agreed to establish a forum of 'non-violent' parties to look at the future of Ireland. On March 22nd, the day before Carrickmore man Seamus Kerr became the first Sinn Fein councillor in the North in over half a century, Thatcher and FitzGerald met in Brussels. On March 29th the Workers' Party announced that they would not participate in the forum, which they described as 'a prop for the SDLP'. On May 5th, as ten more nationalists went on trial in the Diplock Courts on the word of 'supergrass' Kevin McGrady, FitzGerald was visited in Dublin by Prior in order to begin patching up Anglo-Irish relations. Undoubtedly, Prior had extradition top of his agenda.

Finally, on May 30th 1983, under a fanfare of pomp and TV cameras, the 'Forum for a New Ireland' got under way in Dublin. The venue chosen was Dublin Castle, formerly the symbol of British rule in Ireland. No unionist or republican voice was present, the loyalists boycotting the affair and the republicans being excluded. A later attempt by Des Wilson to bring to the Forum some small hint of the feelings of the nationalist working class was vetoed. The forum was to be little more than a mutual admiration society of Irish establishment parties, aided and abetted by the Catholic hierarchy. The oppressed of the Northern ghettoes would not be heard.

On June 9th 1983 a further sense of urgency entered the renewal of Anglo-Irish relations. In the British General Election, in which Thatcher's Conservatives were returned with a 144-seat majority, Sinn Fein took 43 per cent of the nationalist vote in the Six Counties. Gerry Adams defeated sitting MP Gerry Fitt and the SDLP's Joe Hendron to take West Belfast despite some 5,000 tactical votes cast for Fitt by Shankill road loyalists in an attempt to keep the Ballymurphy man out. In Fermanagh–

South Tyrone a split nationalist vote lost Owen Carron his seat, but in Mid-Ulster, Sinn Fein Director of Publicity Danny Morrison came within 79 votes of victory. The British and Irish establishments were appalled at Sinn Fein's success. The Forum life-line had clearly not done its job. Four days after the results were announced Secretary of State for Northern Ireland, James Prior, vowed not to recognise the results of the ballot-box. 'We are not prepared to negotiate with people who are committed to violence', Prior declared on June 14th. Such sentiments, coming from the representative of a government responsible for a campaign of state terrorism in the Six Counties over the previous 15 years, were treated with derision by republicans.

In the 26 Counties Garret FitzGerald and Peter Barry met with visiting US Vice-President George Bush on July 5th, impressing on him the 'dangers' of Sinn Fein's northern successes and asking for the US government's support in countering the threat posed by republicanism. Bush, oddly enough, as part of his official visit, had earlier placed a wreath in the Garden of Remembrance, dedicated to Irish 'terrorists' of an earlier generation! On July 21st, Prior, speaking in the House of Commons, again demanded of Dublin that 'workable extradition arrangements' be made as Britain stepped up its pressure on the Irish government to subvert the Irish Constitution and hand over republican guerrillas.

Ten days later Dublin announced that it too would refuse to recognise the results of the ballot-box and would, in tandem with Prior in the North, pursue its own policy of 'McCarthyism' against Sinn Fein. Peter Barry had earlier appeared on RTE's 'This Week' and in the course of discussion, had offered to debate the Northern issue with Gerry Adams. Shortly afterwards a statement was issued through the Department of Foreign Affairs hurriedly withdrawing the offer with the assertion that 'until Sinn Fein ends and repudiates the use of violence for political objectives, it will not be possible for the Government to have any dealings or debate in public or in private with Sinn Fein'.[12]

As the political manoeuvrings went on in the background, the war continued as before in Ballymurphy. On March 17th 1983, in the first major operation of the year, the IRA launched a gun and rocket attack on a British mobile patrol in full view of Fort Pegasus. After a wait of twelve hours, four Volunteers walked out of a house into Britton's Parade and blasted a Saracen with an RPG-7 rocket, seriously wounding one of the soldiers inside. They then sprayed the vehicle with gunfire before disappearing into Ballymurphy. As a result the British built a 60-foot tower inside the fort so as to command a greater view of the surrounding area.

Two months later, on May 12th, Liz Kirkpatrick, the wife of INLA 'supergrass' Harry Kirkpatrick, was kidnapped from her parents' house in Westrock Drive as part of the INLA's efforts to force Kirkpatrick to retract his statements. (On August 3rd 1983 Kirkpatrick's stepfather and sister were also kidnapped by the INLA. Fifteen days later Irish Gardai raided an INLA hideout in Gortahork, County Donegal, and freed Richard Hill and his daughter Diane. On August 26th, the INLA, realising that

Kirkpatrick was not going to be pressurised, released Liz Kirkpatrick unharmed.)

Windows throughout Ballymurphy were rattled by a massive van-bomb that devastated Andersonstown Barracks on May 24th, in an operation organised by Ballymurphy Volunteers. On June 10th the Volunteers struck again in Ballymurphy Estate itself. Shortly before 9am a 15lb bomb, concealed in a lamp-post, exploded as an army patrol escorted two RUC men through the area. Private Geoffrey Curtis of the 1st Light Infantry took the full force of the blast and was killed instantly.

Two weeks later the area heard the news that Joe Doherty of the M60 squad had been arrested in a Manhattan bar in New York and charged with illegal entry into the USA. Then on August 9th, in one of the most traumatic incidents to hit the district for several years, Thomas 'Kidso' Reilly of Turf Lodge was murdered by the British army in broad daylight and in front of some 60 witnesses, one of whom was the author.

Thomas Reilly (22) was a road-manager with the rock group Bananarama. He had come home to visit his family. On the afternoon of August 9th he and a half dozen friends had gathered at the top of Whiterock Road to take the sun and drink a bottle of cider. At 4.30pm, as they sat stripped to the waist, a military patrol passed by and one of the soldiers made some comment. Thomas Reilly jumped to his feet, punched the soldier, and said 'You won't call me an Irish bastard!'

Immediately several soldiers set upon him with rifle-butts, knocking him to the ground. Emmanuel Cruthers, one of his friends, ran to his defence and he too was attacked, having his mouth smashed open by a rifle-butt. At this point more soldiers rounded the corner and began to run towards the scene, all of this happening in the space of a few seconds. Realising the hopelessness of the situation, Thomas Reilly got up and took off, running around the corner and up the Springfield Road towards Turf Lodge. Some soldiers followed; and one, taking careful aim, fired his SLR at the fleeing shirtless figure. Thomas Reilly was dead before he hit the ground at the gates of St Aidan's school. Afterwards, in a unique verdict, a British soldier received a life sentence for his murder.

The Upper Springfield was incensed at 'Kidso' Reilly's murder and the accompanying taunts of 'That's one less of the bastards'. Within hours the area was engulfed in serious rioting. The following day a small shrine of white stones was cemented into the ground at the gates of St Aidan's where it remains to this day as over 1,000 people, carrying black flags, marched in protest on Fort Jericho. Afterwards rioting again broke out and Fort Pegasus came under IRA fire. A military Land Rover was shot at on Whiterock Road and several vehicles and three Portakabins on a nearby building site were set on fire.

On August 11th fresh rioting erupted after the funeral, which was attended by a large crowd, with the members of Bananarama leading the cortege. This was followed on August 12th by more trouble after soldiers shouted abuse at the Reilly family home and arrested Thomas Reilly's sister's boyfriend and nine-month-old daughter. Then Thomas 'Kidso'

Reilly became another statistic, the 114th person to die in Greater Ballymurphy as a result of the Troubles.

In September 1983 the 'supergrass' system came to the Upper Springfield with a vengeance. During the first week of the month six men had been arrested on the word of William 'Bo' Skelly. On September 5th Ted Jones, solicitor for one of the accused, asked the RUC in court if they were aware that Skelly 'has a history of surrendering himself to the police and claiming that he had committed crimes which, in fact, had not occurred'. The RUC replied that they were not, despite Skelly's first admission being a Browning machine-gun attack on the RUC which had never taken place.

However, one of those arrested on Skelly's word was Robert 'Bido' Lean (37) of Glenalina Park. Lean was a member of the Administrative Staff of the IRA's Belfast Brigade, the body responsible for the policing of republican areas, which was in turn responsible to the Brigade Staff. He had already spent time in jail on the word of 'supergrass' James 'Bimbo' O'Rawe who later retracted, and was now accused by Skelly of numerous war-related acts.

In the early hours of Tuesday, September 6th, Bridie Adams, Lean's 60-year-old next-door neighbour, was alerted by the sound of military vehicles in the street: Lean had become the RUC's 25th 'supergrass'.

> I heard the jeeps and all outside. I never bothered going to the door the way I normally would when the Brits are in. I was just looking out the window. I thought they were maybe raiding further down the street. Then I seen this man with an anorak and the hood pulled up over his head. I says to myself 'There's some fella going to work; they'll pull him in.' But it must have been Lean coming back to get her and the kids. Shortly afterwards, one of the neighbours said she saw them all coming out of the house with a big black bag.[13]

As soon as she could, Bridie Adams contacted a local community activist who raised the alarm throughout West Belfast, but 18 people had already been held in early morning swoops. By the morning of September 27th 27 people were being held and the RUC was cock-a-hoop, claiming that Lean was the IRA's second-in-command and that they had captured the Belfast Brigade's commander and the 'Chief of Staff of the North'.

In reality, Lean's statements consisted of hearsay, rumour, guesswork and RUC prompts, but, as with all the other 'supergrasses' his word would be sufficient to secure life sentences, and there was no possible means of defence. Also, there was no real need on the part of the state to present anything even vaguely resembling a concrete charge. 'Conspiracy' was enough, so that anybody could be charged with an innumerable array of events that never actually happened. For example, George Donnelly Newell of Belfast was charged on the alleged word of John Gibson – who was never produced – of 'conspiring to murder a person or persons unknown between January 1st 1975 and December

31st 1975'! Conviction would have secured a life sentence had the case not collapsed on the RUC.

Lean's recruitment by the RUC had shocked and demoralised republican areas throughout Belfast, but nowhere was the blow as severe as in the Upper Springfield, where the community was riven with suspicion and fear. At this juncture local community groups decided to resist the new tactic. Concerned Community Organisations was established, drawing on the support of over 200 community groups in nationalist areas of the city, and joining the existing Relatives for Justice in taking on the British government in a fight that seemed impossibly weighted against them.

Republican morale received a boost, on September 25th 1983, when 38 IRA men staged a dramatic escape from the H-Blocks of Long Kesh. Despite a huge dragnet, 19 escapees made it safely across the border. Among them were four Ballymurphy men: Robert Russell, serving 20 years for the attempted killing of an RUC superintendent; Gerry Kelly, serving life for the 1973 London bombings; Tony McAllister, doing life for possession of firearms and preparation of an ambush; and Paul Brennan, serving 16 years for possession of a bomb and handgun in Belfast city centre. Paul Brennan was one of eight men, led by IRA prison commander Brendan 'Bic' McFarlane, whose subsequent adventures were to make colourful media headlines.

Having commandeered a car, the group drove towards Moira, then turned off the main road in search of a secluded house. The house they took over belonged to a loyalist couple and their two sons aged 14 and 12. After hiding the car and quizzing the family as to their whereabouts, they discovered they were only a few miles from Long Kesh, and probably still inside the first ring of roadblocks. They then told the family that they could only protect themselves by taking one of the boys hostage or leaving an armed Volunteer behind. However, the family agreed to swear on the Bible not to inform the authorities for 72 hours if the Volunteers left without a hostage; and this agreement was struck.

The men searched the house and found a compass, pocket torch and maps of the area that belonged to the sons, both of whom were Boy Scouts. They also found rucksacks which they filled with food and water. At 10pm they packed the family off to bed and left an hour later.

> There was a heavy fog which helped us in a way because the choppers couldn't pick us out with their lights. We stuck to the back lanes and fields which meant we only managed to cover a few miles before dawn. Then we dug in for the day in a clump of bushes.
>
> By Monday night all the food was gone. We picked up all our rubbish and headed off about eight o'clock across the fields again. We skirted around Gilford and arrived at the Bann. Then we went into a big estate with lots of trees and a big mansion and decided to stay for the day. We kipped down in some undergrowth near a greenhouse and took turns at sleeping ... Some time in the morning a man and women went into the greenhouse. But they didn't see us and we just stayed put. Then, in the middle of the afternoon, we wished we hadn't.

The man, who had an English accent, turned up with these dogs. He went into the greenhouse, but one of the dogs, a big black labrador, kept coming up to where we were and barking at the bushes. Going wild it was. Your man came out and dragged it away. But it came back again with two other dogs and we were sure they'd give us away.

In the end your man went off with the two dogs and about 15 minutes later the RUC arrived and we were sure he'd 'phoned them. They pulled up just up the drive from where we were and three Peelers got out and started talking to the English bloke. Then one of the Peelers came towards us and stared right at us. We were ready to bolt for it. Then he stubbed out a fag and walked away back to the others. And they all got back in the car and drove off. We got out of there as fast as we could.[14]

The group then waded the Bann and waited until dark. Walking through the night, they passed Scarva and Poyntz Pass, and at dawn hid in bushes again. On Wednesday night they took to the fields again, using the compass to find the Belfast–Dublin railway line. Above the town of Newry they crossed the Egyptian Arches and marched on until Newry's lights had vanished. They stayed in the fields, using the line as a guide, until dawn, when they knew they were well over the border. They eventually reported into a safe house to find that the loyalist family had kept their word. The story of their extraordinary encounter with the IRA was just making the news.

Over the following days there were some hopeful developments for the 27 being held on Lean's word. On September 29th Geraldine Coleman, Lean's common-law wife and her five children returned to the area after 24 days in RUC protective custody, having left Lean with a clear message that she would not stand by his actions. Meanwhile the campaign against the 'supergrass' system was further strengthened on October 2nd by the formation at a Dungannon conference of the Stop the Show Trials Committee. By the end of the month the three nationalist anti-'supergrass' organisations: Relatives for Justice (RFJ), Concerned Community Organisations (CCO), and the Stop the Show Trials Committee had banded together to draw up a common strategy, while on the loyalist side, Families for Legal Justice drew up theirs. At the same time British fortunes were again beginning to wane.

In the early hours of Wednesday, October 19th, Robert Lean lifted the car keys of his RUC 'minder', climbed out through a window in Palace Barracks, Holywood, and escaped in his 'minder's' car. Later in the day, after signing an affidavit retracting his statements, the Ballymurphy man appeared at a press conference to denounce the 'supergrass' system. The media attention given to Lean's arrest, and the RUC's claims of the time, now backfired badly.

International attention was focused on Lean as he described how the RUC had given him prepared statements and told him that he would have plenty of time for rehearsal, and how they had wanted him to sign a statement implicating Gerry Adams in IRA activities. Two days later Eddie Carmichael, one of those released after Lean's retractions, also told how he too had been offered £300,000 to sign a statement against the

Sinn Fein Vice-President. Five days after Lean's retraction, in a further embarrassment to the RUC, Patrick McGurk of Dungannon also retracted and nine more men were freed.

As nationalist areas rejoiced, the naked body of Ballymurphy man, Gerard 'Sparkey' Barkley (26) was found dumped in a plastic bag on the Fermanagh/Monaghan border on October 26th. He had been shot by a faction within the INLA, his killing a portent of things to come. Two callers telephoned the media, both using an identical recognised INLA code: one claimed that the Ballymurphy man had been 'murdered by pro-British thugs', the second said that he had been 'executed' for 'using his weapons in criminal activities for gain'. Among the rumours of a sim- mering feud within the INLA following Gerard Barkley's death, the only clear points were that he had been killed by the INLA, and that the INLA had fired a volley over his grave as a mark of respect to a fallen comrade. Then the whole episode was temporarily swallowed up in the continuing saga of the 'supergrasses'.

Somehow, the Lean episode seemed to mark a turning point. Up to then the new form of legalised internment had been running relatively smoothly. In the following weeks it was to be plagued with setbacks and dogged by the escalating anti-'grass' campaign until the British, the RUC and the judiciary found themselves fighting a rearguard action, trying desperately to defend the indefensible. By November twelve of the 27 'supergrasses' so far recruited had withdrawn their statements, many of them relating to the media stories of dubious deals, false statements and intensive RUC schooling.

At the same time the October 26th judgement in the McGrady trial had caused uproar within sections of the legal profession. Three weeks earlier the trial judge, Lord Chief Justice Sir Robert Lowry, had released two of the ten accused and thrown out 13 of the original 45 charges (including murder charges) on the basis that he found McGrady's evi- dence 'so unsatisfactory and inconsistent that I could not contemplate allowing myself, as a tribunal of fact, to say that guilt has been proved beyond a reasonable doubt'.[15]

Nevertheless, in his final summation on October 25th, despite an admission that McGrady's evidence contained 'some glaring absurdities' and was 'contradictory, bizarre and in some respects incredible', and despite throwing out a further 19 charges, Lowry went on to find seven of the accused guilty on 13 charges. Among them was Jim Gibney, former Sinn Fein national organiser who was sentenced to twelve years on two charges, although he had been cleared of another 20. Jim Gibney had, on the RUC's admission, been 'high on the list of people the RUC wished to convict'.

On the one hand the McGrady verdict came as a major blow to the anti-'grass' campaign: it seemed that, regardless of the quality of the chief crown witness, convictions would be secured. Lawyers even took the unusual step of visiting their clients on remand in Crumlin Road Jail to tell them that, in their opinion, there was no longer any possible defence against the new tactic. However, in the long run, Lowry's verdict was to prove a principal weapon in the fight back. It also prompted the first public statement by lawyers.

On November 2nd the Criminal Bar Association, representing most of the solicitors involved in the political courts, called a press conference to condemn the system and recommend to their members that they withdraw from 'supergrass' trials. The following evening 40 barristers and solicitors attended a meeting convened by CCO, and a body of lawyers came forward to campaign publicly alongside the community groups. The meeting was attended by Lord Gifford QC, who had arrived in Belfast to conduct an investigation into the trials.

Gifford was the first of a string of influential people who would visit the political courts over the following years, most at the invitation of the anti-'grass' campaigners, until the judges and the judicial system itself finally found that they too were on trial. By November condemnation of the use of 'supergrasses' had also come from Bishop Edward Daly of Derry and all shades of political opinion in Britain and Ireland other than the Tories, who continued to defend it. In the 26 Counties criticism of the Diplock Courts had crept into all government statements on the North as the Dublin establishment realised that, not only was the nationalist working class being further alienated from the state, but so were the loyalists, and a considerable rump of the nationalist middle class.

Then, within weeks of the McGrady verdict, Lowry further complicated the situation by delivering another verdict which, when placed beside the McGrady judgement, was startling to say the least. In April 1982 RUC detective Charles McCormick was convicted of armed robbery, illegal possession of weapons and hijacking – on the word of Tony O'Doherty, an alleged accomplice – and was sentenced to 20 years. Judge Donald Murray, who later freely convicted on the uncorroborated evidence of Joseph Bennett, threw out 23 other charges, including one of murder, on the grounds that: 'It would be highly dangerous to convict the accused of any of the crimes on the evidence of O'Doherty *unless that evidence is supported by clear and compelling corroboration*' (author's emphasis).[16]

Lowry was one of the judges hearing McCormick's appeal in January 1984. On this occasion the Lord Chief Justice decided that the *corroborating evidence* on which McCormick had been convicted was weak and insufficient! McCormick was duly released; and the anti-'grass' campaign was handed a powerful propaganda weapon.

The first collapse of a 'supergrass' trial also occurred in November 1983 when John Grimley, an INLA 'supergrass' from Craigavon, admitted telling lies in court, setting at least five of those in the dock up at the behest of the RUC, and carrying out armed robberies in Craigavon with the collusion of the Special Branch! Producing Grimley in court heralded the seemingly final abandonment by the RUC of any pretence that normal court standards were any longer required to secure convictions in the political courts. He had over 40 criminal convictions, and in court admitted to: 'Being an exhibitionist ... consistent lying, being a habitual drinker ... being given to acts of violence, having spent six months in a psychiatric hospital and being given to irrational behaviour, and manipulating people to get himself out of unpleasant situations.'[17]

The fact that Grimley had been produced by the RUC as a credible and sole witness was described by visiting US attorney Henry O'Brien as 'obscene'. However, despite Grimley's background and the appalling quality of his 'evidence', the case had been allowed to continue for weeks with all the trappings of a serious trial, until Grimley started revealing some of the seedier sides of RUC activities around Craigavon. The following month, in December 1983, another 'supergrass' trial collapsed when the chief crown witness, John Morgan, admitted, among other things, that he had shot his brother-in-law dead in England while he slept. After this, the flow of 'supergrasses' suddenly dried up as the British attempted to consolidate what they had and fight off the growing international campaign and the increasing pressure from Dublin.

Meanwhile, Sinn Fein held its annual Ard Fheis in Dublin during the second weekend of November and handed over the party leadership to Gerry Adams. The day after Adams' election, William Skelly retracted his statements and those held on his word were released. Earlier, on November 4th, two others had been released in a Ballymurphy brush with 'supergrasses' that was bizarre even by Northern legal standards.

Twenty-eight-year-old Frankie Cahill, son of the former BTA secretary, had been among those arrested on Lean's word. He had been charged with bombings and 'conspiracies'.

Lean retracted on a Wednesday and on the Friday we were brought to court. We were all handcuffed together in pairs. When we were brought over to the cells they came in with forms. They then re-handcuffed us in different batches. I was handcuffed to Jimmy Duff. Then everybody was taken out until there was only three of us left in the cell. Later we were called up – for a bail application! We hadn't applied for bail. We assumed we were getting out. Eilish, our barrister, says, 'But the charges have been retracted!' But the cops said to Lowry, 'We wish to proceed: same charges, a different witness.' At that stage we had never been confronted by Skelly or mentioned by him. Then they got Skelly to make a statement after Lean retracted.

I think they then realised they'd never get away with that one, saying Skelly hadn't 'remembered' such important events until after Lean retracted. The end result was that, 13 days later, I was brought out to Townhall Street Barracks. I knew in the jail that I was being released. I also knew that Skelly had been trying to retract and they wouldn't let him. In Townhall Street they had a judge waiting, and I was released. They held onto Duff for another week. Johnny had to finish a sentence for assaulting Peelers before he was released.[18]

The only real 'conspiracy' in the whole affair appeared to be conspiracy by the state 'to pervert the course of justice'. Afterwards, Frankie Cahill sued the state and was awarded considerable damages for wrongful imprisonment. At his wedding in Dundalk in 1986 he thanked the Northern Ireland Office for providing the money to pay for the fine banquet being eagerly consumed by hundreds of Irish republicans.

Following a series of loyalist murders against nationalists, an offshoot of the INLA burst in on a Sunday prayer meeting at the Mountain Lodge Pentecostal Church in Darkly, County Armagh, on November 20th 1983, and sprayed the congregation with sub-machine-gun fire. Three people were killed and a further seven were wounded. The next day the OUP walked out of the Stormont Assembly, dealing another blow to Prior's rolling devolution'. Amid howls for Prior's resignation, the unionists explained that they were no longer willing to participate in a body that was nothing more than a formal device for ritual protest. Three days later it was reported that one million gallons of nuclear waste was pumped into the Irish Sea each day by the nuclear reprocessing plant at Sellafield in Cumbria. But this piece of news was lost amid the Darkly uproar.

The IRA poured further pressure on Prior by shooting dead OUP Assembly member Edgar Graham outside Queen's University on December 7th. Two days after the Graham killing, the RUC, in a new departure, invaded the small nationalist enclave of Bawnmore in North Belfast to attack the funeral of INLA Volunteer, Joseph Craven, shot by the Protestant Action Force (UVF). This was the first attack on a republican funeral since the shoot-up of Joe McDonnell's. It signalled a new policy whereby the British would attempt to force all republican military displays off the streets of the Six Counties, culminating in some incredibly macabre confrontations in cemeteries and around the homes of dead Volunteers.

By December 31st 1983 the war in the North had cost Britain more than any of the other colonial wars fought since 1945: 507 soldiers (including UDR), 190 members of the RUC and 1,648 civilians (including republican and loyalist guerrillas) had been killed. Another 25,000 people had been wounded. These figures do not include those killed and injured in Britain or in the 26 Counties. In financial terms, it had cost £4,507 million with an additional £3,278 million lost in depressed investment and the collapse of the Northern economy.[19]

* * *

During the early weeks of 1984, as the Forum continued its deliberations in Dublin Castle and the war and 'supergrass' trials continued in the North, Ballymurphy was relatively quiet. The constant patrolling by British forces went on as usual, houses continued to be raided, suspects continued to be arrested for interrogation at Castlereagh, but there was little IRA activity locally. On February 10th the lull ended with an almost disastrous rocket attack on an armoured car on Whiterock Road. At 10.17am the missile was fired from a house in Glenalina Park, which had been occupied by the ASU since midnight. It hit the front of the Saracen, veered off to one side and ended up in a classroom of St Aiden's Primary School. Miraculously nobody was injured.

Twelve days later a 27-year-old man and a soldier were shot by another member of the same foot patrol in New Barnsley Park in an incident similar to that in which Thomas Reilly was murdered. The soldiers had been harassing a group of men when one fired without warning.

At the same time Ballymurphy continued to have a high profile in the campaign against the 'supergrasses'; and the campaign was beginning to bite as was clear from the RUC Chief Constable's Annual Report published on March 12th. In it, Hermon lambasted 'terrorist organisations and their propagandists' for attempting 'to destroy what the police are achieving'.

Throughout 1983 and the early months of 1984 community action in the area had continued as before with varying degrees of success. In Moyard, the tracts of cleared land attested to the first triumph of the demolition campaign. In Ballymurphy, Gaelic street names were being erected as part of a growing revival of the Irish language, begun by the prisoners in Long Kesh. There, the men had used it as a means of frustrating the prison authorities and keeping up their spirits. Once outside, the more fluent speakers joined other language enthusiasts in setting up classes until dozens were operating in West Belfast.

Finally, Liam Andrews, the Ballymurphy artist who taught Gaelic at Springhill Community House, found that his long years of optimism had not been in vain. The revival was becoming a visible entity on the street corners of Ballymurphy. In the end the streets of nationalist areas throughout Belfast would all have Gaelic name-plates alongside the English, thanks to the tireless efforts of Glor na nGael.

Springhill Community House was also spreading its wings. Towards the end of 1982 the Pound Loney Social Club had purchased an old disused flax mill in Conway Street off the Falls Road. One of the smaller buildings on the site was renovated to house the new club, whereas the mill itself was handed over to a management committee of community activists who included Frank Cahill and Des Wilson. Most of the building was to be used to encourage economic development, but one whole floor had been handed over to the Springhill people to be used as an educational and cultural centre. By early 1984 the educational floor had been extensively renovated and much of the mill was in use, a total of 30 jobs having been created. The future for the steering committee looked very encouraging. However, later events were to turn Conway Mill into one of the most contentious political issues in West Belfast.

Housing issues in the Upper Springfield were also dominant throughout the previous twelve months. Ken Livingstone, leader of the Greater London Council, who had visited Belfast in February 1983 at the invitation of Sinn Fein, had described the housing as some of the worst he had ever seen. Three months later, on May 27th, women from all the estates of the Upper Springfield took part in a protest march to the Adelaide Street headquarters of the Housing Executive – to an unexpected and vicious sectarian reception. Once the group of 200 women and children entered Adelaide Street, the RUC sealed off both ends of the street, refused entry to the media, and attacked the marchers. Margaret

Keenan, secretary of the Moyard Housing Action Committee, described the attack later that day to *Resource*:

> You should've seen the hatred on their faces. As soon as the protest started they formed up in a line with Sterlings held by the barrels and butts, then came at us, pushing the guns against our throats. Then as soon as someone pushed back, they went crazy, lashing out like animals. One pulled a revolver on us – just a crowd of women – and another was roaring for a plastic bullet gun. They kicked us and punched us and threw us on the ground. Four of them had one woman up against the wall, one banging her head off the wall, and the other three kicking her.[20]

The presence of Gerry Adams and Sean Keenan undoubtedly contributed to the zeal with which the RUC carried out their duty.

Another grim note of 1983 was the final collapse of the only remaining symbol of the Upper Springfield's co-operative developments that had once offered so much hope. In April Whiterock Pictures Ltd found its debts exceeding its assets and was forced to go into liquidation – just a few weeks before its tenth birthday. Nothing visible remained of the industrial experiment other than the huge military fort that had formerly been Whiterock Industrial Estate. And the knowledge in Ballymurphy that nobody could ever again say that the people didn't try.

Early 1984 also heralded the opening of a relationship between Ballymurphy and the Black community in Britain. Towards the end of February an anti-'supergrass' delegation to London had included two people from the Upper Springfield. Afterwards, a representative of the Troops Out Movement, which had co-ordinated the London end of the visit, contacted the Upper Springfield Resource Centre to ask for assistance in programming for a Black delegation which TOM was bringing to Belfast. As a result the group was accommodated in Ballymurphy, with the Resource Centre organising its programme.

Two days prior to their visit, Gerry Adams, Sean Keenan and three other members of Sinn Fein were returning from a much-publicised court appearance when a UFF gang drew up alongside and pumped their car full of bullets, injuring four of the Sinn Fein men. Gerry Adams had been shot five times and Sean Keenan's injuries included a bullet in the face. Incredibly, none of the wounded were critically injured. The UFF team had apparently panicked – shooting one of their own members in the process – and had afterwards been arrested.

Three days after the attempted assassination of Gerry Adams, Britain was finally rewarded for its years of pressurising the Irish government. On St Patrick's Day 1984 Dominic McGlinchey, Chief of Staff of the INLA, became the first republican in the history of the 26 Counties to be extradited to the North. McGlinchey had been on the run on both sides of the border. An extradition order had been signed against him in December 1982 on an RUC charge of killing Hester McMullan of Toomebridge in March 1977 during a gun-attack aimed at her son who was a member of the RUC. He had jumped bail during the extradition hearing and had since led the Gardai a merry dance around rural Ireland.

However, on March 17th, in the early hours of the morning he and three other men were surrounded by a large force of armed Gardai in a house in County Clare. After a short gun-battle the INLA men surrendered in order to safeguard a women and her two children who were in the house. Legally, McGlinchey should have had to face a 26-County court for his part in the gun-battle, but, in an attempt to appease the British, the Dublin regime rushed him through the extradition formalities to the border. At a special sitting of the High Court, in the County Dublin home of Justice Barrington, the INLA man had been granted a temporary injunction until the following Wednesday against the order. But this was overruled at an emergency session of the Supreme Court and McGlinchey was handed over to the RUC shortly before 1am on March 18th 1984.*

On May 2nd the Forum for a New Ireland published its report. It contained three suggested alternatives for the future of Ireland: a unitary state by agreement; a federal/confederal state; or joint authority by London and Dublin. The document was dismissed by unionists and by the Tories; it caused a temporary rift within the SDLP, with a Hume faction and a Seamus Mallon (deputy leader) faction emerging; and it caused a split in Fianna Fail as Desmond O'Malley opted for a federal Ireland and Charles Haughey insisted on a unitary state. (O'Malley later left Fianna Fail to form the Progressive Democrats, another right-wing party that attracted a huge membership before it had produced a single policy.)

In the North it changed nothing, and the war went on as it always had. On May 18th, as Fianna Fail was expelling O'Malley from its parliamentary party, two British soldiers were killed and two others seriously injured in a booby-trap explosion in Enniskillen. In Camlough in South Armagh a massive culvert bomb killed two RUC men. And in Belfast a nationalist was shot in the Markets by loyalist would-be assassins. And Secretary of State James Prior finally threw in the towel.

Announcing his desire to leave the North on May 21st, he caused a political storm by asserting that if his own constituents at Lowestoft were asked what the British government should do, they would tell them 'to get the hell out of it'. For the dispirited Prior, it was the end of a long political career. A few days later, on May 23rd, the Official Unionists ended their boycott of the Stormont Assembly.

On Friday, June 1st 1984, US President Ronald Reagan arrived in Ireland for a state visit. Some time earlier the village of Ballyporeen in County Tipperary had discovered that Reagan's ancestors had emigrated from there and had invited the President to pay them a call. With a presidential election looming in the USA, Reagan's trip was little more than a gimmick aimed at the huge Irish-American vote and an opportunity to throw his weight firmly behind his old friend Margaret Thatcher. 'I stand

*Afterwards, the RUC failed to prove their case against Dominic McGlinchey and he was re-extradited back to the 26-Counties where he was jailed for his part in the Clare shootout.

with you in condemning any misguided American who supports terrorists in Northern Ireland', Reagan told the Irish establishment after his
visit to Ballyporeen on June 3rd.

Garret FitzGerald in turn asked for the US President's support for the
Forum Report. In his speech to the Dail on June 4th Reagan again
attacked republicanism and the use of violence, despite his own administration's appalling record in Latin America. He was publicly thanked by
Thatcher the following day when he called on Downing Street on his
way home to the White House.

On the same day, in the North, the British commitment to non-
violence was given admirable expression by Judge Maurice Gibson.
While acquitting three RUC men accused of murdering Eugene Toman,
one of the three unarmed IRA Volunteers shot dead in an RUC ambush
in November 1982, he described them as 'blameless' and praised them
for their 'courage' in 'bringing the three deceased men to justice – in this
case, to the final court of justice'.[*]

The Euro poll of June 14th was the first test of the Forum's success in
providing the SDLP with a lifebelt. The results gave the Irish establishment parties little cause for joy. Although John Hume defeated Danny
Morrison for the nationalist seat at the EEC Parliament, the Sinn Fein
vote held solid. Even more worrying was the low-key reception the
Forum Report was still receiving in Britain. On July 2nd, when
Westminster debated the document, only 80 of 650 MPs were present as
the session opened. A half hour later, when James Prior stood up to
speak, the number had been whittled down to 49. The British attitude
was described the following day by Fianna Fail leader, Charles Haughey,
as the 'greatest and most considered rebuff to democratic Irish nationalism ... in modern times'.

Over the following weeks, as the war maintained its now-familiar
pattern, the annual Orange marching season was marked by the usual
attacks on nationalist homes and by rioting in Derry. Then, at the end of
July, the British Home Office banned Martin Galvin, Publicity Director of
the American republican organisation, Noraid, from visiting the Six
Counties. It was to prove a disastrously counter-productive move.

Galvin arrived in Dublin on August 2nd to prepare the ground for the
annual Noraid visit. The rest of the delegation arrived in Belfast a week
later for the anti-internment demonstrations. On August 11th the
Americans attended the funeral in Newry of IRA Volunteer Brendan
Watters who had been killed in action, and were at the receiving end of
yet another RUC attack on a republican funeral. The next day they
attended the Sinn Fein anti-internment parade from Dunville Park on
the Falls Road to the Busy Bee in Andersonstown.

The day's sunshine attracted large crowds from nationalist areas of

---

[*]Three years later, in April 1987, the IRA used Gibson's reference to 'the final
court of justice' when they detonated a 500lb car-bomb as the judge and his wife
drove across the border at Killeen. Both were killed instantly in the meticulously
planned attack which prompted the British establishment to carry out a revenge
attack at Loughgall the following month.

Belfast to take part in the Sunday event that had become an almost festive occasion. The possible appearance of banned Martin Galvin brought the press out in droves. At Connolly House, Sinn Fein's Belfast headquarters, the crowd sat down in the face of a massive RUC/British army presence. A few minutes later Martin Galvin appeared on the Connolly House platform. The RUC brutality that followed was broadcast worldwide. Driving Land Rovers into the peaceful demonstration, the RUC batoned the crowd of men, women and children indiscriminately and fired 167 plastic bullets in a carefully planned police riot. Hundreds of people were injured and 22-year-old John Downes was killed by a plastic bullet fired at point-blank range. Martin Galvin escaped.

The RUC's action was internationally condemned as reporters brought back first-hand personal accounts of the savagery they had experienced at Andersonstown. Paddy Vallelly of Ballymurphy was photographed standing in the middle of the Andersonstown Road clutching two armfuls of shoes and handbags dropped by the terrified victims of the RUC riot. The next day, as Dr Joe Hendron of the SDLP condemned the 'berserk' RUC, thousands of people staged a Black Flag march along the same route in open defiance of British tactics. In Ballymurphy, the rioting that had broken out at news of John Downes' killing lasted three days.

On August 27th a three-day public inquiry, sponsored by Springhill Community House, opened at Conway Street Mill, gathering evidence to be distributed worldwide. Its purpose was to document precisely the events of the August 12th anti-internment rally. Its most immediate effect, however, was to strip Springhill Community House of an annual £500 grant provided by the loyalist-dominated Belfast City Council, a blow that would in time materialise as the first shot of a vicious state campaign against the developments at Conway Street Mill.

Following the international flak from the Downes killing, the Anglo-Irish process was again revived on September 3rd 1984. Thatcher and FitzGerald, meeting in London to discuss EEC issues, also talked about the North and Anglo-Irish relations. In a hint of an unchanging British line, however, NIO Minister Nicholas Scott spoke six days later of the possible 'pooling of sovereignty' by the British and Irish governments on security. The next day Douglas Hurd, a hardline Tory lightweight, replaced James Prior as Secretary of State at Stormont. There would be no change in policy, Hurd said. 'Hurd it all before!' the cover of *Republican News* said. 'Hurd is a turd' a Ballymurphy poet scribbled on the BTA community centre wall.

Meanwhile, the Coalition in Dublin and the SDLP were becoming increasingly desperate as the political plank of the Forum sank further into the depths. On September 24th, three days after 32 men were formally charged on the evidence of 'supergrass' Harry Kirkpatrick, John Hume led an SDLP delegation to see Hurd at Stormont. There they complained bitterly of the British lack of response to the Forum Report and the 'growing alienation' of nationalists, which in fact meant the growing isolation of the SDLP. Britain would have to take steps to counter the growth of Sinn Fein's influence. But Thatcher was too busy with the British miners' strike, then entering its 29th week.

Three weeks later, however, the republican threat was brought home forcibly to Thatcher and the British government. In the early hours of October 12th – the last day of the Conservatives' Annual Conference – the IRA almost succeeded in wiping out the entire British cabinet. A bomb, planted weeks before, exploded at Brighton's Grand Hotel, where the conference was being held. Four people died in the explosion, a fifth died later, and many were injured. 'Today we were unlucky', the IRA grimly warned Thatcher, 'But remember, we have only to be lucky once; you will have to be lucky always.' By the time the dust settled Thatcher was shaken, enraged and in no conciliatory mood towards the Irish. But Ireland was back in the forefront of British politics.

On November 4th, in the lead-up to the next London–Dublin summit, FitzGerald hitched a ride home from Indira Gandhi's funeral aboard Thatcher's RAF jet, but was virtually ignored by the British Prime Minister. On November 18th the Taoiseach left for Chequers to press Thatcher on the need to give the Forum Report some positive consideration. The following day at the post summit press conference, Thatcher listed the Forum's three options, saying firmly after each one that it was 'out'. FitzGerald, fumbling for words, was left humiliated before the international press, the SDLP's constitutional platform collapsed, and London–Dublin relations were in disarray. On September 21st Hurd further incensed Dublin by declaring that it had no role in the future administration of the North. As for this alienation business, there was no real evidence that it existed at all. To which John Hume replied that Hurd would need an 'army of tanks' to visit his (Hume's) home in Derry.

Meanwhile, the extradition question had again surfaced with the arrest in Dublin on May 26th of Robert Russell of Ballymurphy. Russell was one of the Long Kesh escapees, who had been serving 20 years for the attempted killing of an RUC inspector. As soon as news of his arrest broke, the British applied to have him extradited back to the North. Immediately, his family and friends in Ballymurphy began to rally against the threat of extradition that had followed the McGlinchey case. On July 31st these fears were further fuelled by the extradition from the 26 Counties of Seamus Shannon, the first IRA Volunteer ever to be extradited to the North. Shannon was charged with killing former Stormont Speaker Sir Norman Stronge (84) who died along with his son, who was a member of the RUC, during an IRA attack on their Tynan Abbey home. Because Norman Stronge was not a member of the British occupation forces, the courts in the 26 Counties had decided that the killing was not political. (Later Shannon was in fact acquitted in Belfast when the crown failed to produce sufficient evidence for the Diplock Courts to convict him.)

Back in Ballymurphy, Russell's comrades maintained a cautious level of military activity. On May 21st a soldier narrowly escaped sniper fire in Ballymurphy estate. Eight days later a 30lb bomb, packed with nails, was discovered on the Whiterock Road and defused by the British army. On June 22nd a soldier was shot in the neck a short distance from where the bomb had been found. Exactly a month later the INLA in the area shot an 18-year-old man in both arms and both legs near the Whiterock Leisure Centre, accusing him of misusing the organisation's name and defaming a dead INLA Volunteer. The area was also about to have a dramatic encounter with Shankill Road firebrand Assembly member, George Seawright – 'an honest bigot' as he described himself. The occasion was the official opening of Whiterock Leisure Centre. Just to demonstrate the all-pervasive nature of Six-County politics.

Whiterock Leisure Centre had actually opened in January 1984. However, the official opening was scheduled for September 12th. Normally all local elected representatives would be invited to such an affair; but the local MP was Sinn Fein President Gerry Adams. In the apartheid-type state fostered by loyalism, an invitation to Gerry Adams was simply out of the question. This was a calculated insult, not just to the local MP, but to all those who elected him, many of whom lived in the Upper Springfield. It was therefore decided to stage a 'People's Opening', organised by Sinn Fein and sponsored by local community groups, for September 10th. This proved a huge success. Hundreds of local children and most of the area's community groups turned out along with Sinn Fein and People's Democracy councillors to see Gerry Adams unveil a Gaelic plaque after several young men had hoisted an Irish Tricolour over the council building. Orange juice and crisps were in abundance and everyone went home happy.

The City Hall's unionists, however, were furious, not least George Seawright, also a member of the City Council. Seawright had recently attained notoriety when he suggested at the May 30th meeting of Belfast Education and Library Board that 'Taxpayers' money would be better spent on an incinerator and burning the lot of them [Catholics].' He had been suspended from the DUP at the end of June for his remarks and was later expelled from the party, but at a meeting of the City Council's Leisure Services on September 11th, his pyromaniac tendencies erupted again. He wanted Whiterock Leisure Centre 'closed down or burned down'. The next day the centre was 'opened' for the third time by SDLP councillors and maverick unionist John Carson – the only councillors willing to step into the storm. The only community presence was in the form of a protest outside.

On October 8th Seawright called for a special Council meeting to discuss the proposal that Whiterock be closed down until the plaque and Tricolour were removed, but he failed to find a seconder for his motion. So he decided to do the job himself. At 7.55am on October 18th a gun-toting Seawright and two armed loyalists turned up at Whiterock Leisure Centre.

They'd been jamming the 'phones from about 6 o'clock that morning. There should've been only one security man on, but the other had stayed on because he thought something funny was going on. They were watching the cameras when two cars drove up to the Centre. One turned and parked outside and the other parked under a window, out of sight of the cameras. One of the security men went to check it out. There had been a terrible storm the night before and he thought it might be the telephone men. When he got out a man with a ladder forced his way past and started to climb up onto the roof. Other staff pulled the ladder from under him but he got onto the roof. Later on, we came to believe this was John Bingham of the UVF. And he had a gun with him. Another fellow, who turned out to be 'Frenchy' Marchant, had another ladder, but he didn't get on the roof.

When the guy on the roof got back down, our security men chased them and knocked one of them – that was Marchant – down at the top of the steps. As they did, your man shouted 'Get the gun! Get the gun!' A guy in a car pointed a gun, Seawright said it was him, but I don't know if it was. There was so much panic to get away that the door ended up getting barred with one of our security men still outside! And he was the one with the keys! It's worth mentioning that the staff 'phoned 999 at 8.05, saying 'There's gunmen on the roof and they're going to shoot us!' but the RUC didn't show up until 9.20. By then Seawright had already released a statement to the press.[21]*

Seawright had hardly left the area when the flag was replaced, and two others added for good measure, but the threat to the Leisure Centre remained. On January 21st 1985, however, the people of the Upper Springfield mobilised to counter any attempt by the City Council to close the building. At a public meeting, some 40 community organisations joined local residents, trade unionists and all but two of West Belfast's elected representatives to discuss the Council's latest decision to close the Leisure Centre unless the Department of Education took it over.

The opening speaker at the meeting pointed out to the packed hall how deeply sectarian bigotry, and support for it, penetrated into the community: when the ad hoc committee went about organising the meeting, they had found all public buildings in the area closed to them. The only facility available for a simple meeting to discuss an issue of importance to the whole community was the sole building controlled by the people: the BTA community centre. By the end of the evening a provisional management committee had been elected with a mandate to take control of the building, with or without the consent of the Department of Education, should the Council move to close it down. However, the Council realised that they were going nowhere in the face of the united opposition of the community. At a meeting on March 11th 1985 the issue died when the OUP and DUP failed to support one another's motions aimed at pressing on with the controversy.

Two days before Seawright's gun-toting antics, an attempted execution of a joyrider occurred in the centre of Ballymurphy. Just after 2pm on

*Within three years, John Bingham and 'Frenchy' Marchant, leading members of the UVF, had been shot dead by the IRA: and George Seawright by the Irish People's Liberation Organisation. Locally, the affair was compared to the opening of Tutankhamen's tomb.

October 16th 1984 a stolen car was rammed in the Bullring by two jeeps. Stephen McMenamim (18) of Britton's Parade jumped out and ran off. An RUC man gave chase and was within ten feet of the youth when a soldier opened fire and shot Stephen McMenamin in the back. His companion, John Miller (15) was arrested.

The incident came 14 days after a speech by Hurd, in which he claimed widespread acceptance of British forces in areas such as Ballymurphy, and a time when gun-attacks on joyriders were so commonplace that the joyriding terminology for a back-seat passenger was 'sandbagger'.

On November 5th the Upper Springfield was visited by two Fianna Fail TDs who were invited North by Concerned Community Organisations to observe the Gilmour 'supergrass' trial then in progress. On their return to Dublin they assisted Haughey in the preparation of Fianna Fail's case against the use of 'supergrasses' for a forthcoming Dail debate. A few days later, in the lead-up to the Chequers humiliation of Garret FitzGerald, Haughey, who clearly saw what the British were after, declared that 'No court in this country should hand over any of our citizens'. If there were concessions to be had from the British, Haughey felt, the price demanded would be extradition. As it transpired, there were no concessions to be had from the British.

The fallout from the Chequers summit left the Irish government and the SDLP more desperate than ever. The hype built up around the Forum Report rebounded badly. The SDLP rank and file were blaming FitzGerald and, by association, Hume for the debacle, and there was a threat of a split in the party. It also left the way open for the British to push forward with their own plans, having shocked the Dublin establishment and the SDLP leadership into a more 'realistic' position. On November 22nd, the day after Hurd's statement on Dublin's irrelevance, the British ambassador to Ireland visited FitzGerald. Within another fortnight the softening-up process had begun. On December 3rd Thatcher and FitzGerald met in Dublin after a gathering of EEC Heads of State. The next day Hurd began to talk of the need to accommodate the 'Irish identity' of Northern nationalists. It seemed that, perhaps, the British were having second thoughts about the contents of the Forum Report.

However, in reality, the British were back on the offensive, still following the post-Narrow Water line, which had been updated in a policy document published in October 1984. This document, entitled *Britain's Undefended Frontier: A Policy for Ulster*, outlined a framework in which the Dublin government, the SDLP and the loyalists could be moulded into 'the greatest possible resistance to republican terrorism'. The report pointed out that the Dublin government 'in practice ... accords de facto constitutional and diplomatic recognition to Ulster's status as part of the UK'. To mobilise the components of the suggested framework, the report argued, 'an attempt should be made to meet as much of the political aspirations of the Irish Republic as are unequivocally consistent with Britain's obligations to Ulster'.[22]

The report then envisaged a scenario in which Dublin would be 'willing to extradite those accused of terrorist crimes and to establish close and uninhibited co-operation between its security forces and those of the United Kingdom'. If this were done, 'it would be possible to defeat the IRA without reverting to such a contentious measure as internment'. The report, published one month before the Chequers summit, went on to say:

> It should be made clear to the Dublin government that the degree of force which must be used in the attempt to restore order will be in inverse proportion to the degree of effective co-operation on security which can be achieved between the two governments.[23]

By the beginning of 1985, the British plan was being buoyed along satisfactorily by the Dublin government, the SDLP and the Catholic hierarchy who were all clawing for Anglo-Irish negotiations towards a 'political settlement' in the North.

At the same time the real nature of British policy was being represented by SAS death squads and British military repression. On January 15th 1985, Ballymurphy had yet another taste of that policy. Five youths in a stolen car ran into a UDR checkpoint at Kennedy Way. One of the soldiers shouted 'There's the car!' and the youths immediately reversed – straight into another jeep that 'came out of nowhere'. As the car went forward again the UDR opened fire. The car went out of control and crashed into a ditch, but the soldiers continued firing, eye-witnesses reporting up to 60 shots. One of the youths got out of the car, but was shot while trying to run away. When the firing died down 17-year-old Paul Kelly of Whiterock Crescent was dead, two others were seriously wounded and a fourth had a broken knee-cap. No attempts had been made to stop the car other than by riddling the joyriders inside with bullets. Paul Kelly was the twelfth joyrider to be killed in Belfast since 1979, and the first person to die as a result of the Troubles in 1985.

Meanwhile, the 'supergrass' system continued to disintegrate under the constant pressure of the protest groups and its own internal problems. On December 18th the Gilmour case had collapsed. On January 28th the Kirkpatrick trial had opened amid widespread condemnation of the system. On February 21st the James Crockard trial collapsed. The followed day an Amnesty International report condemned the Diplock Courts for flouting international law.

RUC demoralisation at the continued releases from the prisons was further exacerbated on February 28th when an IRA mortar attack on Newry RUC barracks left nine of their number dead. The Newry attack came five days after another SAS stakeout had resulted in the deaths of three IRA Volunteers in Strabane, and heralded the beginning of a series of deadly bomb, mortar and rocket attacks against British bases throughout the North.

On the day the British miners ended their year-old strike, March 3rd, Hurd hinted tantalisingly that there just might be a role for Dublin in the future administration of the North. Both Hurd and British Foreign

Secretary, Sir Geoffrey Howe, arrived in Dublin, on March 22nd, to take the British plans a step further. There they met with FitzGerald's deputy, Labour leader Dick Spring, and Foreign Affairs Minister, Peter Barry, as speculation mounted of a new summit. Three days later Ronald Reagan promised substantial US aid to any political settlement agreed by the two governments, while John Hume hinted of vast sums from Europe to support an Anglo-Irish agreement.

A week later FitzGerald and Peter Barry visited Derry in a pro-SDLP move aimed at influencing the May local government elections. None the less the May 15th poll left Sinn Fein with 59 seats on the North's local councils. In Belfast, Omagh, Strabane and Fermanagh, they took the majority of nationalist seats. In the aftermath of the May 1985 elections, Dublin was even more pliable than before.

Over the following months, as the Anglo-Irish discussions continued, it became clear that something big was in the air. At the same time it became clear that whatever it was, it would not have a smooth run. In the councils the Sinn Fein triumph had caused uproar, with fist fighting breaking out on a regular basis and many of the loyalist-dominated councils expelling Sinn Fein members and suspending business indefinitely in protest at the republican presence. During June and July a British attempt to portray the RUC as an 'impartial' force caused serious rioting across the North as the RUC clashed with loyalists attempting to march through nationalist areas.

The most serious trouble flared in Portadown over the Twelfth of July period as tens of thousands of Orangemen attempted to invade the nationalist 'Tunnel' area to find *their* RUC enforcing a hitherto unheard-of ban. In turn loyalist mobs attacked nationalist homes in vulnerable areas and by mid August had begun to petrol-bomb RUC homes. In return for the cosmetic dabs in the North, Dublin announced in September that security along the border would be massively increased. Loyalists, however, were unimpressed and were preparing for a showdown in the event of Dublin's involvement in Northern affairs.

Throughout the London–Dublin politicking the war went on as always, and life in Ballymurphy remained unchanged. In January the local community groups formally joined the protests against strip-searching, adding more bodies to the white-line pickets along the Falls Road. At the end of the month the area was visited by a delegation of the American Indian Movement who had come to Ireland to express solidarity with the republican struggle and explain the plight of their own people. They went down a treat with the children and younger teenagers of Ballymurphy. On March 21st women from Springhill blocked the Springfield Road to draw attention to the 'slum conditions' of their homes, long neglected by the Housing Executive. On April 24th the Springfield Road was again blocked by residents of Ballymurphy, New Barnsley and Moyard demanding traffic lights at the Springfield/ Whiterock junction. Earlier in the day two ten-year-old girls from Moyard had been knocked down at a nearby zebra crossing. From May 10th to 13th a second Black delegation from Britain stayed in the area.

On the 11th they attended a commemoration for Ballymurphy's IRA dead, during which the Republican Movement handed out crystal plates to the families of each dead Volunteer. On Sunday the 13th, they joined the people of the Upper Springfield as Gerry Adams unveiled a plaque in honour of the republican dead in the centre of Ballymurphy estate.

On June 25th the case of M60 squad member, Joe Doherty, was again brought to mind when Britain and the USA signed a new extradition treaty in Washington. (Joe Doherty was still in jail in the USA despite the refusal of a federal judge to extradite him in December of the previous year.) On July 2nd Fort Pegasus was mortar-bombed for the second time when a single missile scored a direct hit on the kitchen. The kitchen was empty at the time, but that did not prevent the panic-stricken garrison, many in their underpants, from streaming out onto the Whiterock Road to assault passers-by in reprisal.

On July 26th a stolen car crashed near Saintfield killing 18-year-old James Henry from Moyard and fatally injuring 19-year-old Joseph Dorrian from Springfield Park. Another Dorrian boy, 18-year-old Denis, was left fighting for his life. Martin McNally (18) from Moyard described how, after the crash: 'I saw them [RUC] pull James Henry out by the hair and drag Joseph Dorrian by the collar of his jacket. They hit Joseph Dorrian in the back and left him lying on the ground, flat on his back.'[24]

Young McNally was himself batoned and kicked when he tried to run off, and had his arm twisted up his back, leaving him with a dislocated shoulder. Two days later, a few minutes before Joseph Dorrian died, the RUC raided the Royal Victoria Hospital in an attempt to arrest Joseph's brother, Peter, for non-payment of a fine. In the process they beat up three of the Dorrian family and knocked the father unconscious with blows of their batons.

Two weeks later marked the fourteenth anniversary of internment. As was the case all over the Six Counties, the riots in Ballymurphy were the worst for years. In Derry, Martin Galvin had appeared at the funeral of Volunteer Charles English, prompting the RUC to run riot in all nationalist areas, indiscriminately firing volleys of plastic bullets. Less than a month later, on September 2nd, Douglas Hurd was replaced as Secretary of State by Tom King.

On the same day Fort Pegasus was burned to the ground. The base had lain empty for two days, having been hastily deserted by the British. The contractors, who had been given the job of dismantling the structure, notified Sinn Fein and Gerry Adams announced the news. Within an hour the fort was ablaze. Those entering the empty fort said that it reminded them of the story of the *Mary Celeste* – everything was as it should have been, except there was nobody there any more.

On September 8th the IRA executed Gerald Mahon (28) and his wife Catherine (27) in an alley in Turf Lodge, sending shock waves through the Upper Springfield. In a detailed statement issued afterwards the IRA accused the couple, both originally from Ballymurphy, of having acted as British agents for the previous 18 month, since the husband's arrest in 1984 for unpaid fines. The statement charged that in June 1984 they had been responsible for the capture of a 30lb bomb and the arrest of three INLA men, for which they were paid £250. The couple had also offered the IRA the use of their Twinbrook flat as an arms dump. They had then, the IRA alleged, given the Special Branch a key so that the weapons could be 'bugged'.

> In all, three 'bugs' were placed. The first was in a Ruger rifle. The second, which was light sensitive, was in the dump itself, and it gave off a signal each time the dump was opened. The third bug was a special 'bleeper' ... If any IRA Volunteers were in the house, the bleeper was to be triggered twice. If the weapons were being removed they sent four bleeps and six bleeps meant that the handlers had to phone him. If Mahon were arrested by the IRA, his wife was to send a continuous bleep ...
>
> On three occasions, when the RUC thought there was a chance of 'hitting' IRA Volunteers in the flat, they were both sent to Newcastle for the weekend. All expenses were paid by the Special Branch ...
>
> The Mahons were executed because for almost a year and a half they were consciously and unscrupulously working for the RUC. They willingly gave not only information but attempted to assist in the murder of republican Volunteers.[25]

Shortly after the execution of the Mahons, the RUC sealed off their Twinbrook flat. They then claimed to have 'found' two rifles, three two-way radios and three timing power units in shrubbery nearby. The IRA identified the find as one FNC (5.56), a Ruger (5.56), and a .38 Special revolver, adding: 'It was to these that we referred in our earlier statement. After we arrested the Mahons, our personnel attempted to remove this dump but as testing for bugs proved positive we decided not to move them from the vicinity.' The RUC, on arrival, had discovered that the weapons had been tampered with and had sealed off the flat to check for booby-traps.

On September 17th Tom King met Peter Barry and Garret FitzGerald in Dublin as the council turmoil continued in the North and the unionists threatened war should Britain 'capitulate' to pressure from Dublin. Four days later the BBC 'Panorama' programme suggested that the deal being worked out between the two governments would include an Anglo-Irish council with a permanent secretariat in Belfast – one of the proposals put forward by the 1984 Tory policy document, which would seem be hailed by Dublin and the SDLP as a result of the Forum Report and a creation of theirs.

October 1985 was a month of increasing expectations in the North, with the SDLP clearly satisfied with developments, and loyalists and republicans alike lambasting the undemocratic nature of whatever was going on. On the 7th, Spring and Barry met with Howe and King to put the finishing touches to the deal while the RUC and loyalists continued to confront each other amid suggestions that the former would have to quit their homes in loyalist areas and move to fortified RUC cantons.

Towards the end of the month, the anti-'supergrass' groups, who felt that the ending of the crumbling 'supergrass' system would be one of the 'concessions' of any Anglo-Irish deal, were surprised when the RUC recruited Angela Whoriskey in Derry and arrested a group of alleged IRA Volunteers. However, it later transpired that the British had already decided to abandon the 'supergrass' system in the face of international and local opposition (a BBC 'Spotlight' poll conducted in May 1985 showed that only 19 per cent of people in the Six Counties supported the use of 'supergrasses'), and the RUC was acting in opposition to British thinking. In October 1986 the final nail in the 'supergrass' coffin was driven home when all those charged under Whoriskey were released without explanation.

On November 15th 1985 Thatcher, King, FitzGerald, Spring and Barry met at Hillsborough Castle in County Down to formally sign the agreement worked out during the previous months of leaks and speculation. The Anglo-Irish Accord was hailed by the Coalition and the SDLP as a major victory for constitutional Irish nationalism. The British had agreed to a formula in which they would consent to Irish unity if in the future a majority in the North were in its favour. There was to be an 'Irish dimension' – a joint secretariat at Marysfield near Belfast and an intergovernmental Conference that would give the Irish government, and by extension the SDLP, a consultative (but powerless) role in the affairs of the North.

There would also be some cosmetic internal reforms: a vague recognition of the 'tradition' and identity of the Northern nationalists; a promise to recognise cultural rights; hints of unspecified changes to the Diplock Courts; an end to all sorts of discrimination; and changes in the laws governing the display of flags and emblems. In reality, many of the British 'concessions' had already been wrested from them by the republican communities: the 'supergrass' system had been devastated; flags and emblems were being displayed openly; street names were in Irish; and it was unlikely that the British could maintain their occupation of the North anyway without the support of the artificial loyalist 'majority'.

The British government, by contrast, had succeeded in achieving the goal put before it by its generals after Narrow Water, and updated in the 1984 policy document. (It was no coincidence that one of the key figures responsible for setting up the Anglo-Irish Agreement was Sir Robert Armstrong, former chairperson of the Official Committee on Intelligence.) For minimal concessions, none of which threatened British interests in the North, it had secured the active collaboration of the Irish government and the SDLP/Catholic Church in opposing the Irish demand for reunification as enshrined in the Irish Constitution. They had strengthened the old colonial link with Dublin, secured the Irish government's recognition of the Northern state and partition, and its support for a new devolved administration at Stormont. They had also, through the new Conference, incorporated Dublin as the junior partner in the British war machine and – the cornerstone of the British thrust – they had extradition within their grasp as both governments promised to be 'concerned with policy aspects of extradition and extra-territorial jurisdiction as between North and South'.

On November 19th, Fianna Fail leader, Charles Haughey, denounced the Accord as 'an acceptance of British sovereignty over Northern Ireland and Northern Ireland as an integral part of the United Kingdom and what must be done is to smooth out the difficulties which the British government encountered in running this part of this kingdom'.[26] He warned that Dublin would now find itself responsible for security policies over which it had no control and that the Irish establishment was simply being used to legitimise the British military and political presence in the Six Counties. Yet, within two years, Haughey himself would be part of the process.

In Ballymurphy, there was general disbelief that any Irish administration could have signed such a document, in effect putting its seal of approval on partition. King articulated the overall feeling on December 3rd when he said that the Irish government had given up 'in perpetuity' the chance of a united Ireland. Regardless, Dublin pushed ahead. On December 10th 1985 the Secretary General of the Council of Europe, Marcelino Oreja, met with Garret FitzGerald and Dublin's Minister for Justice, Michael Noonan, to discuss legislation that would enable Dublin to sign the European Convention on the Suppression of Terrorism, thus paving the way for the introduction of extradition.

On December 18th 27 men were jailed in the North's Diplock Courts on the word of INLA 'supergrass' Harry Kirkpatrick. The same courts stood internationally condemned as did the whole administration of 'justice' in the Six Counties. These were the courts to which the Dublin government, in violation of the Irish Constitution, was now planning to extradite Irish republicans.

On December 19th Bobby Tohill of New Barnsley, convicted on the uncorroborated word of Harry Kirkpatrick, went on hunger strike in Long Kesh demanding an immediate appeal. His co-convicted threatened to follow him in a fast to the death.

References

1. Gerry Sloan, formerly of Ballymurphy (1987 Interview).
2. Ibid.
3. Ibid.
4. Paddy Adams of Ballymurphy (1988 Interview).
5. *Ballymurphy*, Belfast Areas of Need Sub-Group 1980, Section 2.
6. *Ballymurphy Benefit Campaign* (Upper Springfield Resource Centre, Belfast, 1983).
7. *Belfast Telegraph*, November 2nd 1981.
8. *Belfast Telegraph*, November 7th 1981.
9. *Irish News,* Belfast, July 10th 1982.
10. Maureen McCullough of Ballymurphy (1987 Interview).
11. 1983 Annual Report of RUC Chief Constable, Sir John Hermon.
12. *Irish News,* Belfast, August 1st 1983.
13. Bridie Adams of Ballymurphy (1987 Interview).
14. Paul Brennan, formerly of Ballymurphy (1984 Interview).
15. *Iris* (Irish Republican Information Service, Dublin, November 1983), p. 15.
16. *Supergrasses: Belfast Bulletin No. 11* (Workers' Research Unit, Belfast, summer 1984), p. 30.

17. Andrew Pollock writing in *Fortnight*, Belfast, December 1983/January 1984.
18. Frankie Cahill of Ballymurphy (1987 Interview).
19. Peter Beresford Ellis, *A History of the Irish Working Class* (Pluto Press, London, 1972), p. 334.
20. *Resource*, Upper Springfield Resource Centre, Belfast, June 1983.
21. Interview with member of staff of Leisure Centre who does not wish to be identified.
22. *Britain's Undefended Frontier: A Policy for Ulster* (Independent Study Group, London, October 1984).
23. Ibid.
24. *Irish News*, Belfast, July 29th 1985.
25. *An Phoblacht/Republican News*, Dublin, September 12th 1985.
26. *Irish News*, Belfast, November 20th 1985.

15

'Little Beirut'

The hunger strike did not last long. On January 6th, with Gerard Steenson and Thomas Power having joined Bobby Tohill, the protest was called off after a visit to the prisoners by anti-'supergrass' campaigner, Lord Gifford. A promise of an early appeal had brought an end to the protest. In fact the whole 'supergrass' system was already crumbling under the weight of local protest, international condemnation, and the fact that Dublin was not happy with the effect it was having on Northern middle-class nationalists.

Inside twelve more months every prisoner held on the uncorroborated evidence of a 'supergrass', other than former Sinn Fein organiser, Jim Gibney, would be freed in a series of successful appeals. A campaign co-ordinated by a handful of individuals would have deprived the British of yet another 'solution' to the Irish war. By then, however, the British would have already neatly streamlined their next offensive against Irish republicanism through the Anglo-Irish Accord.

By November 18th 1985 the London–Dublin pact was already beginning to show results as the realignment and consolidation of anti-republican forces got under way. There would be no future electoral pacts with Sinn Fein, the SDLP announced, regardless of how this affected nationalist representation. All establishment forces in Ireland were now rallying in an attempt to politically isolate Sinn Fein while the British government, with the full co-operation of the Irish state, stepped up its campaign against the IRA and the republican communities supporting the guerrillas. In return for the lucrative spoils of the Anglo-Irish Accord, the British were now also, for the first time in the history of the Six-County statelet, willing to confront loyalist atavism and intransigence. To hell with 'democracy'! The loyalists would digest the Accord, with or without their consent.

On November 23rd, eight days after the signing of the pact, some 250,000 loyalists gathered at Belfast City Hall – they were ignored. A few days later, on Westminster's acceptance of the deal, all unionist MPs quit their seats, forcing a mini-General Election for the 15 unionist seats in the North. On January 23rd 1986 the mini election took place. The combined unionist and Sinn Fein vote registered a massive democratically-expressed rejection of the Accord within the Six Counties. The vote was ignored, the establishment parties in London and Dublin taking succour from SDLP Deputy-Leader Seamus Mallon's success in taking one of the loyalist seats, and a drop in Sinn Fein's vote. Although the drop might have been a pro-pact rather than anti-Sinn Fein sentiment, the establishments on both sides of the Irish Sea were ecstatic.

The Accord was already 'working'. The price being paid by Northern nationalists, as loyalists marched, rioted, burned and engaged in sectarian attacks, was also largely ignored. The British were content to see the more extreme arms of loyalism take their toll on nationalist lives and property in order to split the loyalist camp into extremists and moderates. Already, on December 5th, the Alliance Party had walked out of Stormont after a combined unionist vote had set up a grand committee to study the Anglo-Irish Accord. Shortly afterwards Alliance said yes to the Accord.

By early January the Official Unionists were becoming worried by loyalist violence. Media coverage of attacks on nationalist homes and trading premises, and an attack on Marysfield on January 5th, were doing nothing to help the unionist cause. The 'withdrawal of consent' protest, whereby councils suspended business and unionists refused to talk to government ministers, had also degenerated into unseemly scenes of mob violence which again worried Molyneaux' party. On January 18th 30 hooded and uniformed UDA men turned up for an 'Ulster Says No' rally at Ballynahinch, further damaging the unionists' 'democratic' image. (The UDA men were in fact asked by a senior RUC officer to go home again because the rally organisers were not keen on their presence. This was at a time when republican 'paramilitary displays' prompted the same RUC into vicious baton and plastic-bullet attacks on mourners at republican funerals.)

The real crunch came on March 4th 1986 during a 'Day of Action' against the Accord. The OUP was horrified to find itself identified with the hooded men on the countless roadblocks and the mobs burning, rioting and attacking nationalists and the RUC. Although the RUC remained generally inactive during the day of violence and intimidation, they were already being branded by Paisley and his cohorts as agents of Dublin and 'Barry-rule'. As soon as 'law and order' confronted loyalist sectarianism, then it was no longer 'law and order'. Soon, RUC homes began to come under attack and the RUC became targets for loyalist gunmen. Undoubtedly the RUC itself was torn by its divided loyalties – and there were even rumours of a full mutiny within the force – but the ranks held firm alongside their paymasters, holding the line until the brunt of the loyalist violence had spent itself on nationalist towns and nationalist homes.

Within twelve months of the signing of the Accord, the rota of rioting, the attacks on RUC and nationalist homes, and the anti-Accord sectarian assassinations of nationalists had died back to yet another 'acceptable level' and the loyalist backlash was reduced to rhetoric and posturing. Three years after its signing, the Hillsborough Agreement was still there as unionism gradually slipped back into its old role, realising that nothing had really changed, other than the irritating presence of Irish government representatives at Marysfield.

In the meantime the British and Irish establishments had been dangling the carrot of a new Stormont following the axing of Prior's Assembly in June 1986. However, all attempts at devolved government in the North seemed doomed. This time, the SDLP was doing all the offering. They would help stabilise the Six Counties within a partitionist framework, as planned by London and Dublin, but only within the context of the Hillsborough Agreement, which had given them a new credibility among the less radicalised sections of nationalism. The loyalists, on the other hand, were now offering to bend over backwards to accommodate the SDLP – provided the Agreement was scrapped. It was the same deadlock as existed on May 28th 1974 when the power-sharing Assembly fell. The only difference this time was that when it suited British interests, loyalism was confronted head on and worn down.

For a while in 1986, however, the situation had looked grim for the British, particularly after the plastic-bullet killing of Keith White, the first loyalist to be killed by this weapon. The 20-year-old man had been struck during fierce rioting in Portadown on March 31st and had died when his life-support machine was switched off on April 14th. In the build-up to the Twelfth of July period there were even rumours of UDI, but after an orgy of violence against nationalists and a spate of sectarian assassinations and attempted assassinations, loyalist fervour for UDI cooled again. The OUP/DUP alliance, however, had been wrecked in the process.

On other fronts the Accord was running relatively smoothly for the British. In Dublin the Coalition was pushing ahead with its extradition plans and beefing up its border security. It was also turning a blind eye to the mass repression being unleashed by the British army and RUC.

Along the border, large tracts of land were being annexed by the military for a series of spy-forts and look-out posts, a process that had begun in October 1984 when hilltops in South Armagh were commandeered. The 'Hillsborough Wall' gave the British army easy access to the 26 Counties, making cross-border incursions so much easier.

In the republican areas of the North the military were putting the boot in with a vengeance as Peter Barry, Irish Foreign Affairs Minister, talked of how the Accord was solving all ills and 'ending the nationalist nightmare'. Eventually even the traditional enemies of republicanism, such as the Catholic hierarchy, began to protest loudly at military actions. The situation in the Upper Springfield was summed up in an open letter entitled 'Bashing the Nationalists', posted to Garret FitzGerald (with a copy to all Dail members) in October 1986. The letter, written by one of the most prominent community groups in the area, attacked the Coalition for its claim that, as a result of the Accord, state forces were now behaving and were therefore more acceptable in nationalist areas.

We who know listen in stupefaction ... We try to comfort the mother of three-year-old Paul Burns of Springhill who was tossed over a wall like a sack of spuds; we listen to 68-year-old Frank Hardie, who is deaf and had his skull split open for not responding quickly enough to a soldier's question; young Martin Morris who was asked if he had any problems, and was then smashed in the face and told that 'Now you have one'; Ned Ryan who received eight stitches in his head; Susie Vallelly and her children who woke up to find armed RUC men with torches in her bedroom in the middle of the night; Gerry Daly who was kicked in the groin and smashed in the face with a rifle butt for the crime of walking down the street; the McManus children who had to be kept from school because they were beaten and threatened every day by the military; young Jimmy Lennon who had a rifle butt broken across his mouth as he gave his name and address to a soldier; and many, many more ... What do we tell young Irish women who are daily called 'whores' on their own streets? How do we reconcile their reality with the land of delusion currently inhabited by the Irish political establishment? Can somebody somewhere please explain this new era, this 'ending of the nationalist nightmare' of which we recently hear so much ...?[1]

Earlier in the year the people of Ballymurphy had reacted with disbelief to Alan Dukes' statement, when on February 24th he had urged nationalists to join the RUC. Speaking from Strasbourg, where he was formally signing the European Convention on the Suppression of Terrorism, the Coalition's new Justice Minister could hardly have displayed a greater ignorance of the realities of life in the Six Counties. At that point the state forces were stepping up their campaign against the very people to whom Dukes was addressing himself. It was like asking Palestinians on the West Bank to join the Israeli army.

Towards the end of 1986 the military repression was curtailed somewhat when the volume of protest outweighed the advantages for the British. However, it is worth noting that, in October 1986, as the British army dealt out collective punishment to entire communities, neither the Workers' Party nor the SDLP supported any of the efforts of community groups in the Upper Springfield to resist the terror campaign.

It should also be mentioned that, in the period since, those who have been most vocal in their condemnation of republican violence (the Catholic hierarchy, the SDLP, the Dublin government, the Workers' Party and the pro-SDLP/Catholic Church *Irish News*) have been infinitely more silent during the summary roadside executions, the attacks on republican funerals, the strip-searching of women in the jails, the destruction of nationalist homes and the state's assault on radical community groups in nationalist areas. It will also be of interest to students of state repression (and community work) that the British chose this period – when the Irish establishment had been firmly knitted to its war machine – to include community groups in the list of targets to be eliminated.

When outlining his counter-insurgency tactics, Brigadier Frank Kitson had argued that all in the community who disagreed with state policy had to be marginalised, isolated and pushed aside, whereas all those who agreed were to be elevated and rewarded. Every suspect organisation or group was to be stripped of any means of advancing its position within the community. The process had begun in the North shortly after the election of a substantial number of anti-imperialist candidates to the urban and rural councils. Speaking in the House of Commons, then Secretary of State, Douglas Hurd, stated that:

> Some community groups, or persons prominent in the direction or management of some community groups, have sufficiently close links with paramilitary organisations to give rise to a grave risk that to give support to those groups would have the effect of improving their standing and furthering the aims of paramilitary organisations, whether directly or indirectly.[2]

Hurd's blanket categorising was an attempt to isolate all anti-imperialist community activists and encourage community groups to embark on their own witch-hunts in order to save themselves. As well as denting the effectiveness of republican political activists, this move would also relieve some of the pressure from the SDLP, who could not hope to compete with the republican grassroots involvement in the community.

The first target for the new assault was the large independent community venture at Conway Street Mill on the Falls Road, a venture in which Springhill Community House had invested heavily. First, the Mill's management committee was refused grant aid from the Local Enterprise Development Unit (LEDU) on instructions from the NIO. These grants would normally be available to any job-creation scheme. Then, in a letter dated June 27th 1985, the Department of Economic Development informed the creche on Springhill's educational floor at the Mill that their funds were being withdrawn. They were, apparently, a threat to Britain's national security!

In early 1986 the Mill's problems intensified as the SDLP allied itself to the NIO attack. On February 4th North Belfast SDLP councillor, Brian Feeney, accused community groups in West Belfast of being fronts for the IRA and of laundering government funds for the guerrillas. He was immediately challenged by the four umbrella community organisations of West Belfast – representing some 200 community groups – to provide one shred of evidence. He failed to do so.

In the meantime the SDLP itself refused to refute Feeney's allegations, lending them further credibility. On February 5th Feeney was again challenged to name names on RTE's 'Morning Ireland'. He now named Conway Street Mill as 'a front for considerable enterprise for Sinn Fein and the Provos'. He followed this up in a letter to the *Andersonstown News* on February 15th in which he accused community leaders in West Belfast of 'squealing like stuck pigs' because they had challenged his unspecified and unfounded allegations. He then went on to say that 'Provo and Stickie infiltration over years has resulted in depriving West Belfast of funds and facilities. For example the Glen Community Centre and Horn Drive both had to close for periods.'

In a reply, the umbrella groups of West Belfast pointed out that Glen Community Centre had been closed due to fire damage, and Horn Drive for renovations. Facts that should have been well known to Feeney, who was a member of Belfast City Council – which managed both centres! However, the damage was done: all community groups in West Belfast were now suspect and the NIO could move against them with full SDLP consent. Not to mention the fact that workers and management had been set up by Feeney as 'legitimate' targets for loyalist assassins.

In the months that followed the hit list grew. However, Conway Mill remained the biggest target. Not alone was the Mill management denied job-creating grants and Springhill Community House deprived of its ACE grants, but every single group wishing to set up shop in the Mill was told that no government grants would be forthcoming unless they found an alternative location. The NIO then threatened the Ulster People's College and the Workers' Educational Association that funding would be withdrawn if they continued to operate courses in Conway Mill and, in August 1987, Belfast Education and Library Board informed Springhill Community House (by telephone) that all funding for educational tutors at the Mill was to cease forthwith.

Concurrent with the assault on independent community groups, the British set in motion another facet of Kitson's doctrine. By then, the British guru of counter-insurgency had seen his philosophy translated into reality in the Six Counties through the 'screening' and mass disorientation techniques of Motorman, Diplock Courts and 'supergrass' trials, subversion of the media, mass surveillance, blackmail, extortion, pseudo-gangs, counter-gangs and death squads. It had produced the mass terror tactics deployed against the civilian population; the military control of housing, planning, the environment and the economy; the redistribution of population to compress the combat-zones; and the public summary executions of suspected guerrillas and republican Volunteers apprehended in action.

The one final aspect – which still presented difficulties – was co-optation, what Kitson called 'drowning the revolution in babies' milk'. This required the recruitment of compliant elements of the rebellious communities into active involvement in the suppression of the rebellion. The payoff would be a share in the cake. By channeling this share through the collaborating elements to the rebellious population at large, support for the militants would be drained away until they were left isolated and exposed. The launching pad for this drive had already been set in place through the signing of the Hillsborough Agreement and the vehicle chosen by the British was the Catholic Church, particularly the Church in West Belfast.

After a series of meetings and dinners between the NIO and the Church leaders, a string of companies was established by the Diocese of Down and Connor, under the direct control of Bishop Cahal Daly. Simultaneously, other community-controlled organisations and proposed employment schemes were attacked and destroyed, or aborted before they could get off the ground, while funds were diverted from many quarters, including the above-mentioned schemes, to bolster and develop the expanding economic empire of Friars Bush Ltd, the umbrella for the entire Church operation.

The ultimate aim of the affair was that the SDLP and the Catholic hierarchy would be afforded the ability to exercise economic patronage towards the nationalists of West Belfast, thus drawing away support from the republicans. On September 13th 1986 the *Andersonstown News* reported that the Bishop of Down and Connor was about to become the biggest employer in West Belfast, having 350 ACE jobs under his control by the end of the year. A month later, *Scope* community magazine added that Down and Connor would be receiving £2.5 million per annum for the creation of ACE jobs. Cathedral Community Enterprises would co-ordinate the work of a huge team of 'environmental workers', engaged in one-year contracts.

Although the scheme would not lay any economic base in West Belfast, it would, the Church hoped, provide the hierarchy with the bandwagon from which to launch a concerted campaign against the Republican Movement and independent community groups that opposed British policies. Meanwhile, as the plan got under way, the community groups and local economic projects under attack in West Belfast were appealing to the SDLP and the Catholic hierarchy for support – unaware of the extent of the plot being hatched against them.

At the time of writing, Conway Mill is still in business, struggling defiantly against the NIO campaign, a campaign foreseen in part as far back as 1984. At that time, a legal adviser was asked to assess the Mill's future.

He advised that the government would, according to the pattern of what happened in the past, refuse to direct industry towards the project, would refuse to help create industry within it, would delay or refuse grants, and if in the end the project survived, it would send in the troops ... it has all proved true apart from the last resort of sending in the troops. However, since that was done with the Whiterock Industrial Estate we cannot have confidence that it will not be done in the case of the Conway Street complex.[3]

Throughout this period British military and political actions were constantly being bolstered by the Northern nationalist establishment, who maintained a concentrated assault on republicanism. The Catholic hierarchy, through its principal politician, Bishop Cahal Daly of Down and Connor, poured out an endless tirade of vitriol. No matter what the subject matter, Daly could turn his homily into a bitter attack on republicanism. On August 30th 1986 he was joined by Bishop Edward Daly of Derry who told all republicans that they should leave the Catholic Church.

In reply, Derry Sinn Fein leader, Martin McGuinness, asked Edward Daly if the Catholic Church was now open only to supporters of the SDLP or those who accepted the continued presence of an occupying army and administration. He reiterated Sinn Fein's call for the Church to morally pronounce on the partition of Ireland, the British presence, and what advice, if any, the Church offered to Catholic members of the British army. Daly did not reply. But the *Irish News*, now the unofficial organ of the SDLP/Catholic Church alliance, responded with an attack on McGuinness, calling the Sinn Fein stance 'a blasphemous challenge to Christ himself'. Writing 'under our motto, *Pro Fide et Patria* (for Faith and

Fatherland)' the leader went on to say that the British had 'made determined efforts to remedy past wrongs.'[4] The writer obviously did not live in Greater Ballymurphy or along the Falls Road.

Meanwhile, the IRA increased its operational level during 1986 to demonstrate its contempt for the Hillsborough Agreement. In the twelve months following the signing of the pact 22 mortar and bomb attacks were carried out against British bases, many of which were totally demolished. An IRA warning to all contractors and suppliers to cease working for British forces meant that soldiers had to be drafted in to carry out basic repairs and rebuild on a temporary basis. At the same time gun and bomb attacks against the military and RUC continued to take their toll.

In September the IRA turned its attention to the North Belfast UVF which had carried out a number of sectarian assassinations of nationalists. In the early hours of September 14th an ASU sledgehammered its way into the home of John Bingham, the local UVF commander. After shooting the lock off an upstairs steel security gate, they found Bingham cowered in the corner of a blacked-out room and shot him dead.

A month later the IRA held its first Army Convention for 16 years. In preparation for the coming debate on abstentionism at November's Sinn Fein Ard-Fheis, the constitution of Oglaigh na hEireann was amended to remove the ban on support for republican candidates who took their seats at Leinster House. A month later, absentionism was abolished at a historic Sinn Fein Ard-Fheis. As a result, some of the old guard walked out and formed Republican Sinn Fein, but there was no repeat of the split of 1969/70. The vast majority of republicans had decided that old romanticisms had no further relevance in an Ireland plagued by the problems of the late twentieth century.

In the Upper Springfield the Volunteers went on with the war as they had for the past 16 years. As members of the Belfast Brigade they engaged the military and RUC across the city. As local experts they harassed them on the ground in Greater Ballymurphy. On October 7th 1985 they had hit the Taggart with a 50lb mortar, causing serious damage to buildings inside and leaving a hole in the perimeter wall. The mortar had been fired from the top of Springhill Avenue. Immediately the military raced to the spot, only to find that it was cut off by its own security barrier at the top of the street. On January 16th 1986 one of the area's former Volunteers made international headlines. Gerry Kelly, who had escaped from Long Kesh while serving life for the 1973 London bombings, was arrested in the Netherlands. With him were Brendan 'Bic' McFarlane, fellow escapee and former H-Block commander, and Billy 'Blue' Kelly from the Springfield Road. They were accused of possession of weapons found in a container some distance from their flat. When no evidence could be produced to support this charge Billy Kelly was released, but the British applied for the extradition of the two escapees. After a protracted battle in the Dutch courts they were eventually sent back to Long Kesh in early December. One of the conditions, however, was that Gerry Kelly's earlier prison sentence be dropped as the London bombings were deemed political. The escape from Long Kesh, on the other hand, was not. So, in a bizarre verdict, 'Bic' McFarlane was returned to face life and Gerry Kelly to face charges relating to the 1983 escape.

On February 17th the case of M60 squad member, Joe Doherty, surfaced once more when a US appeals court again refused to extradite him. None the less he was re-imprisoned as the US government continued its attempts to satisfy Thatcher's demands for the IRA man's return. Five months later the US Senate approved the Anglo-US extradition treaty. Joe Doherty, still in jail, now awaits almost certain extradition. On May 12th 1986 the Taggart was one of three British bases in West Belfast to come under hand grenade attack.

In July Whiterock Leisure Centre was back in the political limelight. Folk singer Christy Moore had given a concert at the centre, during which Gerry Adams announced that the singer's fee was being donated to the Kelly/McFarlane anti-extradition fight – unionist howls could be heard for miles. On August 4th the British army came under blast-bomb attack in Ballymurphy estate. Two months later, on October 11th, an ASU launched another single mortar at the Taggart. They had coolly waited for an end to a British army saturation operation in the area before firing the 50lb missile. The mortar exploded over the Taggart, killing RUC Constable Desmond Dobbin and causing leg injuries to a passing civilian. Then the area remained relatively quiet until the beginning of 1987.

* * *

The final collapse of the 'supergrass' system had taken place on December 23rd 1986 when all those convicted under INLA 'grass', Harry Kirkpatrick, were freed on appeal. In the Upper Springfield, the general consensus was that there would be trouble now.

Ever since the death of Seamus Costello, the INLA leadership had constantly been undermined from within, while the IRSP had been relegated to a propaganda organ. At the end of 1979 and the beginning of 1980, as several of the ex-prisoners returned to the IRSP and INLA, two factions were locked in struggle for control of the organisation. One was led by Gerard Steenson of Clonard, the other by Harry Flynn of Ballymurphy. This culminated in a spate of shootings, the victims including Harry Flynn, wounded in a Dublin attack in December 1981.

In 1982, with the conflict still unresolved, the movement was hit by the first of its 'supergrasses', Jackie Goodman of Ballymurphy. Goodman was followed by a series of others, ending with Harry Kirkpatrick from Divis Flats. (Kirkpatrick had originally offered to work for the British in March 1982 but was not accepted until April 1983.) Simultaneously, allegations of corruption were being levelled at senior members of the INLA. They were being accused from within the organisation of carrying out 'homers' – robberies for personal gain – and feeding weapons to criminals in return for a cut of subsequent armed robberies.

Kirkpatrick's recruitment by the British left the Belfast INLA and IRSP in disarray. A large number of arrests also meant that the simmering conflict shifted to Crumlin Road Prison. Again, accusations of corruption began to fly, and a feeling emerged among some of the prisoners that the IRSP and INLA had lost direction and degenerated to a point where they could not be redeemed. At this stage, Gerard Steenson, who adhered to this belief, began to canvass for support inside and outside the jail, building up a caucus of followers, among them Jimmy Brown, former Belfast chairperson of the IRSP.

At the beginning of 1984 an attempt to poison Kirkpatrick was foiled because of lax security among some of the prisoners. This further exacerbated tensions in Crumlin Road. The dissidents then charged that John O'Reilly, a leading member of the opposite faction, had agreed to work for the RUC in 1979. The leadership outside, who supported O'Reilly, was furious. They accused Steenson of corruption. At the same time, they declared themselves Marxist-Leninist, breaking from the broad-front politics espoused by Costello and still nurtured by the dissidents in the jail. Eventually, the divisions erupted into violence in October 1984. According to one of the dissidents:

> O'Reilly got bail on October 4th 1984. He was involved in the shooting of Jimmy McCrystal in Farnham Street on October 12th. He shot Jimmy with a .25 which we had got and was to have been used in an escape attempt by us (the dissidents). At first the O'Reilly faction denied it. They put out a statement saying it was the Red Hand Commandos. But the UVF commander in the Crum denied this emphatically.[5]

The situation continued to deteriorate throughout 1985 with several more gun attacks in Belfast and the dissidents in Crumlin Road becoming worried about the intentions of their fellow prisoners:

> During the same period there was a .32 revolver in the Crum. It was meant for another escape attempt, but the story was that they were going to try and shoot either Gerard Steenson or Jimmy Brown. As well as that they had control of the poison, so that our lads stopped eating canteen food, and only ate from food parcels sent in by relatives.[6]

Eventually, in an effort to stem the fragmentation, the Belfast branch of the IRSP contacted Des Wilson at the end of 1985 and asked him to mediate. A compromise was reached whereby: 'The INLA leadership gave an undertaking that nothing would happen to Steenson and his followers in or out of jail provided they refrained from acting against the leadership or describing themselves as INLA. Steenson and his followers were to take on "neutral" status under the IRA prison command.'[7] Steenson was then suspended from the INLA. In 1985 he was expelled. Jimmy Brown, the other leading dissident within the jail, resigned from the IRSP. By then two men were already dead.

Gerard 'Sparkey' Barkley, the Ballymurphy man whose body was found at the border on October 26th 1983, had been one of the Steenson tendency. He and the Clonard man had been friends since 1976. He had supported Kirkpatrick and Steenson in 1980 when they were attempting to wrest the Six-County INLA from the control of Jackie Goodman and Sean Flynn, brother of Harry Flynn. He had also supported Steenson's drive against corruption within the movement, and was identified with Steenson when he in turn was accused of corruption. By October 1983 Gerard Barkley was being accused by the INLA of having purchased two houses with the proceeds of 'homers'. He was shot dead by the O'Reilly faction without any court of inquiry. The 'INLA volley' fired in his honour had actually been fired by his friends. According to the INLA, two of the weapons used belonged to the UDA, and had been acquired through loyalist underworld channels. Afterwards, the INLA swooped on Gerard Barkley's 'firing party' and confiscated the guns.

Meanwhile, another drama with violent conclusions was unfolding. Seamus Ruddy, one of Harry Flynn's men, had been arrested in 1979 crossing the Greek–Turkish border in possession of weapons acquired from the Palestinians. Shortly after his return to Dublin he was involved, as Quartermaster-General of the INLA, in the import of another shipment of weapons. However, before the weapons could be collected, he was arrested outside a Dublin bar by the Garda Special Branch. In his pockets they found receipts for a container of arms then sitting in Dublin's docks. Ruddy went on the run. According to the INLA he told nobody of his encounter with the Gardai and thus endangered other Volunteers going to collect the weapons. The dissidents flatly deny this allegation. Either way, Seamus Ruddy next appeared working as an English teacher in Paris. In 1985 he disappeared without trace. He is believed buried in a wood outside the French capital, having been shot dead, according to the dissidents, by John O'Reilly.

Nevertheless, despite the troubled past, things appeared to have settled after the Kirkpatrick trial. The sentenced men were sent to the H-Blocks where Bobby Tohill and Thomas 'Ta' Power embarked on a hunger-strike along with Gerard Steenson. The dissidents, meanwhile, maintained their 'neutral' status under the IRA command.

Following the release of the INLA prisoners (including dissidents) in December 1986, Thomas Power, loyal to the existing leadership of the IRSP, instigated a series of meetings in an attempt to rebuild the organisation. By now, the INLA Chief of Staff, Tom McAllister, had given his allegiance to the dissidents. Power approached all past members, including the Steenson/Brown faction, to see what common ground still existed, in the hope that past members could be reintegrated into the movement.

Unknown to Power and his faction, however, an alliance was already being forged between the Steenson/Brown faction, a faction led by Harry Flynn and Gerry Roche, and the INLA Revolutionary Command led by the new Chief of Staff, Tom McAllister. The alliance would become known as the 'INLA Army Council'.

At the same time, another group of ex-INLA Volunteers had formed the Irish People's Liberation Organisation, which had already killed former INLA man Tom McCartan and an RUC man. The IPLO supported the INLA Army Council Alliance, and in the confusion of terms that followed, both names were used by nationalists to describe the Army Council Alliance. Eventually, after the 1987 feud, both groups merged and adopted the IPLO title. The INLA Volunteers loyal to the IRSP and the O'Reilly/Power faction called themselves the 'INLA GHQ'.

By mid-January 1987 it was accepted by all sides that no common ground existed between the IRSP/INLA and the alliance. A meeting was arranged for the Rossnaree hotel close to Drogheda to formalise an agreement to differ. It was agreed that, once this meeting began, Thomas Power would ring Des Wilson in Belfast so that he could arrive at the end of the meeting to witness the 'peaceful parting of the ways'. 'In fact', Des Wilson recalled, 'what happened was that Thomas Power phoned me to say not to bother coming, that the others hadn't turned up and they would just head on home.'

Shortly afterwards, as the four INLA GHQ representatives sat at a table, two men walked into the Rossnaree hotel and opened fire on them. John O'Reilly (26) and 'Ta' Power (34) were shot dead. A man from Ballymurphy was hit in the hand. The INLA Army Council claimed the attack as the shock waves rolled across Belfast. Over the next month the city reeled in confusion as nationalists tried to differentiate between the INLA Army Council and the INLA GHQ. And the shooting and killing went on as the INLA Army Council attempted its forced dissolution of the INLA, and the INLA GHQ struck back.

On February 18th the INLA feud began to centre around Ballymurphy. By this stage, the GHQ faction had concentrated its forces in the Springhill/Westrock area. The allied IRSP had simultaneously switched its operational headquarters to the Springfield Park home of its vice-chairperson, Kevin McQuillen, across the street from the Taggart. On the night of February 18th, three Army Council units arrived in Springhill. One of them, consisting of four Volunteers, took over a house in Springhill Avenue. They were spotted by GHQ members, who surrounded the house.

According to the GHQ Volunteers, the others then made a break out through the back and were immediately engaged. The Army Council, however, says that its unit had simply lured the GHQ men into a trap, and was waiting in ambush at the side of the house when they arrived. One way or another, GHQ Volunteer, Michael Kearney of New Barnsley, was shot dead. The Army Council unit then withdrew into Ballymurphy Estate. Later that evening, local IRA sympathisers 'secured' Springhill to facilitate an interview between Kevin McQuillen and the BBC. 'Micky Kearney was well known and well liked in Ballymurphy', McQuillen later recalled. 'As well as that, there had been a lot of previous co-operation between the IRA and INLA in the Upper Springfield. There was also a feeling in the area that we were the ones under attack for no apparent reason.'[8]

On February 27th, however, Gerry Adams expressed the Republican Movement's growing exasperation over the feud. 'In order that there be no misrepresentation of the republican position,' he said, 'it is quite clear that both factions have long ceased to play any role in the anti-imperialist struggle. They should both disband.'[9] By then, nationalists were disgusted and angry at the apparently senseless killings; and Springhill which had become a focus of the fighting, had become known locally as 'Little Beirut'. At night, its streets were deserted as people stayed indoors rather than risk an INLA fusillade. Sinn Fein was also becoming concerned that its own supporters were beginning to take sides in a conflict not of their making.

During the last week of February there was a lull in the shooting as Des Wilson and Clonard priests, Alex Reid and Gerry Reynolds attempted to mediate an end to the killing. The talks ended on March 1st when the INLA GHQ wounded John 'Bap' Campbell in Turf Lodge. Two days later an alleged GHQ supporter was shot in the legs in a bar on the Stewartstown Road. On March 8th an Army Council sympathiser was shot dead at the border. Then the feud returned to Ballymurphy. On March 9th the Army Council hit the IRSP base in Springfield Park – directly across the street from the Taggart. Late at night Kevin McQuillen's brother, Eamon (17), answered a knock at the door. Two armed men told him to lie on the floor, then shot him in the head, leaving him partially paralysed. Kevin McQuillen was then shot in the head and back. However, he was not seriously wounded. The IRSP accused the British of collusion in the attack and called on 'all anti-imperialist, republican and socialist groupings in Ireland' to isolate the Army Council.

On March 14th the INLA GHQ shot dead Fergus Conlon (31), one of its own members, accusing him of informing. The following day 25-year-old Ian Catney, Kevin McQuillen's cousin, was wounded as he sat in a parked van in New Barnsley. The Army Council claimed that the van had been used during a GHQ raid in Divis Flats. That night, Gerard Steenson (29) – considered by many nationalists to be the driving force behind the feud – and Tony 'Boot' McCarthy (31) were shot dead in Springhill Avenue. Steenson had gone into the area to kill the Ballymurphy man wounded in the Rossnaree Hotel attack. He was spotted by GHQ lookouts.

> There were two carloads of them. They were cruising, looking for targets in Springhill. They had already been up Springhill Avenue and out through the top. The second time they arrived in Springhill Avenue, our Volunteers had closed the Brit security barrier at the top. We had been expecting the other car to come in first, but as it happened Steenson's was first ... They seen the gate was closed – they had full beams on. At the pull-in, where the Loughgall mural is, they turned. A very slow U-turn. Then it happened. They seen our people with the weapons. Afterwards, we took two weapons and documents from the car.[10]

On March 17th the funerals took place. Tony McCarthy was buried under a massive RUC presence at the City Cemetery, within a stone's throw of Ballymurphy. Although his wife, Ann-Marie, was a native of the area, very few people attended, such was the community's revulsion at the feud and people's wish not to be identified in any way with either faction. Five days later, the final killings took place. Emmanuel Gargon, recovering from earlier feud wounds, was blasted with a shotgun in the Hatfield bar on the Ormeau Road. The killing was claimed by the Army Council, as was that of Kevin Barry Duffy, a GHQ Volunteer shot dead in Armagh. On March 27th Fr Alex Reid and Fr Gerry Reynolds announced a truce. The conditions were that: 'Both parties accept the right of any group to organise politically and they commit themselves unreservedly to the resolution by peaceful mediation of their own present dispute and of any further disputes that may arise.'[11] Nobody other than the British, had apparently achieved anything out of the killings or the legacy of hatred and bitterness left in their wake.

Throughout the early months of 1987, as republican areas of the North despaired at the INLA feud, political developments and the war continued apace. On January 16th in a year already punctuated by IRA attacks, the British and Irish governments' attempts to politically isolate Sinn Fein suffered a grievous setback; Peter Archer, British opposition spokesperson on the Six Counties, was a member of a high-ranking Labour delegation who met with the republicans in Belfast. Less than a week later Garret FitzGerald's Coalition collapsed after losing a vote on proposed budget measures. During the second weekend of February, with the Hillsborough Agreement a significant election issue in the 26 Counties, Peter Barry, former Foreign Affairs Minister, accused Fianna Fail of denigrating the 'progress' made under the Agreement, progress that was scant on the ground in the Upper Springfield. At the same time, the UFF, in its own effort to denigrate the Accord, fire-bombed shops in Dublin and Donegal, causing £1 million property damage.

A few days later, in the General Election of February 17th, Fianna Fail won 81 of the 166 Dail seats. Shortly afterwards, Haughey announced the formation of a minority government, supported by Independents. After weeks of attacking Haughey, the Irish and British media grudgingly accepted the result. Haughey, it seems, was too 'republican'. There were fears that he would not deliver on the more contentious aspects of the Agreement.

The fact that the British were delivering nothing was conveniently overlooked. Long gone were the days when any section of the Irish or British media would raise a storm about issues like the continued strip-searching of women prisoners; the blatantly differential sentencing in the Diplock Courts; the beatings in Castlereagh; the indiscriminate blasting of nationalists with plastic bullets; or the ongoing brutality at republican funerals. In the Upper Springfield, arrests, beatings, house searches and the wanton destruction of homes and property went on as they had for the past 18 years.

On April 2nd, as the dust began to settle on the INLA feud, new Public Order legislation came into effect in the North. Under its provisions, it became illegal to stage any march unless seven days' notice was given to the RUC, a feature guaranteed to create problems for the Republican

Movement. In Ardoyne, on the same day, IRA Volunteer Larry Marley was shot dead in his home by the UVF. Four days later, Larry Marley's home became an international focus for the struggle of wills between republicans and the British.

Already, on March 13th, the funeral issue had been pushed to a new pitch. Following an IRA warning, two RUC men were injured in a car-bomb explosion at Roselawn Cemetery an hour before the arrival of the body of an RUC member killed by the IRA. The republicans stated that this was a warning shot, coming after four years of RUC attacks on 25 IRA and INLA funerals.

In reply, the NIO Minister, Nicholas Scott, said that, 'Even in war people are allowed to bury their dead in peace and dignity.' In Ballymurphy, people wondered if he could hear himself talking.

On March 6th the Marley family put Scott's assertion to the test. The IRA man's body was taken from his home to be buried. Immediately, in an attempt to surround the coffin, the RUC baton-charged the mourners. Fighting broke out, and the Marley family brought the body back inside. Over the next two days the RUC laid siege to the Marley home, taunting the family and mourners about 'the smell', and baton-charging the crowd each time an attempt was made to proceed with the funeral. The IRA responded with a spate of attacks as riots erupted in republican areas. In the Upper Springfield, the Taggart came under gun-attack and mortars were fired into Fort Jericho.

On the afternoon of the 7th, as the Falls Black Taxis suspended all services to provide a shuttle to Ardoyne, the Marley family pleaded with Bishop Cahal Daly to intercede on their behalf. The Bishop was not to be found. Finally, after another night of rioting, international attention forced the RUC and NIO into a compromise: the RUC agreed to stay a dignified distance form the cortege. By then the mourners were several thousand strong and it was this image, of a dignified disciplined popu-lace, that triumphed over the 64 military vehicles, the hundreds of RUC and troops, and the riot gear, helmets and weaponry. After taking seven hours to cover the 2.5 miles from Ardoyne to Milltown Cemetery, the Marleys eventually buried a husband and father six days after his death. Then the thousands of mourners turned, each staring defiantly into the eyes of the nearest RUC member, for a minute's silence for Larry Marley. [*]

Earlier in the afternoon, the author was among a crowd of Ballymurphy, Turf Lodge and Upper Falls residents waiting at the bottom of Whiterock Road for the funeral to pass. The RUC were there in force, jeering and taunting. The people on the roadside, united behind the Marleys in their ordeal, ignored them. The RUC, plastic bullet guns loaded and ready, continued to provoke. Then crack! A single shot was fired from Whiterock. And in an instant reversal of roles, the RUC dived for the cover of their Land Rovers while the crowd cheered wildly at the distant invisible IRA sniper. Afterwards, on the Whiterock Road, the

---

*On April 28th the IRA shot dead UVF leader, William 'Frenchy' Marchant, accusing him of direct involvement in the killing of Larry Marley.

author met with Bridie Adams of Ballymurphy and one of her friends. The two women, both pensioners, had been at the funeral. 'You don't want to be hateful,' Bridie's friend said, 'but, God love us, they make you hate.'

In early May the funeral issue flared again when the RUC attacked the mourners at Volunteer Finbarr McKenna's funeral with batons and plastic bullets. A week later the NIO appeared to have capitulated: no attempt was made to interfere with the funerals of the eight Volunteers killed in an SAS ambush at Loughgall on May 8th.

Throughout April and May, sporadic IRA attacks took place in the Upper Springfield. Riots also followed Finbarr McKenna's funeral and the Loughgall killings. On June 11th, as Britain voted Margaret Thatcher into her third term of office, a soldier was wounded by a sniper in New Barnsley. The following day it was announced that, despite a concerted campaign by the British and Irish establishments, the Catholic hierarchy and the *Irish News*, Gerry Adams had retained his West Belfast seat, actually increasing his vote. His support in the Upper Springfield ran at 73 per cent. In its continuing commitment to democracy, the RUC greeted the result with an attack on a carload of Sinn Fein workers leaving Belfast City Hall. Windows in the car were smashed and a gang of a dozen RUC batoned and kicked its five occupants after dragging them into the street. (Less than a month later, the RUC attempted to kill Sinn Fein worker, Michael Ward, riddling his car on a quiet road in County Tyrone.)

At the beginning of July, unionist-dominated councils were again in uproar over the Agreement and the presence of Sinn Fein councillors. Loyalists were also angry at the removal of flags, bunting and Orange 'arches' in Six-County factories, the result of a campaign initiated in the USA by veteran Irish statesperson, Sean MacBride. The 'MacBride Principles', being widely adopted under Irish-American pressure, were designed to end displays of loyalist triumphalism, and promote equality of opportunity, in American-controlled firms in the North. Simultaneously, the loyalist campaign against the Agreement was beginning to crack: already, on May 2nd, Paisley and Molyneaux had agreed to engage in 'talks about talks' with the NIO.

Bombs and bullets continued to dominate Six-County politics, as on July 23rd Whitehall extended its military corridor of spy-forts along the border, and British Home Secretary, Douglas Hurd, agreed to look at 'new evidence' in the case of the Guildford Four, who included New Barnsley man, Paul Hill. In January Hurd had agreed to refer the case of the Birmingham Six to the Court of Appeal, giving new hope to Lily Hill and her family.

There were strong hints from the Irish establishment and the SDLP that such movement was a direct benefit of the Anglo-Irish Agreement. In fact, everything achieved by nationalists was now being attributed to the Agreement: the demolition of Divis; the abandonment of the 'supergrass' system; the proposed demolition of Unity and Rossville flats; the demolition scheme for Springhill; and the relaxation of assaults on funerals. All of which were in fact the result of years of campaigning and direct action by local communities. By the end of July, when the Alliance Party confirmed that the housing decisions had been the result of purely internal Housing Executive management policies, not one real concession had been granted to nationalists, nor had a single strand of British policy changed. If anything, the drive towards a military solution in the North was being intensified, now that Dublin had been safely neutralised.

In Dublin an unofficial coalition of Haughey's government and Fine Gael, under its new leader Alan Dukes, attempted to patch up a shattered economy with drastic budgetary measures. As the screw was tightened on the Irish working class, already decimated by chronic unemployment, emigration and a crumbling network of state support, there was no mention of any U-turn on the Hillsborough Agreement. After all, the British just might come up with a few concessions that could alter the political climate in the North and draw mass support away from the IRA. If the IRA and Sinn Fein were isolated, the war might end and Dublin would be spared the IR£150 million annually being spent to maintain the partition of Ireland.[12] British actions, however, belied any real intentions of changing the political climate: on August 6th, in the build-up to the annual internment commemorations, the RUC sprayed bullets into a stolen car in Belfast's Hamill Street. Whiterock teenager Joe Miller was critically wounded in the attempted summary execution.

The IRA, meanwhile, was showing no sign of either being isolated or defeated. In June it had been reported that Colonel Gaddafi of Libya had re-established his support for the Republican Movement. His support was said to have intensified after the killing of his adopted daughter during the British-aided US bombing of Tripoli and Benghazi in 1986. Among the war materiel said to have been sent by Gaddafi was the powerful plastic explosive, Semtex, which had recently been used in letter-bombs to top British civil servants and in a car-bombing of a British army/RAF base in West Germany back in March.

IRA warnings to firms and businesses, including a number of multinationals, to cease supplying British forces in Ireland, had also largely succeeded in isolating crown forces and was hampering the rebuilding of the many bases blitzed in the previous 18 months. IRA operations too were very much on the increase, with British forces slipping back into a defensive position. This was evidenced in Ballymurphy on March 30th when Volunteers mounted a gun and mortar attack on the Taggart. No attempt at a follow-up was made until the next day and then only at a snail's pace as the military and RUC, fearful of sophisticated booby-traps, fine-combed the approach to the discarded launching-tube. On August 9th the British were pushed further onto the defensive.

An impact grenade, a new IRA weapon already used twice (causing one British fatality), was hurled at an RUC Land Rover in Belfast's Dawson Street. It destroyed the armour-plated vehicle and injured five RUC men. It also shattered the confidence of the RUC's Divisional Mobile Support Units (DMSUs). Previously the three-vehicle patrols had been relatively immune to IRA attacks in cities and towns, but the new device – a drogue-guided pound of Semtex with a copper cone that vapourised on impact – cut through the armour of the Land Rovers, blasting the occupants with shrapnel and molten metal. Overnight, military vehicles became potential death-traps.

On August 10th, after two days of gun attacks on the Taggart amid the annual ritualistic internment riots, Volunteers in Ballymurphy Road hit a second DMSU with two impact grenades, injuring three RUC men. From then on, the new grenade became a standard weapon against mobile patrols, its only disadvantage being that the Volunteers using them had to get within 30 yards of their intended target to ensure a smooth flight for the hand-held device. Other home-made weapons now being used by the IRA included massive 50lb mortars and rocket-propelled grenades, both of which were used regularly during 1987 in Greater Ballymurphy. On September 20th, in another demoralising attack on the RUC, the Ballymurphy IRA drove into the centre of loyalist Highfield and mortar-bombed Springfield Parade Barracks.

By the end of August 1987 the Hillsborough Agreement was beginning to cause problems in Dublin. Taoiseach Charles Haughey, so vociferously opposed to extradition when in opposition, was now faced with having to finalise the deal. Pressure from London was daily mounting despite the fact that Britain had refused to honour its side of the extradition deal (cosmetic changes in the Diplock Courts and within the RUC and UDR). The hype from London intensified further in early October as the Tory Conference, scheduled for Blackpool, drew near. Such was the IRA threat, the British claimed, that warships and submarines would be patrolling the coast keeping an eye out for republican commandos. (The warship, HMS *Cuxton*, was actually deployed to keep 24-hour radar watch throughout the Conference.) However, with the British still refusing to budge on concessions, resistance to extradition began to grow within Fianna Fail.

By mid-October, with the Opposition demanding that Haughey press the British for reforms, the Irish cabinet was becoming desperate, the 'republican' party could not be seen extraditing republicans in the face of Thatcher's colonial arrogance. On October 17th Foreign Affairs Minister Brian Lenihan flew to London to see Hurd and King. Two days later an all-party Irish delegation again met with Hurd to urge some change of heart before the coming Anglo-Irish Conference. However, the Conference wound up on October 21st with no British concessions and threats by King that Dublin's failure to sign the Extradition Bill would have 'serious implications'. The following day Thatcher further compounded Haughey's problems. Dismissing Dublin's demands – now reduced to increasing the number of judges in Diplock Courts from one to three – she declared that the future of Six-County courts was 'not a bargaining point'. For the time being, extradition seemed all but dead.

October 1987 was also a turbulent month in Ballymurphy. Early in the month an anti-extradition committee was put together to become part of a nationwide campaign, hindered by the general republican belief that Haughey could not go through with extradition. Community activists, meanwhile, had joined a city-wide campaign against proposals contained in the Belfast Urban Area Plan, which envisaged a vast landscaping of Belfast while generally ignoring West Belfast.

Local people were also discovering that, yet again, Housing Executive work in Ballymurphy was anything but satisfactory. According to tenants in Ballymurphy estate, solid fuel central heating systems installed as part of the earlier refurbishing scheme, were causing illness and death by leaking toxic fumes.

Tommy Norton of Glenalina Crescent complained that his budgie had keeled over dead while the refurbishing contractor was checking his appliance for escaping gases. By October 1987 the Executive was admitting that they 'no longer use the appliance fitted in Ballymurphy' and that the ceramic flues installed 'may have led to some faults'. The result was that homes in the area, many having just redecorated after the initial refurbishing, were again ripped apart from fireplace to chimney, with all the attendant disruption, rubble and expense. Then, on October 9th, the assassins returned to Ballymurphy.

Two days earlier, two local men, Micky Vallelly and Geordie Hagans, had been arrested on the Antrim Road a short distance from a military/ RUC barracks. They were among five people accused of possession of two mortars. On October 8th, the British army swamped the Upper Springfield with dogs and detectors looking for the source of the mortars. The operation lasted all day, and came on top of weeks of military saturation and concentrated house-searches.

Yet, on the morning of October 9th, not a soldier was to be found anywhere near Ballymurphy as two gunmen drove into the centre of the estate at 7.30am. Dressed in boiler suits, they burst into a house in Whitecliff Parade and shot dead 65-year-old Francisco Notarantonio as he lay in bed with his wife Edith. 'Fra' Notarantonio was an IRA veteran of the 1940s who had been interned for a while in the early 1970s. He was the 126th person to die as a result of the Troubles in the one square mile of Greater Ballymurphy. The gunmen's car was later found abandoned in Springmartin. There was widespread belief in Ballymurphy that the area had been 'frozen' by the military and RUC to facilitate the loyalist (or SAS/SSU) gunmen.

On October 13th the long-standing problem of the 'hoods' was highlighted by the first of three attacks on the new Whiterock Family Centre. A group of young men climbed over the perimeter railings late at night and smashed 24 windows along the front of the building. They then took two chairs and lit themselves a wee fire directly outside the railings of the centre. The following morning the RUC discovered blood at the scene. On checking the hospitals they found a young man from the district undergoing micro-surgery for lacerations to his hand at Dundonald Hospital. On October 17th the hoods struck again. Windows were once more smashed and filing cabinets, desks and a door were destroyed. Baby foods were strewn about and the very optimistic or AIDS-conscious intruders made off with 300 condoms. The following night the *coup de grace* was delivered. A car was driven through the railings, and straight through the front door of the Family Centre. Two public meetings resulted, demonstrating community support for the centre and anger at the hoods. Demands were also made that the IRA take more effective action against anti-social elements in the area.

West Belfast's joyriding epidemic had also taken a nasty twist, with several deliberate attempts to run down pedestrians, including the Belfast secretary of Sinn Fein. These in turn prompted a spate of punishment shootings and the banishment from the country of two young men from Whiterock. They also caused the resurfacing of the 'non-existent' Official IRA whose Belfast Brigade distributed leaflets in Turf Lodge, warning the joyriders that they would 'act harshly' against them – deeply embarrassing the Workers' Party who consistently claimed to have stood down their armed wing. On October 17th a prominent member of the Workers' Party shot and wounded another man at the top of Whiterock Road, using a legally-held weapon, one of many such weapons in the hands of Workers' Party members. Why the RUC should issue gun-licences to people who are involved in, or connected to, the Official IRA is one of the intriguing mysteries of the North of Ireland.

On Sunday, November 1st, delegates at Sinn Fein's annual Ard-Fheis in Dublin debated whether or not the party's candidates in Northern elections should sign a 'non-violence' declaration being proposed by the British as a means of debarring republicans from the political arena. It was generally agreed that if Tom King could sign such a declaration, then so could Sinn Fein. Shortly afterwards, the proposal was quietly dropped by the NIO who would have to search for another more suitable refinement to British 'democracy'.

The following day several Ballymurphy people were in Derry for the double funeral of IRA Volunteers Paddy Deery and Eddie McSheffrey, killed when the bomb they were transporting exploded prematurely. A masked IRA man fired a volley from the protection of the huge crowd. The RUC immediately launched a savage baton and plastic-bullet attack on the mourners, injuring over a hundred people, many seriously.

Four days later, the same force, praised by the Dublin establishment and Bishop Cahal Daly for its 'impartiality', gave another display of naked sectarian hatred at the Springfield/Whiterock junction. Throughout the evening, RUC gangs in Land Rovers had been touring the neighbourhood, shouting sectarian abuse at passers-by. When that failed to provoke sufficiently, they waited until the local social clubs closed, then drew up at the Whiterock/Springfield junction, deliberately to promote trouble. Nineteen-year-old Ann Bradley, the Clerical Officer at the Upper Springfield Resource Centre, described her own experiences over the next few minutes:

The Peelers went over and started pulling at 'Gillso' for absolutely no reason. Some people went over to see what was happening. An argument started and the Peelers pulled the batons out and just got into everyone who was there ... All I remember is a Peeler grabbed me by the coat and he was batoning me. I got out of my coat. Next thing, plastics started to be shot. Everybody ran into the two chippies. I was running with the others and then I was on the ground and the Peelers were batoning the head off me and the others who were lying around me. Ernie McCrory came over to help me away and as he was trailing me off they were batoning him too.[13]

Within seconds of the initial attack, a convoy of Land Rovers, which had been concealed in nearby streets, obviously awaiting the signal, raced to the scene, and in a clearly pre-arranged ambush plan, hemmed in the fleeing Ballymurphy people. Gerard Heath (31) who was hit at point-blank range with a plastic bullet, described how the RUC had 'no guns and no flak-jackets. When do the Peelers walk about Ballymurphy with no guns and no flak-jackets? They had just the green jumpers on. They were out to do it. It was premeditated alright.' Ann Bradley went on to describe the scene in Raffo's chip shop:

They were shooting at the chippies. Somebody locked the chippie door. They were trying to get in and couldn't so they started firing plastic bullets at the windows covered by grilles and at the people outside. Then they started ramming the door with a Land Rover – reversing it and ramming and reversing and ramming. The people inside were all screaming and trying to get out the back, but the back door was locked ... [Outside] the Peelers were shooting plastics. Just walking around and shooting plastics at anyone who was there. It was just a slaughter.[14]

Although a support column between the window and door of Raffo's was fractured and shifted, the Land Rover attempt to bring the front of the building down on those inside failed. However, by the time the RUC had adequately vented their 'policing' instincts, several people had been seriously injured, many with broken limbs and severe lacerations from the salvos of plastic bullets. Despite two decades of political upheaval, little had changed in the nature of the RUC. Meanwhile, on the broader front, the IRA and a maverick INLA unit led by 'Border Fox', Dessie O'Hare, were easing Fianna Fail off the extradition hook.

On Friday, October 30th, a Panamanian-registered ship, the *Eksund*, had been arrested by French customs officers off the coast of Brittany. On board were 150 tons of IRA arms, including SAM-7 missiles, en route from Libya. Dublin described the find as a threat to the 26-County state. Then, on November 5th, dentist John O'Grady, kidnapped by the 'Border Fox' on October 13th and held for a IR£1.5 million ransom, was freed in a Dublin shoot-out. O'Grady's account of how two fingers sent to his millionaire father-in-law had been severed with a hammer and chisel horrified the whole island.

Three days later, on Sunday, November 8th, an IRA bomb killed eleven people at Remembrance Day commemorations in Enniskillen. The remote-controlled device, believed by republicans to have been prematurely detonated by an electronic sweep of the area by the British army, had been intended for military and RUC personnel. Although RUC Chief Constable, Sir John Hermon, admitted that the empty building housing the bomb had not been searched because only civilians (normally protected in IRA attacks) gathered at that particular point prior to the ceremonies, the bombing was none the less presented as a deliberate slaughter of loyalist civilians.

Enniskillen was an international propaganda disaster for republicans; the British, gloating, were back on the offensive; and Fianna Fail was handed the mandate to proceed with extradition, British concessions or not. At the same time Whitehall pushed home to its post-Narrow Water goal of making Dublin the junior partner of its war machine in Ireland.

At the Anglo-Irish Conference on November 16th 1987 the Irish delegation agreed to launch a nationwide dragnet for four other shiploads of IRA arms, believed smuggled into Ireland prior to the capture of the *Eksund*. The British army also now had limited permission to cross the Irish border. London then agreed to loan Dublin sophisticated military equipment to assist the detection of underground dumps. The subsequent search, which began on November 23rd, was used by the Garda Special Branch as a means of gathering intelligence on all dissidents within the state. It was also the first time since the Civil War of 1921–3 that a Dublin regime had used British military equipment against Irish republicans.

The day after the beginning of the search, as two of the Long Kesh escapees were picked up in the 26 counties, Fianna Fail published 'safeguards' to be incorporated into the Extradition Bill. These were designed to relieve the party's 'republican' conscience, and were to be reviewed in a year. Thatcher and King were furious that the Dublin government should attempt to act independently. On December 1st, Thatcher claimed that Britain would now be 'the least favoured nation in this matter'. On December 3rd, the Extradition Bill and its 'safeguards' were ratified by Dail Eireann. The next day Haughey met Thatcher at an EEC summit in Copenhagen to reassure her about the 'safeguards'. If they didn't work (for the British), that would be taken into account at the review in twelve months' time. Thatcher apparently went home happy.

Seven weeks later, on January 20th 1988, Ballymurphy man Robert Russell, who had escaped from Long Kesh in 1983 and was subsequently imprisoned in Portlaoise, became the first person to be processed since the new legislation was passed. The Supreme Court in Dublin, consisting of five judges, agreed by a three to two majority to reject his appeal against extradition.

In a convoluting judgement, Chief Justice Finlay decreed that any organisation other than Dail Eireann that attempted to reintegrate the national territory was subverting the Irish Constitution: its members could therefore not be protected by the political offence exception to extradition contained in that Constitution. Dublin had finally rubberstamped Britain's criminalisation policy in the North. No mention was made of how Irish courts could also subvert the Irish Constitution.

In a dissenting judgement, Justice Hederman said that if an offence was political, it remained so whether or not the Dail approved. He was unaware, he said, of 'any law in this state which prohibits anybody publicly urging the raising of an armed revolt in another state, or urging Irish support for any such revolt.'[15]

References
1. Letter to Garret FitzGerald from Upper Springfield Resource Centre, October 20th 1986.
2. Douglas Hurd, in reply to John Taylor MP (Solihull), House of Commons, June 27th 1985.
3. Fr Des Wilson of Springhill (1986).
4. *Irish News*, Belfast, September 2nd 1986.
5. Interview with author (1988).
6. Interview with author (1988).
7. Fr Des Wilson of Springhill (1988 Interview).
8. Kevin McQuillen of Springfield Park (1988 Interview).
9. *Belfast Telegraph*, February 27th 1987.
10. Interview with author (1988).
11. Statement on cessation of hostilities, March 27th 1987.
12. *Sunday Press,* Dublin, April 26th 1987.
13. Ann Bradley of Upper Springfield Resource Centre (1987 Interview).
14. Ibid.
15. *An Phoblacht/Republican News*, Dublin, January 21st 1988.

16

Britannia Waives the Rules

On Sunday, November 29th 1987, as Dublin, through a receptive Irish media, churned out its extradition propaganda to a public psychologically cut off from the North, Des Wilson spoke at the annual Kilmichael commemoration in County Cork where republicans of the 1920s were being honoured. There he denounced the decision to go ahead with the extradition of political refugees to a regime that stood internationally condemned.

Two days later, in a further example of the Irish establishment's fulsome support for British policies in the Six Counties, the *Cork Examiner* devoted an 850-word editorial to attacking the Ballymurphy priest. His views were 'coloured', the newspaper pronounced dismissively, because he 'speaks from a nationalist enclave'. Two decades of untiring humanitarian effort among the poor and oppressed of Belfast were apparently irrelevant as far as the *Examiner's* leader-writer – who had never in 19 years of war visited a Northern area of conflict – was concerned.

The editorial went on to link the conflict with the 'international terrorism' myth so beloved of Europe's right wing: the Northern revolt was part of some vague nefarious worldwide conspiracy. Throughout, republican violence was described as 'terrorism', while British violence translated into 'excesses'. The *Examiner's* only concession was an admission that there '*possibly* still is harassment of the nationalist community' (author's italics)! However, it countered this by assuring its readership that Britain was now an honest broker and an honourable partner in the European Community. Britain and Ireland together were 'all committed to the elimination of terrorism' (but not 'excesses').

On December 9th, Criostoir De Baroid, secretary of the Cork-based Between Community Organisation, replied. Basing his letter on 18 years of assisting the community efforts of loyalist and nationalist communities in the North, and a 16-year acquaintance with Des Wilson, he condemned the propagandist nature of the *Examiner's* editorial, written by a scribe 'who has no first hand information on which to base his judgement', and challenged the leader-writer to deny this.

The following day, the newspaper's editorial and the whole of the Val Dorgan column (34 column-inches in all) were given over to a bitter personalised attack on the Between secretary. 'Over the years, we have had many people visit the troubled areas of the North', the editorial declared in reply to the charge of being ill-formed.

Community groups in the Upper Springfield, on December 15th, angry at the tone and content of the editorials and Dorgan's column, and the continuous distortion of events in the North by the Irish and British media, wrote to the *Examiner*. The letter, signed by 23 organisations 'of Greater Ballymurphy, where Fr Wilson lives and works', was sent by courier mail to avoid the Christmas post. It arrived in Cork on December 17th. The *Examiner* initially refused to publish the letter. Then, after six weeks of pressure, a censored version appeared in its January 30th edition – two months after the original editorial, when the issue had safely died. The edited paragraphs (reproduced below) demonstrate how carefully the public in the far south is cocooned from the realities of life in the North and the nature and extent of media censorship. Only two sentences were published from the second paragraph. Omitted was:

> Despite your assertions that you write from an informed background, we in West Belfast cannot recall a single occasion on which *Cork Examiner* journalists ever visited this, the most troubled quarter of the Six Counties, to investigate the realities of our existence and the true nature of 'terrorism' and who owns that 'terrorism'. (We are only vaguely aware of a certain Peter Martin, an American living in South Belfast, who reported for you on general matters.)

In relation to translations of violence into 'terrorism' and 'excesses', omitted was:

> Even you, of course, must concede that such distinctions/distortions are the essence of propaganda. However, we have grown to expect nothing more. We are seldom disappointed.

In relation to British 'excesses':

> We might remind you that, among the 'excesses' of the British forces in this small area, where 120 people have died since 1969, are: the murder of eleven civilians, including a Catholic priest, in two days during internment week; the massacre of five civilians, including a 13-year-old girl and a second Catholic priest, in a ten-minute period in July 1972; the killing of two-year-old Francis McGuigan in early 1970; an ongoing campaign of random murder and maiming, torture and indiscriminate destruction of property, none of which, strangely, has ever been described by the *Cork Examiner*, or anyone else, as 'terrorism' ... We could go on but we would only exhaust ourselves, and at this stage feel the effort to be hardly worthwhile. Perhaps you will recognise the voice of despair; perhaps not.

Although receiving a courier-delivered letter signed by 23 community organisations in response to published material was unprecedented in the newspaper's history, the *Examiner* had at first suppressed the entire letter. When it did publish it, most of the punch, all references to British terror and the rump of the accusations of distortion and misrepresentation were omitted. Even while printing an accusation of distortion, the *Examiner* had found it necessary to distort, thus depriving its readership of both the content and spirit of the Belfast letter. The challenge from the North could not be answered, or even faced, by the most influential newspaper in the southern counties of Ireland. Better to continue the deceit.

Meanwhile, Des Wilson, in private correspondence, had invited the *Examiner* to co-sponsor an open discussion on the North, to be held in Cork at a later date. The newspaper refused. The case rests.

* * *

By the beginning of 1988 Britain's propaganda war was moving along nicely after the setbacks of the hunger strike and the 'supergrass' system. Its post-Narrow Water military strategy, neatly incorporated into the Hillsborough Agreement, had been sold to the international community and the Irish government as a major political development. Extradition had been achieved, Dublin had been integrated into the British war machine and a united Ireland was no longer on the agenda. Dublin, duped into a belief that Britain had 'gone political', was also busily making excuses for British actions in the North, playing down the seriousness of continuing army/RUC brutality, pardoning all intrusions on Irish sovereignty, redoubling its efforts against the IRA, and largely ignoring the wholesale confiscation of farmland along the border as Britain drove home its military corridor. At the same time, the Irish people were being bombarded by a government-sponsored anti-republican tirade fully supported by the Irish media and the Catholic bishops. Since 1969, political conditions in Ireland had never favoured the British more.

However, the British, having gained all and given nothing, were overcome by their own arrogance. Despite the best efforts of Dublin, the long-established pattern of humiliating successive Irish governments was resumed in January 1988 with a crassness that was almost unbelievable. So far, Dublin had accepted two years of British pussy-footing on the Hillsborough Agreement with only the occasional grumble of discontent. The most recent had been in December 1987 when questions were asked about the criteria governing the allocation of the International Fund for Ireland set up as a result of the Hillsborough Agreement. The SDLP had also added its voice to this protest, complaining that nothing had gone to economically starved West Belfast. There had also been some discord in Dublin and within the Northern nationalist establishment at British refusals to grant any concessions in the lead-up to extradition. But nothing in 20 years of British political bungling could match the ineptitude shown by the string of events that began on January 25th 1988.

On that date Sir Patrick Mayhew, the British Attorney General, announced in the Commons that no prosecutions would be brought against any RUC personnel as a result of the Stalker/Sampson Inquiry into the Armagh death-squad killings of 1982. Furthermore, the report was not to be published, nor would it be shown to the Irish government. There was uproar within the Irish establishment, while in the Commons,

Ken Livingstone MP accused Mayhew of being 'an accomplice to murder'.

Dublin immediately cancelled a scheduled meeting between the RUC and Garda chiefs, and called for 'clarification'. The deliberately low-key response was accompanied the following day by an expression of continuing collaboration on the war front: Gardai and Irish troops confiscated a huge IRA arms dump hidden under an isolated beach in northern Donegal, their first success in the hunt for the Libyan arms. The British praised Dublin.

Things appeared to be steadying, and were widely expected to be further calmed by the inevitable release of the Birmingham Six whose appeal verdict was to be announced on the 28th. While nothing could ever compensate for the 13 years spent behind bars under most brutal conditions, the release of the men – widely acknowledged to have been victims of hysterical British racism – would at least ease Dublin's position in trying to convince Northern nationalists, and the Irish public in general, that they could now have some confidence in 'the administration of justice' in the Six Counties. After all, did not extradition guarantee this?

The verdict was a bombshell: the men's appeal was dismissed despite the avalanche of evidence in their favour. Peter Barry, former Irish Foreign Affairs Minister, emerged from the courthouse shocked. Bishop Edward Daly of Derry came out in tears. The British legal system, they argued, had chosen to keep in jail six innocent men rather than face the fact that they were brutalised into forced confessions and framed to satisfy British public opinion. Anglo-Irish relations were rocked to their foundations.

The Irish people, and much of the international community, were outraged. Coming on the heels of the decision not to prosecute RUC men involved in what most Irish people considered to have been state murders, or for the cover-up that followed, the dismissal of the 'Brum Six' appeal was greeted with disbelief. Immediately, there were suggestions from the Irish establishment that Britain should invoke the Royal Prerogative of Mercy. The next day British Home Secretary Douglas Hurd said that he had no intention of doing so. Dublin called for an urgent meeting of the Anglo-Irish Conference.

On February 2nd, amid rumours that extradition was threatened, the Conference met at Stormont. The meeting was adjourned in impasse. In an effort to defuse tension, another meeting was arranged, the Irish government hoping that there would be some British change of heart in the meantime. But now John Stalker's book had been released. Its allegations further incensed the Dublin government and the Northern nationalist middle class. Britain was simply helping the IRA, they proclaimed, by not reversing its decision on the Stalker/Sampson report. Then more bad news: the British army had erected a post and checkpoint outside a nationalist school in Newry, making hostages of the children.

Dublin had to make some gesture: on February 8th Fianna Fail Minister John Wilson visited the Newry school. The British and loyalists were furious. The following day they were further irked by a European Parliament vote, condemning the decision not to prosecute over the Stalker/Sampson Inquiry. Meanwhile, the London–Dublin meeting planned for February 10th was postponed so that Haughey could first voice his government's 'concerns' to Thatcher herself at an EEC summit in Brussels on the same day.

Early on the 10th, Dublin Ministers Gerry Collins and Ray Burke met with King and his deputy, John Stanley, in London. There was no shift in the British stance. They went on to Brussels to brief Haughey. On February 11th Haughey met with Thatcher, only to find the same intransigence. On February 12th he told the Dail that, 'The response of the British government was totally unsatisfactory – and I have to say that relations are at an impasse.'

On February 15th, as the crisis deepened, it became known that the British attorney general was ignoring the extradition 'safeguards' set up by Dublin. Warrants were simply being accompanied by a note from Mayhew instead of a *prima facie* case as required under the December legislation. On February 16th, in another twist, the Anglo-Irish Conference met again at Stormont amid reports that the anti-Irish Prevention of Terrorism Act was to be made permanent by the British. King denied this to the media before the meeting got under way. That evening Hurd confirmed the reports. Dublin was at this stage going berserk at the stupidity and contempt being displayed by London. But the Dail was still doing its utmost to play things down. The British can only have been further encouraged. On February 18th the Birmingham Six were formally refused leave to appeal to the House of Lords. They were, however, given permission to apply for a hearing 'on a point of public importance' following the outcry over the appeal verdict.*

By the end of the third week of February Anglo-Irish relations were at their lowest ebb for years. Despite Dublin's best attempts to appease the British, Whitehall seemed intent on sabotaging all its efforts. On Sunday, February 21st, the screw was turned again. Aidan McAnespie, a 24-year-old from Aughnacloy, who had been continuously threatened by the British, was crossing the border checkpoint close to his village when he was shot dead from a sangar. He had been monitored every inch of the way by soldiers on both levels of the two-storey tower. One soldier's finger then happened to 'slip' onto the trigger of a general purpose machine-gun, which just happened to be aimed at the Aughnacloy's man's back. At the funeral, two days later, Cardinal Tomas O Fiaich

---

*Two months after the appeal, the last legal avenue was closed to the Birmingham Six. On April 14th, 1988, the British House of Lords refused to hear the case, giving no reason for the decision. Calling it a 'black day for justice', the Belfast-based *Irish News* commented: 'This means that the highest court in the United Kingdom has washed its hands of this whole dirty affair. It has turned its back on justice for fear of having to find its own judges guilty of wrongdoing ... The world knows they are innocent and today British justice once again stands before the dock of international opinion – in total disgrace.' (Editorial, April 15th 1988)

described the killing as 'murder', echoing the outrage of people throughout Ireland. Meanwhile, Dublin had announced the setting up of a Garda inquiry into the incident, and Deputy Commissioner Eugene Crowley had been despatched to Monaghan to carry it out.

The British were again furious. Dublin had misinterpreted the Hillsborough Agreement, Thatcher told the Commons, if it thought it could investigate the Aughnacloy killing. The Irish had no right to interfere in anything that happened north of the border, or to comment on the decisions of the British Court of Appeal. She then went on to commend the 'most excellent' statement made by Mayhew about the non-prosecution of RUC personnel involved in the Armagh death-squad killings. The Commons debate of February 23rd could hardly have better illustrated the real nature of Dublin's position within the framework of the Accord.

Dublin's role was to give, as it had been doing for the past two years, under intense British bullying. When it came to demands being made on London by Dublin, the Irish side could 'put forward views and proposals', which the British could promptly reject. As for partnership? That clearly ended where British interests were at stake. Finally, when a frustrated Dublin set up a Garda investigation into the killing by British forces of an Irish citizen in the occupied part of the national territory, it was definitely overstepping itself. A parallel inquiry (although there was no question of a joint inquiry) demonstrated a lack of confidence in the British investigation and in the 'administration of justice' in the North.

In another masterful piece of British sensitivity, Lord Denning, ex-judge and former Master of the Rolls, stated on February 21st that innocent people should stay in jail if freeing them meant risking a loss of public confidence in British 'justice'. 'The general course of upholding our system is that I would put aside all those ... cases in favour of upholding our system of justice', Denning said.[1] The statement clearly demonstrated what the Birmingham Six were up against.

Denning was the judge who dismissed their appeal in 1980 when the men had sought leave to sue the British police for the brutality meted out to them in 1974. At that time he had said that the significance in the vindication of the men – which would have meant that the police had lied and the men had been framed through the courts – was such an 'appalling vista' that the case could not be allowed to proceed. Continuing this line in February 1988, he attacked journalists for seeking fresh evidence in cases such as those outlined in the 'Rough Justice' and 'Out Of Court' TV programmes, which had questioned twelve convictions.

I'm quite sure it's better for society as a whole that the series of 'Rough Justice' should not have been produced. It is better that the system should be in there, as it is, and that those twelve stories ought not to have been put.[2]

Granada Television's unearthing of new evidence in the case of the Birmingham Six was doing 'a great disservice to British justice', the ex-judge concluded.

Just when it seemed that Britain had exhausted its entire store of offensive acts, it produced another. On the day of Aidan McAnespie's funeral, it was disclosed that Private Ian Thain, convicted of murdering Thomas 'Kidso' Reilly at the Whiterock/Springfield junction in 1983, had been freed at the beginning of 1987 after serving only 26 months of a life sentence. He had also rejoined his regiment. In the Six Counties the announcement was greeted with disgust but not surprise. As for the fact that a murderer was walking about in British army uniform, people in Ballymurphy quipped, 'What's new about that?'

The Anglo-Irish Conference met on February 24th in Dublin with the whole Hillsborough Agreement overshadowed by the yawning rift between Dublin and London. Although Dublin still attempted to gloss over the resounding humiliation delivered by the British over the previous weeks, there was no more talk about having 'confidence in the administration of [British] justice'. Fianna Fail was by now seething. None the less, King could not resist another jab. After the meeting he told the media that a meeting on security, to be attended by RUC and Garda chiefs, was again on the agenda. Dublin responded in exasperation that it had no idea where King could have picked that up as nothing of the sort had been decided.

On the night of February 24th and 25th, buses were burned at the Whiterock/Springfield junction in protest at the release of 'Kidso' Reilly's murderer.

On February 29th 1988 Gerry Adams revealed that talks between the SDLP and Sinn Fein, initiated a month earlier, would continue in an attempt to fuse together the common interests of all Northern nationalists. That evening, General James Glover, author of the 1978 assessment of the IRA, stated in a televised interview that, 'In no way can or will the Provisional IRA ever be defeated militarily.' Meanwhile, the IRA, responding to speculation on the nature of recent shipments of Libyan weaponry, said, 'When we connect right, the British government will find that they cannot take what we can give.' That statement was to prove clairvoyantly prophetic over the next twelve months.

The first blow, however, was to be struck by the British. On the afternoon of Sunday, March 6th, Mairead Farrell, Dan McCann and Sean Savage, all from West Belfast, were assassinated in Gibraltar by plain-clothes SAS gunmen. All three were members of an IRA unit attached to GHQ staff and were on active service.

Immediately, the British issued a story of a 'gun battle', purported to have followed the planting of a 500lb bomb which, they claimed, had subsequently been defused. By lunchtime the next day the truth began to emerge. There had been no gun battle. The Volunteers were unarmed. And there was no bomb. West Belfast erupted while the British army and RUC vanished from the streets – to remain out of sight for the next two days. In Ballymurphy vehicles were hijacked and burned; the Taggart came under petrol bomb and sniper attack; and in keeping with a long-standing tradition, an attempt was made to set fire to Corry's timberyard.

Eight days after the Gibraltar killings the bodies were flown home amid fears of further bloodshed at the funerals. Continuing attacks on republican funerals and the anticipated massive turnout seemed a certain recipe for another round of state carnage.

However, as was transmitted worldwide, there was no RUC or British army presence as the 20,000-strong funeral procession made its way from the heart of Andersonstown to Milltown Cemetery. The IRA guarantee that there would be no firing party seemed to have been accepted by the British, who used it as a means of finally conceding that attacking funerals was bad propaganda. At the cemetery there was a feeling of relief that all had passed peacefully. Then loyalist assassin, Michael Stone, launched his televised gun and grenade attack that left three dead and 68 injured.

Three days later, the funeral of IRA Volunteer Caoimhin Mac Bradaigh, shot in pursuit of Stone, was approaching Milltown when a car ploughed into the crowd. Believing themselves under another loyalist attack, a section of the crowd dragged the two armed occupants (one of whom fired a shot) from the car and beat them up. When it was discovered that they were undercover soldiers, the IRA took them away and shot them.

The incident provoked widespread outrage in Britain and brought the RUC back in force to republican funerals. It also illustrated British thinking. 'It was no secret', Tom King said in the Commons, 'that the first impression was that it might have been a further attempted bomb attack on the funeral ... As soon as it was clear that the matter was very much more serious, the police acted with considerable determination.'[3] A bomb attack on a crowd of Irish mourners was not, apparently, a serious matter.

Over the next five months the IRA concentrated a large number of attacks on British servicemen (RUC and UDR personnel were also being attacked) in the North, Britain and mainland Europe. This, they explained, was to bring the reality of the war home to the British public. Twenty-one soldiers and three airmen were killed and many others wounded. Among the dead was Alexander Bannister (21) who died on August 8th, three weeks after being shot outside the Taggart.

Politically, the picture was equally bleak for Britain. In a UTV/*Fortnight* magazine poll, published on March 24th, over 80 per cent of nationalists said that the Hillsborough Treaty had failed them. On the devolution front, there seemed no hope: Haughey was adamant that it was no answer; Hume was favourable only within the framework of the Treaty; while the unionists retreated further into their laager, refusing to talk to anyone until the Treaty was scrapped. At the same time, Amnesty International was demanding inquiries into the Gibraltar killings and the shoot-to-kill policy, much to the chagrin of Thatcher, who vociferously attacked the human rights organisation in the House of Commons.

London–Dublin relations again took a temporary tumble when, on April 14th, the Law Lords refused the Birmingham Six the right to appeal to the House of Lords; and the issue looked set to continue, as did the cases of the Guildford Four, the Maguires and Judith Ward, all victims of the same rough justice. (On July 20th the Guildford Four campaign denounced the British Home Office after New Barnsley man Paul Hill was transferred for the 47th time in 14 years. He had already spent 1,641 days in solitary confinement and was in poor health. The campaigners accused the British of attempting to destroy Paul Hill's physical, mental and emotional health, and accompanied their statement with a photo of the emaciated prisoner.)

Other British problems included a badly functioning extradition agreement and an increasing opposition to extradition within Haughey's ruling party; attacks on the allocation of monies from the International Fund for Ireland; the spectre of collapse hanging over Harland and Wolff and Shorts, two of Belfast's biggest employers; the revival of a civil rights movement in the form of the '68 Committee; and council chambers disintegrating into chaos and inertia as unionists attempted to prevent Sinn Fein's participation in local government. (The July 4th meeting of Belfast City Council culminated in a massive brawl.)

The British nerve finally cracked with the August 20th Semtex bombing of a busload of soldiers near Ballygawley, County Tyrone, that left eight dead and 28 injured. The process was further accelerated the following week-end, August 27th/28th, when the extradition of Robert Russell was accompanied by 200 attacks carried out in less than 24 hours, demonstrating the depth of the republican reservoir of operational capacity. In response the SAS was sent into Tyrone, where they lured three IRA Volunteers into an ambush close to Ballygawley and shot them dead. This was followed by a 'package' of measures aimed at destroying Sinn Fein and the IRA – along with a few time-honoured British civil liberties.

New powers were given to the RUC to forcibly take mouth swabs so that suspects could be genetically 'finger-printed'. It was then proposed that personal and business bank accounts could be scrutinised, and persons jailed or businesses closed down if they were suspected of providing or holding funds belonging to guerrilla organisations.* Sinn Fein was banned from radio and television, and an anti-violence oath (earlier abandoned) was introduced in an attempt to keep the republicans out of the political arena. It was also decided to reduce the 50 per cent remission available to prisoners to 33.3 per cent, and to make those who were caught a second time serve the remission gained during the previous incarceration before starting the new sentence. And a suspect's right to silence – a cornerstone of the British legal system for centuries – was ended.

Meanwhile, the SDLP/Sinn Fein talks had ended inconclusively during the first week of September. On the 6th of the same month the Gibraltar inquest opened. It ran through to the 30th, with the SAS and MI5 officers screened from the public. Despite overwhelming evidence of state-

*This measure became law in March 1988.

sponsored premeditated murder, a verdict of 'lawful killing' was returned.

Two weeks later the Tory Annual Conference returned to Brighton for the first time since the IRA bombing of the Grand Hotel. From the rebuilt hotel, Thatcher proclaimed to the world that she was not afraid of the IRA while Brighton experienced a £1.5 million security clampdown that included the scouring of the sewers by the SAS, 50,000 computer checks on people in the area, the sea patrolled by a missile-carrying minesweeper and the Special Boat Squadron, and a three-mile air exclusion zone.

On October 28th three young Irish people were convicted at Winchester court of conspiring to kill Tom King at his Wiltshire home the previous summer. The evidence against them amounted to the possession of car licence numbers, some names and addresses and a map detailing the location of British army bases. They were given 25-year jail sentences. The Dublin government expressed shock at the verdict and sentences. Less than a month later a female member of the UDR was convicted at Belfast Crown Court of an almost identical offence: she was found guilty of passing on details of car registrations and the movement of their owners to the UDA. She was sentenced to six months' imprisonment.

The treatment of the Winchester Three, and their trial-by-media, was followed by a new twist in the extradition wrangle. On November 3rd Fr Patrick Ryan, held in a Belgian jail on immigration charges, went on hunger-strike against a British bid to have him extradited on various IRA-related 'conspiracy' charges. On November 25th, after he had embarked on a thirst-strike, the Belgian government flew him to Dublin. Thatcher and the British media were livid. Ryan was tried and convicted in the Commons and the tabloids while demands were made that Dublin extradite him forthwith.

At an EEC summit in Rhodes in early December Thatcher attacked Belgium and was snubbed by Haughey, who returned to Dublin emphasising the need to renew the 'safeguards' in the Extradition Act when it came up for review on December 6th. A week after the renewal of the Act, Dublin also refused to extradite Ryan on the grounds that he could not expect a fair trial in Britain, further infuriating Thatcher who described the Irish Attorney General's decision as 'an insult to all the people of this country'. The following day's London–Dublin Conference was described as a series of 'angry and blunt' exchanges, while Haughey's popularity soared in the 26 Counties and London–Dublin relations sunk to yet another all-time low.

In the meantime, as the Ryan affair erupted towards the end of November, Britain was found guilty of human rights' violations by the European Court. At the very point when the Tories were presenting a bill seeking a more repressive version of the PTA, the detention of suspects for more than four days was declared illegal. Two months later, in January 1989, London decided to derogate and ignore the Court of Human Rights' decision.

And as the image of British 'justice' all but ceased to exist, new problems were developing in the USA where demands were growing for a Congressional Hearing on the 'misuse of funds' allocated from the International Fund for Ireland, and where, despite the massive British effort against them, the MacBride Principles continued to gain ground, seriously threatening the sectarian economic base of the Six Counties.

Throughout, life in Ballymurphy remained fettered to the war, but with the addition of renewed conflict between Springhill and Springmartin. During May and June loyalists began to launch attacks on a regular basis. When young people came out to defend their homes, the RUC and British army came into Springhill to blast residents and homes with plastic bullets. During June 7th/8th there was continuous rioting during which 300 plastic bullets were fired, the result of RUC provocation which included the firing of 40 plastic bullets at a group of Springhill children during a period of calm on the 8th.

Finally, on June 9th, Gerry Adams arrived in Springhill and successfully appealed to the young people not to be drawn by provocation. After a brief respite, however, the attacks from Springmartin were resumed and were further facilitated by the RUC at the end of July when they removed a barrier erected by local people at the top of Springhill Avenue.

The IRA too continued its attacks. On June 22nd a soldier was seriously wounded during a military saturation of Westrock. Another died as a result of injuries received on July 15th. Bomb, rocket and gun attacks continued without further casualties until a soldier was wounded by a booby-trap on October 7th. Three weeks later an IRA Volunteer was injured by return fire during an attack on the Taggart. And on January 4th 1989 two RUC men were injured in a booby-trap attack in New Barnsley.

At the same time the area spiralled into further poverty and debt with the removal in April 1988 of most welfare benefits. On July 19th, Tom King, under pressure to do something about unemployment in West Belfast, announced a £10 million package for the north and west of the city. A month later the West Belfast Community Festival brought a temporary relief from the pressures of poverty, a relief countered in Ballymurphy by yet another bout of flooding. One family in Divismore Park reported its 25th experience of being inundated by the run-off from Black mountain. Meanwhile, the campaign to have Springhill demolished was finally successful and the first houses were being boarded up, bringing hope of better times to the families who had lived in its appalling conditions.

West Belfast – the Way Forward published on September 8th, put Tom King's £10 million package into perspective. In it, Des Wilson and Oliver Kearney, both prominent MacBride Principle campaigners, outlined the Catholic Church's role in new forms of counter-insurgency and social control through economic patronage. They showed how the Church's pro-British stance, particularly the vehement anti-republicanism of Bishop Cahal Daly, had been rewarded with huge financial dividends enabling the hierarchy to gain an undeserved credibility in the area of job-creation; undeserved because very few real jobs were being created and no economic base was being established. King's £10 million, they suspected, would simply go towards the creation of more useless ACE jobs to add to the hundreds of useless ACE jobs already in existence. 'The price', they concluded, 'is nothing less than the total and unequivocal support by the Church of Down and Connor for all policies and actions (however immoral) of the British government.'[4]

Five weeks later *The Obair Report*, launched in Conway Mill, added further to the unemployment debate, supporting the Wilson/Kearney findings and outlining how the very government advocating remedies to West Belfast's unemployment had created the problem – from the Industrial Revolution to the present day. In relation to the apparent change of heart, it explained:

> In the last two decades at least West Belfast has not been a government priority in any sense other than 'security' ... Now that the area's economic problems have moved closer to the centre of the political stage the conclusion must be that 'security' rather than economic development as such is still a major determinant of government action. Not only is the money ... insufficient for economic recovery, but it is also being used for political ends, building up supposedly safe church-backed groups to the detriment of other groups.[5]

In Ballymurphy they said that the leopard never changes it spots.

In November 1988 Ballymurphy's community groups unexpectedly found themselves again in the vanguard of the conflict with the British. The muzzling of Sinn Fein in October had been followed by an immediate increase in repression. By early November nationalist areas of Belfast were in the grip of martial law. Whole areas were being sealed, as houses were torn apart by sledgehammer-wielding soldiers in random blanket searches. It soon became clear that the 'searches' were in fact a form of collective punishment against republican communities, and a return to Kitson's 'polluting the water' tactics. The *Andersonstown News* commented:

> When Brigadier Frank Kitson ... was serving his apprenticeship in Cyprus, a favourite tactic of his when an EOKA attack took place in a certain area, was to move in, cordon it off, and deliberately blow up a few buildings ...
> We suspect that something similar has been happening in nationalist areas of Belfast.[6]

The mass destruction of homes led to street protests, the bombing by the IRA of British army housing in Lisburn and Derry, and the resurfacing of Concerned Community Organisations which had been active on the 'supergrass' issue. A full-page advertisement in the *Andersonstown News* of December 10th, condemning the raids and accompanying assaults, was signed by 90 community groups representing all of nationalist Belfast. The community groups then set about monitoring the situation, using their credibility within the community and beyond to publicise and lobby against the latest round of state terror.

Meanwhile, on November 21st, Gerry Sloan, the last of the 1981 Crumlin Road escapees was arrested as he boarded a plane at Dublin Airport. In the Upper Springfield there was a feeling of collective loss.

On December 22nd the relationship between the state forces and loyalist squads was again confirmed by a newssheet that appeared in loyalist areas. It contained names and mugshots of several Ballymurphy republicans, mugshots taken by the RUC in Castlereagh interrogation centre. It coincided with an increased UDA and UVF onslaught against republican activists and nationalist civilians. There were also several attacks on Ballymurphy residents by the RUC during December and a renewal of rioting in Springhill from the 11th to the 20th of the month. There were daily attacks by loyalists from Springmartin, who on most occasions were supported by the RUC and British army firing plastic bullets. On Saturday, January 14th, a loyalist gunman fired into the estate from the roof of Glenravel School, in full view of the Taggart, and on the 20th troops harassing the residents during a loyalist attack cut TV aerial wires and telephone lines.

The rioting was punctuated by other ongoing events affecting the area. January 16th saw an announcement by British Home Secretary, Douglas Hurd, that an appeal by the Guildford Four had been given the go-ahead – 14 years on. There was new evidence, he said; it included the fact that Carole Richardson had been drugged with Pethidine before her 'confession' was extracted.*

The next day Home Office minister, Douglas Hogg, made another statement that was to have terrifying consequences for nationalists involved in the North's legal profession. Some solicitors, Hogg claimed, were 'unduly sympathetic' to groups such as the IRA. On February 12th 38-year-old Pat Finucane, who had worked with the Ballymurphy community groups against the 'supergrass' system, was murdered in his North Belfast home by the UFF.

Finucane had been a tireless champion of civil liberties and human rights, and a thorn in the British side. On several occasions, when republicans were being questioned in Castlereagh, Special Branch officers had promised 'We'll stiff Finucane.' In the end somebody did, and Geraldine Finucane, his grieving widow, laid the blame at Hogg's doorstep. In the wake of the killing several other solicitors found that they too were on a loyalist death-list.

By the time Pat Finucane was killed, it was already clear that the loyalists were back with a vengeance. And Ballymurphy had been hit again. The first nationalist to die at the assassins' hands in 1989 was Ian Catney

---

*On October 19th 1989, after the completion of this book, the Guildford Four were released. On that morning Mr Roy Amlot QC, acting on behalf of the Director of Public Prosecutions, stated that the 'confessions' of the Four – the only evidence against them – had been fabricated by the Surrey police. There was no apology from the Court of Appeal, the DPP nor the state. The Guildford Four had spent almost 15 years in jail.

(27) of Springfield Park, shot in his mother's shop in Smithfield on January 18th by two gunmen. He had previously survived a gun attack during the INLA feud when he was targeted because of his family connections. The inferences drawn by the UVF from that attack subsequently cost him his life.

The last week-end in January was dominated by the Sinn Fein Ard Fheis, at which it was again decided that all prospective election candidates would sign the British anti-violence declaration. In his presidential address, Gerry Adams urged the IRA to be 'careful and careful again' after a year in which there were several bungled operations that had cost the lives of innocent civilians.

On the evening of January 29th Springhill again came under loyalist attack. Two bursts of gunfire were directed at three men and a young boy standing by a bonfire. Immediately afterwards, as they ran for cover, a British mobile patrol opened up on them from the Springfield Road, several of the bullets smashing into the home of Patrick and Elizabeth Lowe. The soldiers said they were shooting at 'gunmen'.

February began with the BBC revelations that 'talks about talks' had taken place in Duisburg, West Germany, between the DUP, OUP, SDLP and Alliance parties. But there were problems – the Hillsborough Treaty for example. A week later the talks were scuppered when the British and Irish governments agreed to strengthen the Agreement, throwing the unionists back to the laager. Nobody showed much concern up in Ballymurphy.

Then the shooting and bombing went on.

* * *

Almost 40 years have passed since the land was purchased for Ballymurphy estate. For over half of that period the area that subsequently became known as Greater Ballymurphy has been to the fore of the present phase of the 800-year-old Anglo-Irish conflict. In that period British policies in Ireland have transformed a transient working-class community with little interest in politics into a square mile of solid anti-state conspiracy. The boys and girls who roamed the streets of 1968, as the handful of local politicised residents attended the first civil rights marches, have since grown into a deadly efficient guerrilla army. In one square mile 128 people have died as a result of the Troubles; hundreds more have been injured, interned and imprisoned.

During the 20 years of the war much of Ballymurphy has changed beyond recognition: the aluminium bungalows of Westrock are gone; Moyard's flats are gone; new houses have been built in Springhill, Westrock and Moyard; the Bullring flats have been pulled down, the Bullring itself is now a small shopping centre; the waste ground that was once the IRA's firing range now boasts a council-run community and leisure centre, a library and a family and health centre; there are youth clubs and social clubs; and there are the military forts. There are also the huge murals on the gable walls of houses throughout the area depicting images of the war and its related political struggle.

The community, too, has changed. Where transience, apathy and despair had reigned, there is cohesion, dynamism and determination. There is a purpose in life that had not been there before, a purpose encapsulated in two lines of graffiti on a wall of the BTA community centre: 'The people are the Provos; and the Provos are the people.' The community is at war, and is adamant that it will see this through, no matter what the cost.

Twenty years ago, adults in Ballymurphy were set on raising their children in a society free from British colonial repression. Today, their children raise families of their own to the pulse of that same inherited goal. It is this that the British, and their allies in Ireland, are up against. They are not attempting to defeat an army: they are attempting to defeat an ideal. 'You may kill the revolutionary,' a Falls Road mural screamed during the 1981 hunger-strike, 'but you cannot kill the revolution.'

For 800 years Irish men and women have resisted British imperial might through force of arms. In the last four centuries, more than three million Irish people have died as a direct result of the British presence in Ireland. Some 2,000 of those Irish deaths have occurred in the present low-intensity war that has now lasted as long as the Vietnam War. Tens of thousands of others have been injured. There is no reason to suspect that, even if the British somehow manage to crush the present revolt, it will not resurface again in five or ten years' time. There is no reason to believe that, unless the British pack their bags and go, the Anglo-Irish conflict will not go on for another century, or, as Brigadier J.M. Glover assessed in 1978, for as long as the British remain in Ireland.

In the meantime, the only certain thing is that many more names will have been added to the list of Ballymurphy's dead. Children playing tag in the streets today, children who could grow up a credit to any society, will one day have their lives snuffed out violently as a result of the continuing colonial presence in Ireland. Other children, growing up in Britain, will also one day find sudden death on Irish streets or in the green undulating landscape of the Six Counties.

Undoubtedly, there will be difficulties in Anglo-Irish relations, and hiccups in collaboration; and Dublin will continue to absorb humiliation and contempt. Then the ship will roll on towards the goal of 'defeating terrorism'. Over the past 20 years the British have pumped every resource at their disposal into this one narrow objective. Ballymurphy people can only hope that, some day, they will realise that, as happened to the French in Algeria, the degree of force required to stamp out the Irish revolt would also precipitate an ignominious British withdrawal.

The British cannot win this war. Neither can they impose a political settlement while remaining in colonial stewardship of part of Ireland.

To date, all British 'solutions' have failed. The only solution that remains – a phased orderly withdrawal from the occupied counties of Ireland – is the only one that holds any future for the Irish or British people. It will then be up to the people living on this island to find compromise and accommodation of one another's way of life. That cannot be accomplished while a foreign power continues to manipulate the situation for its own ends. It cannot be accomplished in an atmosphere of black propaganda, state murders, strip-searching, 'supergrasses' and the provocative military saturation of Six Counties of Ireland. Nor can the most brutal repression destroy the ideal of freedom from British imperialist domination that has fuelled Irish politics for eight centuries.

Tom Barry, the famous West Cork IRA leader of the Black and Tan War, often quoted Terence McSwiney: 'Not all the armies of all the empires of the whole world can crush the spirit of one true man.' It is a sentiment that the British might well consider.

Meanwhile the Ballymurphy story goes on ...

References

1. *Irish News*, Belfast, February 22nd 1988.
2. Ibid.
3. Reply given by Tom King to Kevin McNamara, Labour Shadow Secretary for Northern Ireland, House of Commons, March 21st 1988.
4. Des Wilson and Oliver Kearney, *West Belfast – The Way Forward*, September 1988, p. 24.
5. Bill Rolston and Mike Tomlinson, *The Obair Report* (Beyond the Pale Publications, Belfast, 1988), p. 102.
6. *Andersonstown News*, Belfast, November 19th 1988.

The Dead of Ballymurphy

Republican Personnel
Liam McParland (43) car accident while on active service, November 6th 1969.
Michael Kane (35) premature explosion, September 4th 1970.
Dorothy Maguire (19) by British army, October 23rd 1971.
Maura Meehan (31) by British army, October 23rd 1971.
Michael Sloan (16) accidental shooting, January 11th 1972.
Eamon McCormick (17) by British army, January 16th 1972.
Patrick Campbell (16) accidental shooting, March 25th 1972.
Michael Magee (15) accidental shooting, May 13th 1972.
John Dougal (16) by British army, July 9th 1972.
Bobby McCrudden (19) by British army, August 3rd 1972.
Michael Clarke (22) premature explosion, August 11th 1972.
Anne Parker (18) premature explosion, August 11th 1972.
Jimmy Quigley (18) by British army, September 29th 1972.
Eddie O'Rawe (27) by British army, April 12th 1973.
Eileen Mackin (14) by loyalists, May 17th 1973.
Cathy McCartland (12) killed in a fall, August 12th 1973.
Patrick Mulvenna (19) by British army, August 31st 1973.
Anne Marie Pettigrew (19) premature explosion, September 1st 1973.
Jim Bryson (25) by British army, September 22nd 1973.
Paddy Teer (20) died Long Kesh, July 2nd 1974.
John Stone (22) premature explosion, January 21st 1975.
Jim McGrillen (25) by British army, February 15th 1976.
Tommy Tolan (31) by Officials, July 27th 1977.
Paul McWilliams (17) by British army, August 9th 1977.
Billy Carson (32) by loyalists, April 25th 1979.
Kevin Delaney (26) premature explosion, January 17th 1980.
Terence O'Neill (23) by RUC, July 1st 1980.

British Forces
Peter Taunton ( ) accident or suicide, September 26th 1970. British army.
George Hamilton (21) by IRA, October 17th 1971. British army.
Stephen Maguire (20) by IRA, November 4th 1971. British army.
Sean Russell (30) by IRA, December 8th 1971. UDR.
Peter Sime (22) by IRA, April 7th 1972. British army.
Alan Buckley (22) by IRA, May 13th 1972. British army.
Eustace Handley (20) by IRA, May 23rd 1972. British army.
George Lee (22) by IRA, June 6th 1972. British army.
James Jones (18) by IRA, July 18th 1972. British army.
Brian Thomas (20) by IRA, July 24th 1972. British army.
Francis Bell (18) by IRA, September 20th 1972. British army.
John Joesbury (18) by IRA, December 8th 1972. British army.
Michael Doyle (20) by IRA, February 21st 1973. British army.
Anton Brown (22) by IRA, March 6th 1973. British army.

Reginald Roberts (25) by IRA, July 1st 1973. British army.
David Smith (26) by IRA, July 4th 1974. British army.
Louis Harrison (20) by IRA, August 9th 1977. British army.
Christopher Shanley (21) by IRA, May 11th 1979. British army.
Stephen Rumple (19) by IRA, May 18th 1979. British army.
Paul Wright (21) by IRA, October 8th 1979. British army.
Errol Price (21) by IRA, January 26th 1980. British army.
Samuel Vallelly (23) by IRA, May 14th 1981. RUC.
David Brown (35) by IRA, April 16th 1982. RUC.
Leon Bush (22) by INLA, September 27th 1982. British army.
Geoffrey Curtis (20) by IRA, June 10th 1983. British army.
Desmond Dobbin (42) by IRA, October 11th 1986. RUC.
Alexander Bannister (21) by IRA, August 8th 1988. British Army.

Civilians
Francis McGuigan (2) by British army, April 1st 1970.
Alexander McVicker (35) by IRA, November 16th 1970.
Arthur Mckenna (35) by IRA, November 16th 1970.
Fr Hugh Mullan (37) by British army, August 9th 1971.
Frank Quinn (20) by British army, August 9th 1971.
Joan Connolly (50) by British army, August 9th 1971.
Daniel Teggart (44) by British army, August 9th 1971.
Noel Philips (20) by British army, August 9th 1971.
Eddie Doherty (28) by British army, August 10th 1971.
John Lavery (19) by British army, August 10th 1971.
Paddy McCarthy (44) stress of internment week, August 11th 1971.
John McKerr ( ) of Andersonstown by unknown pro-British gunmen, possibly soldiers, August 11th 1971.
Joseph Murphy (41) by British army, August 22nd 1971.
Joseph Corr (43) by British army, August 27th 1971.
Thomas McIlroy (29) by British army, February 2nd 1972.
Tommy McIlroy (50) of Andersonstown, by loyalists, May 13th 1972.
Robert McMullan (32) by loyalists or British army, May 13th 1972.
Martha Campbell (13) by loyalists, May 14th 1972.
John Moran (19) of Turf Lodge, by loyalists, May 23rd 1972.
James Bonner (19) of Iveagh, by British army, June 25th 1972.
Bernard Norney (38) by IRA, June 27th 1972.
Margaret Gargan (13) by British army, July 9th 1972.
Fr Noel Fitzpatrick (40) by British army, July 9th 1972.
Paddy Butler (38) by British army, July 9th 1972.
David McCafferty (14) by British army, July 9th 1972.
Patrick McKee (25) by loyalists, September 30th 1972.
Jimmy Gillen (21) by loyalists, October 18th 1972.
Jack Mooney (31) by loyalists, January 2nd 1973.
David McAleese (38) by loyalists, February 18th 1973.
David Glennon (45) by loyalists, March 8th 1973.
Gerard Barnes (31) by loyalists, May 31st 1973.
Robert Clarke ( ) by loyalists, July 5th 1973.
Joseph Murphy (30) by loyalists, August 10th 1973.
Joseph Murphy senior ( ) heart attack at news of son's murder, August 10th 1973.
Bernard Teggart (15) by IRA, November 12th 1973.
Vincent Clarke (43) by loyalists, February 4th 1974.
James Corbett (20) by IRA, April 20th 1974.

Joseph Duffy (16) Brain haemorrhage after beating by British army, May 26th 1974.
Geraldine Macklin (20) by loyalists, November 22nd 1974.
Kevin Kane (18) by loyalists, April 5th 1975.
George Quinn (41) by loyalists, September 9th 1975.
Sean McNamee (24) by Officials, October 10th 1975.
James Fogarty (22) ex-Official, by IRA, November 3rd 1975.
John McAllister (19) by IRA, November 11th 1975.
Maureen Fogarty, suicide, a year after her husband was shot dead during the Official/Provisional feud of 1975.
Mary Fegan (56) heart attack while attempting to prevent son's arrest, March 23rd 1976.
John Ritchie (31) by loyalists, May 30th 1976.
John Savage (17) of Ardoyne, by British army, December 18th 1976.
Kevin McMenamin (10) by loyalists, April 10th 1977.
John Short (49) by IRA, April 10th 1977.
Kevin Dyer (25) by loyalists, June 16th 1978.
Joseph McKee (34) by loyalists, June 9th 1979.
Hugh O'Halloran (28) by Officials, September 10th 1979.
Gabriel Wiggins (56) by loyalists, September 12th 1979.
John McGuinness (31) by IRA, shot in February 1971, died of injuries on October 21st 1979.
Doreen McGuinness (16) of Distillery Street, by British army, January 1st 1980.
Hugh Maguire (9) accidentally killed while stoning military, February 10th 1980.
Hugh O'Neill (21) accidentally shot, July 10th 1981.
Francis Toner (26) by loyalists, May 2nd 1982.
Joseph Donegan (48) by loyalists, October 23rd 1982.
Thomas 'Kidso' Reilly (22) of Turf Lodge, by British army, August 9th 1983.
Paul Kelly (17) by UDR, January 15th 1985.
James Henry (18) crashed stolen car while being chased by RUC, July 26th 1985.
Joseph Dorrian (19) crashed stolen car while being chased by RUC, July 26th 1985.
Gerald Mahon (28) by IRA, September 8th 1985.
Catherine Mahon (27) by IRA, September 8th 1985.
Francisco Notarontonio (65) by loyalists, October 9th 1987.
Ian Catney (26) by loyalists, January 18th 1989.

Others
MRF operative, by IRA, autumn 1972.
Hugh Ferguson (19) IRSP member killed by Officials, February 20th 1975.
Michael Kearney (33) INLA member killed by IPLO, February 18th 1987.
Gerard Steenson (29) IPLO member from Falls killed by INLA, March 15th 1987.
Tony McCarthy (31) from Lenadoon killed with Gerard Steenson by INLA, March 15th 1987.
Gerard 'Sparkey' Barkley (26), INLA member killed by INLA, October 26th 1983.